*f*P

Also by David Swensen:

Unconventional Success:
A Fundamental Approach to Personal Investment

Pioneering Portfolio Management

An Unconventional Approach to Institutional Investment

Fully Revised and Updated

DAVID F. SWENSEN

FREE PRESS

New York   London   Toronto   Sydney   New Delhi

FREE PRESS
A Division of Simon & Schuster, Inc.
1230 Avenue of the Americas
New York, NY 10020

This Free Press hardcover edition January 2009

For information about special discounts for bulk purchases,
please contact Simon & Schuster Special Sales at 1-800-456-6798
or business@simonandschuster.com

Manufactured in Italy

20   19   18   17

Library of Congress Cataloging-in-Publication
Data Control Number: 2008021556

ISBN-13: 978-1-4165-4469-2
ISBN-10:   1-4165-4469-0

To Tory, who excels as a student and shines as a writer, while approaching life with compassion and sensitivity that enrich all those who know her.

To Alex, who programs computers (without being a geek) and modifies cars (without being a gearhead), while inspiring all who know him with his courage.

To Tim, who avidly plays sports of any ilk and just as avidly roots for Yale's bulldogs, while thrilling teammates and spectators with his infectious enthusiasm.

To my parents, who invariably showed me the right path, even though I sometimes failed to take it.

Contents

Foreword
by Charles D. Ellis

Correctly and increasingly widely recognized as the best book ever written on managing institutional investment portfolios, *Pioneering Portfolio Management* presents in plain language the knowledge and understanding David Swensen has developed over thirty years of intensive research and extensive experience—most particularly during the most recent twenty-three years, over which he and his team at Yale have produced simply astounding serial successes as innovative professional practitioners. Swensen has proven himself one of the world's truly great investment professionals.

Some of the obvious consequences—please fasten your seatbelts—are inspiring:

- Yale has enjoyed the happy benefits of Swensen's remarkably good investment results. Funds flowing to the University have increased over the past twenty years by nearly $3 million *every day*.
- Endowment support for Yale University's expanding budget has increased from 10 percent of expenditures in 1985 to 45 percent of a much larger total in 2009.
- Swensen has produced in current purchasing power for his favorite university—as defined by the *incremental* superior performance over and above the average results achieved by

the nation's other university endowments—multiples more
than any of Yale's most generous benefactors.*

- During the past twenty-three years, the value added by
David Swensen, Dean Takahashi, and their colleagues—
over and above their endowment peers—has been an astonishing $16.5 billion.

- With President Richard C. Levin's wise and creative leadership, Yale has used this financial strength to position itself
as a leader among the world's great universities for the benefit of all people. Alumni and friends of Yale, encouraged by
Swensen's investment results and Levin's leadership, have
proven themselves remarkably generous in their gifts for
their university and its future.

On seven major dimensions, Yale's investment management stands
out:

- Returns over long periods are outstanding.
- The consistency of these returns is remarkable.
- The structural strength of the portfolio against market
adversities is robust. Charming as achievements on offense
have been, the first priority has always been on active
defense—defense in portfolio structure, defense on manager selection, and defense in manager relationships.
- The innovative and assertive search for superior opportunities—by asset class and by manager—is exemplary.
- The linkage of endowment investment management to
Yale's overall financial management continues to be innovative, constructive, and prudent.
- The organizational effectiveness and teamwork efficiency
shown consistently by the Yale Investments Office is
admirable.
- The series of very favorable working relationships between
Yale's Investments Office and its quite numerous external
managers bring many important advantages to Yale's
endowment—including identifying possible new managers.

*Only King Abdullah of Saudi Arabia who recently funded the new King
Abdullah University of Science and Technology with $20 billion, has done
more for a university anywhere in the world.

Happily, these advantages have a compounding benefit for the endow-ment and, therefore, for Yale University and its capacity for public service.

Original and innovative as he continues to be, Swensen incorporates in his book the cream of others' best thinking. John Maynard Keynes criticized fiduciaries for preferring to "fail conventionally" rather than taking, as Swensen so often does, direct responsibility for independent, even pioneering thought and action. When Bob Barker of the Advisory Committee on Endowment Management reported to the Ford Founda-tion how important it was in theory for the nation's endowments to take the truly long-term view that would lead them to an appropriate emphasis on equity investing, he would have celebrated Swensen's extraordinary successes in practice. Sometimes explicitly and often implicitly, Tobin, Markowitz, Samuelson, Sharpe, Buffett, Black, Scholes, Ross, Liebowitz, Litterman, and other great thinkers are all here.

Nothing is so powerful as a theory that works, and Swensen has integrated the abstract conceptual work of the Academy with the prag-matic rough and tumble of the Street to make theory work *and*, as a gifted teacher, share his best understandings in this remarkable book— a gift to those who share his devotion to rigorous thinking that pene-trates complexity while rejecting the temptations of oversimplification.

As innovative and successful as Yale's many investment initiatives have been—and Yale's extraordinary achievement in superior long-term results quite naturally attracts all the attention—close observers know that the real secret in Yale's investment success is *not* the pro-foundly pleasing performance produced over the past five, ten, *and* twenty years. Just as the secret of real estate is location, location, loca-tion, the real secret to Yale's remarkable continuing success is defense, defense, defense.

But how, you might ask, can defense be so important to Yale's remarkably positive results? Starting with those great truisms of long-term success in investing—"If you lose 50 percent, it will take a 100 percent win just to get even," or "If investors could just delete their few large losses, the good results would take care of themselves"—all experienced investors will gladly remind us of the great advantages of staying out of trouble. Delete a few disasters and compounding takes care of everything. (The equivalent in driving is simple: No serious accidents.)

Consistency of strong results over many years—plus indications that even as competition gets stronger, Yale's results are still improving comparatively—provides evidence of the advantages of Swensen's giving first priority to a strong and assertive defense. On a strong "defense first" foundation, he and his team conduct a repetitively active search for better ways to manage the total portfolio—from individual manager selection *and* manager creation to pioneering concepts of asset classes. Yale continues to demonstrate that the best defense in free and dynamic markets is neither fixed nor cautious, but rather, is resourceful, bold, and active on every level.

The architecture of Yale's portfolio structure is designed to enable the endowment to weather with confidence the storms and disruptions that are sure to come—but at unknowable times—to the world's capital markets and to position the endowment portfolio on the efficient frontier in trade-offs between risk and return. Using Monte Carlo simulations that incorporate many years of past market experience, Yale's portfolio is carefully structured to achieve optimal, non-covariant results—with particular attention to understanding and thereby avoiding unrewarded market adversities.

Having established a secure foundation through its aggressive defense, Yale then seeks specific ways to create comparative advantages that can contribute significantly to the endowment's superior results over the long term, including: unorthodox *and* rational asset class allocations; pioneering *and* logical strategies within each asset class; unconventional *and* timely commitments to out-of-favor asset classes; original *and* disciplined selection of little known asset managers; training *and* empowerment of relatively young professionals; sensible *and* innovative structures of investment manager relationships; and disciplined leadership in the integration of endowment management with the overall financial management of the university.

Yale's portfolio structure strategy and explicit assumptions are stress-tested in three different ways: Simulated returns are forced through a variety of possible "nightmare" scenarios; the Investment Committee devotes a full meeting each year to challenging every aspect of the portfolio structure in the classic tradition that only the well-tested decision merits strong, sustained commitment; and pragmatic "Street smarts" are always used in the professional implementation of strategy when selecting managers and allocating funds—protecting against adversities by searching out potential difficulties in an assertive, preemptive defense.

Selection of specific external managers adds another powerful defense—and has added significantly to Yale's superior returns. The obvious risks in manager selection are two: hiring managers at or after their best results and terminating managers at or near their nadirs. Yale carefully avoids short-term "dating" relationships and strongly favors long-term, continuing "marital" commitments to very carefully chosen

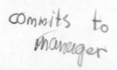
commits to manager

managers, often hiring them at an early stage in their development when terms can best be negotiated to align the manager's incentives with Yale's long-term interests. As a result, serial additions to each manager's mandates are frequent, and turnover is very low among Yale's manager relationships.

Yale's process for selecting managers is unusually rigorous: partly because staff professionals are so experienced and so in touch with the markets; partly because extensive "due diligence" probes are made; and partly because Yale selects only those managers who demonstrate considerable strength on several criteria—investment skill, organizational coherence, clarity of business strategy, appropriate fees and incentives, and, most importantly, personal and professional integrity.

Excellent investment managers know that Yale works closely with each manager to be a "tough" *and* ideal client. By maintaining unusual currency in all investment markets and an unusually effective staff of skilled decision makers, Yale is organized to engage promptly in rigorous evaluations of new opportunities. Managers know they will get a thoughtful evaluation of their ideas and investment strategies *and* their firm's organizational strategy, governance process, and compensation, *and* an early decision. One happy result is that Yale often gets an early opportunity to work with the best new managers. Of course, one negative is that Yale's high standards and selectivity mean that each year many managers are told "No" because of the consistent rigor of decisions.

Each new manager is recommended through a formal memorandum that details all "due diligence" research; explains the manager's record, investment philosophy, and decision-making process—and the strengths or limits of its organization; and provides the personal/professional record of each principal. Each of these in-depth background briefings—typically fifteen to twenty pages long—is studied by Investment Committee members in advance of their quarterly meetings at which any questions are discussed openly with staff professionals before a final decision is made.

Committee meetings are much like an advanced seminar in investment theory and practice, led by two Yale Ph.D.s: Rick Levin and David Swensen. (David Swensen and Richard Levin have developed a very special relationship based on the language and concepts of institutional economics in which they both earned their doctorates, their shared love of sports, and the good-humored intensity with which their teams compete annually in softball. These strong affectionate realities may be hidden from the casual observer as they strive for rigorous thinking about investing.) Committee members are chosen for their

their selected for opinions

devotion to Yale, their ability to work unusually well in a small group, their expertise in investment management, and most particularly, their capacity to provide effective oversight for and work well with the investment professionals.

The best part of a good defense is, of course, avoiding major error, but the disciplined removal of small errors through rigorous thinking and attention to detail can accumulate beneficially too. Consistently superior achievement by any investment organization depends ultimately on the people who do the important work, and Yale has a remarkable team of highly skilled investment professionals, each with a different area of focus and expertise, who share objectivity when making qualitative decisions, a continuous commitment to teamwork, tenacity of purpose when searching out or nurturing relationships with investment managers, and deep appreciation of the importance of serving the university unusually well.

As clearly and fully—and quite generously—as David Swensen shares and explains his investment philosophy in this wonderful book, and as grateful as all readers will surely be for having convenient access to a treasure trove of remarkably useful expertise graciously presented in Swensen's typically rigorous *and* completely understandable explanations, I feel obliged, after many happy years of sitting in the front row of the bleacher seats at the fifty-yard line, watching wonderful results unfold, to warn serious readers that for all his candor and openness, David is too modest to reveal certain salient ingredients of *Swensen's Secret Sauce* that only a close observer would know are central to Yale's success. They are too valuable to stay secret, so here they are.

First, as already noted, while all the excitement centers on the splendid high returns Yale has so enjoyed, the essential foundation underpinning all the creative and innovative decisions to invest boldly in unconventional asset classes and to commit significant millions to little known, often newly formed, managers is a carefully constructed, rigorously tested portfolio structure and decision-making process that are clearly defensive.   *Structure*

Second, the most remarkable reality about Yale's Investments Office—unless, of course, you would rank even higher the very extraordinary investment results achieved—is the rich culture of professional respect and personal affection that bonds so many talented and committed individuals into a superbly effective team whose collective efforts excel. If you spend much time with the core group at Yale's Investments Office—particularly if you've spent time with many other investment organizations of different types in various nations as I've

Defensive

Want to invest in sure things

been able to do over a long career—you will marvel at how very unusual Yale's team of star performers is in combining rigor and objectivity with the personal warmth and trust that avoids "politics" or "positioning" and maximizes real listening for full understanding every day.

Third, those bonds of professional respect and personal friendship extend out to the hundreds of key people working at Yale's many investment managers and engage them in unusually beneficial ways, both in their own work as investment managers and in the new ideas and insights they send Yale's way.

Fourth, Swensen & Co. are extraordinarily thoughtful about and engaged with their client, Yale University. Recognizing the potential consequences of the endowment's supporting a larger and larger proportion of the university's annual budget and the importance of stability in the flow of spendable funds from the endowment to the budget of the university—which is, by nature, so people-intensive and therefore needs consistent support—they recently initiated yet another increase in the annual spending rate *and* a modification of the spending rule *and* a complementary modification of the portfolio structure to increase its stability. Taking a very broad view of their long-term responsibilities, they took the lead in initiating a creative reconsideration of the optimal way to conceptualize the amortization of university buildings. The happy result is a shift from inherently misleading bookkeeping data to usefully informing management information. This kind of "above and beyond" thoughtfulness about an institution's best interests significantly enhances qualitatively the quantitative support Swensen & Co. give to the university.

The fifth secret may well be the most important: personal respect and affection. Visitors to Yale's Investments Office are invariably impressed by the open architecture and informal "happy ship" climate that is almost as obvious as the disciplined intensity with which the staff work at their tasks and responsibilities. Positive professionals perform at their peak productivity and teams get better with low turnover. David Swensen and Dean Takahashi have both made Yale a breeding ground for great careers at Yale and in leadership positions at such other endowed institutions as MIT, Bowdoin, Carnegie, Princeton, and Rockefeller *and* have established a team at Yale with the longest tenure in their field.

Equally important to Yale's own success has been its extensive network of professional friendships throughout the world of investing. Among the very bright and well-connected, how they spend their time is always a matter of free choice because everyone has lots of alternatives about how they share insights and information—and with whom. David Swensen is so well liked personally and admired professionally by such an extraordinarily extensive network of professional friends—and has long been a leader in helping others—it can be no surprise that he is at the vortex of insight and valuable information coming to him from many, many others. This is no accident. One of his great secrets of success is how many people are looking for opportunities to be helpful to David because it gives them so much pleasure and satisfaction and serves such high purpose and because he has been so helpful to them.

The sixth secret is that, as Charles Darwin tried to explain, survival of the fittest is *not* determined by competitive strength, but rather by social desirability. There's more money than certified talent in the world of investing, so outstanding investment managers have many choices because so many investors want to be their clients. Given their freedom of choice, managers prefer to work for and with clients they like and admire, and they like and admire David Swensen very much. They want to work with him and his team. This is why, despite its very high and rigorous screening standards, Yale attracts so many nimble, creative investment managers who are repetitively able to outperform. And the odds are high that most managers do their best work for Yale because Swensen & Co. work so conscientiously to facilitate and encourage them.

One last secret: David Swensen is almost unique in the way he has defined what he does. Yes, he is Yale's CIO; yes, he is a leader among investment professionals; and yes, he is driven to excel. But he maintains the gentler qualities of a personal and academic life while he silently defines his purpose-driven life's work as figuring out the really right way to manage not only Yale's endowment, but all endowments; sharing very generously through this book the concepts and practices developed over many years of creativity and discipline; striving to improve the practices of the investment management profession; integrating endowment investing and university financial management into a coherent system; and encouraging others to achieve personal and professional fulfillment by choosing meaningful, purpose-driven lives by devoting their careers to creating financial strength for our world's great educational and philanthropic institutions.

Along the way, David Swensen has done more to strengthen our educational and cultural institutions than anyone else on our planet—and he's still developing and sharing his best thinking with everyone in a genial and inspiring illumination of how much good one very fine man can do. Not too bad, David, not too bad.

Tobin's Friend—
Foreword to the 2000 Edition

Jim Tobin grew up during the Great Depression in Champaign, Illinois, where his father went each day to the public library to read the *New York Times*. He learned that Harvard University had decided to reach out beyond New England for students, and Illinois was one of the seven midwestern states selected for special effort in the Harvard recruiting plans, which included several generous national scholarships. He suggested to his son, "You might apply."

Jim Tobin did apply, proved to be a first-rank scholar and went on to earn his Ph.D., when economics at Harvard was going through a revolutionary reconsideration, shifting its orientation away from deductive "reasoning" from declared truths over to a rational commitment to empirical analysis of real world data.

Harvard would prove to be an exciting environment for undergraduate and doctoral students as gifted and engaged as Jim Tobin. Filled with the excitement of realizing how useful and how intellectually absorbing a career in economics could be, Tobin accepted a faculty appointment at Yale. He held his position at Yale for nearly four decades, with intellectual distinction, great personal warmth, and important influence on many, many students. At Yale, Tobin headed the celebrated Cowles Foundation for Economic Research, taught and advised students (many of whom went on to careers of great distinction in business, government, and academia), and earned a Nobel

Prize. Among his many Ph.D. advisees at Yale, he developed a deep "father-son" friendship with David Swensen, who was headed for a career on Wall Street.

Jim Tobin made two enormously important contributions to Yale's very successful endowment management. First, he led a team that designed the smoothing, inflation-responsive spending rule that would link the endowment fund with the university's annual budget in a rational, continuously adaptive process that works—and is being increasingly adopted by others. (Yale's endowment currently provides 20 percent of the university's annual budget.) Second, with his colleague and later provost Bill Brainard, Jim Tobin recommended David Swensen to the Yale administration and persuaded Swensen to abandon his promising career on Wall Street and take up the task of managing Yale's endowment. This would lead to Swensen's designing the architecture for the overall portfolio, crystallizing investment objectives and policies for each component and then selecting and supervising dozens and dozens of investment managers tasked with implementing the endowment's investment strategies.

Yale's endowment was just over $1 billion when David Swensen arrived in 1985; it's over $7 billion now. During the intervening fifteen years—within a rigorous, risk-controlled portfolio structure that has very little in bonds, relies almost entirely on outside managers and, during the longest and strongest bull stock market in American history, has been quite deliberately and substantially underinvested in publicly traded U.S. equities—David Swensen and his team have achieved an annualized rate of return for Yale's endowment superior to 96 percent of endowments and 98 percent of such institutional funds as pensions.

Public interest naturally centers on David Swensen's fine results—observers conventionally citing the unconventional structure of the portfolio and the superior returns realized, but usually overlooking the complementary strength of the long- and short-term controls used to avoid, minimize, and manage risk.

Those closer to Yale will recognize that David Swensen's risk-controlling portfolio structure and persistent discipline have enabled the endowment to provide more and more funding for Yale's educational program. Yale's endowment has not only increased quite wonderfully in market value, but has also enabled the Yale Corporation to increase with prudence the rate of annual spending—not once, but twice—because of the structural strength and resilience built into the endowment's portfolio. All told, the dollars flowing each year from Yale's endowment to the university have increased over David

Swensen's fifteen years from $45 million to $280 million.

The timing couldn't be better: Yale is experiencing a great renaissance under the gifted leadership of President Richard C. Levin and his extraordinary colleagues. And as the Medicis knew so well, any renaissance is costly.

Most of the Western world's great educational and cultural institutions—universities, colleges, libraries, museums, and foundations—depend, to varying degrees, on their endowments and the spendable funds they produce. Usually, the difference between "mediocre" and "excellent" is that margin of assured fiscal strength that only an endowment can produce. In this way, our society depends on endowments for that vital margin of fiscal strength that facilitates institutional excellence. Yale's leadership in endowment management—a leadership Yale cheerfully shares with Harvard, Princeton, and Stanford—is important far beyond the university campus and well beyond the Yale community.

At Yale, superior endowment management has generated the vital extra funding that has enabled President Richard Levin and the Yale Corporation to assure "need-blind" admission and to lead the way in limiting annual increases in tuition. These policies contribute importantly to Yale being a first-choice college for our future leaders to study and mature. And in a "virtuous circle," wonderful students attract, stimulate, and reward great teachers to come to Yale. When Yale set a record by raising $1.7 billion to support its educational mission, the university's alumni and friends were obviously encouraged to be particularly generous by the fine investment record of the Yale endowment.

These lofty consequences are clearly important to David Swensen and his team over the long run, but their real work is also very "daily." They meet regularly with nearly 100 current investment managers; analyze many, many potentially interesting proposals; conduct due diligence on scads of prospective new managers; examine each manager's investment performance versus expectations; and run Monte Carlo simulations to "stress test" the portfolio under various possible market scenarios to work out the probable impact of both intended and unintended risks. This rigorous process of operational management enables Yale to sustain its long-term investment policy commitments through market disruptions, because they are so soundly documented and carefully conceived. The clarity of policy also enables Yale to take swift, bold action when opportunities present themselves.

The operational framework within which David Swensen and his team work each day is the lineal descendant of a conceptual framework that was originated at Yale (and Stanford, MIT, and Chicago) and became known as Modern Portfolio Theory. This conceptual framework, converted into rigorously defined investment policies, gives structural strength to the present portfolio and consistency to its path through time and through markets' turbulence. The discipline to make hundreds of day-to-day decisions in the "real" world to convert this conceptual framework into a very large portfolio of very real investments that fulfill the promise of the theory is the "bottom-up" complement to the "top-down" concept and theory. If nothing is so useless as an "ivory tower" academic theory that goes unused, nothing is so very practical as the theory that works. At Yale, as David Swensen and his team keep demonstrating, the theory works very well.

One of the many ways in which Yale is special among great universities is the traditionally collegial process of decision making. So David Swensen is not alone: He has a committee of trustees and investment experts to work with, and on campus, he's in the proverbial "goldfish bowl." An engaging, warm personality and a first-class mind are wonderfully helpful, but could be insufficient in successfully working with a committee of bright, informed volunteers who are keen to "make a difference." In managing his several constituencies, David Swensen is stellar.

One secret in Yale's success has been David Swensen's ability to engage the committee in *governance*—and not in investment *management*. Contributing factors include: selection of committee members who are experienced, hard-working, and personally agreeable; extensive documentation of the due diligence devoted to preparing each investment decision; and full agreement on the evidence and reasoning behind the policy framework within which individual investment decisions will be made. As a result, the whole investment committee is always conceptually "on board" with overall policy, before turning to specific investment decisions. This preempts *ad hoc* decision making by individuals determined to be "helpful." Of course, good results and careful adherence to agreed and articulated policies help too. But the decisive factor is the great confidence David Swensen has earned by constant fidelity to purpose, rigorous rationality, and open, full review of all investment decisions with staff, investment managers, and members of his committee.

Clearly a descendant of Norway, David Swensen is a man with a deep sense of mission to serve. Personally modest, in a sober Scandinavian way, Swensen is frequently enthusiastic about the achievement of others—particularly successful investment managers. He teaches a popular undergraduate course on investing and a rigorous investment seminar at Yale's School of Management. He lives by *both* aspects of being a "man of principle": on the one hand, devoting quality time to his children and to members of his staff (and to his continuing close friendship with mentors like Jim Tobin); and on the other hand, being almost prim in his insistence on the proper behavioral integrity of the managers and the deals in which Yale invests. Significantly, his moral gyroscope has enabled him to see and make unusual investment decisions that have proven financially beneficial to the University.

Finally, David Swensen has made it fun to work on investing for Yale—recruiting a team of exceptionally talented Yale graduates, who in their first professional jobs get a wide exposure to the world of investing; early responsibility for enquiry, analysis, and decisions; and an exemplary exposure to teamwork at work. David Swensen's "alumni" have gone on to important endowment management posts at the Carnegie and Rockefeller foundations, as well as Duke and Princeton universities. As Churchill observed, "People like *winning* very much." Sharing the joys of victory and the discipline necessary to sustain championship performance, David Swensen infuses the process of investing with a sense of the important mission of enabling Yale's faculty, students, and administration to aspire to achieve.

David Swensen was reluctant to write this book when the idea was first proposed to him. His reasoning illustrates the remarkable integrity of the man. First, he worried that his writing the story would draw attention to him individually and away from his team—and particularly his senior colleague and friend, Dean Takahashi. He also worried that a "how-to" book might make it look "too easy." He was concerned that other institutions (particularly those with smaller endowment funds) might be attracted by the impressive results achieved in the past several years for Yale. But they might not have the internal staff or the organizational structure and discipline required to sustain commitments through the good *and* bad markets that will be encountered in the future. He knows sustained commitment is necessary for success with out-of-the-mainstream portfolio structures.

Fortunately, David Swensen was persuaded to go ahead with the book. He has a lot to show us and we all have a lot to learn as he shares of the lessons taught by his experience.

Consider this: Over and above the investment returns earned by the average endowment, the incremental investment results achieved by David Swensen and his team have added well over $2 billion to Yale's endowment and comfortably more than $100 million this year to Yale's annual budget. How many can aspire to make as much of a real difference to an important institution as does David Swensen in his value-added work for Yale?

Charles D. Ellis

Pioneering
Portfolio
Management

1
Introduction

When I wrote the introduction to the first edition of *Pioneering Portfolio Management* in early 1999, Yale's pathbreaking investment strategy had produced excellent results, both in absolute and relative terms, but had not yet been tested by adverse market conditions. In fact, Yale's return for the ten years ending June 30, 1998 amounted to 15.5 percent per annum, more than three full percentage points short of the S&P 500's 18.6 percent result. The endowment's deficit relative to the then-highest-performing asset class of domestic equity caused naysayers to question the wisdom of undertaking the difficult task of creating a well-diversified equity-oriented portfolio.

The years following the first edition's publication proved the worth of Yale's innovative asset allocation. The continuation of the bull market in 1999 and early 2000 produced wonderful results for Yale, culminating in a 41.0 percent return for the year ending June 30, 2000, a result that trounced the average endowment return of 13.0 percent. Yet, the real test of Yale's approach took place in 2001 and 2002 as the Internet bubble burst and marketable equities collapsed. Yale posted positive returns of 9.2 percent in 2001 and 0.7 percent in 2002, even as the average endowment reported deficits of 3.6 percent and 6.0 percent, respectively. In short, equity orientation continued to drive Yale's strong results, while diversification kicked in to preserve the university's assets.

From a market perspective, the vantage point of early 2008 differs dramatically from that of early 1999. For the ten years ending June 30, 2007, Yale's 17.8 percent return emphatically exceeded the S&P 500's

7.1 percent. Twenty-year results tell a similar tale with Yale's 15.6 percent trumping the S&P's 10.8 percent. In fact, Yale's conspicuous success attracted the attention of many investors, making the university's strategy seem less radical and more sensible, less pioneering and more mainstream.

In spite of widespread imitation of Yale's portfolio management philosophy, the university posted stunning returns relative to peers. For the year ended June 30, 2007, Yale reported a 28.0 percent return, which exceeded the results of all of the educational institutions that participated in the 2007 Cambridge Associates *Annual Analysis of College and University Pool Returns*. More significantly, Yale's results led the pack for five-, ten-, and twenty-year periods. The university's pioneering portfolio management works in theory and in practice.

The most important measure of endowment management success concerns the endowment's ability to support Yale's educational mission. When I arrived at Yale in 1985, the endowment contributed $45 million to the university's budget, representing a century-low 10 percent of revenues. For Yale's 2009 fiscal year, in large part as a result of extraordinary investment returns, the endowment will transfer to the budget approximately $1,150 million, representing about 45 percent of revenues. High quality investment management makes a difference!

Institutions versus Individuals

When I wrote my second book, *Unconventional Success*, I characterized its message as "a sensible investment framework for individuals," in contrast to the institutional focus of *Pioneering Portfolio Management*. I erred in describing my target audiences. In fact, I have come to believe that the most important distinction in the investment world does not separate individuals and institutions; the most important distinction divides those investors with the ability to make high quality active management decisions from those investors without active management expertise. Few institutions and even fewer individuals exhibit the ability and commit the resources to produce risk-adjusted excess returns.

The correct strategies for investors with active management expertise fall on the opposite end of the spectrum from the appropriate approaches for investors without active management abilities. Aside from the obvious fact that skilled active managers face the opportunity to generate market-beating returns in the traditional asset classes of domestic and foreign equity, skilled active managers enjoy the more important opportunity to create lower-risk, higher-returning portfolios with the alternative asset classes of absolute return, real assets, and private equity. Only those investors with active management ability sensibly pursue market-beating strategies in traditional asset classes and portfolio allocations to nontraditional asset classes. The costly game of active management guarantees failure for the casual participant.

No middle ground exists. Low-cost passive strategies, as outlined in *Unconventional Success*, suit the overwhelming number of individual and institutional investors without the time, resources, and ability to make high quality active management decisions. The framework outlined in *Pioneering Portfolio Management* applies to only a small number of investors with the resources and temperament to pursue the grail of risk-adjusted excess returns.

The World of Endowment Management

The fascinating activity of endowment management captures the energy and imagination of many talented individuals charged with stewardship of institutional assets. Investing with a time horizon measured in centuries to support the educational and research missions of society's colleges and universities creates a challenge guaranteed to engage the emotions and the intellect.

Aside from the appeal of the eleemosynary purposes that endowments serve, the investment business contains an independent set of attractions. Populated by unusually gifted, extremely driven individuals, the institutional funds management industry provides a nearly limitless supply of products, a few of which actually serve fiduciary aims. Mining the handful of gems from the tons of mine ore provides intellectually stimulating employment for the managers of endowment portfolios.

The knowledge base that provides useful support for investment decisions knows no bounds. A rich understanding of human psychology, a reasonable appreciation of financial theory, a deep awareness of history, and a broad exposure to current events all contribute to development of well-informed portfolio strategies. Many top-notch practitioners confess they would work without pay in the endlessly fascinating money management business.

The book begins by painting the big picture, discussing the purposes of endowment accumulation and examining the goals for institutional portfolios. Articulation of an investment philosophy provides the underpinnings for developing an asset-allocation strategy—the fundamentally important decision regarding the portion of portfolio assets devoted to each type of investment alternative.

After establishing a framework for portfolio construction, the book investigates the nitty-gritty details of implementing a successful investment program. A discussion of portfolio management issues examines situations where real world frictions might impede realization of portfolio objectives. Chapters on traditional and alternative asset classes provide a primer on investment characteristics and active management opportunities, followed by an outline of asset class management issues. The book closes with some thoughts on structuring an effective decision-making process.

The linearity of the book's exposition of the investment process masks the complexities inherent in the portfolio management challenge. For example, asset allocation relies on a combination of top-down assessment of asset class characteristics and bottom-up evaluation of asset class opportunities. Since quantitative projections of returns, risks, and correlations describe only part of the scene, top-notch investors supplement the statistical overview with a ground-level understanding of specific investments. Because bottom-up insights into investment opportunity provide information important to assessing asset class attractiveness, effective investors consider both top-down and bottom-up factors when evaluating portfolio alternatives. By beginning with an analysis of the broad questions regarding the asset allocation framework and narrowing the discussion to issues involved with managing specific investment portfolios, the book lays out a neat progression from macro to micro, ignoring the complex simultaneity of the asset management process.

Rigorous Investment Framework

Three themes surface repeatedly in the book. The first theme centers on the importance of taking actions within the context of an analytically rigorous framework, implemented with discipline and under-girded with thorough analysis of specific opportunities. In dealing with the entire range of investment decisions from broad-based asset allocation to issue-specific security selection, investment success requires sticking with positions made uncomfortable by their variance with popular opinion. Casual commitments invite casual reversal, exposing portfolio managers to the damaging whipsaw of buying high and selling low. Only with the confidence created by a strong decision-making process can investors sell mania-induced excess and buy despair-driven value.

Establishing an analytically rigorous framework requires a ground-up examination of the investment challenges faced by the institution, evaluated in the context of the organization's specific characteristics. All too often investors fail to address the particular investment policy needs of an institution, opting instead to adopt portfolio structures similar to those pursued by comparable institutions. In other cases, when evaluating individual investment strategies, investors make commitments based on the identity of the co-investors, not on the merits of the proposed transaction. Playing follow-the-leader exposes assets to substantial risk.

Disciplined implementation of investment decisions ensures that investors reap the rewards and incur the costs associated with the policies adopted by the institution. While many important invest-ment activities require careful oversight, maintaining policy asset-allocation targets stands near the top of the list. Far too many investors spend enormous amounts of time and energy constructing policy port-folios, only to allow allocations, once established, to drift with the whims of the market. The process of rebalancing requires a fair degree of activity, buying and selling to bring underweight and overweight allocations to target. Without a disciplined approach to maintaining policy targets, fiduciaries fail to achieve the desired characteristics for the institution's portfolio.

Making decisions based on thorough analysis provides the best foundation for running a strong investment program. The tough com-petitive nature of the investment management industry stems from the prevalence of zero-sum games where the amount by which the win-ners win equals the amount by which the losers lose. Carefully consid-ered decisions provide the only intelligent basis for profitable pursuit of investment activities, ranging from broad policy decisions to nar-row security selection bets.

Agency Issues

A second theme concerns the prevalence of agency issues that inter-fere with the successful pursuit of institutional goals. Nearly every aspect of funds management suffers from decisions made in the self-interest of the agents, at the expense of the best interest of the princi-pals. Culprits range from trustees seeking to make an impact during their term on an investment committee to staff members acting to increase job security to portfolio managers pursuing steady fee income at the expense of investment excellence to corporate managers diverting assets for personal gain. Differences in interest between fund beneficiaries and those responsible for fund assets create potentially costly wedges between what should have been and what actually was.

The wedge between principal goals and agent actions causes problems at the highest governance level, leading to a failure to serve the interests of a perpetual life endowment fund. Individuals desire immediate gratification, leading to overemphasis of policies expected to pay off in a relatively short time frame. At the same time, fund fiduciaries hope to retain power by avoiding controversy, pursuing only conventional investment ideas. By operating in the institutional mainstream of short-horizon, uncontroversial opportunities, committee members and staff ensure unspectacular results, while missing potentially rewarding longer term contrarian plays.

Relationships with external investment managers provide a fertile breeding ground for conflicts of interest. Institutions seek high risk-adjusted returns, while outside investment advisors pursue substantial, stable flows of fee income. Conflicts arise since the most attractive investment opportunities fail to generate returns in a steady predictable fashion. To create more secure cash flows, investment firms frequently gather excessive amounts of assets, follow benchmark-hugging portfolio strategies, and dilute management efforts across a broad range of product offerings. While fiduciaries attempt to reduce conflicts with investment advisors by crafting appropriate compensation arrangements, interests of fund managers diverge from interests of capital providers even with the most carefully considered deal structures.

Most asset classes contain investment vehicles exhibiting some degree of agency risk, with corporate bonds representing an extreme case. Structural issues render corporate bonds hopelessly flawed as a portfolio alternative. Shareholder interests, with which company management generally identifies, diverge so dramatically from the goals of bondholders that lenders to companies must expect to end up on the wrong side of nearly every conflict. Yet, even in equity holdings where corporate managers share a rough coincidence of interests with outside shareholders, agency issues drive wedges between the two classes of economic actors. In every equity position, public or private, management at least occasionally pursues activities providing purely personal gains, directly damaging the interests of shareholders. To mitigate the problem, investors search for managements focused on advancing stockholder interests, while avoiding companies treated as personal piggy banks by the individuals in charge.

Every aspect of the investment management process contains real and potential conflicts between the interests of the institutional fund and the interests of the agents engaged to manage portfolio assets. Awareness of the breadth and seriousness of agency issues constitutes the first line of defense for fund managers. By evaluating each participant involved in investment activities with a skeptical attitude, fiduciaries increase the likelihood of avoiding or mitigating the most serious principal-agent conflicts.

Active Management Challenges

The third theme relates to the difficulties of managing investment portfolios to exploit asset mispricings. Both market timers and security selectors face intensely competitive environments in which the majority of participants fail. The efficiency of marketable security pricing poses formidable hurdles to investors pursuing active management strategies.

While illiquid markets provide a much greater range of mispriced assets, private investors fare little better than their marketable security counterparts as the extraordinary fee burden typical of private equity funds almost guarantees delivery of disappointing risk-adjusted results. Active management strategies, whether in public markets or private, generally fail to meet investor expectations.

In spite of the daunting obstacles to active management success, the overwhelming majority of market participants choose to play the loser's game. Like the residents of Lake Wobegon who all believe their children to be above average, nearly all investors believe their active strategies will produce superior results. The harsh reality of the negative-sum game dictates that, in aggregate, active managers lose to the market by the amount it costs to play in the form of management fees, trading commissions, and dealer spread. Wall Street's share of the pie defines the amount of performance drag experienced by the would-be market beaters.

The staff resources required to create portfolios with a reasonable chance of producing superior asset class returns place yet another obstacle in the path of institutions considering active management strategies. Promising investments come to light only after culling dozens of mediocre alternatives. Hiring and compensating the personnel needed to identify out-of-the-mainstream opportunities imposes a burden too great for many institutions to accept. The alternative of trying to pursue active strategies on-the-cheap exposes assets to material

danger. Casual attempts to beat the market provide fodder for organizations willing to devote the resources necessary to win.

Even with adequate numbers of high quaility personnel, active
management strategies demand uninstitutional behavior from institutions, creating a paradox few successfully unravel. Establishing and
maintaining an unconventional investment profile requires acceptance of uncomfortably idiosyncratic portfolios, which frequently
appear downright imprudent in the eyes of conventional wisdom.
Unless institutions maintain contrarian positions through difficult
times, the resulting damage of buying high and selling low imposes
severe financial and reputational costs on the institution.

Even though the investment lessons in this book focus on the challenges and rewards of investing educational endowment funds, the
ideas described in these pages address issues of value to all participants in financial markets. Perhaps most important, readers might
develop an understanding of the extraordinary requirements for successful pursuit of active management strategies. Rigorous self-assess-
ment leads to segregation of those with active management ability
from those without, increasing chances for investment success by
understanding which activities to avoid and which activities to pursue.

Beyond the pragmatic possibility of improving investment outcomes, students of finance might enjoy exploring the thought process
underlying the management of a large institutional fund. Because
fund managers operate in an environment that requires insights into
tools ranging from the technical rigors of modern finance to the qualitative judgments of behavioral science, the funds management problem spans an improbably wide range of disciplines, providing material
of interest to a broad group of market observers.

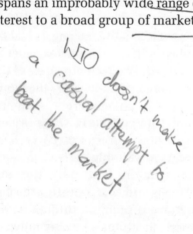

2

Endowment Purposes

Institutions accumulate endowments for a number of purposes. A significant level of endowment support for university operations enhances institutional autonomy and provides an independent source of revenues, thereby reducing dependence on government grants, student charges, and alumni donations. Financial stability increases with the level of sustainable endowment distributions, facilitating long-term planning and increasing institutional strength. Finally, since colleges and universities tend to post strikingly similar tuition levels, better-endowed institutions enjoy an incremental income stream, providing the means to create a superior teaching and research environment.

Institutions without permanent financial resources support day-to-day operations with funds from sources that frequently demand a voice in organizational governance. Government grants expose colleges and universities to a host of regulations concerning matters far afield from the direct purpose of the activity receiving financial support. Gifts from alumni and friends often contain explicit or implicit requirements, some of which may not be completely congruent with institutional aspirations. In an organization's early years, when any source of income might represent the difference between survival and failure, institutions prove particularly vulnerable to the strings attached to external income flows.

Universities frequently make long-term commitments as part of the regular course of operations. For example, awarding tenure to a faculty member represents a financial obligation that might span decades. Funding such an enduring obligation with temporary sources of funds exposes the institution (and the individual) to the risk of disruption in revenue flows. The permanent nature of endowment funds matches nicely the long-term character of tenure commitments.

Some institutional constituencies view endowments with a decidedly short-term horizon. Students generally prefer greater levels of support today, expecting that higher expenditures translate into better, less expensive education. Faculty recognize that current resources provide the wherewithal to pursue a more comprehensive set of scholarly activities, while administrators see enhanced financial flows as the means to relax the binding constraint of budgetary discipline. Some donors suggest increasing endowment payout as a means to reduce the pressures associated with raising current use funds. Trustees ultimately face the difficult-to-resolve tension between desire to support current programs and obligation to preserve assets for future generations.

Colleges and universities stand among the most long-lived institutions in society. By charting an independent course in fulfilling a mission of teaching and scholarship, the academy adds immeasurably to the quality of life. Endowment funds contribute to the educational enterprise by providing institutions with greater independence, increased financial stability, and the means to create a margin of excellence.

MAINTAIN INDEPENDENCE

Endowment accumulation facilitates institutional autonomy, since reliance on impermanent income sources to support operations exposes institutions to the conditions attached by providers of funds. For example, when the government awards grants to support specific research projects, university-wide activities frequently face requirements and regulations even though the affected operations may be far removed from the grant beneficiary. Similarly, colleges relying on donor gifts for current use often find that benefactors demand a significant voice in the institution's activities. Even educational institutions that rely heavily on tuition income may be constrained by that dependency, perhaps by responding to current trends and fashions to attract sufficient numbers of students to maintain operations. Greater institutional needs for current income correspond to greater degrees of external influence.

Educational institutions certainly must respond to government policy and take into account donor wishes and student desires. However, at times such influences detract from the ability of trustees to pursue well-considered institutional goals. Endowment accumulation allows educational institutions to be accountable to their constituencies without being held hostage by them.

Donors to endowment often attach meaningful restrictions to gifts, stipulating that funds provide permanent support for designated purposes. Occasionally, such requirements come into conflict with institutional goals, as might be the case when an endowment supports a field of study long since abandoned by scholars. More frequently, endowment gifts provide restricted support to fund activities central to organizational aspirations, such as teaching and financial aid. Even though donors exercise considerable influence in negotiating the initial terms of an endowment gift, after establishing the fund, donor influence wanes.

Attracting short-term sources of income requires institutions to respond to a combination of explicit and implicit pressures. Institutions that benefit from a stable stream of endowment income stand a greater chance of maintaining independence from external pressures. Support of the operating budget by endowment fosters academic freedom and allows independent governance.

Yale and Connecticut

The survival of the fledgling Yale in the early eighteenth century depended on generous legislative and financial support from the Colony of Connecticut. In October 1701 the General Assembly of the Colony of Connecticut approved a proposal put forth by five Connecticut ministers to charter a college: "Wherein Youth may be instructed in the Arts and Sciences who through the blessing of Almighty God may be fitted for Publick employment both in Church and Civil State." Support for Yale included grants of land, special grants for construction or repair of college buildings, authorization for briefs or lotteries, duties on rum, and the exemption of ministers, ministers' tutors, and students from taxes. Brooks Mather Kelley, in his *Yale—A History*, estimates that "throughout the eighteenth century, Connecticut's contribution amounted to more than one half the total gifts to the college."[1]

The colony's support came with a price. For instance, in 1755, the general assembly voted to refuse the annual grant to Yale, ostensibly because of wartime expenditures, but in fact to retaliate for a controversial position taken by Yale President Clapp concerning the religious character of the college. In 1792, in exchange for renewed financial support, the governor, lieutenant governor, and six legislators became fellows of the Yale Corporation. The presence of the state-appointed representatives on the Yale governing board caused discord and conflict, with disagreements ranging from the proper religious faith of the faculty to the general assembly's rights in reforming abuses in the running of the college.

State-appointed representatives served on the Yale Corporation until the termination of state support for Yale in 1871, which resulted in the withdrawal of the state senators from the Yale Corporation.[2] With the replacement of the six legislators by fellows elected by Yale's alumni body, control became more firmly centered in the college. Yale's experience mirrored national trends. With the end of the Civil War and the rise of Darwinism and laissez-faire philosophies, the previous view of the major role of the state in the support of private education had shifted. As historian Frederick Rudolph noted, "a partnership in public service, which had once been essential to the colleges and inherent in the responsibilities of government . . . [became] insidious or . . . forgotten altogether." Fortunately for Yale, this withdrawal of public support was replaced by organized alumni support.[3]

The appointment of elected officials to the university's governing board in exchange for financial support illustrates in the starkest fashion the loss of control associated with reliance on external sources of funds. While the nearly eighty years of direct state influence on Yale's governance represents an extreme case, more subtle issues of outside influence continue to test the wisdom of today's trustees. Balancing the legitimate interest of providers of funds in having a voice with the fundamental need of private institutions to maintain ultimate control poses a difficult challenge to fiduciaries responsible for managing educational organizations.

Federal Support for Academic Research

The benefits and dangers of reliance on government support have shaped private educational institutions throughout their history. Many scholars credit the influx in the 1960s of federal dollars for research in higher education with the rise to preeminence of the American research university. However, the costs of this support to the administrative flexibility of the universities became painfully evident in the 1970s.

In their extensive study of the American research university, Hugh Graham and Nancy Diamond note that federal support for research resulted in "increased congressional involvement, an emphasis on targeted research, and a general trend toward government regulation of the private sector."[4] During the late 1960s and early 1970s federal regulation of universities slowly but steadily embraced issues such as hiring, promotion, and firing of university personnel (including faculty); research; admissions; toxic waste disposal; human and animal subjects of research; access for the handicapped; wage and salary administration; pensions and benefits; plant construction and management; record keeping; athletics; fund-raising; and in some cases, curricula.[5]

With this new web of federal regulation came increased costs and bureaucracy for the universities. In a widely quoted claim, Harvard President Derek Bok noted that compliance with federal regulations at Harvard consumed over sixty thousand hours of faculty time and cost almost $8.3 million in the mid 1970s. A 1980 study found that meeting regulatory costs absorbed as much as 7 to 8 percent of total institutional budgets.[6]

The reduction in administrative autonomy poses a significant threat to institutional governance. In his *Report of the President for 1974–1975*, Yale President Kingman Brewster stated: ". . . the experience of recent years gives fair warning that reliance upon government support for *any* university activity may subject the entire university to conditions and requirements which can undermine the capacity of faculty and trustees to chart the institution's destiny."

When well-endowed institutions accept external financial support, compliance with the accompanying requirements no doubt influences institutional policies. That said, such compliance generally poses no fundamental threat to the integrity of the institution. The greater the independent flow of financial resources from endowment assets, the greater the ability of an institution either to avoid external funds with onerous requirements or to negotiate changes mitigating undesirable regulations. In cases where organizations lack substantial independent means, external funds providers wield the potential to reshape the institution, threatening to alter the fundamental character of the college or university.

University of Bridgeport

In the early 1990s, severe financial distress caused the University of Bridgeport to lose its independence after a desperate fight to survive. From a peak of more than 9,000 students in the 1970s to fewer than 4,000 in 1991, declining enrollment created budgetary trauma, forcing the school to consider radical measures. In spite of the institution's dire straits, in October 1991, the University of Bridgeport rejected an offer of $50 million from the Professors World Peace Academy, an arm of the Reverend Sun Myung Moon's Unification Church. Preferring to pursue independent policies, the institution's trustees elected to take the drastic step of eliminating nearly one-third of its ninety degree programs, while petitioning a judge to dip into restricted endowment funds to meet payroll costs.

After running out of options in April 1992, the trustees of the university reversed course, ceding control to the Professors World Peace Academy in exchange for an infusion of more than $50 million over five years. As board members associated with the Unification Church took control, the sixty-five-year-old institution received a new mission:—to serve as "the foundation of a worldwide network of universities striving for international harmony and understanding."[7]

Three years later, the Reverend Sun Myung Moon received an honorary degree from the University of Bridgeport, which recognized him as a "religious leader and a man of true spiritual power."[8] During Reverend Moon's appearance on campus, he took credit for the fall of communism and promised to resolve conflicts in the Middle East and Korea. Claiming that "the entire world did everything it could to put an end to me," the Reverend Moon said that "today I am firmly standing on top of the world."[9] According to the *New York Times*, the speech provided further evidence to critics that the "once sturdy university" sold its independence for an infusion of capital from "a religious cult with a messianic and proselytizing mission."

The University of Bridgeport's demise resulted from a number of factors, yet a more substantial endowment might have allowed the institution to maintain its independence. The lack of a stable financial foundation exposed the university to wrenching change, causing varying degrees of distress among important institutional constituencies.

External support for colleges and universities frequently comes with collateral requirements designed to influence institutional behavior. In extreme cases, outside agents seek to change the fundamental character of an organization. The greater the extent to which endowment funds provide support for operations, the greater the ability of an institution to pursue its own course.

completely independent

PROVIDE STABILITY

Endowments contribute to operational stability by providing reliable flows of resources to operating budgets. Nonpermanent funding sources fluctuate, and may diminish or disappear, as government policies change, donor generosity diminishes, or student interest wanes. By reducing variability in university revenues, endowments enhance operational viability and promote long-term planning.

Yale and Josiah Willard Gibbs

Yale's history is riddled with instances of budgetary problems due to fluctuating current income. On numerous occasions the university operated at a deficit, forcing faculty to forego full salaries. In an extreme example, the "greatest scholar Yale has ever produced or harbored," Josiah Willard Gibbs, renowned for his seminal research in physics and engineering, received an appointment as professor of mathematical physics without salary in 1871, indicating "not any lack of esteem for Gibbs, but rather the poverty of Yale." In 1880, officials at Johns Hopkins University attempted to woo Gibbs from Yale with an offer of a $3,000 salary.

The well-known geologist and mineralogist, Yale Professor James Dwight Dana, convinced Yale President Noah Porter to provide Gibbs with a salary of $2,000 and a promise to increase the salary as soon as funds were available. In a letter to Gibbs, Dana implored the brilliant professor to stay loyal to Yale: ". . . I do not wonder that Johns Hopkins wants your name and services, or that you feel inclined to consider favorable their proposition, for nothing has been done toward endowing your professorship, and there are not here the means or signs of progress which tend to incite courage in professors and multiply earnest students. But I hope nevertheless that you will stand by us, and that something will speedily be done by way of endowment to show you that your services are really valued . . . Johns Hopkins can get on vastly better without you than we can. We can not."[10]

Gibbs eventually received Yale's prestigious Berkeley fellowship for postgraduate scholarship, endowed in 1731 by George Berkeley with the gift of a ninety-six-acre farm in Newport, Rhode Island. Funded by income from the farm, the fellowship supported some of Yale's most illustrious graduates including Eleazer Wheelock, the first president of Dartmouth College, and Eugene Schuyler, the first American to hold the Ph.D.

Today, endowed chairs serve largely to confer honor on distinguished faculty members; in Gibbs's era support from the endowment conferred both prestige and financial security. That said, even today, the credibility of an institution's promise to provide ongoing financial support creates an important competitive edge in recruiting and retaining faculty.

Stanford University

Endowment distributions occasionally provide more than year-to-year stability in funding operations. In times of severe economic stress, well-endowed institutions employ extraordinary distributions to weather the storm, while those with meager permanent resources face the consequences of substantial financial trauma more directly.

In 1991, Stanford lost significant amounts of financial support from the federal government in a controversy over cost recoveries that the university claimed in connection with federally sponsored research activity. Stanford allegedly overbilled the government, seeking reimbursement for headline-grabbing charges associated with the seventy-two-foot yacht *Victoria*, a nineteenth century Italian fruitwood commode, and a Lake Tahoe retreat for university trustees.[11] Primarily as a result of the "continued impact of the disputes with the federal government," the university posted a 1992 operating deficit in excess of $32.5 million, representing nearly 3 percent of revenues.

Facing projected deficits aggregating $125 million over three years, Stanford sought to "finance the expected losses while expense reduction programs were implemented." A critical component of the "financing" plan involved increasing the endowment payout rate from 4.75 percent to 6.75 percent for 1993 and 1994, releasing a projected incremental $58 million to support operations during Stanford's period of adjustment.

The combination of increased endowment spending, reduced expenditures, and incremental borrowing placed the university on firm financial footing. In 1995, basking in the glow of a substantial operating surplus, Stanford lowered the payout rate to 5.25 percent, nearly returning to the "customary rate of 4.75 percent."[12] The extraordinary increase in the endowment spending rate provided a cushion for Stanford's operations, allowing the university to deal with a sudden, significant loss of funds with minimal disruption.

Yet the use of permanent funds to finance temporary operating shortfalls imposed substantial costs on Stanford. In the five years following the university's extraordinary payout rate increase, strong investment returns led to more than a doubling in asset values. Certainly, with twenty-twenty hindsight, Stanford would have benefited by using much lower-cost external borrowing to fund the budget deficits, leaving the payout rate at its "customary" level of 4.75 percent. Considering the longer-term impact of withdrawal of permanent funds reinforces concerns regarding the ultimate cost of unusually high rates of spending from endowment.

Reliable distributions from endowment contribute to the stability of educational institutions. Under normal operating circumstances, greater levels of endowment serve to improve the quality of an organization's revenue stream, allowing heavier reliance on internally generated income. When faced with extraordinary financial stress, endowment assets provide a cushion, either by paying out unusually large distributions or by serving as support for external borrowing, giving the institution the capacity to address disruptive fiscal issues. A substantial endowment creates a superior everyday budgetary environment and enhances the ability to deal with unusual financial trauma.

CREATE A MARGIN OF EXCELLENCE

Endowments produce resources that allow an institution to establish a superior educational environment. On the margin, endowment income attracts better scholars, provides superior facilities, and funds pioneering research. While financial resources fail to translate directly into educational excellence, incremental funds provide the means for the faculty, administration, and trustees to develop an unusually robust educational institution.

Endowments and Institutional Quality

Endowment size correlates strongly with institutional quality. A survey of major private research universities shows that larger, better-endowed organizations score more highly in the *U.S. News and World Report* rankings of educational institutions.[13] While the *U.S. News and World Report* rankings garner a fair share of controversy, much of the debate centers around the rank order of institutions. Placing the major research universities into quartiles reduces the focus on numerical order and produces a set of categories that group like with like. The quartile groupings show a strong correlation between excellence and endowment size.

Public universities fall outside of the study because budgetary issues for state-supported institutions differ significantly from those of private universities. For example, government appropriations play a much greater role for public institutions than for private. If public authorities wish to support institutions at a particular level, changes in levels of endowment income might be offset by altering levels of state support for the universities. Strong endowment distributions may correspond to weak state subventions, while weak endowment support may elicit higher state contributions. Public institutions face investment and spending problems that differ fundamentally from those of private universities.

Major private research universities have strikingly similar tuition streams. In 2004, among the top twenty research universities in the survey, undergraduate tuition ranged from $19,670 to $32,265, a reasonably tight band. Eliminating the high and low outliers produces a range of $24,117 to $29,910. Among the top five institutions, tuition charges fell in an even narrower band from $28,400 to $29,910. Price discrimination, at least with respect to posted tuition levels, appears to be quite weak among leading universities.

Large private universities operate substantial enterprises, with 2004 revenues ranging from $74 million to nearly $2.8 billion, averaging $722 million. To put the revenue numbers in a corporate context, eleven of sixty-one institutions run budgets sufficiently large to rank among the Fortune 1000 companies.[14]

Student income provides the largest single source of income to research universities, accounting for more than 48 percent of revenues. Grants and contracts supply nearly 25 percent of cash flow, investment income about 13 percent, and contributions 8 percent. The catch-all remainder amounts to less than 6 percent of revenues.

Ranking institutions by quality poses a host of challenges, because such rankings involve reducing the characteristics of a complex, multifaceted institution to a single number. Nonetheless, a cottage industry, led by *U.S. News and World Report*, produces widely followed annual ratings of colleges and universities.

In part, because of the impossibility of making precise distinctions where none exist, the ratings engender controversy. In the *U.S. News and World Report* evaluation, the magazine assesses academic reputation, student retention, faculty resources, admissions selectivity, financial wherewithal, graduation rates, and alumni giving rates.[15] Combining measures such as SAT scores, class size, and graduation rates, the publication fashions a ranking scheme of colleges and universities. While the precise rank order causes much debate, the general groupings of institutions make intuitive sense.

Dividing the large private universities into quartiles according to their academic ranking allows examination of the relationship between investment income and institutional quality. Table 2.1 lists (alphabetically) the institutions falling into each particular group.

Quality ranking and endowment size exhibit a strong correlation, with top quartile institutions benefiting from endowments averaging just in excess of $6.0 billion, in contrast to the bottom quartile average of $324 million. Moving from one quartile to the next, a clear step pattern emerges, indicating a direct relationship between endowment assets and institutional achievement.

The level of endowment per student tells the same story. Top quartile universities enjoy nearly $530,000 in endowment assets for each full-time equivalent (FTE) student. After dramatic declines to approximately $190,000 for the second quartile and just over $61,000 for the third quartile, bottom quartile institutions average only $43,000 per student. Endowment size correlates clearly and strongly with institutional quality.

The degree to which investment income supports research institution budgets varies dramatically. As seen in Table 2.2, top quartile university investment assets produce 19.1 percent of revenues. In contrast, bottom quartile institutions receive roughly one-third the relative support, with investments contributing 6.8 percent of income.

Since higher quality institutions tend to be larger, greater relative levels of investment income translate into dramatically greater numbers of dollars. Top quartile institutions operate with an average draw of $274 million, while lower quartile universities receive only $17 million.

Student charges provide the complement to investment income. As institutional quality increases, budgetary dependence on student charges decreases. Top quartile institutions rely on student income for 24.5 percent of revenues, while bottom quartile universities obtain 64.5 percent of revenues from such charges, a spread of 40 percent. Lower quality institutions rely heavily on tuition. Yet viewed on a per capita basis, student charges show a remarkably consistent pattern across the quartiles, with figures ranging from $26,800 for the top quartile to $19,400 for the bottom quartile. Better-endowed universities use their financial strength to create a richer educational environment.

Grants and contracts display a strong relationship with institutional quality, providing nearly 38 percent of revenues for top quartile institutions and declining monotonically to just over 16 percent of revenues for bottom quartile universities. As in the case of investment income, the combination of the top institutions' larger budgets and larger shares

Table 2.1 Endowment Size Correlates Strongly with Institutional Quality

Data as of Fiscal Years Ending 2004

	Institution		Average Size of Endowment ($mm)	Average Endowment per Student	Average Age of Institution
Top Three	Harvard Princeton Yale		$14,934	$1,255,667	310
1st Quartile	Brown Cal Tech Columbia Cornell Dartmouth Duke Harvard Johns Hopkins	MIT Northwestern Princeton Stanford Penn Washington Univ. Yale	$6,053	$529,573	196
2nd Quartile	Boston College Brandeis Carnegie Mellon Case Western Emory Georgetown Lehigh Notre Dame	NYU Rice Tufts Chicago Rochester USC Vanderbilt Wake Forest	$1,802	$189,379	143
3rd Quartile	RPI Baylor Baylor BU Clark Fordham George Washington Pepperdine SMU	St. Louis University Stevens Institute Tech. Syracuse Tulane Miami WPI Yeshiva	$569	$61,517	137
4th Quartile	American Catholic Univ. of America Drexel Howard Illinois Institute of Tech. Loyola Marquette Northeastern	TCU Univ. of Denver Univ. of Tulsa Univ. of Dayton Univ. of the Pacific USD USF	$324	$43,429	123
Average			$2,181	$205,703	150

Source: Moody's Investors Service.

Table 2.2 Investment Income Provides More Support at Top Universities

Data as of Fiscal Years Ending 2004

	Institution	Average Total Revenues ($mm)	Student Income	Grants/ Contracts	Contri- butions	Investment Income	Other
Top Three	Harvard Princeton Yale	1,736	19.7%	23.5%	6.0%	31.2%	8.6%
1st Quartile	Brown Cal Tech Columbia Cornell Dartmouth Duke Harvard Johns Hopkins	MIT Northwestern Princeton Stanford Penn Washington Univ. Yale	1,463	24.5%	37.7%	8.4%	19.1%	8.1%
2nd Quartile	Boston College Brandei Carnegie Mellon Case Western Emory Georgetown Lehigh Notre Dame	NYU Rice Tufts Chicago Rochester USC Vanderbilt Wake Forest	733	45.2%	25.9%	9.0%	14.5%	5.4%
3rd Quartile	RPI Baylor BU Clark Fordham George Washington Pepperdine SMU	St. Louis University Stevens Institute Tech. Syracuse Tulane Miami WPI Yeshiva	422	58.9%	19.0%	6.9%	9.4%	5.8%
4th Quartile	American Catholic Univ. of America Drexel Howard Illinois Institute of Tech. Loyola Marquette Northeastern	TCU Univ. of Denver Univ. of Tulsa Univ. of Dayton Univ. of the Pacific USD USF	271	64.5%	16.2%	8.1%	6.8%	4.3%
Overall		722	48.2%	24.7%	8.1%	12.5%	5.9%

Source: Moody's Investors Service.

translates into substantially more grant and contract income for research activity at large, high quality universities.

Annual giving numbers fall into a reasonably narrow range from 6.9 percent to 9.0 percent of revenues and exhibit no particular pattern. Even though top quartile universities receive a smaller percentage of revenues from current gifts, the dollars given to top quartile institutions exceed the dollars for all other institutions combined.

While endowment size clearly correlates with institutional quality, the direction of causality remains unclear. Do higher quality institutions attract higher levels of endowment support, creating a self-reinforcing virtuous cycle? Or do larger endowments provide the resources required to build superior institutions, facilitating the creation of a margin of excellence? Regardless of the direction of causation, greater financial resources correlate with superior educational environments.

CONCLUSION

Endowments serve a number of important purposes for educational institutions—allowing greater independence, providing enhanced stability, and facilitating educational excellence. Institutions of higher education best serve society as independent forums for free and open inquiry, promoting unfettered pursuit of ideas regardless of convention or controversy. The conditions attached to sources of outside financial support contain the potential to create institutional sensitivities, limiting healthy debate and impairing open inquiry.

For established institutions, endowments enhance operating independence and budgetary stability. Sizable reserves of permanent funds allow trustees to resist government interference and unreasonable donor requirements. Large endowments enable administrators to smooth the impact of financial shocks, buffering operations against disruptive external forces.

For less established institutions, endowments sometimes determine the difference between survival and failure. In the decade ending June 2007, more than one hundred degree granting institutions closed, representing approximately 3 percent of the total number of such institutions in the United States.[16] Well-endowed institutions enjoy a level of fiscal support that cushions financial and operating blows. Even modest endowments make a significant difference.

Endowments provide the means to produce a margin of excellence. Better-endowed institutions enjoy an incremental source of funds available for deployment to create a superior educational environment. By contributing to the excellence of superior colleges and universities, endowments play an important role in the world of higher education.

Understanding the purposes that drive endowment accumulation represents an important first step in structuring an investment portfolio. By defining the reasons endowments exist, fiduciaries lay the groundwork for articulation of specific investment goals, shaping in a fundamental manner the investment policy and process.

3
Investment and Spending Goals

*endowment
exempt from
taxes.*

Endowment managers pursue the conflicting goals of preserving purchasing power of assets and providing substantial flows of resources to the operating budget. If fiduciaries produce spending and investment policies that deal successfully with the tension between the goals, the institution receives a sustainable contribution from endowment assets to support academic programs. Asset preservation and stable budgetary support, if achieved, satisfy the purposes of endowment accumulation—maintaining independence, providing stability, and creating a margin of excellence.

Benjamin Franklin observed that death and taxes represent life's only certainties. Managers of endowment assets suspend those certainties, as educational institutions aspire to exist in perpetuity and endowment assets enjoy exemption from taxes. The perpetual nature of colleges and universities makes endowment management one of the investment world's most fascinating endeavors. Balancing the tension between preserving long-run asset purchasing power and providing substantial current operating support provides a rich set of challenges, posing problems unique to endowed educational institutions.

Purchasing power preservation represents a long-term goal, spanning generations. Successfully managed endowments retain forever the ability to provide a particular level of institutional support, justifying the classification of endowment funds as permanent assets. Pur-

24

suit of long-term asset preservation requires seeking high returns, accepting the accompanying fundamental risk and associated market volatility.

Stable operating support constitutes an intermediate-term goal, reflecting the demands of a shorter-term budgetary planning cycle. Since academic programs contract only with great difficulty, institutions rely on reasonably predictable flows of funds from endowment to support operations. Supplying stable distributions for current operations requires dampening portfolio volatility, suggesting lower levels of fundamental risk with the accompanying lower levels of expected returns.

The high risk, high return investment policy best suited to serve asset preservation conflicts with the low risk, low return investment approach more likely to produce stable distributions to the operating budget. Spending policies deal with the conflict, in part by dampening the transmission of portfolio volatility to budgetary distributions. Further, by specifying institutional preferences regarding the trade-off between purchasing power preservation and stability of flows to fund operations, spending policies determine the degree to which endowments meet the needs of current and future generations.

INVESTMENT GOALS

The late Yale economist James Tobin captured the essence of the investment problem facing fiduciaries:

> The trustees of an endowed institution are the guardians of the future against the claims of the present. Their task is to preserve equity among generations. The trustees of an endowed university like my own assume the institution to be immortal. They want to know, therefore, the rate of consumption from endowment which can be sustained indefinitely. . . . In formal terms, the trustees are supposed to have a zero subjective rate of time preference.
>
> Consuming endowment income so defined means in principle that the existing endowment can continue to support the same set of activities that it is now supporting. This rule says that the current consumption should not benefit from the prospects of future gifts to endowment. Sustained consumption rises to encompass and enlarge the scope of activities when, but not before, capital gifts enlarge the endowment.[1]

Tobin's concept of intergenerational equity comports with the goals of purchasing power preservation and stable operating budget support. By preserving endowment assets adjusted for inflation, the institution retains the ability to "support the same set of activities that it is now supporting." In supplying a stable flow of resources for operations, the endowment provides continuity of support, avoiding disruptive interruptions in distributions to academic programs.

Gifts and Endowment

When making an endowment gift, donors intend to provide permanent support for the designated activity. If financial managers maintain only the nominal value of gifts, inflation ultimately reduces to insignificance the impact of the fund. Yale's oldest surviving endowment fund dedicated to the support of teaching, the Timothy Dwight Professorship Fund established in 1822, entered the university's books at an historical cost basis slightly in excess of $27,000. Because price levels rose nearly twenty-seven fold in the intervening 185 years, a 2007 distribution from an endowment of $27,000 pales in comparison to an 1822 distribution from the same size fund. While during the Dwight Professorship's existence, the fund grew more than eighteen times to nearly $500,000, the current value falls short of the inflation-adjusted target by nearly one-third. Even though the university continues to benefit from the Timothy Dwight Professorship in the early twenty-first century, after accounting for inflation the fund fails to provide the same level of support available in the early nineteenth century. While fiduciary principles generally specify only that the institution preserve the nominal value of a gift,* to provide true permanent support institutions must maintain the inflation-adjusted value of a gift. *must adjust for inflation always*

Explicitly stating that new gifts allow an institution to "enlarge the

---

*Section 2 of the Uniform Management of Investment Funds Act (UMIFA), which has been adopted in forty-eight states and the District of Columbia as of June 30, 2007, codifies this obligation by requiring that an institution maintain the historic dollar value of an endowment gift. Some states have strengthened this law to include preservation of purchasing power.

In 2006, the National Conference of Commissioners on Uniform State Laws proposed adoption of the Uniform Prudent Management of Institutional Funds Act (UPMIFA), which explicitly suggested that states consider preservation of purchasing power when drafting their statutes. As of June 30, 2007, twelve states had adopted statutes based on UPMIFA.

scope of activities," Tobin recognizes a principle important to endowment benefactors. Some institutions factor gifts into spending considerations, targeting a consumption level equal to the portfolio's expected real return *plus* new gifts. Harvard University, in fashioning its 1974 spending policy, assumed that "university expense growth would exceed [the long-term inflation] rate by two points."[2] Yet the institution's targeted reinvestment rate offset only the general level of inflation, not the higher university expense growth. Obviously, supporting the "same set of activities" required keeping pace with university expense growth, not general inflation, rendering the reinvestment rate inadequate to its purpose. To maintain endowment purchasing power, Harvard articulated a goal of accumulating sufficient new capital gifts to offset the difference between the general inflation rate and university expense growth. In so doing, the university explicitly employed new gifts to replenish inflationary losses.[3]

Using new gifts to offset part of the impact of inflation on asset values fails to "enlarge the scope of activities" supported by endowment. If a fund devoted to supporting a chair in the economics department loses purchasing power, establishing a new chair in the law school does nothing to replenish the economics department's loss. From a bottom-up basis, donors have the right to expect that each individual endowment fund will retain purchasing power through time.

Trade-off Between Today and Tomorrow

Fund managers charged only with preserving portfolio purchasing power face a straightforward task. Simply accumulating a portfolio of Treasury Inflation Protected Securities (TIPS) allows investors to generate inflation-sensitive returns guaranteed by the government. Unfortunately, the excess of university inflation over general price inflation may well consume any incremental returns from TIPS, providing almost no real return to the institution. Such single-minded focus on asset preservation fails to meet institutional needs, as merely accumulating a portfolio of assets with stable purchasing power provides little, if any, benefit to the academic enterprise.

Endowment assets benefit educational institutions primarily by generating substantial reliable distributions to support operations. Fund managers with a narrow focus on providing generous predictable spending flows face little problem, particularly when operating with an intermediate time horizon. By holding assets that promise low levels of volatility, managers create a stable portfolio that allows budget planners to forecast payouts with reasonable certainty. Unfortunately, low risk investment portfolios deliver returns insufficient both to support substantial distributions and to preserve purchasing power. Exclusive pursuit of stable support for current operations favors today's generation of scholars over tomorrow's beneficiaries.

A clear direct trade-off exists between preserving assets and supporting operations. To the extent that managers focus on maintaining purchasing power of endowment assets, substantial volatility influences the flow of resources delivered to the operating budget. To the extent that managers emphasize providing a sizable and stable flow of resources to the operating budget, substantial volatility influences the purchasing power of endowment assets.

Consider two extreme policies to determine the annual spending from an endowment. One extreme, placing maintenance of asset purchasing power at center stage, requires spending each year only the real returns generated by the portfolio. Assume a particular year produces investment returns of 10 percent and inflation of 4 percent. Distributing 6 percent of assets to the operating units provides substantial support to operations, while reinvesting 4 percent in the endowment offsets inflation and maintains purchasing power. The following year, in an environment with 2 percent investment returns and 7 percent inflation, the institution faces a serious problem. Compensation for inflation requires a 7 percent reinvestment in the endowment, but the fund generated a return of only 2 percent. The endowment manager cannot ask the operating units for a 5 percent rebate to maintain portfolio purchasing power. At best, the institution can declare no distribution, hoping to generate positive real returns in following years to replenish lost purchasing power and, perhaps, to provide operational support. From an operating budget perspective, a policy that places year-by-year maintenance of purchasing power above all else proves unacceptable.

The other policy extreme, pursuing a goal of providing a completely stable flow of resources to the operating budget, requires spending amounts that increase each year by the amount of inflation. In the short term, the policy provides perfectly stable inflation-adjusted distributions from the endowment to the operating budget. While under normal market conditions such a policy might not harm the endowment, serious damage results when faced with a hostile financial environment. In a period of high inflation accompanied by bear markets for investment assets, spending at a level independent of the value of assets creates the potential to permanently damage the endowment fund.

Spending policies specify the trade-off between protecting endowment assets for tomorrow's scholars and providing endowment support for today's beneficiaries. Cleverly crafted rules for determining annual endowment distributions reduce the tension between the objectives of spending stability and asset preservation, increasing the likelihood of meeting the needs of both current and future generations.

SPENDING POLICY

Spending policies resolve the tension between the competing goals of preservation of endowment and stability in spending. Sensible policies cause current-year spending to relate both to prior-year endowment distributions and to contemporaneous endowment values, with the former factor providing a core upon which planners can rely and the latter factor introducing sensitivity to market influences.

Yale's Spending Policy

Based on a structure created by economists James Tobin, William Brainard, Richard Cooper, and William Nordhaus, Yale's policy relates current year spending both to the previous level of spending from endowment and to the previous endowment market value. Under Yale's rule, spending for a given year equals 80 percent of spending in the previous year plus 20 percent of the long-term spending rate applied to the endowment's market level at the previous fiscal year end. The resulting figure is brought forward to the current year by using an inflation adjustment. Since previous levels of spending depend on past endowment market values, present spending can be expressed in terms of endowment levels going back through time. The resulting lagged adjustment process averages past endowment levels with exponentially decreasing weights.

The accompanying chart, Figure 3.1, shows weights applied to endowment values of previous years (ignoring the inflation adjustment). Multiplying the weights by the endowment values for the respective years and summing the results determines spending for the current year. Note that years farther in the past have less influence on the calculation than more recent years. In contrast, a simple four-year average would apply equal 25 percent weights to each of the four most recent years.

By reducing the impact on the operating budget of inevitable fluc-

**Figure 3.1 Yale's Spending Policy Insulates
the Budget from Market Fluctuations**

Influence of Past Endowment Levels in Determining Current Spending

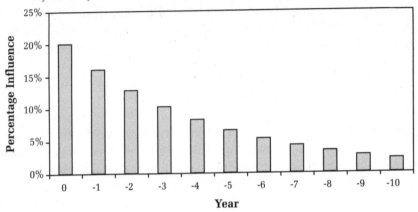

Source: Yale University Investments Office.

tuations in endowment value caused by investing in risky assets, spending rules that employ an averaging process insulate the academic enterprise from unacceptably high year-to-year swings in support. Because sensible spending policies dampen the consequences of portfolio volatility, portfolio managers gain the freedom to accept greater investment risk with the expectation of achieving higher return without exposing the institution to unreasonably large probabilities of significant budgetary shortfalls.

By doing a particularly effective job of smoothing contributions to the operating budget, Yale's elegant spending rule contributes an important measure of flexibility to the university's investment policy. Instead of employing a simple averaging process that unceremoniously drops the oldest number in favor of the new, as time passes Yale's exponentially declining weights gradually squeeze out the influence of a particular year's endowment value. The superior smoothing characteristics reduce the transmission of investment volatility to the operating budget, allowing pursuit of portfolio strategies promising higher expected returns.

The 80 percent weight on previous year's spending and the 20 percent weight on current target spending reflect institutional choices regarding the trade-off between spending stability and purchasing power preservation. Different institutions may well exhibit different preferences. Moreover, institutional preferences may change over time. In fact, as Yale's endowment support moved from one-tenth of revenues in the mid 1980s to one-third of revenues in the mid 2000s, the university opted for greater stability in operating budget support. By changing the weight on previous year's spending from 70 percent to 80 percent, Yale reduced the likelihood of a disruptive spending drop (at the expense of greater risk to purchasing power preservation).

Other Spending Policies

Throughout most of the twentieth century, institutions typically followed a practice of distributing for current expenditure only income generated in the form of interest, dividends, and rents. Yale, which in 1965 began spending "a prudent portion of the appreciation in market value," noted two reasons for adopting the new policy:

> First, it is only by coincidence that Yield will be a correct balance between the present and the future. . . . Second, when Yield is the sole measure of what can be spent for present needs, a situation of annually increasing needs, such as has obtained for many years and seems likely to continue for many more, forces investment policy to seek to improve current Yield. But this, in turn, under market conditions prevailing most of the time since World War II, could only be done at the loss of some potential Gain.[4]

Concerns about "invading principal" no doubt underlie the policies of institutions that base spending on the income generated by a portfolio. As Yale recognized, the distinction between current income and capital appreciation proves too easily manipulated to provide a sound foundation for spending policy.

Consider the spending implications of discount, par, and premium bonds with comparable levels of sensitivity to changes in interest rates, as set forth in Table 3.1. Although these bonds exhibit remarkably similar investment attributes, spending implications differ dramatically for an institution pursuing a policy of consuming all current income. The zero coupon bond provides no current cash flow, the par bond generates a 6 percent yield, and the premium bond pays out a well-above-market rate of 12 percent. Naturally, holding low coupon bonds leads to lower current spending and higher future portfolio value, while the opposite consequences stem from owning high coupon bonds. Fortunately, income-based spending rules determine spending for far fewer institutions today than in the late 1980s, when

Table 3.1 Otherwise Similar Bonds
Generate Dramatically Different Cash Flows
Coupon, Duration, Price, and Yield for Three Different Types of Bonds

	Coupon	Duration[a]	Price	Yield
Zero coupon	0%	10 years	55.4	6%
Par	6	10 years	100.0	6
Premium	12	10 years	166.5	6

[a]*The maturity of the zero coupon bond is 10 years, the par bond 15 years, and the premium bond 18.5 years.*

nearly one in five of educational institutions followed a policy of spending portfolio yield.[5]

Today, seven in ten educational institutions determine spending by applying a prespecified percentage to a moving average of endowment values. Including past endowment values provides stability, because those past values determined in part the previous year's spending. Incorporating the current endowment value ensures that spending responds to market conditions, avoiding potential for damage caused by spending at levels unrelated to endowment value.

Some institutions spend a prespecified percentage of beginning endowment market value, thereby transmitting portfolio volatility directly to the operating budget. On the opposite end of the spectrum, some colleges and universities spend a prespecified percentage of the previous year's spending, potentially threatening endowment purchasing power preservation with market-insensitive spending levels.

A number of institutions decide each year on an appropriate rate, or have no established rule. This practice, although superficially appealing, fails to instill the financial discipline provided by a rigorous spending rule. In the absence of a well-defined spending policy, budgetary balance becomes meaningless. Spend enough to bridge the gap between revenues and expenses to produce a balanced budget. Spend less to create a deficit. Spend more to fashion a surplus. Balance, distress, and prosperity rest in the hands of the spending committee. Fiscal discipline disappears.

Target Spending Rate

The target rate of spending plays a critical role in determining the degree of intergenerational equity. Spending at levels inconsistent with investment returns either diminishes or enhances future endowment levels. Too much current spending causes future endowment levels to fall, benefiting today's scholars; too little current spending causes future endowment levels to rise, benefiting tomorrow's scholars. Selecting a distribution rate appropriate to the endowment portfolio balances the demands of today with the responsibilities of tomorrow.

Target spending rates among endowed institutions range from a surprisingly low 0.1 percent to an unsustainably high 15.5 percent. More than 70 percent of institutions employ target rates between 4.0 percent and 6.0 percent, with about one in six using a 5.0 percent rate.[6] The appropriate rate of spending depends on the risk and return characteristics of the investment portfolio, the structure of the spending policy, and the preferences expressed by trustees regarding the trade-off between stable budgetary support and asset preservation.

Analysis of investment and spending policies leads to the conclusion that distribution rates for educational institutions generally exceed the return-producing capacity of endowment assets. According to a series of simulations conducted by the Yale Investments Office, the average endowment faces a nearly 20 percent intermediate-term probability of a disruptive decline in operating budget support. More troubling may be the almost 40 percent long-run likelihood of losing one-half of endowment purchasing power.* High probabilities of intermediate-term spending volatility and long-term purchasing power decline indicate an inconsistency between expected portfolio returns and projected spending rates. Institutions faced with likely failure to meet the central goals of endowment management need to consider reducing spending levels or increasing expected portfolio returns.

In contrast to the average institution's high probability of failing to achieve endowment goals, institutions that follow sensible investment and spending policies face much better probabilities of success. For example, Yale has a long history of implementing well-articulated, disciplined policies. The university currently projects a 5 percent probability of a disruptive spending drop (as opposed to nearly 20 percent for the broader universe of institutions) and a 15 percent probability of purchasing power impairment (as opposed to 40 percent

---

*The simulations assume returns consistent with the average endowment target asset allocation as reported in the 2006 NACUBO Endowment Study, employing a spending rate of 5 percent applied to a five-year moving average of endowment values. The intermediate term spending decline consists of a 25 percent real decline over five years. The time horizon for evaluating purchasing power preservation is fifty years.

for the broader universe). Superior investment and spending policies lead to dramatically higher chances for success.

Endowment spending policies balance the competing objectives of providing substantial stable budgetary flows to benefit today's scholars and preserving portfolio assets to support tomorrow's academicians. Responsible fiduciaries face the challenging task of evaluating the ability of investment and spending policies to meet the long-term goal of purchasing power preservation and the intermediate-term goal of stable operating budget support. Employing the tools of portfolio construction and spending rules, trustees ultimately select policies based on preferences regarding the trade-off between the central goals of endowment management.

PURCHASING POWER EVALUATION

Preserving purchasing power requires that each individual gift to endowment forever maintain its ability to "support a specific set of activities." In aggregate, then, after deducting spending distributions, endowment assets must grow by the rate of educational inflation and increase by the amount of new gifts.

Appropriate measurement of inflation allows institutions to assess the continuing ability to consume a basket of goods and services peculiar to higher education. Since expenses of colleges and universities differ dramatically from those of individuals, and from those of the economy as a whole, inflation measures appropriate to individuals (the Consumer Price Index) or the broad economy (the GNP deflator) work poorly for higher education.

The Higher Education Price Index (HEPI) measures costs specific to educational institutions. Heavily weighted toward salaries and other personnel costs, over its forty-six-year history HEPI advanced at a rate approximately 1.4 percent per annum in excess of the GNP deflator. Lack of productivity gains in education accounts for the greater inflation in academic costs. A labor-intensive enterprise, teaching cannot be made more efficient without impairing the process. For example, applying technology by using video terminals to replace in-person lectures improves productivity in a superficial sense, but diminishes the educational experience. Likewise, increasing class sizes improves productivity, but undoubtedly reduces quality at the same time. As long as productivity gains disproportionately accrue to the rest of the economy, costs for higher education can be expected to grow at a rate higher than the general level of inflation.

HEPI is better predictor

Yale's Endowment Purchasing Power

Figure 3.2 illustrates the Yale endowment's purchasing power from 1950 to 2006. The analysis begins in 1950, because prior to that date the university lacks clean data on gifts, spending, and investment performance. Throughout much of the twentieth century, financial statements recorded only book values of financial assets, providing little information for students of markets. Unit accounting, which enables institutions to distinguish between various inflows and outflows, gained wide acceptance only in the early 1970s, causing earlier data to be disentangled only with great difficulty.

Purchasing power analysis starts with the 1950 endowment value and subsequent inflation rates. Increasing the 1950 portfolio value by the amount of inflation in each subsequent year creates a series of purchasing power targets. Since gifts "enlarge the scope of activities" supported by endowment, each year the purchasing power target increases by the amount of new gifts, which in subsequent years undergo a similar adjustment for inflation.

Note the importance of new gifts to the endowment, with nearly three-quarters of 2006's targeted value stemming from gifts made since

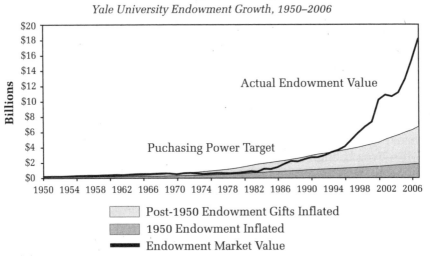

**Figure 3.2 Endowment Values Vastly Exceed 1950
Purchasing Power Target**

Yale University Endowment Growth, 1950–2006

Post-1950 Endowment Gifts Inflated
1950 Endowment Inflated
Endowment Market Value

*Sources: Yale Financial Statements. Higher Education Price Index data from
Research Associates of Washington.*

1950. In other words, in the absence of new gifts over the preceding fifty-six years, Yale's 2006 endowment would likely total only about one-quarter of its actual value.

A comparison of actual endowment values with targeted levels illustrates the degree of success in meeting purchasing power goals. Based on the difference between the June 30, 2006 market value of $18.0 billion and the purchasing power goal of $6.7 billion, Yale succeeded admirably in increasing asset values.* Yet the bottom line success includes periods in which the overall picture appeared far less rosy.

The 1950s witnessed a rough balance between endowment growth and purchasing power preservation, with a surplus of approximately 17 percent shown by 1959. After keeping pace through most of the 1960s, the endowment began to suffer as inflationary pressures grew, setting the stage for serious problems to come. During the 1970s, disastrous markets for financial assets and high inflation caused the endowment to end the decade 56 percent below its target level. By 1982, Yale's endowment reached a low point, with assets representing only 42 percent of the targeted purchasing power goal. Fortunately, the 1980s bull market reversed the problems of the 1970s, ultimately allowing the 1994 endowment to achieve the targeted level of the 1950 endowment inflated and adjusted for gifts. Extraordinary market returns subsequently boosted the June 30, 2006 endowment to a 170 percent surplus over the target.

Recent dramatic increases in endowment purchasing power cause some to question whether by accumulating assets, Yale's fiduciaries favor future generations of scholars at the expense of the current generation. While the question of the appropriate spending level generates spirited debate, the current increase in assets results from a combination of strong markets and reasonable spending rules, creating a cushion that will be drawn down in tough times to come.

Dramatic swings in purchasing power relative to targeted levels come as little surprise to veteran market observers. In 1982, Yale's endowment registered a nearly 60 percent deficit versus the desired level. Twenty-four years later, the portfolio shows a 170 percent surplus. Even though market swings cause institutions to feel alternately poor and rich, sensible portfolio managers base investment and spending decisions on assumptions regarding long-term capital market char-

---

*In fact, a significant portion of Yale's increase in purchasing power results from value added in the investment process. Over the last two decades, Yale's portfolio increased by approximately $12.4 billion relative to the median result achieved by colleges and universities.

acteristics. Evaluating purchasing power preservation requires appreciation of the positive and negative consequences of market volatility, considered within the perspective of a distinctly long time frame.

Human nature reacts to unexpectedly handsome investment returns by looking for ways to consume newfound wealth. Responding to strong markets by increasing spending rates creates the potential for long-term damage to endowment. First, increases in the rate of spending following extraordinary investment returns put the institution at risk of consuming part of the cushion designed to protect against a less robust future. Second, increases in spending soon become part of an institution's permanent expense base, reducing operational flexibility. If the rate of spending rises in a boom, an institution facing a bust loses the benefit of a cushion and suffers the burden of a greater budgetary base.

Target spending rates sit at the center of fiscal discipline, leading responsible fiduciaries to alter rates with great reluctance. Rather than seeing strong recent performance as an encouragement to increase payouts, skeptical managers wonder about the sustainability of past good fortune and prepare for the possibility of a less rewarding future. Only fundamental improvements in an institution's investment and spending policies justify altering target spending rates.

Evaluating maintenance of purchasing power requires an extremely long time horizon. Reacting to a decade of disastrous losses by reducing payout formulas or responding to a decade of extraordinary returns by increasing distribution rates may harm the academic enterprise. Bear market–induced cuts in programs and bull market–driven expansions of offerings needlessly buffet the institution, causing the endowment to fail in its mission of buffering university operations from financial market volatility. Responsible fiduciaries look past the inevitable short-run swings in endowment value caused by market gyrations, keeping attention firmly focused on the long-run preservation of asset purchasing power.

SPENDING SUSTAINABILITY EVALUATION

Stewards of endowment assets strive to provide a substantial, sustainable flow of resources to support the academic enterprise. In Tobin's words, to "support the same set of activities" throughout time, distributions must grow by at least the rate of inflation for the goods and services consumed by endowed institutions. When new gifts "enlarge the scope of activities," distributions from endowment must increase to support and sustain the new activities.

In contrast to the long-term nature of the purchasing power preservation goal, providing a sustainable flow of support to the operating budget constitutes an intermediate-term objective. Since large fluctuations in endowment spending flows wreak havoc with a budgetary process that thrives on stability, endowment managers strive to deliver reasonably predictable distributions to support operations.

Yale's Endowment Distributions

A spending sustainability analysis, portrayed in Figure 3.3, mirrors the purchasing power evaluation illustrated earlier. Beginning with 1950 spending from endowment as a base, the targeted spending levels increase each year by inflation and by the amount of spending from new gifts. For purposes of analysis, 4.5 percent represents the assumed spending rate on new gifts, a level consistent with Yale's long-run spending pattern.

Over the fifty-six years covered in the spending analysis, Yale managed to increase or maintain nominal spending year-in and year-out.

Figure 3.3 Spending Growth Surpasses Inflation

Yale University Spending Growth, 1950–2006

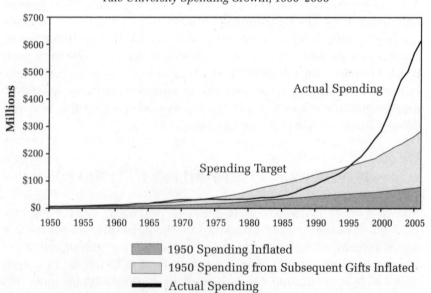

1950 Spending Inflated
1950 Spending from Subsequent Gifts Inflated
Actual Spending

Sources: Yale University Financial Statements. Higher Education Price Index data from Research Associates of Washington.

Inflation-adjusted spending does not boast the same unblemished record. After keeping pace with the inflation-adjusted target in the 1950s and 1960s, Yale's spending failed to keep up with the virulent inflation of the 1970s. Beginning in the mid 1980s, spending flows grew rapidly, posting sizable real gains and closing the gap between actual distributions and inflation-adjusted goals. In spite of extraordinary growth in the 1980s and 1990s, not until 1996 did Yale's spending from endowment exceed the inflation-adjusted target.

The two-year lag between the endowment's recapture of the 1950 gift-adjusted purchasing power level in 1994 and the spending flow's achievement of the same goal in 1996 stems largely from the dampening effect of the spending policy's smoothing mechanism. As endowment values rose rapidly beginning in the early 1980s and continuing through the 1990s, the averaging process in the spending rule kept endowment distributions from adjusting fully to the endowment's price appreciation.

More evidence of the impact of the smoothing mechanism comes from the spending level for 2006. Even though applying the target spending rate of 5.25 percent to the endowment's $15.2 billion value (as of June 30, 2005) results in a projected distribution of $799 million (ignoring the inflation adjustment), the actual spending level for fiscal 2006 amounted to only $618 million. As time passes, the spending rule causes actual payouts to move toward the targeted level, implying that if Yale were to maintain a $15.2 billion endowment, spending would approach $799 million within a few years.

While current beneficiaries of endowment distributions sometimes complain about the lag between endowment growth and spending increases, the smoothing mechanism performs a necessary function in muting the transmission of volatility in endowment values to spending flows. Yale's policies dampen volatility effectively, as evidenced by the fact that over the past fifty-six years the dispersion of year-over-year percentage changes in endowment value (12.4 percent standard deviation) exceeds by a fair margin the dispersion of changes in spending level (6.9 percent standard deviation). Effective spending rules allow assumption of greater investment risk, without transmitting the associated volatility to budgetary distributions.

At times, even the most effective set of policies provides little protection against turbulent markets. The greatest failure in providing stable budgetary support occurred in the 1970s. Operating in an environment where the rate of inflation exceeded returns on domestic stocks and bonds, endowment managers faced a grim set of choices. In spite of beginning the decade with actual spending comfortably ahead of the adjusted 1950 target level, by 1980 actual spending amounted to less than one-half the inflation-adjusted goal. In the face of hostile financial market conditions from 1970 to 1980 the university managed only to maintain the nominal payout, which proved woefully inadequate in the face of the decade's inflation. Even though nominal spending flows began to rise after 1980, the target level rose faster, causing actual spending at 1984's nadir to represent only 44 percent of the goal.

Viewed from the perspective of individual, but not independent, five-year periods, Yale experienced real spending declines of more than 25 percent six times in a succession of miserable years from 1971 to 1981. Such significant drops represent a failure to provide a stable flow of resources to support operations.

Providing stable, substantial, sustainable flows of resources to support operations represents the ultimate test of the effectiveness of endowment investment and spending policies. Even though at times financial market conditions preclude reasonable satisfaction of endowment objectives, by fashioning a sensible package of asset management and distribution policies, investors increase the likelihood of achieving reasonable balance between the competing goals of protecting endowment assets from inflation-induced erosion and providing high, reliable levels of current budgetary support.

FOUNDATION INVESTMENT GOALS

Foundations share some characteristics with educational endowments. Along with their counterparts at colleges and universities, trustees of foundation assets often ignore Ben Franklin's certainties of life, enjoying favorable tax status and operating with a perpetual horizon. For many foundations, however, permanency constitutes a choice, not an obligation. If a foundation pursues a mission with a particular sense of urgency, for example, funding research to cure a terribly virulent disease, the trustees may decide to expend all available resources in an attempt to reach the goal with deliberate speed. Even without a time-sensitive mission, spending at rates designed to extinguish foundation assets constitutes a legitimate option for trustees.

A number of characteristics separate academic institutions from foundations. College and university endowment managers control both the management of assets, by determining the portfolio allocation, and the specification of liabilities, by defining the spending policy. The lack of constraints on investment and spending strategies provides great flexibility for fiduciaries, increasing the likelihood of meeting institutional goals.

Foundations exercise complete control over asset-allocation policies, similar to the flexibility enjoyed by educational institutions. On the spending side, however, foundations must achieve a minimum payout of five percent of assets to support charitable purposes, or face tax penalties. The mandated distribution level causes foundations to face an investment problem materially different from the challenge facing educational endowment managers.

While academic institutions benefit enormously from high levels of endowment distributions, in the event of a serious disruption in endowment support other revenue sources play a compensating role in the budgetary base. Endowment distributions generally support only a modest portion of educational institution operating budgets, with major research universities relying on endowment payout to fund an average of 12.5 percent of expenditures.[7] For most such institutions, a significant decrease in spending from endowment poses difficult problems, but fails to threaten institutional viability.

Foundations rely almost exclusively on investment income to support operations. In 2006, eight of the ten largest grant-making foundations received essentially 100 percent of total revenues from investment portfolios. Even though grant programs grow and shrink somewhat more readily than academic operations, foundations require reasonably stable flows of funds to avoid disruption, particularly when activities involve multiyear commitments. The great reliance of foundations on distributions from investment assets calls for structuring portfolios with lower risk profiles.

Colleges and universities benefit from the generosity of alumni and friends, with gifts providing an important source of support for academic programs. In difficult times, inflows from donors serve to dampen shortfalls in endowment support for operations. In prosperous times, gifts allow educational institutions to expand the scope of their activities. Over time, the cumulative impact of giving makes an enormous difference to colleges and universities.

The Impact of Gifts

The experience of Harvard, Yale, and the Carnegie Institution over the course of the twentieth century provides insight into the importance of donor support. The Carnegie Institution of Washington, one of

Andrew Carnegie's many philanthropies, pursues pure, cutting-edge scientific research in astronomy, plant biology, embryology, global ecology, and earth sciences. Carnegie established the Institution in 1902 with a $10 million gift, increased the endowment by a further $2 million in 1907, and added $10 million in 1911. Carnegie's $22 million endowment nearly equaled Harvard's 1910 fund balance of $23 million and vastly exceeded Yale's $12 million.

Over the course of nearly a century, the Carnegie Institution endowment more than kept pace with inflation, with June 30, 2006 assets of $720 million comfortably ahead of the $490 million needed to match the rise in price levels. But the formerly comparable Harvard endowment, with a June 30, 2006 value of $29.2 billion, and the previously smaller Yale endowment, with a value of $18.0 billion, dwarf the Carnegie fund. While differences in investment and spending policies no doubt explain some of the gap, the absence of gift inflows constitutes the fundamental reason for Carnegie's failure to keep pace with Yale and Harvard.

In desiring to supply a stable flow of operating income, hoping to exist forever and wishing to comply with minimum IRS distribution requirements, foundation fiduciaries face a fundamentally conflicting set of goals. Without a safety net of external sources of support, foundations feel the impact of poor investment results. Short-term stability in distributions argues for a less volatile portfolio, while long-run maintenance of purchasing power and high payout rates point toward a higher risk allocation. Foundations generally opt for lower risk portfolios, sensibly providing stable flows of resources to support the institutional mission. As a result, the foundation community spends at rates inconsistent with preservation of capital, suggesting that in the long run the role of most foundations will diminish as purchasing power erodes.

In spite of superficial similarities, endowments and foundations differ in important ways, including the amount of control over spending streams, the degree of programmatic reliance on portfolio distributions, and the availability of continuing external support. While endowments and foundations share some important characteristics, dissimilarities between the two types of funds lead to articulation of meaningfully different purposes and goals. That investment objectives of such closely related organizations differ so significantly highlights the importance of careful consideration of the relationship between investment funds and institutional objectives. Understanding the raison d'etre of a fund and expressing the related institutional aspirations serve as an important starting point in the fund's management process.

THE SKEPTICAL VIEWPOINT

In a healthy academic community, controversy abounds. In the case of endowments, debate generally revolves around intergenerational issues, with some current beneficiaries suggesting that endowment payout levels provide insufficient support for university operations.

Henry Hansmann, the Augustus E. Lines Professor of Law at Yale Law School, questions the advisability of any endowment accumulation, raising issues that go far beyond the question of appropriate payout rates. In an August 2, 1998 *New York Times* interview, Hansmann suggests that "a stranger from Mars who looks at private universities would probably say they are institutions whose business is to run large pools of investment assets and that they run educational institutions on the side that can expand and contract to act as buffers for investment pools."[8] Hansmann suggests that trustees pursue a "real objective" of accumulating a large and growing endowment, viewing the educational operations as a constraint to unfettered financial asset accumulation. Administrators and faculty seek endowments to provide job security, a light workload, and a pleasant physical environment, while alumni focus on reputational capital, hoping to bask in the reflected glory of a wealthy educational institution.

In a paper entitled "Why Do Universities Have Endowments?" Hansmann uses the experience of the 1960s and 1970s to bolster his argument. He notes the "financial crisis of the 1970s" damaged higher education as "private demand declined, government support abruptly stopped its former upward trajectory, and energy costs increased dramatically."[9] Recognizing that universities found themselves squeezed between costs that were continuing to rise and income sources that were shrinking, Hansmann observes "little affirmative evidence that universities have viewed their endowments principally as buffers for their operating budgets."[10]

Yale's Endowment Buffer

An analysis of the behavior of Hansmann's own institution belies his claims. His employer, Yale University, used endowment spending policy to dampen growth in the boom times of the 1960s and to cushion the financial trauma of the 1970s. During the decade of the 1960s, Yale released an average of 4.4 percent of the endowment to support the academic enterprise. Strong budgetary results and superior investment performance accompanied endowment distributions that provided support at levels consistent with long-term sustainability.

In contrast, during the 1970s, spending from endowment averaged 6.3 percent, as Yale sought to offset, at least in part, the impact of hostile economic forces. Despite following a policy that released support for the operating budget at unsustainable rates, Yale posted deficits in every year of the decade. The policy of "leaning against the wind" cost the endowment dearly, as the purchasing power of assets declined by more than 60 percent between 1968 and 1982, in spite of the infusion of substantial amounts of new gifts.

The historical record indicates that Yale uses endowment assets to shield the operating budget from disruptive fluctuations in income streams. Sustainable spending rates in the range of 3.8 percent to 4.4 percent in the 1950s, 1960s, 1980s and 1990s correspond to reasonably stable operating environments. In contrast, the deficit-plagued 1970s saw spending peak at the stunning rate of 7.4 percent in 1971. Without extraordinary endowment support in the 1970s, Yale's operational troubles would have been magnified, perhaps causing long-term damage to the institution.

Not only does historical experience suggest that Yale employed endowment assets to insulate academic programs from economic stress, but the very nature of the university's spending policy places budgetary stability in a prominent place. Each year Yale spends 80 percent of last year's spending adjusted for inflation *plus* 20 percent of the targeted long-term spending rate applied to the previous year's endowment market value adjusted for inflation. By emphasizing budgetary stability, the university expresses a strong preference for using the endowment to reduce the impact of financial shocks.

Spending Policy Extremes

endowment as a fallback in case of turmoil

Examining Yale's spending decisions in the context of policy extremes favoring, on the one hand, spending stability and, on the other hand, endowment preservation, highlights the university's substantial bias toward providing reliable support for operations. If universities treat academic operations as a sideshow to endowment accumulation, spending distributions would correspond to levels consistent with maintenance of asset purchasing power. In the extreme case, institutions would distribute only returns in excess of inflation, placing preservation of investment assets above even a modicum of stability in supporting academic programs. At the other end of the spectrum, if universities focus exclusively on consistent payouts from endowment, spending would rise with inflation, tracing a pattern independent of fluctuations in the market value of endowment assets.

Figure 3.4A illustrates the spending patterns resulting from two extreme spending policies using market returns from the 1960s and 1970s. The first panel shows the constant flows from maintaining inflation-adjusted spending, while the second depicts the volatile flows from maintaining inflation-adjusted endowment values. Note that an exclusive focus on endowment purchasing power stability fails to allow any distribution to support operations in more than one-half of the simulated periods.

Figure 3.4B shows the impact of the extreme spending policies on endowment levels. Pursuing stable spending flows, as illustrated in the first panel, produces enormous volatility in real endowment values. In contrast, preserving endowment purchasing power promotes stability in asset values, as depicted by the relatively smooth pattern in the second panel.

Policies designed to provide a constant level of inflation-adjusted support for operations, illustrated in the top panels of Figures 3.4A and 3.4B, depend on benign financial markets to operate successfully. Consider the dramatically different results from simulations conducted using financial data from the 1960s and the 1970s.

The 1960s provided substantial rewards to investors. Stocks returned 7.8 percent per annum and bonds 3.5 percent in an environment where inflation grew by only 2.5 percent. Investors pursuing stable spending policies did little damage to endowments, causing a purchasing power decline of only around 10 percent.

In contrast, economic and financial conditions in the 1970s posed grave threats to endowed institutions, as high inflation and poor marketable securities returns exacted a terrible toll. Inflation, consuming 7.4 percent annually, exceeded returns on domestic stocks at 5.9 percent per annum, bonds at 7.0 percent, and cash at 6.3 percent. Investors found no place to hide. Simulations show that in 1970, if a traditional portfolio followed a stable spending policy, more than 60 percent of the purchasing power of a fund evaporated by the end of the decade.

Policies focused solely on endowment preservation, shown in the middle panels of Figures 3.4A and 3.4B, failed to release any distribution to the operating budget in twelve of the twenty years between 1960 and 1979, highlighting the impracticality of a single-minded focus on asset protection. Even in the hospitable environment of the 1960s, investment results provided no support for current operations

Figure 3.4A: Spending Flow Comparison Illustrates Impact of Extreme Policies

Stable Spending Policy Simulation Provides
Consistent Inflation-Adjusted Budgetary Support
Spending Flows, 1960–1979
Spend 5% of Market Value, Increased by Inflation

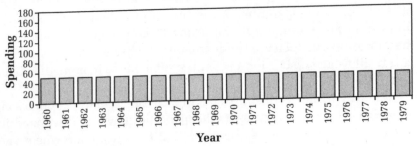

Stable Endowment Policy Simulation Generates Unreliable Budgetary Support
Spending Flows, 1960–1979
Spend Only Returns Generated in Excess of Inflation

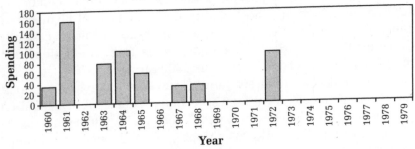

Yale Policy Provides Stable Budgetary Support
Spending Flows, 1960–1979
Actual Yale Policy

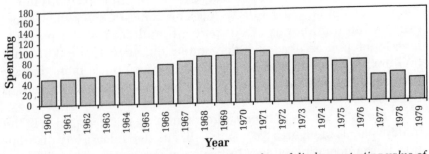

Note: Data are adjusted for inflation. Hypothetical portfolio has a starting value of $1000 and is readjusted to an asset allocation of 60 percent stocks and 40 percent bonds yearly. Actual Yale experience includes impact of new gifts while simulations do not.

Figure 3.4B: Endowment Level Comparison Illustrates Impact
of Extreme Policies

Stable Spending Policy Simulation Erodes Inflation Adjusted Endowment Values
Endowment Levels, 1960–1979
Spend 5% of Market Value, Increased by Inflation

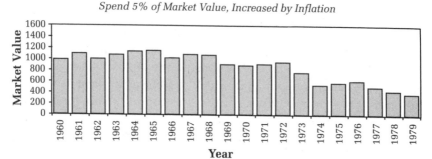

Stable Endowment Policy Simulation Protects Inflation Adjusted
Endowment Values
Endowment Levels, 1960–1979
Spend Only Returns Generated in Excess of Inflation

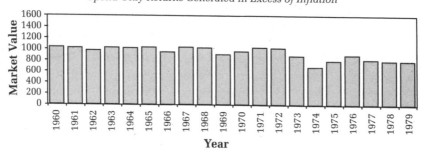

Yale Policy Favors Budgetary Flows at the Expense of Endowment Preservation
Endowment Levels, 1960–1979
Actual Yale Experience

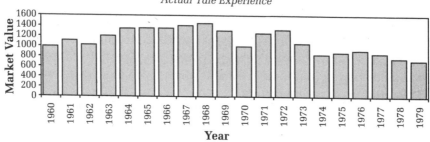

Notes: Data are adjusted for inflation. Hypothetical portfolio has a starting value $1000 and is readjusted to an asset allocation of 60 percent stocks and 40 percent bonds yearly. Actual Yale experience is indexed to 1000 in 1960 to facilitate comparison with the simulations, but includes the impact of new gifts while simulations do not.

in three of ten years. So hostile were the 1970s that even with only one meaningful distribution to the budget, stable endowment policies failed to preserve assets, as purchasing power declined by nearly 24 percent.

Yale's policies, as reflected in spending flows and endowment levels depicted in the bottom panel of the figures, track the stable spending policy much more closely than the stable endowment policy. Similar to other endowed institutions, in the 1970s Yale experienced an extraordinary decline in endowment purchasing power as the institution sought to supply flows of funds to support the university's academic mission. By spending at unsustainably high rates, purchasing power of assets declined dramatically, dropping more than 40 percent during the 1970s. Yale's actions belie Hansmann's suggestion that endowment preservation dominates institutional thinking.

CONCLUSION

Investment and spending policies support the purposes for which educational institutions accumulate endowments, providing the framework for producing enhanced stability, increased independence, and greater excellence. By achieving the long-term goal of purchasing power preservation and the intermediate-term goal of substantial, stable budgetary support, colleges and universities meet economist James Tobin's requirement that an endowment "continue to support the set of activities that it is now supporting."[11]

Fiduciaries face a challenge in balancing the conflicting goals of preserving assets and supporting current operations. Spending policies resolve the tension by specifying the relative importance of sensitivity to current endowment market values (contributing to asset preservation) and sensitivity to past spending levels (contributing to stable budgetary support). The target spending rate plays an important role in determining a fund's ability to meet the objective of intergenerational equity, with too-high rates favoring current scholars and too-low rates favoring tomorrow's.

Donors to endowment expect to provide permanent support to a designated activity, requiring endowment managers to maintain each specific fund's ability to purchase the associated goods and services throughout time. Rates of inflation faced by educational institutions exceed general price-level increases since human-resource-dependent academic enterprises generally fail to achieve productivity gains, increasing the difficulties inherent in maintaining endowment purchasing power. New gifts fail to relieve the pressure to maintain asset values, as contributions to endowment expand the set of activities funded by an institution's permanent funds and enlarge the size of the portfolio to be preserved.

The process of articulating purposes and defining goals benefits fund managers of all stripes, leading to substantially different conclusions for different investors. In the case of institutions as similar as endowments and foundations, differences in institutional character cause purposes to vary. Variations in operating environments lead to expression of different investment goals that accommodate the particular institution's specific opportunities and constraints.

By providing the ultimate test against which to measure the desirability of various investment and spending policies, investment goals serve as an essential foundation for the funds' management process. Investment objectives influence the philosophical tenets that underlie the creation of investment portfolios, generating important guidance for fund managers. Investors evaluate combinations of portfolio asset allocations and spending policies in terms of ability to meet institutional goals, placing articulation of portfolio objectives at the heart of the investment process.

A mix of purchasing power and budget support

4
Investment Philosophy

1. Asset Allocation
2. Market timing
3. Security selection

Successful investors articulate coherent investment philosophies, consistently applied to all aspects of the portfolio management process. Philosophical principles represent time-tested insights into investment matters that rise to the level of enduring professional convictions. The central tenets of an investor's approach to markets emanate from fundamental beliefs regarding the most effective means to generate investment returns to satisfy institutional goals.

Investment returns stem from decisions regarding three tools of portfolio management: asset allocation, market timing, and security selection. Investor behavior determines the relative importance of each aspect of portfolio management, with careful investors consciously constructing portfolios to reflect the expected contribution of each portfolio management tool.

Asset allocation, the starting point for portfolio construction, involves defining the asset classes that constitute the portfolio and determining the proportion of the fund that resides in each class. Typical institutional asset classes include domestic equities, foreign equities, fixed income, absolute return, real assets, and private equities. The policy portfolio describes the target allocation to each of the asset classes employed by the fund.

Market timing consists of short-run deviation from the long-term policy targets. For example, assume that a fund's long-term targets are 50 percent stocks and 50 percent bonds. A fund manager who identifies stocks as temporarily cheap and bonds as temporarily expensive might tactically weight the portfolio 60 percent to stocks and 40 percent to bonds. The return resulting from the overweighting of stocks and underweighting of bonds constitutes the return attributable to market timing.

Security selection derives from active management of individual asset classes. If a manager creates portfolios that faithfully replicate the markets (i.e., passive portfolios), that manager makes no active bets. To the extent that a portfolio differs from the composition of the overall market, active management accounts for a portion of investment results. For example, the security selection return for the U.S. equity asset class would be the difference between returns from the U.S. equity portfolio's securities and returns from the overall domestic equity market, as defined by a benchmark index of U.S. equities, such as the Wilshire 5000.

The Role of Asset Allocation

Many investors believe that a law of finance dictates that policy allocation decisions dominate portfolio returns, relegating market timing and security selection actions to secondary status. In a 2000 study, Roger Ibbotson and Paul Kaplan survey a number of articles on the contribution of asset allocation to investment returns. The authors note that "[o]n average, policy accounted for a little more than all of total return," implying that security selection and market timing make no material contribution to returns.[1] In another nod to the centrality of the asset-allocation decision, Ibbotson and Kaplan conclude that ". . . approximately 90 percent of the variability of a fund's return across time is explained by the variability of policy returns."[2]

Investors often treat asset allocation's central role in determining portfolio returns as a truism. It is not. The Ibbotson and Kaplan study describes investor behavior, not finance theory. Imagine a buy-and-hold portfolio consisting of one (particularly idiosyncratic) stock—portfolio returns follow largely from security selection. Or, consider the strategy of aggressively day trading bond futures—market timing dominates returns.

Obviously, institutional portfolio managers usually buy more than one stock and rarely pursue aggressive day trading strategies. Instead, investors hold broadly diversified portfolios and avoid market timing, leaving asset allocation to determine investment results. Given the difficulties in timing markets and the challenges of security selection, such behavior provides a rational foundation for investment management. By avoiding extreme allocation shifts and holding diversified portfolios, investors cause asset allocation to account for the largest share of portfolio returns.

Recognizing that decisions regarding the relative importance of asset allocation, market timing, and security selection lie within an investor's purview serves as an important starting point for policymakers. Instead of passively accepting the overwhelming importance of asset allocation, knowledgeable investors consider each source of return as a significant independent factor. Ultimately, in articulating a philosophy regarding the respective roles of asset allocation, market timing, and security selection, investors determine the fundamental character of the investment management process.

By choosing to place asset allocation at the center of the investment process, investors ground the decision-making framework on the stable foundation of long-term policy actions. Focus on asset allocation relegates market timing and security selection decisions to the background, reducing the degree to which investment results depend on mercurial, unreliable factors.

Selecting the asset classes for a portfolio constitutes a critically important set of decisions, contributing in large measure to a portfolio's success or failure. Identifying appropriate asset classes requires focus on functional characteristics, considering potential to deliver returns and to mitigate portfolio risk. Commitment to an equity bias enhances returns, while pursuit of diversification reduces risks. Thoughtful, deliberate focus on asset allocation dominates the agenda of long-term investors.

The principles of equity ownership and diversification underlie asset allocation deliberations of serious long-term investors. Both historical experience and finance theory point to the conclusion that owning equities provides higher returns than owning bonds. Investors seeking to generate high rates of return naturally gravitate toward substantial allocations to equity assets. At the same time, risks associated with concentrating portfolios in a single asset type give investors pause, causing prudent market participants to diversify portfolio exposures. Expressing an equity bias and maintaining appropriate diversification provide the foundation for building strong investment portfolios.

The Role of Market Timing

Market timing, according to Charles Ellis, represents a losing strategy. "There is no evidence of any large institutions having anything like consistent ability to get in when the market is low and get out when the market is high. Attempts to switch between stocks and bonds, or between stocks and cash, in anticipation of market moves have been unsuccessful much more often than they have been successful."[3]

Market timing causes portfolio characteristics to deviate from those embodied in the policy portfolio, producing inevitable differences in risk and return attributes. If market timers bet against the stock market by reducing equity holdings and increasing cash positions, long-run expected portfolio returns decline as the market timer's position decreases risk levels. Because such activity lowers anticipated returns, market timers must succeed substantially more than 50 percent of the time to post a winning record. The wind in the speculator's face, combined with transactions costs and market impact, provide a high hurdle for those who would beat the market by holding abnormally high cash positions.

If market timers increase the risk profile of a portfolio by overweighting a risky asset at the expense of lower-risk positions, fiduciaries must consider the advisability of moving risk beyond policy portfolio levels. If riskier portfolios produce characteristics consistent with institutional goals, portfolio managers ought to consider adopting a higher risk policy portfolio. If the market timer's enhanced risk gives fiduciaries pause, then prudence demands rejecting even temporary moves to increase risk. Serious investors avoid timing markets.

The Role of Security Selection

In efficient markets, active portfolio management, like market timing, tends to detract from aggregate investment performance. In the context of relative performance, security selection constitutes a zero-sum game. Since IBM (and every other tradeable stock) represents a finite, measurable proportion of the market value of the U.S. equity market, an investor can only hold an overweight position in IBM when other investors hold a corresponding underweight position in IBM. The active manager who overweights IBM creates market impact and incurs transaction costs in establishing the position; on the other side of the trade are other active managers who underweight IBM, incurring those same transactions costs and creating that same market impact. Only one of those positions can be right in light of IBM's subsequent performance. Measured by the change in IBM's price relative to the market, the amount by which the winners win equals the amount by which the losers lose. Since active managers pay a high price to play the game, in the aggregate active investors will lose by the amount of manager fees, transactions costs, and market impact.

In less efficient markets, active management produces potentially sizable rewards. In fact, passive replication of benchmark returns proves impossible in private markets, such as venture capital, leveraged buyouts, real estate, timber, and oil and gas. Even were the market return obtainable, investors would almost certainly prefer to pursue more selective approaches. When examined over reasonably long periods of time, in aggregate, illiquid asset classes generally produce mediocre returns relative to less risky marketable security alternatives.

An inverse relationship exists between efficiency in asset pricing and appropriate degree of active management. Passive management strategies suit highly efficient markets, such as U.S. Treasury bonds, where market returns drive results and active management adds little or nothing. Active management strategies fit inefficient markets, such as private equity, where market returns contribute very little to ultimate results and investment selection provides the fundamental source of return.

Market participants willing to accept illiquidity achieve a significant edge in seeking high risk-adjusted returns. Because market players routinely overpay for liquidity, serious investors benefit by avoiding overpriced liquid securities and by embracing less liquid alternatives.

Pursuit of value-oriented strategies enhances opportunities to achieve security selection success. Value can either be purchased, by identifying assets trading at below fair value, or created, by bringing unusual skills to improve corporate operations. Value investors operate with a margin of safety unavailable to less conservative investors.

The degree of active management opportunity in various asset classes provides important input into the portfolio management process. Emphasizing inefficiently priced asset classes with interesting active management opportunities increases the odds of investment success. Intelligent acceptance of illiquidity and a value orientation constitute a sensible, conservative approach to portfolio management.

In structuring portfolios, investors make choices, either explicitly or implicitly, regarding the respective roles of asset allocation, market timing, and security selection. A strong portfolio management framework rests on asset allocation decisions and incorporates a bias toward equity assets with an appropriate level of diversification. Since market timing actions generally prove unrewarding and always cause portfolios to deviate from desired characteristics, serious investors avoid market timing. Security selection decisions, while extremely difficult to execute with consistent success, contain the potential to add value to portfolio returns. Investors enhance opportunity for beating the market by pursuing excess returns where the degree of opportunity appears largest, by accepting reasonable degrees of illiquidity, and by maintaining a value orientation.

ASSET ALLOCATION

Equity Bias

Sensible investors approach markets with a strong equity bias, since accepting the risk of owning equities rewards long-term investors with higher returns. High returns contribute mightily to meeting the goals of preservation of purchasing power and of provision of sustainable operating budget support. In fact, the tension between the conflicting goals of preserving assets and spending for operations can be relaxed only by increasing investment returns.

Finance theory posits that acceptance of greater risk leads to the reward of higher expected returns. In a happy coincidence, historical capital markets data, collected by Roger Ibbotson and Rex Sinquefield, support the theoretical conclusion. Consider the wealth multiples for investments in various U.S. asset classes and inflation outlined in Table 4.1.

Table 4.1 Equities Generate Superior Returns in the Long Run

Wealth Multiples for U.S. Asset Classes and Inflation

December 1925–December 2005

Asset Class	Multiple
Inflation	11 times
Treasury bills	18 times
Treasury bonds	71 times
Corporate bonds	100 times
Large-capitalization stocks	2,658 times
Small-capitalization stocks	13,706 times

Source: Ibbotson Associates, Stocks, Bonds, Bills and Inflation, 2006 Year Book.

Historical Evidence

The data indicate that a dollar invested in Treasury bills at the end of 1925, with all income reinvested, would have grown eighteen times by December 31, 2005. At first glance, having multiplied the original investment by a factor of 18 appears satisfactory. However, given that more than 60 percent of the increase would have been lost to inflation, the result loses some luster. The low return of Treasury bills should not come as a surprise. On at least two measures Treasury bills have been close to risk free. Investors face virtually no credit exposure, as the U.S. government represents, perhaps, the most creditworthy entity in the world. In addition, Treasury bills have provided a hedge against inflation, with returns that closely track price increases. The price of these attractive characteristics has been an extremely low real return. Thus, at least with twenty-twenty hindsight, Treasury bills would not have been an appropriate investment for an institution investing to earn substantial after-inflation returns.

Moving farther out the risk spectrum, the same dollar invested in longer-term government bonds at the end of 1925 would have multiplied 71 times by the end of 2005. Government bonds share with Treasury bills extremely high credit quality. Unlike shorter-term instruments, however, bonds have a highly uncertain real return. Twenty-year bonds, which are used in the Ibbotson-Sinquefield analysis, face two decades of inflation rates, unknown and unknowable at the time of purchase. Not only do real returns vary greatly, nominal returns also fluctuate over holding periods of less than the term-to-maturity. The higher risks of longer-term bonds have been rewarded with higher returns, although such returns fail to provide meaningful support for an institution that consumes only after-inflation returns.

Corporate bonds provide an alternative to investment in government securities. Over the eighty-year period, corporate bonds provided a wealth multiple of 100, exceeding the multiple of 71 for default-free government bonds. The incremental return reflects compensation for credit risk and call risk embodied in corporate obligations.* In essence, high-grade corporate bonds are a hybrid instrument, combining bond-like characteristics with some equity risk and some optionality.

The 18 multiple for investing in Treasury bills, the 71 multiple for

---

*Call risk represents the risk that an issuer will redeem bonds at a fixed price prior to maturity. Bondholders generally suffer when issuers call bonds, since calls usually occur in an environment in which interest rates have declined.

investing in Treasury bonds and the 100 multiple for investing in corporate bonds represent long-term rewards for lending money. Loans are relatively low risk assets. In the case of Treasury obligations, the full faith and credit of the United States Government stand behind the commitment to pay interest and return principal in a timely manner. In the case of corporate bonds, the instruments have a senior claim on the assets of a corporation. That is, payments on bonds take precedence over distributions to the owners of a company, its equity holders.

Obviously, as residual claimants, equity holders face substantially greater risks than do bondholders. In extreme cases, when corporations fail to meet fixed obligations, equity owners may be wiped out. In spite of (or, perhaps, because of) these risks, in the United States, over long periods of time equities have outperformed bonds by impressive margins.

A dollar invested in common stock at the end of 1925 would have multiplied 2,658-fold during the eighty-year holding period. An enormous difference exists between the return expected from the conservative investment in cash (18 times) or government bonds (71 times) and that expected from taking the greater risk in owning equity securities (2,658 times).

The long-term benefits of owning equities increase as investments move farther out the risk continuum. When investors assume the risk of investing in smaller capitalization equities, the dollar grows 13,706 times during the period, a staggering amount relative to returns for other asset classes. While some controversy surrounds the methodology used by Ibbotson-Sinquefield's measurement of returns for small stocks, their work gives a sense of the long-term rewards for accepting greater equity risk.

Although eighty years of Ibbotson-Sinquefield data show persuasive results, longer periods of time produce even more dramatic conclusions. Wharton Professor Jeremy Siegel, in his book *Stocks for the Long Run,* examines investment returns from 1802 to 2001. By using Ibbotson's recent data to extend Siegel's return series, over the more than two centuries from 1802 to 2005, a dollar in the U.S. stock market grows to $10.3 million. During the same period, cash investments generate a multiple of only 4.8 thousand. The return-generating power of equity investment over long periods of time dominates the multiples obtained by investing in bills and bonds as shown in Table 4.2.

As a footnote, gold "bugs" will be disappointed to learn that their favorite precious metal returned a multiple of only 27, trailing by a large margin the returns of low risk Treasury bills and only modestly exceeding the 16-fold impact of inflation.

Table 4.2 Equities Provide Astonishing Results in the Very Long Run

Wealth Multiples for U.S. Asset Classes and Inflation
December 1802–December 2005

Asset Class	Multiple
Inflation	16 times
Treasury bills	4.8 thousand times
Treasury bonds	19.5 thousand times
Large-capitalization stocks	10.3 million times

Sources: Ibbotson Associates, Stocks, Bonds, Bills and Inflation, 2006 Year Book; *Jeremy Siegel,* Stocks for the Long Run *(New York 2002);* Bloomberg.

equity => return

These findings suggest that long-term investors maximize wealth by investing in high-return, high-risk equity rather than buying debt instruments of governments and corporations. As with many broad generalizations, this seemingly obvious conclusion requires further examination.

Market studies focusing only on returns for securities in the United States miss important information. Recent academic work by Will Goetzmann and Philippe Jorion on investor experience in other countries reduces confidence in the long-run superiority of equity investing.[4] At the turn of the twentieth century, active stock markets existed in Russia, France, Germany, Japan, and Argentina, all of which have been interrupted ". . . for a variety of reasons, including political turmoil, war, and hyper-inflation. Obviously, these markets provide little grist for the mill of long-term capital market studies. Even the most continuous of markets, those in the United States and United Kingdom, were shut down for several months during World War I."[5] Studies of long-term returns in the United States ignore the fact that investors in foreign markets experienced less favorable outcomes, with sometimes dramatically worse results.

In addition to the possibility that enthusiasm for equities might be based on parochial experience, survivorship bias* inflates percep-

---

*Survivorship bias occurs when data exclude markets (or investment funds or individual securities) that disappear. Since lower returning, higher-risk markets (or investment funds or individual securities) tend to fail at a higher rate than their higher-returning, lower-risk counterparts, the sample of survivors describes an environment that overstates the real world return and understates the real world risk.

tions of historical returns. One study suggests that ". . . the 5 percent real capital appreciation return on U.S. stocks is exceptional, as other markets have typically returned 3 percent less than U.S. equities." Were this conclusion to influence expectations for long-run equity returns, the case for stock investments becomes considerably less compelling.

Ultimately, the argument for an equity bias in a long-term investment portfolio rests on more than historical experience. Finance theory sensibly teaches that acceptance of greater risk accompanies an expectation of greater return. While future stock market returns might not be as robust as they have been for U.S. equity investors, long-term investors will be well served with an equity bias.

Diversification

Even though market return studies indicate that high levels of equity market exposure benefit long-term investors, the associated risks come through less clearly. Significant concentration in a single asset class poses extraordinary risk to portfolio assets. Fortunately, diversification provides investors with a powerful risk management tool. By combining assets that vary in response to forces that drive markets, investors create more efficient portfolios. At a given risk level, properly diversified portfolios provide higher returns than less well diversified portfolios. Conversely, through appropriate diversification, a given level of returns can be achieved at lower risk. Harry Markowitz, pioneer of modern portfolio theory, maintains that portfolio diversification provides investors with a "free lunch," since risk can be reduced without sacrificing expected return.

That's why you diversify!

Yale and the Eagle Bank

An extraordinary example of the risk in portfolio concentration comes from a catastrophic event in the early history of the Yale endowment. An overwhelmingly large, ill-advised investment in a single bank nearly bankrupted the college, with consequences that lasted for decades.

In 1811, Yale College treasurer James Hillhouse and his illustrious colleagues, Eli Whitney, William Woolsey, and Simeon Baldwin, acquired the charter for the formation of the Eagle Bank of New Haven. At that time, only one other bank served New Haven's healthy economy and developing merchant class. Hoping to pursue a mission of fostering industry and commerce, at its opening the Eagle Bank commanded a significant level of public confidence.

William Woolsey, a shrewd and experienced merchant and banker, served as the bank's first president, returning to New Haven from a lucrative business career in New York as a speculative sugar trader, hardware merchandizer, and merchant banker. With Woolsey at the helm and a roster of New Haven's finest citizens as founders, the financial officers at Yale were so convinced of the soundness of the bank that they applied for a special dispensation from the State of Connecticut to invest more than the statutory limit of $5,000 in the stock of any one bank. Yale not only invested far in excess of the limit, the trustees also leveraged the college's investment with borrowed funds. In 1825, with the exception of a few shares in municipal projects, the entire endowment was invested in the Eagle Bank.

Sadly, Yale's confidence was misdirected. Upon William Woolsey's return to his business ventures in New York in 1825, he selected George Hoadley, a Yale graduate, practicing lawyer, and mayor of New Haven, to succeed him as bank president. The founders of the bank were too busy with other endeavors to oversee Hoadley. In September of 1825, after Hoadley had loaned out nearly the entire value of the bank in inadequately collateralized loans, the bubble burst and the Eagle Bank declared bankruptcy. Yale College lost over $21,000, bringing the total value of the endowment down to $1,800. Unpaid debts for the college at the time amounted to well over $19,000, causing Yale president Jeremiah Day to obtain emergency sources of financing. The collapse of the bank was catastrophic to the City of New Haven, precipitating a depression in the local economy. In disgrace, George Hoadley quietly moved to Cleveland, where he finished out his days as a justice.

The Clark Foundation and Avon

While Yale's early nineteenth century portfolio exhibited unusual concentration, similar situations exist today. Of the fifteen largest foundations in the United States, two (the Lilly Endowment and the Starr Foundation) hold nearly all assets in a single stock, another (the Robert Wood Johnson Foundation) holds well over half of assets in a single stock, and yet another (the Annie E. Casey Foundation) holds over a quarter of assets in a single stock. Oblivious to the measure of good fortune that contributed to the undiversified portfolio's rise to the top of the charts, trustees use past success to justify continuing to concentrate

assets in one security. For each institution with a wildly successful concentrated portfolio, any number of other institutions with undiversified
holdings languish in obscurity. Unfortunately, many single-stock foundations ultimately experience the costs of holding radically undiversified portfolios.

Even when investors make good faith efforts to diversify, results
sometimes disappoint. In the early 1970s, trustees of the Edna
McConnell Clark Foundation decided to reduce exposure to Avon
Products, the company that provided the wherewithal to establish the
institution. By selling shares of Avon to fund a diversified external
equity manager, the trustees hoped to reduce heavy dependence on
the fortunes of a single security. The timing of the decision made
exquisite sense, as prices of Avon and other members of the "Nifty
Fifty" had climbed to unprecedented heights in an extraordinary bull
market for large-capitalization growth stocks.*

The trustees chose J.P. Morgan to manage the portfolio, selecting
the era's dominant money management firm. Pursuing a strategy that
had served the firm and its clients well, Morgan promptly diversified
the foundation's assets into other high quality growth stocks. By
exchanging one member of the "Nifty Fifty" for others of the same
cohort, the Clark Foundation's portfolio received little protection from
the subsequent dramatic collapse in quality growth stocks.

Yale's experience with a single security—shares of the Eagle
Bank—and the Clark Foundation's ill-fated investments in the Nifty
Fifty provide cautionary tales regarding portfolio concentration. True
diversification requires owning assets that respond differently to fundamental forces that drive markets.

Stocks and the Great Crash

Even broadly defined asset classes sometimes produce risks too great
for investors to bear. Consider the wealth multiples for small-cap
stocks around the time of the Great Crash in October 1929 shown in
Table 4.3.

According to the data in Table 4.3, small stock prices peaked in
November 1928. Had a dollar been invested at the peak, it would have

---

*A phenomenon of the early 1970s, the "Nifty Fifty" consisted of approxi-
mately fifty high quality growth stocks. Investors believed these securities faced
such extraordinary prospects that some called them "one-decision" stocks, the
decision being when to buy since selling was out of the question.

Table 4.3 High Risk Assets Hit Occasional Air Pockets
Wealth Multiples for Small Capitalization Equities November 1928–June 1932

Date	Multiple
November 30, 1928	1.00 times
December 31, 1929	0.46 times
December 31, 1930	0.29 times
December 31, 1931	0.14 times
June 30, 1932	0.10 times

Source: Ibbotson Associates, Stocks, Bonds, Bills and Inflation, 2006 Year Book.

declined 54 percent by December 1929, an additional 38 percent by December 1930, an additional 50 percent by December 1931, and a final 32 percent by June 1932. From November 1928 to June 1932, market action nearly destroyed the original investment. No investor, institutional or individual, could tolerate the trauma. As market forces turned dollars into dimes, investors sold small-cap stocks, placed the proceeds in Treasury bills, and swore never to invest in the equity market again. Of course, selling equities in June of 1932 represented precisely the wrong response. Ten cents invested at the depths of the Great Depression in small-capitalization stocks would have grown more than 137,000 fold by December 31, 2005.

The sense of the skepticism with which investors viewed stocks in the 1930s runs through Robert Lovett's "Gilt-Edged Insecurity," which appeared in the April 3, 1937 edition of *The Saturday Evening Post.* Lovett begins his examination of historical market returns by suggesting that his readers "[c]onsider the absurdity of applying the word security to a bond or a stock." Lovett's analysis showed that an investor buying "100 shares of each of the more popular stocks" at the turn of the century would have turned nearly $295,000 into just $180,000 by the end of 1936. He concludes by warning his readers to remember: "(1) that corporations . . . die easily and frequently; (2) to be extra careful when everything begins to look good; (3) that you are buying risks and not securities; (4) that governments break promises just as businesses do; and (5) that no investments worth having are permanent."[6] Lovett's commentary vividly illustrates why so few investors came up with the dime to invest in small stocks in June of 1932.

Diversifying Strategies

Institutions generally respond to the risk in stocks by holding as much domestic equity as tolerable, mitigating portfolio volatility by adding significant amounts of bonds and cash to the mix. At June 30, 2005, the average educational endowment held 53 percent in domestic equity, 23 percent in domestic fixed income, and 5 percent in cash, for a total of 81 percent in domestic marketable securities.[7]

The large concentration of assets in bonds and cash, with fully 28 percent of the average portfolio in these low return assets, creates significant opportunity costs. Instead of owning equity assets where dollars in the past eighty years grew more than 2,600-fold, investors diversifying with fixed income assets held positions that grew 100-fold with corporate bonds, 71-fold with Treasury bonds and 18-fold with cash.

The outsized exposure of more than 80 percent to securities of the U.S. market, with fully half of assets invested in domestic equities, violates sensible diversification principles. Committing more than fifty percent of a portfolio to a single asset type—domestic stocks—exposes investors to unnecessary asset-concentration risk. The significant correlation between domestic stocks and bonds further exacerbates the consequences of overreliance on domestic equities. Interest rates play an important role in markets. Increasing rates definitely cause bond prices to decline and may cause stock prices to decline, eliminating or reducing the hoped for diversification effects. The converse also applies. Under many circumstances, the average educational institution has more than four-fifths of the portfolio driven in the same direction by the same economic factor.

By identifying high-return asset classes that show little correlation with domestic marketable securities, investors achieve diversification without the opportunity costs of investing in fixed income. The most common high-return diversifying strategy for a U.S. investor involves adding foreign equities to the portfolio. Other possibilities include venture capital, leveraged buyouts, real estate, timber, oil and gas, and absolute return. If these asset classes provide high equity-like returns in a pattern that differs from the return pattern of the core asset (U.S. domestic equities), investors create portfolios that offer both high returns and diversification. Although on an asset-specific basis, higher expected returns apparently come with the price of higher expected volatility, the lack of correlation between individually risky asset classes actually reduces overall portfolio risk. Diversification represents "a free lunch" that allows investors to reduce risk without sacrificing expected returns.

The combination of an equity bias and appropriate diversification provides a powerful underpinning for establishing policy asset allocation targets. Responding to the tenets of equity bias and diversification, sensible institutions identify a variety of high expected return assets that derive returns in ways fundamentally dissimilar from one another. By spreading assets across a variety of asset types, investors diminish the risk that undiversified exposure to a single market will cause significant damage and enhance the possibility that well-diversified exposure to a variety of markets will generate high returns with low levels of risk.

MARKET TIMING

Explicit market timing lies on the opposite end of the spectrum from disciplined portfolio management. John Maynard Keynes, in a Kings College Investment Committee memo, wrote that "the idea of wholesale shifts is for various reasons impracticable and indeed undesirable. Most of those who attempt to, sell too late and buy too late, and do both too often, incurring heavy expenses and developing too unsettled and speculative a state of mind."[8] Deliberate short-term deviations from long-term policy targets introduce substantial risks to the investment process.

On the surface, arguments used to attack market timing sound uncomfortably similar to those advanced when making asset allocation decisions. For example, investors might reject market timing because it requires making a few focused, undiversifiable bets. Or, investors might avoid market timing because of the insurmountable challenges in identifying and predicting the multitude of variables that influence asset prices. While similar factors influence both market timing and policy asset allocation, differences in time frame clearly separate one from the other.

Market timing, defined as a short-term bet against long-term policy targets, requires being right in the short run about factors that are impossible to predict in the short run. Yet investors can reasonably deal with the important drivers of returns in the long run as short-term anomalies disappear into predictable long-term patterns. Sensible investors avoid concentrated bets against the institution's adopted asset allocation, thereby eliminating the risk of inflicting serious damage by holding a portfolio inconsistent with long-term objectives.

Tactical Asset Allocation

In the 1950s, many investors played a market timing game with stock and bond yields, based on ". . . practically an article of faith that good stocks must yield more income than good bonds . . ."[9] When dividend yields on stocks exceeded bond yields by a fair margin, investors viewed stocks as attractive, overweighting equities relative to bonds. Conversely, when bond yields neared stock yields, investors favored bonds. History provided a solid foundation for the strategy. "Only for short periods in 1929, 1930, and 1933 [had] stocks yielded less than government bonds."[10] This valuation-based technique worked well until 1958, when stock yields last exceeded bond yields. In the late 1950s and early 1960s, as the yield advantage of bonds increased relative to stocks, market timers became more invested in fixed income and less invested in stocks. Of course, investors incurred significant opportunity losses while futilely waiting for stock yields to signal a buying opportunity. Ultimately, the failure of the relative yield market timing technique forced its practitioners to identify an alternative form of employment.

A modern, somewhat more sophisticated version of the 1950s relative yield game, tactical asset allocation (TAA), moves assets above and below policy weights based on recommendations of a sophisticated quantitative model. After gaining institutional favor based on strong performance during the crash of 1987, in subsequent years TAA's appeal waned, as successes of the late 1980s faded from memory. Even though TAA's recommendations stem from superficially sensible quantitative disciplines, the system suffers from the faults of other market timing mechanisms.

A notable problem with standard three-way (stock, bond, and cash) TAA relates to the resolution of model identified "mispricings." TAA models tend to prefer cash when short-term interest rates equal or exceed long-term rates, that is in flat or inverted yield curve environments.* When TAA holds significant cash positions, investors receive meaningful protection in environments where interest rates increase. The increase in rates causes bond prices to decline and may

---

*Yield curves represent graphically the relationship between yield and term to maturity for bonds with the same credit quality. Normal yield curves slope upward with higher yields for longer maturities. Flat yield curves reflect constant yields, regardless of maturity. Inverted yield curves depict environments where short-term rates exceed longer term rates.

cause stock prices to decline as well. (While the relationship between stocks and bonds is complex, higher interest rates generally lead to lower stock prices.) By holding cash, TAA practitioners protect portfolio assets from interest-rate-induced declines in bond and stock prices.

In contrast, if investors hold cash as the yield curve moves down sharply, portfolios might sustain irreversible opportunity losses. Downward shifts in the yield curve result from bond rallies, which generally cause stocks to rally. TAA investors, stuck with substantial cash positions, receive modest income returns while bonds and stocks post significant gains. In this case, losses are irreversible in the sense that while cash originally appeared to be the cheapest asset class, an across-the-board decline in interest rates resolved cash's cheapness in a fashion that provided little benefit to holders of cash. In a declining rate environment, handsome returns to holders of bonds and stocks make the relatively paltry cash returns a bitter pill for TAA investors to swallow.

Because cash represents a poor asset class for investors with long time horizons, market timing strategies employing cash pose particularly great dangers to endowment assets. If investors mistakenly overweight cash and underweight higher expected return assets, subsequent rallies in long-term asset prices might cause permanent impairment of value. While less severe damage may result from mistakes made in timing one high expected return asset class relative to another, the ultimate consequences depend on disciplined contrarian responses to initial market timing losses. Such discipline might be a lot to expect from parties engaged in market timing in the first place.

Rebalancing and the 1987 Market Crash

While relatively few investors admit to explicit pursuit of market timing strategies, most portfolios suffer from drift as market forces move actual allocations away from target levels. Circumstances surrounding the market crash in 1987 illustrate the meaningful costs incurred by failing to conduct disciplined rebalancing activity in the face of dramatic market moves.

During the period surrounding the 1987 stock market collapse endowment portfolios first exhibited aspects of disciplined rebalancing in the run up before the crash and then showed signs of perverse market timing in the carnage of the crash. In June 1987, the average endowment invested slightly more than 55 percent of assets in domestic equities and committed almost 37 percent to bonds and cash.[11] The 1987

mid-year allocations marked the end of a period of extraordinary portfolio stability, as between 1985 and 1987 stock allocations ranged from
55.0 percent to 55.4 percent and fixed income allocations ranged from
36.7 percent to 36.9 percent. It appears that in the two years prior to June
1987 endowment investors engaged in rebalancing activity, offsetting
market price movements. Since equities outperformed bonds by a
margin of 70 percent to 25 percent for the two-year period, only by leaning against the bull market wind could investors file three consecutive
fiscal year reports indicating essentially constant allocations to domestic stocks and bonds.

After the October 1987 crash, portfolio stability disappeared as
market forces drove down allocations to stocks and pushed up allocations to bonds. Responding to the collapse in stock prices with fear,
the average endowment manager exacerbated the market-induced dislocation by selling stocks. Reacting to the rally in high quality bond
prices with greed, the average endowment manager enhanced the market-induced increases by purchasing more bonds. From June 1987 to
June 1988, equity holdings declined from 55.3 percent to 49.1 percent,
more than can be explained by the market drop during the year.
Roughly offsetting the equity decline, fixed income increased from
36.7 percent to 41.9 percent, more than can be explained by the market rally. In retrospect, educational institutions bought high and sold
low, following a poor recipe for investment success.

By reallocating more than 5 percent of assets from domestic stocks
to bonds and cash in the aftermath of the 1987 market crash, endowment investors incurred significant opportunity costs as the market
staged a reasonably rapid recovery. Even in the face of stronger prices,
fear of the U.S. stock market persisted, as endowment bond and cash
allocations remained above the pre-crash level until 1993. College
and university portfolios incurred substantial opportunity costs by
maintaining lower risk portfolios for years after the stock market crash.

One charitable interpretation of post-crash equity sales involves
the possibility that institutions inadvertently allowed equity allocations to drift above desired levels in the strong stock market of the
early 1980s. Perhaps the 1987 crash highlighted the degree to which
equities dominated institutional portfolios, causing fiduciaries to sell
stocks to reach a lower desired portfolio risk profile. If so, post-crash
reductions in equity allocations represent a belated, costly, inelegant
response to excessive portfolio risk.

Another fundamental justification for reduced equity holdings
stems from the possibility that the 1987 crash caused investors to conclude that risk characteristics of equities differed from previous

assumptions. Perhaps past assessments of stock market variability materially understated true risk. Maybe equity returns exhibit more frequent extreme moves than market participants previously believed. Certainly, the unprecedented market collapse forced investors to reassess the character of equity return patterns, possibly contributing to a portfolio shift from equities to less risky assets.

Unfortunately for those seeking a reasonable explanation for institutional behavior, increases in stock allocations during the 1990s argue against interpreting November and December 1987 sales as a rational portfolio adjustment. Investors motivated by greed held high allocations going into the crash, only to reduce holdings significantly thereafter. As confidence returned, equity allocations began to rise, reversing the allocation decisions made only a short time before. Educational institutions, greedy and fearful in turn, damaged portfolios in their perverse response to the crash in October 1987.

With the benefit of hindsight, post-crash equity purchases made enormous sense, enriching those with the courage to go against the crowd. In fact, the apparently easy money made by buying common stocks in late 1987 encouraged investors to follow a policy of "buying the dips" with increasing enthusiasm.

As the bull market continued its run through the 1990s, the public saw every modest decline in stock prices as an opportunity to buy equities "on sale." Did investors learn an important rebalancing lesson from the 1987 stock market crash, or did the relatively quick rebound in prices point market participants in the wrong direction?

Drawing conclusions from the 1987 stock market crash about the easy profits gained from "buying the dips" places far too much weight on a shaky foundation, since the extraordinary circumstances surrounding the October break in markets constitute a unique occurrence. The extreme one-day decline of 23 percent in the S&P 500 represents a 25 standard deviation event, an occurrence so rare in a normally distributed variable that it staggers the imagination.* Basing future behavior on the 1987 crash and subsequent market recovery exposes investors to the danger that less extreme market declines contain far less information regarding future price behavior. While near-

---

*In a normally distributed variable, a one standard deviation event occurs approximately one out of every three trials, a two standard deviation event occurs one of every twenty trials, and a three standard deviation event occurs one out of 100 trials. An eight standard deviation event occurs once every six trillion years, based on a 250 business day year. The frequency of a 25 standard deviation event defies description.

term profitability of post-crash equity purchases illustrate a positive aspect of rebalancing activity, investors face the possibility of confusing the important risk control function of rebalancing with the unreliable return-oriented activity of "buying the dips."

Excess Volatility

Yale economist Robert Shiller argues that markets exhibit excess volatility.[12] That is, security prices tend to fluctuate more than necessary to respond to fundamental factors, such as earnings and interest rates, that determine intrinsic value. In other words, "if price movements were rescaled down . . . so as to be less variable, then price would do a better job of forecasting fundamentals." Shiller's self-described "controversial claim" provides "evidence of a failure of the efficient markets model."[13] Anyone attempting to understand October 1987's market crash from a fundamental perspective sees merit in Shiller's position.

In a world with excess volatility, investors care about the direction of security price fluctuations. Price declines provide opportunities to buy and price increases provide opportunities to sell. Under some circumstances, following a significant decline in price an asset actually becomes less risky, since it can be acquired more cheaply. The common-sense conclusion of bottom-fishing investors contrasts with the statistician's conclusion that a dramatic drop in price increases observed (historical) volatility, implying a higher risk level for the asset. Of course, price volatility creates opportunity only when prices change more than necessary to reflect changes in underlying fundamentals.

Real-Time Rebalancing

Frequent rebalancing activity allows investors to maintain a consistent risk profile and to exploit return-generating opportunities created by excess security price volatility. Moreover, real-time rebalancing tends to cost less, as trades generally prove accommodating to the market. Frequent rebalancers buy in the face of immediate declines and sell in the face of immediate increases, in both cases supplying liquidity for traders pursuing the opposite, predominant tack. Although few investors commit the time and resources necessary to conduct real-time rebalancing, an examination of the benefits of intensive rebalancing provides context for understanding the value of the strategy.

Consider Yale University's rebalancing activity. Yale possesses a number of advantages unavailable to most investors. The university's endowment enjoys tax-exempt status, allowing frequent trading without adverse tax consequences associated with realization of gains. A sophisticated team of investment professionals manages the funds on a day-to-day basis, providing the staff support needed for management-intensive activities. Yale's special tax status and dedicated investment staff permit the university to engage in real-time rebalancing activity.

Yale's trading activity during the fiscal year ending June 30, 2003 provides some insight into the potential magnitude of rebalancing profits. During the year, the U.S. equity market, as measured by the Wilshire 5000, produced a total return of 1.3 percent. Investors undertaking an annual review of portfolio allocations would likely do little to rebalance domestic equity holdings (unless returns of other asset classes caused the domestic equity allocation to change markedly). In fact, in Yale's case the overall portfolio return for the fiscal year amounted to 8.8 percent, implying reasonable stability in portfolio allocations and suggesting modest annual rebalancing requirements.

For Yale's fiscal 2003, the placid surface of the equity market concealed some powerful undercurrents. Early in the fiscal year, markets collapsed. In July, the Wilshire 5000 posted a peak-to-trough decline of more than 18 percent. The market subsequently rebounded, nearly regaining the July peak in late August with a greater than 19 percent return. From the August high the market once again fell, declining by more than 19 percent to what proved the fiscal-year low on October 9th. The hidden currents continued to roil the markets with a 21 percent increase by November followed by a 14 percent decrease through March. A powerful surge lifted the market by nearly 27 percent to the fiscal-year high in mid June, from which the market drifted down to close the twelve-month period essentially where it started.

The stock market volatility provided numerous opportunities to execute rebalancing trades. Every substantial drop and every meaningful increase allowed investors to buy the dips and sell the peaks. During the university's fiscal 2003, rebalancing activity produced a host of profit-generating transactions.

As a matter of course, at the beginning of every trading day Yale estimates the value of each of the components of the endowment. When marketable securities asset classes (domestic equity, foreign developed equity, emerging market equity, and fixed income) deviate from target allocation levels, the university's investments office takes steps to restore allocations to target levels. In fiscal year 2003, Yale executed approximately $3.8 billion in domestic equity rebalancing trades, roughly evenly split between purchases and sales. Net profits from rebalancing amounted to approximately $26 million, representing a 1.6 percent incremental return on the $1.6 billion domestic equity portfolio.

Even though rebalancing profits produce a nice bonus for investors, the fundamental motivation for rebalancing concerns adherence to long-term policy targets. In the context of a carefully considered policy portfolio, rebalancing maintains the desired risk level. Generating profit while controlling risk represents an unbeatable combination.

Few institutions and even fewer individuals possess the resources to conduct daily rebalancing of investment portfolios. Yet regardless of the frequency of rebalancing, fidelity to asset allocation targets proves important as a means of risk control and valuable as a tool for return enhancement. Thoughtful investors employ rebalancing strategies to maintain policy asset allocation targets.

Investors hoping to profit in the short run from rebalancing trades face nearly certain long-run disappointment. Over long periods of time, portfolios allowed to drift with capital markets returns tend to contain ever increasing allocations to risky assets, as higher returns cause riskier positions to crowd out other holdings. The fundamental purpose of rebalancing lies in controlling risk, not enhancing return. Rebalancing trades keep portfolios at long-term policy targets by reversing deviations resulting from asset class performance differentials. Disciplined rebalancing activity requires a strong stomach and serious staying power. Conducted in a significant bear market, rebalancing appears to be a losing strategy as investors commit funds to assets showing continuing relative price weakness.

Contrast the positive rebalancing experience of investors in 1987 or Yale's rebalancing experience in 2003 with the fate suffered by investors in the bear market of 1973 and 1974. Price declines required purchases of equities, followed by further declines that impaired asset values, which in turn led to further purchases. Losses incurred on rebalancing trades proved particularly painful as investors second-guessed the wisdom of buying into a bear market. For investors seeking to maintain long-term targets in the early 1970s, two years of nearly uninterrupted price deterioration produced seemingly relentless incremental losses.

Rising equity prices provide a similar set of challenges. In a sustained bull market, rebalancing appears to be a losing strategy, as investors constantly sell assets showing relative price strength. Years go by without reward, other than the knowledge that the portfolio embodies the desired risk/reward characteristics.

The alternative of not rebalancing to policy targets causes portfolio managers to engage in a peculiar trend-following market timing strategy. Like many contrarian pursuits, rebalancing frequently appears foolish as momentum players reap short-term rewards from going with the flow. Regardless of potentially negative reputational consequences, serious investors maintain portfolio risk profiles through disciplined rebalancing policies, avoiding the sometimes expedient appeal of moving with market forces.

Burton Malkiel, in *Managing Risk in an Uncertain Era*, writes that "we are particularly averse to the suggestions that a university try to move in and out of the stock market according to its capacity to forecast market trends. Investors who wish to play this timing game must possess an unusual degree of prescience about the course of the general economy, corporate profits, interest rates, and indeed the entire set of international economic, political, and social developments that affect the securities market. The existence of such omniscience, to say the least, is hard to document."[14] More succinct advice to those who wish to time the market comes from a nineteenth century cotton trader: "Some think [the market] will go up. Some think it will go down. I do, too. Whatever you do will be wrong. Act at once."

Market timing explicitly moves the portfolio away from long-term policy targets, exposing the institution to avoidable risks. Because policy asset allocation provides the central means through which investors express return and risk preferences, serious investors attempt to minimize deviations from policy targets. To ensure that actual portfolios reflect desired risk and return characteristics, avoid market timing and embrace rebalancing activity to keep asset classes at targeted levels.

SECURITY SELECTION

Market Efficiency

Investors wishing to beat the market by actively managing portfolios face daunting obstacles. While no market prices assets precisely at fair value all of the time, most markets price most assets with reasonable efficiency most of the time, providing few opportunities for easy gains. Moreover, active management costs increase the hurdle for success as active investors pay management fees, incur transactions costs, and create market impact. Intelligent investors approach active strategies with a healthy sense of skepticism.

Sensible active managers favor markets with inefficiently priced assets and avoid those markets with efficiently priced assets. Unfortunately, no clear measures for pricing efficiency exist. In fact, financial economists engage in a quasi-religious debate regarding efficiency, with one end of the spectrum represented by those who believe in the impossibility of finding risk-adjusted excess returns and the other end of the spectrum by those who argue that human behavior creates a range of active management opportunities.

Degree of Opportunity

In the absence of direct measures of market efficiency, active manager behavior provides clues about the degree of opportunity in various markets. In those markets with limited opportunities for active management, managers deviate little from the market portfolio, leading to market-like returns. Why do managers in efficient markets tend to "hug" the benchmark? In a world of efficiently priced assets, consider the business consequences of holding portfolios that differ markedly from the market portfolio. Substantial deviations from the market portfolio's security holdings cause a manager's portfolio results to vary dramatically from the benchmark. Underperforming managers lose clients and lose assets. While overachievers may temporarily gain clients and gain assets (and gain public adulation), because efficient markets present no mispricings for active managers to exploit, good results stem from luck, not skill. Apparent success proves transitory for active managers in efficient markets. As a result, over time, managers in efficient markets gravitate toward "closet indexing," structuring portfolios with only modest deviations from the market, ensuring both mediocrity and survival.

In contrast, active managers in less efficient markets exhibit greater variability in returns. In fact, many private markets lack benchmarks for managers to "hug," eliminating the problem of closet indexing. Inefficiencies in pricing allow managers with great skill to achieve great success, while unskilled managers post commensurately poor results. Hard work and intelligence reap rich rewards in an environment where superior information and deal flow provide an edge.

Manager behavior causes the magnitude of active management opportunity to relate to the distribution of actively managed returns in

Table 4.4 Dispersion of Active Management Returns
Identifies Areas of Opportunity

Asset Returns by Quartile. Ten Years Ending June 30, 2005

Asset Class	First Quartile	Median	Third Quartile	Range
U.S. fixed income	7.4%	7.1%	6.9%	0.5%
U.S. equity	12.1	11.2	10.2	1.9
International equity	10.5	9.0	6.5	4.0
U.S. small-capitalization equity	16.1	14.0	11.3	4.8
Absolute return	15.6	12.5	8.5	7.1
Real estate	17.6	12.0	8.4	9.2
Leveraged buyouts	13.3	8.0	-0.4	13.7
Venture capital	28.7	-1.4	-14.5	43.2

Sources: Data for marketable securities are from Russell/Mellon. The absolute return, real estate, leveraged buyout, and venture capital data are from Cambridge Associates. Real estate, leveraged buyout, and venture capital data represent returns on funds formed between 1995 and 1999, excluding more recent funds so that immature investments will not bias results downward.

a particular asset class. Any measure of dispersion provides some sense of the degree of active management opportunity. Table 4.4 shows the spread between the first and third quartiles of returns for actively managed portfolios, illustrating the extent to which more efficiently priced assets provide less opportunity for active managers and less efficiently priced assets provide more opportunity.

High quality fixed income securities, arguably the most efficiently priced asset in the world, trade in markets dominated by savvy financial institutions. Since nobody (possibly excepting the Federal Reserve) knows where interest rates will be, few managers employ interest rate anticipation strategies. Without potentially powerful differentiating bets on interest rates, institutional portfolios tend to exhibit market-like interest rate sensitivity, or duration. As a result, managers generally limit themselves to modest security selection decisions, causing returns for most active managers to mimic benchmark results. The spread between first and third quartile results for active fixed income managers measures an astonishingly small 0.5 percent per annum for the decade ending June 30, 2005.

Large capitalization equities represent the next rung of the efficiency ladder, with a range of 1.9 percent between top and bottom quartiles. Stocks provide more difficult pricing challenges than bonds. Instead of discounting relatively certain fixed income cash flows, valuation of equities involves discounting more-difficult-to-project corporate earnings. The greater volatility in equity markets contributes to the wider active manager spread. Less efficiently priced foreign developed equities exhibit a first-to-third-quartile range of 4.0 percent per annum, while small-capitalization stocks in the United States show a range of 4.8 percent per annum over the decade. The progression of degree of opportunity across types of marketable securities makes intuitive sense.

The radical break comes when moving from liquid public to illiquid private opportunities. Absolute return, real estate, leveraged buyouts, and venture capital exhibit dramatically broader dispersions of returns. For the ten-year period, absolute return shows a range of 7.1 percent between first and third quartiles, while real estate and leveraged buyouts exhibit even more extreme 9.2 percent and 13.7 percent per annum spreads. Venture capital captures the dispersion prize with a stunning 43.2 percent first-to-third quartile range.

Selecting top quartile managers in private markets leads to much greater reward than in public markets. In the extreme case, choosing a first quartile fixed income manager adds a meager 0.3 percent per annum relative to the median result. In contrast, the first quartile venture capitalist surpasses the median by 30.1 percent per annum, providing a much greater contribution to portfolio results. Ironically, identifying superior managers in the relatively inefficiently priced private markets proves less challenging than identifying skillful players in the efficiently priced marketable securities markets.

Active Manager Returns

Regardless of the scope of active management opportunities, investors face serious headwinds in the race to beat the market. In the two most significant institutional asset classes, domestic fixed income and domestic equity, fee-adjusted median manager returns fall somewhere in the neighborhood of benchmark results. As shown in Table 4.5, in the extremely efficiently priced U.S. bond market, the median fixed income manager loses 0.2 percent per year net of fees relative to the benchmark, while a first quartile manager ekes out a gain of only 0.1 percent per annum. Active fixed income management fails miserably. Before managing bonds actively, investors should ponder Warren Buffett's famous dictum: "Remember, if you are at a poker table and can't identify the patsy, you are the patsy."

**Table 4.5 Efficiently Priced Markets Challenge
the Average Active Manager**

Median Returns Relative to Benchmark. Ten Years Ending June 30, 2005

Asset Class	Median Return	Bench-mark	Estimated Fees	Net-of-Fee Relative Return
U.S. fixed income	7.1%	6.9%	0.4%	-0.2%
U.S. equity	11.2	9.9	0.8	0.5
U.S. small-capitalization equity	14.0	12.9	0.9	0.2

Sources: Data on fees from Cambridge Associates Investment Manager Database, rounded to the nearest ten basis points. Benchmarks: Lehman Brothers U.S. Government Credit Index for U.S. Fixed Income, S&P 500 Index for U.S. Equity, and S&P 600 Index for U.S. Small Cap Equity.

Domestic equity markets produce slightly more hopeful results. With fee adjustments, the median active manager exceeds the benchmark by 0.5 percent per year. A first quartile manager adds real value, however, exceeding the benchmark by 1.4 percent per annum net of fees. The median small-capitalization manager beats the market by a scant 0.2 percent per annum. In contrast, a first quartile manager adds 2.3 percent per annum, reflecting the greater investment opportunity in less efficiently priced securities.

In the case of domestic marketable securities, the proximity of median returns and benchmarks tells the same story for bonds, stocks, and small-cap stocks. Avoid active management, or undertake active strategies with great caution and realistic expectations.

Consider the markets in which the various securities trade. Domestic fixed income operates in a market dominated by institutions. The returns contained in the active manager universe represent the results of sophisticated investors trading against sophisticated investors. Traders gain an advantage with extraordinary difficulty. As a result, active managers post results in a narrow range, with median managers losing relative to the benchmark and top quartile managers posting exceedingly modest incremental returns. The highly efficient, highly competitive fixed income market stands at one end of the continuum.

Domestic equities trade in a brutally competitive environment, but with a greater degree of opportunity. As might be expected in the negative sum game of active management, the median domestic equity manager produces market-like returns. That said, top quartile managers of both large-capitalization and small-capitalization stocks appear to add value net of fees, with less efficiently priced small-cap securities offering the greater opportunity.

Greater inefficiency in the market environment may not lead to greater average success. Private markets provide a case in point. Median results for venture capital and leveraged buyouts dramatically trail those for marketable equities, despite the higher risk and greater illiquidity of private investing. Over the decade ending June 30, 2005, deficits relative to the S&P 500 amounted to 11.3 percent annually for venture capital, and 1.9 percent annually for leveraged buyouts, numbers that would be higher after risk adjustment. In order to justify including private equity in the portfolio, managers must select top quartile managers. Anything less fails to compensate for the time, effort, and risk entailed in the pursuit of nonmarketable investments.

investments must be worth the time

Survivorship Bias

Although comparisons of active management returns to benchmark results already paint a bleak picture, managers hoping to beat the market face a challenge even greater than suggested by a first reading of the data. Survivorship bias causes active managers as a group to appear more successful than would be indicated by a true picture of reality, since current data on manager returns contain only the results of the strong (survivors), having purged the returns of the weak (failures).

Errors of underinclusion and overinclusion bias manager performance data, limiting the usefulness of consultant reports in understanding active management results. Underinclusion occurs when managers disappear without a trace, while overinclusion occurs when new entrants contribute historical results to the database.

Compilations of return data generally include only results of managers active at the time of the study. Discontinued products and discredited managers disappear, coloring the return data with an optimistic tint. Were the generally poor results of nonsurvivors included in the database, the challenge of beating the market would appear even more daunting.

only successful investors stay in database

Even if the data gatherer undertakes to include results of failed managers, the figures provide reasonable guidance only when considering returns on a year-by-year basis. The shortest time frame produces the highest quality data, because the number of dropouts tends to be smaller for the shorter time periods. More serious problems arise when examining results spanning several years, since more managers disappear during any given multiple-year period. Because managers tend to disappear after posting poor relative results, multiple-year comparisons suffer from return inflation driven by the superior results of survivors.

Errors of overinclusion arise when data gatherers add new firms to the database and incorporate the new additions' historical records. Since the new entrants necessarily produced superior results to attract the attention of the institutional investment community, the addition of the new entrants' historical track record (a.k.a. backfill bias) provides an artificial boost to reported active management returns.

An examination of investment return data produced by the Russell Investment Group illustrates in high relief the impact of survivorship bias on reported returns. Russell, a highly regarded consulting firm, compiles and publishes one of the most widely used investment return databases.

Russell's database suffers significant survivorship bias. Consider the U.S. equity median manager returns as recorded in Table 4.6. In 1996, according to Russell, the median U.S. equity manager produced a return of 22.4 percent based on reports from a sample size of 307. As failing managers departed and up-and-coming managers entered, the reported results for 1996 steadily improved. By 2005, the reported median manager return for 1996 jumped to 23.5 percent, more than one percentage point above the originally recorded result. Strikingly, the 2005 report on 1996 includes only 177 observations, a full 130 fewer than the 1996 report.

The Russell data suffer from overinclusion and underinclusion. Note that from 1997 to 1998, the number of managers increases by nine, indicating some degree of backfill bias. Because Russell does not provide year-by-year information on gross additions to and gross subtractions from the database, observers do not have the information necessary to gauge the relative importance of entries and departures. That said, the more than 40 percent decline over ten years in the number of firms reporting 1996 results indicates that departures of failed managers dominate the survivorship scene.

Precise assessment of the impact of survivorship bias on the Russell database proves impossible. Poor returns of declining managers disappear. Strong returns of rising managers appear. Yet some idea of the magnitude of survivorship bias comes from the deviations between the originally reported returns and the later-reported, biased returns. The deviations, outlined in Table 4.6, range from an increase in the

Table 4.6 Survivorship Bias Paints an Unrealistic Picture of U.S. Equity Returns

U.S. Equity Manager Median Returns

	Year of Return									
	1996	1997	1998	1999	2000	2001	2002	2003	2004	2005
1996	22.4%									
1997	22.8%	30.6%								
1998	23.3%	31.5%	23.0%							
1999	23.4%	31.6%	24.5%	18.0%						
2000	23.5%	31.6%	25.9%	20.1%	-3.1%					
2001	23.5%	31.7%	26.4%	20.9%	-3.3%	-10.8%				
2002	23.5%	31.5%	25.9%	21.1%	-2.9%	-9.9%	-22.1%			
2003	23.5%	31.6%	25.5%	20.5%	0.7%	-8.7%	-21.3%	30.0%		
2004	23.5%	31.5%	25.8%	21.2%	-0.1%	-8.3%	-21.2%	30.2%	11.9%	
2005	23.5%	31.5%	25.3%	20.6%	1.2%	-7.6%	-21.0%	30.2%	12.3%	7.4%

Difference

	1996	1997	1998	1999	2000	2001	2002	2003	2004	2005
	1.1%	0.8%	2.2%	2.6%	4.3%	3.2%	1.2%	0.2%	0.4%	0

(Year of Report is indicated on the left for rows 1996–2005.)

Number of Reporting Managers

	Year of Return									
	1996	1997	1998	1999	2000	2001	2002	2003	2004	2005
1996	307									
1997	303	326								
1998	312	342	365							
1999	278	307	334	352						
2000	265	294	323	346	361					
2001	237	269	299	341	369	393				
2002	230	262	285	325	363	398	412			
2003	205	230	253	292	331	373	403	424		
2004	188	211	233	275	322	367	401	423	446	
2005	177	199	223	265	314	361	389	415	445	471

Net change

	1996	1997	1998	1999	2000	2001	2002	2003	2004	2005
	-130	-127	-142	-87	-47	-32	-23	-9	-1	0

(Year of Report is indicated on the left for rows 1996–2005.)

Source: Frank Russell Company

(handwritten annotation: very prevalent survivorship bias)

reported median return for 2000 of 4.3 percentage points, which transformed an originally reported median loss of 3.1 percent into a later revised median gain of 1.2 percent, to no change for the median return in 2005, the final year of the analysis. On average, survivorship bias increases the reported median returns by 1.6 percent per year.

One imperfect estimate of the longer term impact of survivorship bias comes from linking the annual median returns with and without survivorship bias. The imperfection of the measure stems from the fact that linked median returns do not (except by coincidence) represent the experience of any individual manager. Even if the linked returns by chance reflected an individual manager's record, that manager would not likely represent the median. Yet applying the same technique of linking medians both to the data with survivorship bias and to the data without survivorship bias produces a rough-justice estimate of the magnitude of the impact.

Fully Loaded Active Manager Hurdles

The cumulative impact of manager fees, survivorship bias, and backfill bias completely transforms the active management picture. The results, contained in Table 4.7, disappoint advocates of market-beating strategies. Even in the benchmark-hugging world of fixed income, survivorship bias subtracts an estimated 0.2 percent from already disappointing ten-year active returns. Adding the survivorship adjustment to the post-fee active management deficit of 0.2 percent produces a median active shortfall of 0.4 percent relative to the benchmark return. The market poses a tough test for active managers.

After accounting for survivorship bias, the domestic equity net-of-fee active management advantage of 0.5 percent morphs into a deficit of 1.2 percent per annum, changing an optimistic story into a pessimistic tale. Simple and cheap benchmark matching strategies crush most stock market mavens.

Survivorship bias in distributions of active manager returns fundamentally alters investor attitudes toward active management. Data indicating that the majority of managers beat the index encourage investors to play the active management game, while numbers showing a preponderance of managers failing to match index returns dis-

[handwritten note: promising data, but very biased]

Table 4.7 Estimated Survivorship Bias Adjustments Reduce Appeal of Active Management
Ten Years Ending June 30, 2005

Asset Class	Net-of-Fee Relative Return	Estimated Survivorship Impact*	Estimated Relative Return
U.S. fixed income	-0.2%	-0.2%	-0.4%
U.S. equity	0.5%	-1.7%	-1.2%

Estimated survivorship bias impact represents the difference between: (a) the linked annual median manager returns with survivorship bias; and (b) the linked annual median manager returns without survivorship bias.

courage active management. The positive bias introduced by survivorship bias no doubt leads to excessive confidence in active management strategies.

Consider the numbers that institutional investors use to evaluate active managers. Shown in Table 4.8, the pre-fee, survivorship-bias-inflated numbers encourage would-be market beaters. Active fixed income management appears to be a winning strategy, with nearly three-quarters of managers besting the benchmark. Adjustments for fees and survivorship bias flip the odds and reduce the chance of winning to less than one-fifth. The naïve comparison shows 80 percent of domestic equity managers beating the market. Adjustments for fees and survivorship reduce the chance of winning to less than one quarter. In the aggregate, fee-collecting asset managers win at the expense of fee-paying institutional investors.

A cynic might argue that the money management industry benefits from inflating returns in databases used to assess active managers. Both the active managers and the consultants that compile data on active management want to encourage clients to engage active managers. Painting an unrealistically rosy picture of past active management successes no doubt motivates many investors to pursue the all-too-often-false promise of market-beating returns.

A further note regarding the efficacy of active management relates to the dollar value added by purported market-beating strategies. Simple return numbers tend to overstate value added since early strong results, necessary to attract institutional interest, generally apply to rel-

Table 4.8 Naïve Performance Comparisons Encourage Active Management

Fully Adjusted Returns Consider Fees and Survivorship Bias

Ten Years Ending June 30, 2005

Asset Class	Median Return	Bench-mark	Percentile Rank	Fully Adjusted Benchmark Hurdle	Fully Adjusted Benchmark Hurdle Rank
U.S. fixed income	7.1%	6.9%	74	7.5%	18
U.S. equity	11.2%	9.9%	80	12.4%	23

Benchmarks: Lehman Brothers U.S. Government Credit Index for U.S. Fixed Income and S&P 500 Index for U.S. Equity.
Note: Benchmark hurdles include estimates for fees and survivorship bias.

atively small amounts of money. As size is the enemy of performance, more established managers with greater funds under management tend to produce less eye-catching results. Because investment management return compilations weight each manager equally, the new managers (presumably with smaller portfolios) exert disproportionate influence in the manager rankings. A dollar-weighted evaluation of active management would no doubt provide even less encouragement to those hoping to employ market-beating strategies.

In an ironic twist, survivorship bias causes active managers to appear less successful relative to peers than reality would indicate. Consider the U.S. equity manager that preserves capital in 2000. According to results reported in 2000, as shown in Table 4.6, a zero percent return handily beats the -3.1 percent median result. As survivorship issues inexorably alter the landscape, by 2005 the 2000 median return morphs into a gain of 1.2 percent. As time passed, the erstwhile median-beating zero percent return moves from the respectable second quartile to the not-so-respectable third quartile. Survivorship bias darkens the relative performance picture.

Active portfolio managers face high hurdles, which require that investors approach purported market-beating strategies with great skepticism. Issues of survivorship bias cloud understanding of historical records, causing general problems in evaluating the efficacy of active management strategies and specific problems in assessing individual manager performance. After adjusting for fees and survivorship bias, investors face long odds on winning the domestic marketable securities active management game. In the world of marketable securities, passive management provides the obvious low-cost alternative to high-cost active management. If investors undertake active approaches, focusing on less efficient markets increases the chance of realizing substantial gains. In the least efficient private markets, no passive alternative exists. Even were a passive alternative available, market-like results would likely disappoint. In sum, sensible investors engage in active management with reasonable caution and realistic expectations.

Liquidity

Serious managers who attempt to identify inefficiencies frequently gravitate toward relatively illiquid markets, since rewarding investments tend to reside in dark corners, not in the glare of floodlights. Such out-of-the-way, undiscovered opportunities receive little attention from Wall Street, which thrives on markets that generate large trading volumes.

Market players seek liquid positions, allowing immediate disposition of yesterday's loser and rapid acquisition of today's hot prospect. Speculators and asset gatherers pay a premium price for liquid assets, expecting markets to accommodate reversal of a trade with immediacy and with little or no impact on price.

Illiquidity induces appropriate, long-term behavior. Rather than relying on liquid markets to trade out of mistakes, investors in illiquid securities enter into long-term arrangements, purchasing part ownership in a business with which they have to live. As a consequence, increased care, thoroughness, and discipline represent hallmarks of successful investors in less liquid assets.

By avoiding the highly liquid securities favored by market players, serious active investors focus on much more interesting investments. In embracing less liquid assets, investors often identify opportunities to establish positions at meaningful discounts to fair value.

Full Faith and Credit Obligations

Examples of illiquid opportunities in marketable securities abound. In the realm of full faith and credit obligations of the U.S. government, otherwise identical bonds trade at different prices solely because market liquidity differs. The most actively traded Treasury bonds, so-called on-the-run issues, command a price premium, which produces yields as much as 5 to 10 basis points below those of off-the-run bonds. Based on current issuance patterns by the government, on-the-run offerings carry terms to maturity of two, five, ten, and thirty years. When the Treasury auctions a new ten-year bond, market attention shifts from the old ten-year instrument to the new. Since the premium enjoyed by on-the-run issues relates solely to superior market liquidity, the premium price disappears once a new issue supplants the old.

Regular opportunities exist to purchase full faith and credit instruments of the U.S. government at spreads of 40 to 50 basis points above otherwise comparable, but more liquid Treasury issues. Because such offerings tend to contain structural complexities, cautious investors undertake careful due diligence before committing funds. Moreover, opportunities tend to be relatively small, requiring portfolio managers to "fill a bathtub with a teaspoon." Nonetheless, dogged pursuit of unusual, illiquid securities can result in the accumulation of an attractively priced portfolio of high quality assets.

Markets occasionally offer extraordinary opportunities to investors willing to accept illiquidity. In the aftermath of a market panic in the fall of 1998, less frequently traded assets provided enormous returns relative to highly liquid positions. On November 12, 1998, an intermediate term off-the-run Treasury issue, the 5⅞'s of February 2004, yielded 18½ basis points more than the on-the-run 4¼'s of November 2003.

Beyond the extremely high reward for accepting modest illiquidity in an off-the-run Treasury issue, in late 1998, investors willing to invest in a private placement backed by the full faith and credit of the United States faced incredible opportunity. The Overseas Private Investment Corporation, an agency of the United States devoted to promoting economic growth in developing nations, offered securities with an effective maturity date of March 2004 that carried a spread of more than 100 points over the comparable on-the-run Treasury issue. Receiving a full percentage point in yield over Treasuries for simply bearing the illiquidity of a private placement raises serious questions about rationality of markets.

Even in times of normalcy, investors receive unreasonably large incremental returns in illiquid securities. For example, in early 2006, investors could consider bonds issued by National Archives Facility Trust, acting through the National Archives and Records Administration, an independent government agency devoted to preservation, appraisal, and regulation of the disposition of the permanently valuable records of the United States government. The bonds, with an effective maturity date of September 2019 and a coupon of 8.5 percent, carried a spread of more than 45 basis points over the comparable on-the-run Treasury issue. The National Archives issued approximately $300 million of bonds, a small figure relative to a comparably timed ten-year U.S. Treasury issue of approximately $22.5 billion. Yet patient investors received a reward of almost a half of a percentage point in yield over Treasuries for simply bearing the illiquidity of a small issue of the United States government.

illiquidity = more reward, but can't cash

Emerging Market Debt *at for a while*

In emerging markets, U.S. dollar-denominated debt of sovereign issuers frequently trades at a substantial premium to non-dollar debt of the same issuer. This phenomenon presents itself most dramatically in times of crisis, when investors place extraordinary value on the greater liquidity of U.S. dollar-denominated instruments. To arbitrage this discrepancy investors require only a set of currency forward contracts to eliminate the foreign exchange risk. Arbitrageurs can buy relatively cheap non-dollar debt, sell relatively expensive dollar debt, and eliminate currency risk with forward foreign exchange transactions. Investors paying a premium for dollar-denominated debt create an attractive opportunity for harder working investors.

Throughout 1998, investors found some extraordinary investments amid dislocations caused by the collapse in Asian markets. While the successful resolution of many investments depended on market recovery, other positions promised almost certain rewards to investors. Samsung, a highly leveraged Korean diversified electronics manufacturer, issued debt in a variety of currencies including U.S. dollars, Korean won, Japanese yen, and German marks. Dollar-denominated bonds generally traded at premium prices, reflecting superior liquidity characteristics. In the fall, pricing discrepancies reached an extreme with Samsung 9.75 percent dollar bonds due May 2003 trading at a yield to maturity of 16 percent (approximately 1,200 basis points over U.S. Treasuries), and Samsung 3.3 percent yen bonds due April 2003 trading at a yield of 18 percent (approximately 1,700 basis points over Japanese government bonds). Investors could create a stream of dollar cash flows by buying the relatively cheap yen bond and swapping all future yen flows for dollars. By using the forward currency markets to translate the Samsung yen cash flows into dollars, investors created a synthetic dollar asset with a yield to maturity of 21 percent. The spread between the synthetic bond yield of 21 percent and the Samsung dollar bond yield of 16 percent rewarded arbitrageurs who purchased the relatively cheap synthetic dollar asset cash flows and sold the relatively expensive dollar bond.* If spreads narrow, the investor unwinds the trade with a profit; if not, the investor collects a stream of payments until the bonds mature. By applying modest amounts of leverage to the trade, investors could expect holding period returns in the neighborhood of 24 percent, while without leverage the position carried an 18 percent return.

---

*Execution of the Samsung corporate bond arbitrage required a short sale of the relatively expensive dollar bonds. Short sellers must borrow bonds to consummate the transaction. One risk in executing the arbitrage lies in losing the "borrow," causing the investor to unwind the short position prematurely. In well functioning capital markets, maintaining short positions poses little problem; however, in well functioning capital markets nearly identical streams of cash flows (as represented by the Samsung hedged yen and dollar bonds) do not trade at substantially different prices.

Sallie Mae Stock

Different classes of equity frequently trade at prices reflecting, *inter alia*, liquidity differences. The Student Loan Marketing Association ("Sallie Mae"), established in 1973 to provide liquidity for entities involved in programs supporting the credit needs of students, originally raised equity capital from institutions participating in the Federal Government's Guaranteed Student Loan Program. In 1983, creation of a new class of more broadly held nonvoting stock increased the company's equity base, funding a corporate growth program designed to meet the needs of hundreds of thousands of students. The newly issued nonvoting stock traded at a premium that generally ranged between 15 percent and 20 percent, a spread attributed by market participants to the illiquidity of the original shares. In an attempt to reduce the discount, Sallie Mae made regular offers to convert the cheaper, less liquid voting stock to the more expensive, more liquid nonvoting stock. The discount persisted despite annual conversion of between 28 percent and 41 percent of shares tendered from 1984 to 1989. Curiously, a substantial number of shareholders who owned voting shares failed to take advantage of the opportunity. During the final tender offer in March 1989, at the height of market participant familiarity with the program, of the 8.7 million shares outstanding, 1.5 million shares ignored an offer of $91.875 in cash for shares trading at $83.50, exhibiting behavior difficult to reconcile with notions of market efficiency. In 1991, Congress authorized creation of a single class of stock for Sallie Mae, eliminating the discount and removing a trading opportunity for arbitrageurs willing to play in less liquid markets.

Illiquidity and Information

Less information tends to be available on illiquid securities, creating an opportunity to be rewarded for uncovering insights that are not reflected in a stock's market price. Highly liquid large-capitalization stocks receive widespread coverage, generating enormous amounts of publicly available information. During calendar year 2006, Exxon Mobil, the largest stock by capitalization, was covered by twenty-two Wall Street analysts and was mentioned 659 times in the *Wall Street Journal*. In contrast, Avistar Communications, the 5,000th company by market capitalization, had no research analysts and *Wall Street Journal* references totaled only three.

Table 4.9 Large Companies Receive More Intense Research Scrutiny

Small Companies Offer Opportunities to Develop an Information "Edge"

Companies	Capitalization Rank	Average Market Capitalization	Average Number of Analysts	Average Number of *Wall Street Journal* Citations
Exxon Mobil Corp				
General Electric Co				
Microsoft Corp	1-5	$327.5 Billion	25	954
Citigroup Inc				
Bank of America Corp				
U S Bancorp				
United Technologies Corp				
Qualcomm Inc	50-54	$62.2 Billion	24	119
Medtronic Inc				
Tyco International Ltd				
Capital One Financial Corp				
Halliburton Co				
Kimberly-Clark Corp	100-104	$31.0 Billion	22	90
Valero Energy Corp				
Carnival Corp/Plc (Usa)				
Navistar International Corp				
Teleflex Inc				
Dresser-Rand Group Inc	1000-1004	$2.5 Billion	7	10
Aspen Insurance Holdings Ltd				
Big Lots Inc				
Avistar Communications Corp				
Daily Journal Corp				
Beverly National Corp	5000-5004	$63.7 Million	0	1
Antares Pharma Inc				
Jl Halsey Corp				

Sources: Bloomberg and The Wall Street Journal Online

At first glance, Exxon Mobil, which operates a complex set of global businesses, appears to present a great opportunity for active managers. In fact, security analysts face a tough challenge in developing an "edge" in light of competition from other analysts, all of whom benefit from mountains of publicly available information. With Avistar Communications, the bottom-up stock analyst finds greater opportunity. Information will no doubt be harder to obtain, but its value will be enhanced by its proprietary nature.

Obviously, private markets present more extreme information advantages. Wall Street research analysts do not follow private companies. Press coverage tends to be less intense, in part because less information becomes public through government-mandated regulatory filings. The lack of easily obtainable information about private companies poses a challenge and creates an opportunity. Superior information flows lie at the heart of private investing, contributing to the results of all successful partnerships.

Liquidity's Ephemeral Nature

Investors prize liquidity because it allows trading in and out of securities. Unfortunately, liquidity tends to evaporate when most needed. The crash of October 1987, described in the *Report of the Presidential Task Force on Market Mechanisms*, provides a case in point: "as the rate of decline accelerated on October 19, the efficiency with which the equity market functioned deteriorated markedly. By the late afternoon of October 19, market makers on the major stock exchanges appear to have largely abandoned serious attempts to stem the downward movement in prices. In the futures and options markets, market makers were not a significant factor during that time. . . . Price changes and trading activity were highly erratic from late Monday afternoon through most of the day on Tuesday, October 20, as market makers were overwhelmed by selling. . . . Realistically, in the face of October's violent shifts in selling demand for equity-related securities, a rational downward transition in stock prices was not possible. Market makers possessed neither the resources nor the willingness to absorb the extraordinary volume of selling demand that materialized."[15] Just when investors most needed liquidity, it disappeared.

John Maynard Keynes argues in *The General Theory* that "[o]f the maxims of orthodox finance none, surely, is more antisocial than the fetish of liquidity, the doctrine that it is a positive virtue on the part of investment institutions to concentrate their resources upon the holding of "liquid" securities. It forgets that there is no such thing as liquidity of investment for the community as a whole."[16]

Keynes toyed with the idea of reducing market liquidity to increase the prevalence of long-term investing. He writes "[t]he spectacle of modern investment markets has sometimes moved me towards the conclusion that to make the purchase of an investment permanent and indissoluble, like marriage, except by reason of death or other grave cause, might be a useful remedy for our contemporary evils.

For this would force the investor to direct his mind to the long-term prospects and to those only."[17]

Success matters, not liquidity. If private, illiquid investments succeed, liquidity follows as investors clamor for shares of the hot initial public offering. In public markets, as once-illiquid stocks produce strong results, liquidity increases as Wall Street recognizes progress. In contrast, if public, liquid investments fail, illiquidity follows as investor interest wanes. Portfolio managers should fear failure, not illiquidity.

Value Orientation

Investment success follows most reliably from pursuing value-based strategies, in which investors acquire assets at prices below fair value, "buying dollars for fifty cents." Investors who wish to implement value oriented programs require unusual skill, intelligence, and energy. Without a significant edge relative to other market participants, investors face likely failure. Moreover, value opportunities tend to be out of favor with mainstream investors, demanding courage of conviction to initiate and maintain positions.

Tobin's "q"

John Maynard Keynes in *The General Theory* articulated this concept of value: ". . . there is no sense in building up a new enterprise at a cost greater than that at which a similar existing enterprise can be purchased; whilst there is an inducement to spend on a new project what may seem an extravagant sum, if it can be floated off . . . at an immediate profit."[18] James Tobin and William Brainard formalized this concept as "q," the ratio of market value to replacement cost.

In equilibrium, under a reasonable set of conditions, Tobin-Brainard "q" equals one as the market value of assets equals replacement cost. If market value exceeds replacement cost, a "q" greater than one encourages entrepreneurs to create companies, offering them for sale at an immediate profit in the public markets. If replacement cost exceeds market value, a "q" of less than one leads entrepreneurs to acquire corporate assets in the public market instead of building enterprises from the ground up. Value investors thrive in environments where "q" measures less than one.

Margin of Safety

Renowned investor Benjamin Graham distills the central tenet of value investing into a single concept—margin of safety—the cushion in value created by owning shares of a company with "expected earning power considerably above the going rate for bonds." Graham notes: "The margin-of-safety idea becomes [most] evident when we apply it to the field of undervalued or bargain securities. We have here, by definition, a favorable difference between price on the one hand and indicated or appraised value on the other. That difference is the safety margin. It is available for absorbing the effect of miscalculations or worse than average luck. The buyer of bargain issues places particular emphasis on the ability of the investment to withstand adverse developments. For in most such cases he has no real enthusiasm about the company's prospects. True, if the prospects are definitely bad the investor will prefer to avoid the security no matter how low the price. But the field of undervalued issues is drawn from the many concerns—perhaps a majority of the total—for which the future appears neither distinctly promising nor distinctly unpromising. If these are bought on a bargain basis, even a moderate decline in the earning power need not prevent the investment from showing satisfactory results. The margin of safety will then have served its proper purpose." [19]

In today's highly efficient securities markets, few opportunities exist to acquire assets at less than a fair price. Even with twenty-twenty hindsight, investors may not know whether positions were purchased below intrinsic value. Adjusting for risk and assessing the impact of subsequent external events, positive or negative, complicate evaluation of the initial acquisition decision. Because of the difficulty of proving the efficacy of value-investing strategies, investors accept the approach almost as an article of faith.

Perhaps the most compelling argument for value-based investment approaches rests on contrarian principles. Markets frequently move to extremes, with high valuations for the popular and low valuations for the out-of-favor. By looking for opportunity in neglected securities, contrarian investors increase the likelihood of identifying profitable investments.

Yet mindless contrarian investing poses dangers to portfolios. Sometimes popular companies deserve premium valuations. Sometimes out-of-favor companies deserve discounted valuations. Identifying out-of-favor assets serves as a starting point for serious investors, leading to further analysis. Only if careful analysis confirms expectations of superior future performance should investors purchase securities.

Purchasing stocks with low price-to-earnings ratios or price-to-book ratios represents a naïve strategy. Simply selecting the cheapest stocks, measured relative to current earnings or book value, neglects important factors such as the quality of a business's management and future earnings prospects.

Historically, naïve value strategies have delivered superior rates of return, while exposing investors to relatively high levels of fundamental risk.[20] Jeremy Grantham of Grantham Mayo Van Otterloo warns of the "sixty year flood" that may wipe out years of gains garnered by simply purchasing the cheapest stocks. True value can be acquired by purchasing assets at prices below fair value, a forward-looking concept that considers anticipated cash flows with adjustment for the level of risk.

Value investors need not limit choices to low growth or distressed companies. Even high growth industries contain companies with appealing valuations. One technology stock manager, Sy Goldblatt of S Squared, when attending industry conferences, avoids the rooms crowded with analysts pursuing the "flavor of the month." Instead, operating out of the mainstream, he meets with companies that cannot attract an audience. While many find the concepts of value and technology strange bedfellows, combining the two creates a powerful combination. Value investors seek to purchase companies at a discount to fair value, not to purchase low growth or distressed assets *per se.*

Benjamin Graham recognized that careful investors might identify value in unusual precincts. He writes: ". . . the growth-stock approach may supply as dependable a margin of safety as is found in the ordinary investment—provided the calculation of the future is conservatively made, and provided it shows a satisfactory margin in relation to the price paid. The danger in a growth-stock program lies precisely here. For such favored issues the market has a tendency to set prices that will not be adequately protected by a *conservative* projection of future earnings. The margin of safety is always dependent on the price paid. It will be large at one price, small at some higher price, nonexistent at some still higher price. If, as we suggest, the average market level of most growth stocks is too high to provide an adequate margin of safety for the buyer, then a simple technique of diversified buying in this field may not work out satisfactorily. A special degree of foresight and judgment will be needed, in order that wise individual selections may overcome the hazards inherent in the customary market level of such

issues as a whole."[21] While Graham recognizes the occasional opportunity to identify growth stocks exhibiting a margin of safety, value oriented investors choosing among out-of-favor securities face a richer set
of attractive portfolio alternatives.

Contrarian Investing

Superb opportunities to purchase assets at prices significantly below
fair value tend to be hidden in deeply out-of-favor market segments. At
market bottoms, the broad consensus so loathes certain asset types that
investors brave enough to make commitments find their sanity and
sense of responsibility questioned. In fact, Keynes writes of the contrarian investor that ". . . it is in the essence of his behavior that he should
be eccentric, unconventional, and rash in the eyes of average opinion."[22] Managers searching among unloved opportunities face greater
chances of success, along with almost certain tirades of criticism.

The real estate market in the early 1990s provided obvious opportunities to acquire dollars at a discount. In January 1994, Yale participated in the purchase of a real estate asset with a lease that promised
a rate of return of 14.8 percent. Over the term of the lease the return
would be fully realized in cash, paying back the entire investment
along with a profit and leaving a valuable asset in the partnership's
possession. Even without ascribing any residual value to the property,
the real estate return of nearly 15 percent exceeded, by a dramatic
margin, comparable returns on U.S. Treasury Notes of approximately
5.75 percent. Based on the above facts, the transaction may or may not
have represented good value. Perhaps the risk of nonperformance by
the tenant justified the large spread between the lease payments and
the riskless Treasury rate. In reality, the responsibility of the U.S. government for lease payments rendered the quality of the rental stream
equivalent to the U.S. Treasury Note. Rarely do investors face clearer
opportunities to buy dollars at a discount. (Ironically, the opportunity
to purchase a risk-free stream of cash flows at a bargain price came
from an agency of the U.S. Government, the Resolution Trust Corporation (RTC). While the RTC generally did an effective job of disposing
of assets, attractive deals occasionally surfaced.)

The opportunity to purchase real estate assets at bargain basement prices had its seeds in the excesses of the late 1980s. Real estate
was an institutional favorite, topping the list of attractive categories in
asset allocation studies. Investors characterized regional malls as "irre-

placeable assets" with "monopoly positions," purchasing them at cash yields below 5 percent. Downtown office buildings were treated with similar reverence.

In the early 1990s the story changed dramatically. The overbuilding, over-leveraging and overpaying of the previous decade became apparent as real estate prices went into free fall. Regional malls, in reverse evolution, became dinosaurs, threatened by competition from "power centers" and other new retailing concepts. Central business district office buildings, too, were headed for extinction, as working at home was about to replace commuting to the city.

Value-oriented investors recognized that circumstances were not as good as they seemed in the late 1980s and were not as bad as they appeared in the early 1990s. By simply looking at the relationship between market value and replacement cost, an investor would be a late 1980s seller and an early 1990s buyer. Buying low and selling high beats the alternative.

Performance Chasing Behavior

Far from exhibiting the courage required to take contrarian stands, most investors follow the crowd down the path to comfortable mediocrity. Investor cash flows into and out of actively managed funds provide a case in point. Ideally, serious investors would provide funds to managers after a period of understandable underperformance and before a period of expected outperformance. In fact, investors consistently do the opposite.

Stunning evidence, compiled by Russel Kinnel, Morningstar's Director of Fund Research, shows remarkably consistent dismal decision making by mutual fund investors. The Morningstar study, summarized in Table 4.10, compares mutual fund industry returns that appear in offering documents and advertisements (time-weighted returns) with mutual fund investor returns that consider cash inflows and outflows (dollar-weighted returns). The analysis looked at ten years of results, covered all domestic equity funds and divided them into seventeen categories. In each instance actual experience fell short of reported results. In other words, investors put money into funds after good performance (and before bad performance) and took money out of funds after bad performance (and before good performance).

Kinnel notes that "volatility adds to the problem." Technology funds show a stunning 13.4 percent per annum gap between reported

Table 4.10 Mutual Fund Investors Consistently Chase Performance

Returns for Ten Years Ending April 30, 2005

Category	Dollar-Weighted Return	Time-Weighted Return	Gap
Technology	-5.7%	7.7%	-13.4%
Communications	3.0	8.4	-5.4
Health	8.5	12.5	-4.0
Large growth	4.4	7.8	-3.4
Small growth	5.4	8.4	-3.1
Mid growth	6.3	8.8	-2.5
Small blend	9.0	11.3	-2.4
Natural resources	10.3	12.4	-2.1
Small value	11.6	13.6	-2.0
Real estate	13.4	15.4	-2.0
Mid value	10.4	12.2	-1.7
Large Blend	7.5	9.1	-1.6
Financials	12.8	14.4	-1.6
Moderate allocation	7.3	8.4	-1.2
Mid blend	10.6	11.4	-0.8
Large value	9.6	10.0	-0.4
Conservative allocation	7.2	7.5	-0.3

Note: Figures may not add due to rounding
Source: Morningstar Fund Investor. July 2005, Volume 13 Number 11.

results and actual experience. Sector funds specializing in communications and health care along with small, mid, and large growth stock funds round out the list of failure-prone investment vehicles.

While all fund groups show poor investor decision making, less volatile funds produce less gruesome results. The conservative allocation group boasts the best record, posting the smallest, but still disappointing gap of 0.3 percent per annum. Other low volatility offerings in which investors behave relatively well include large value, mid blend, and moderate allocation.

The Morningstar study indicates that individual investors exhibit return-damaging performance-chasing behavior with remarkable consistency. Adding the effects of persistently perverse cash flows to the costs of active management leaves little room for individual investor success.

Unfortunately, no comparable comprehensive data exist on institutional flows to active managers. That said, available evidence indicates that institutions suffer from precisely the same performance-chasing problem as do individuals. Consider the case of Grantham Mayo Van Otterloo (GMO), an extraordinary Boston-based institutional money manager. Despite boasting one of the best long-term records in the funds management business, when the firm hit a rough patch clients deserted in droves.

GMO's rational, valuation-oriented systematic style failed to keep pace with the late 1990s' manic markets. Investors panicked. Between 1998 and 1999 GMO's asset base declined from $30 billion to $20 billion even as stock markets raced ahead.[23] Departing investors lost thrice: once, by selling GMO at a low point; once, by redeploying assets to momentum-driven managers destined to fail; and once, by failing to participate in GMO's recovery. In a stunning indictment of active management, investors intelligent enough to choose GMO in the first place exhibited the stupidity to abandon the firm's disciplined approach at the point of maximum opportunity.

Consider the specific story of GMO's quantitatively driven International Intrinsic Value Strategy. From inception in early 1987 to the end of 2006, the fund produced returns of 11.1 percent per annum, generating a significant excess return relative to the EAFE index result of 7.0 percent per annum. Long-term investors in International Intrinsic Value fared extremely well.

Yet, in the aggregate, investor behavior managed to turn success into failure. Superb returns in the early 1990s attracted investor interest, as shown in Table 4.11. Average annual excess returns of 8.7 percent from 1990 to 1993 boosted assets in the strategy from $378 million to $2.6 billion! As long as trailing three-year performance showed market-beating returns, inflows continued, increasing assets under management to a peak of $2.8 billion at the end of 1996. Supposedly rational institutions chased GMO's performance.

In 1997, after the trailing three-year performance numbers turned negative, the exodus began. Client withdrawals took assets in International Intrinsic Value from the 1996 peak of $2.8 billion to the 2002 low point of $578 million. GMO's poor relative returns from 1994 to 1999 caused fickle clients to abandon a sensible active strategy.

Of course, exiting clients failed to benefit from GMO's dramatic recovery. As rationality returned to markets after the early 2000 collapse of the Internet bubble, GMO posted average excess returns of 9.5

Table 4.11 GMO's Institutional Investors Buy High and Sell Low
International Intrinsic Value Strategy

Year	Return	EAFE Index	Excess Return	Client Flows (millions of dollars)	Assets Under Management (millions of dollars)
1990	-8.1%	-23.2%	15.1%	256	378
1991	14.4	12.5	1.9	503	990
1992	-1.1	-11.9	10.7	182	1,218
1993	39.9	32.9	7.0	471	2,595
1994	4.2	8.1	-3.9	(23)	2,234
1995	10.3	11.6	-1.2	307	2,606
1996	9.6	6.4	3.2	85	2,838
1997	0.9	2.1	-1.1	(1,257)	1,607
1998	13.6	20.3	-6.7	(784)	1,095
1999	14.6	27.3	-12.7	(190)	1,057
2000	-1.4	-14.2	12.8	(220)	802
2001	-12.1	-21.4	9.3	(27)	647
2002	-0.6	-15.9	15.4	(7)	578
2003	43.5	38.6	4.9	1,116	1,981
2004	25.3	20.2	5.0	597	3,162
2005	14.3	13.5	0.7	886	4,680

Source: GMO.
Note: This does not include accounts where GMO has discretion to allocate across multiple strategies.

percent per annum in the ensuing five years. Buying high and selling low, as practiced by so many of GMO's clients, produced permanent damage to portfolios.

Over the period from 1993 to 2003, GMO's International Intrinsic Value Strategy beat the market by 2.8 percent per year. Client cash flows turned GMO's stellar results on their head. On a dollar-weighted basis, clients underperformed by 2.0 percent per year. Poorly considered commitments to and withdrawals from GMO's International Intrinsic Value Strategy transformed a winning investment vehicle into a losing investment alternative.

In the closed world of marketable security investing, simple logic dictates that a majority of assets fail to beat the market, as the impact of management fees and transaction costs guarantee poor results for most participants. Widespread active management failure makes the unusual success all the more valuable. When foolish clients of high quality managers destroy value by responding perversely to past performance, the already tough case for active management becomes tougher still.

Value investing provides a sturdy foundation for building an investment portfolio, as the acquisition of assets below fair value provides a margin of safety. In many instances, value investing proves fundamentally uncomfortable, as the most attractive opportunities lurk in unattractive or even frightening areas. As a result, many investors abandon sensible strategies to pursue the fashion du jour. If pursued in a steadfast manner, value strategies provide a measure of stability to investment programs, reducing dependence on the vicissitudes of the market and serving to mitigate risks faced by portfolio managers.

CONCLUSION

Investment philosophy defines an investor's approach to generating portfolio returns, describing in the most fundamental fashion the tenets that permeate the investment process. Market returns stem from three sources—asset allocation, market timing, and security selection—with each source of return providing a tool for investors to use to satisfy institutional goals. Sensible investors employ the available tools in a manner consistent with a well defined, carefully articulated investment philosophy.

Investor behavior causes policy asset allocation to dominate portfolio returns, since institutions tend to hold stable commitments to broadly diversified portfolios of marketable securities. Creating a diversified portfolio with a range of equity-oriented asset classes that respond to drivers of returns in fundamentally different fashion provides important underpinning to the investment process.

Market timing causes investors to hold portfolios that differ from policy targets, jeopardizing a fund's ability to meet long-term objectives. Often driven by fear or greed, market timing tends to detract from portfolio performance. Many institutions practice an implicit form of market timing by failing to maintain allocations at long-term policy targets. Risk control requires regular rebalancing, ensuring that portfolios reflect institutional preferences.

Active security selection plays a prominent role in nearly all institutional investment programs despite the poor relative results posted by the overwhelming majority of investors. Fund managers increase their probability of success by focusing on inefficient markets that present the greatest range of opportunities. Accepting illiquidity pays outsized dividends to the patient, long-term investor, while approaching markets with a value orientation provides a margin of safety. Even if investors execute active management programs with intelligence and care, efficiency in pricing assets poses a significant challenge to identifying and implementing market-beating strategies. In the all-too-frequent situation where investors chase strong returns and abandon weak performance, the odds of beating the market lengthen dramatically. Reasonable market efficiency and unreasonable investor behavior combine to make security selection a tough game.

5
Asset Allocation

The process of asset allocation illustrates the importance of combining art and science in investment decision making, as neither informed judgment nor quantitative analysis alone produces consistently successful results. At one extreme, seat of the pants decisions lack rigor, omitting some information and either underemphasizing or overemphasizing the information that remains. At the other extreme, mechanistic application of quantitative tools produces naïve, sometimes dangerous, conclusions. Marrying the art of seasoned judgment with the science of numeric analysis creates a powerful approach to allocating portfolio assets.

Defining and selecting asset classes constitute initial steps in producing a portfolio. Many investors simply allocate among the asset classes popular at the time in proportions similar to those of other investors, creating uncontroversial portfolios that may or may not address institutional needs. By relying on the decisions of others to drive portfolio choices, investors fail to take responsibility for the most fundamental fiduciary responsibility—designing a portfolio to meet institution-specific goals.

Asset Classes and Fashion

The asset classes from which investors construct portfolios change over time. Snapshots of Yale's portfolio throughout the past 150 years provide an impression of the evolution of portfolio structure. Real

99

estate constituted nearly half of the 1850 portfolio, with "bonds and notes mostly secured by mortgages" and stocks making up the remainder. At the turn of the twentieth century, dominant asset categories included mortgage bonds, railroad bonds, and real estate, with relatively small allocations to "stocks in sundry corporations" and "corporation bonds other than railroad." In the 1950s, the university held domestic bonds, domestic common stocks, preferred stocks, and real estate. At the turn of the twenty-first century, Yale's well-diversified portfolio included domestic bonds, domestic common stocks, foreign common stocks, absolute return, real assets, and private equity.

Just as sartorial styles change, investment fashions ebb and flow. Railroad bonds earned special consideration in asset allocation discussions in the late nineteenth and early twentieth centuries because of the dominant role railroads played in the developing U.S. economy. Investors willingly lent money for hundred-year terms to ostensibly secure rail companies, knowing that even if a particular concern failed, valuable rail-bed right of way provided unimpeachable security.

Imagine the surprise of an 1890s-vintage portfolio manager upon learning the fate of the Lehigh Valley Railroad 4½'s due 1989. Offered at 102½ in January 1891 by the distinguished syndicate of Drexel, J.P. Morgan, and Brown Brothers, the bonds attracted little notice for the next four decades as required payments arrived in full and on time. Widespread economic distress in the 1930s hurt the Lehigh Valley Railroad, leading to relief in the form of the 1938 Debt Adjustment Plan. Initial concessions failed to put the rail line on sound financial footing, leading to further negotiations that resulted in the 1949 Debt Adjustment Plan. Ultimately, restructuring proved insufficient to solve the Lehigh Valley's woes, culminating in failure to meet the October 1, 1970 interest payment. Bondholders, beneficiaries of a first lien on 14.4 miles of track (7.9 miles from Hazle Creek Junction to Hazleton, Pennsylvania and 6.5 miles from Ashmore to Highland Junction, Pennsylvania) received little comfort from the security interest, seeing the obligations trade as low as 5 percent of face value in 1972. Although not all railway debt suffered the fate of the Lehigh Valley bonds, railroad obligations generally failed to meet expectations.[1]

Railroad bonds no longer constitute a separate institutional asset class, since the rail industry proved less enduringly robust than investors of the 1890s believed. With a heavy concentration in railway debt, late nineteenth century investors allocated relatively little to domestic common stocks, missing an opportunity to create portfolios with vastly superior return potential. Twenty-twenty hindsight provides obvious conclusions regarding what would have produced profits in the past. The basic challenge for investors lies in fashioning portfolios positioned to succeed in the environment to come.

Investors begin by selecting asset classes and combining them in a way that promises to meet fundamental investment goals. Institutional portfolios require assets likely to generate equity-like returns, such as domestic and foreign equities, absolute return strategies, real assets, and private equities. To mitigate asset-class-specific risks, investors diversify aggressively, holding assets in proportions that allow the asset class to matter, but not matter too much. By understanding and articulating the role played by each asset class, investors create a strong foundation for an institutional investment program.

Asset Class Definition

Purity of asset class composition represents a rarely achieved ideal. Carried to an extreme, the search for purity results in dozens of asset classes, creating an unmanageable multiplicity of alternatives. While market participants disagree on the appropriate number of asset classes, the number should be small enough so that portfolio commitments make a difference, yet large enough so that portfolio commitments do not make too much of a difference. Committing less than 5 percent or 10 percent of a fund to a particular type of investment makes little sense; the small allocation holds no potential to influence overall portfolio results. Committing more than 25 percent or 30 percent to an asset class poses the danger of overconcentration. Most portfolios work well with around a half a dozen asset classes.

half - dozen asset classes

Functional attributes play the dominant role in defining asset classes, with structural and legal characteristics taking secondary positions. Asset class distinctions rest on broad sweeping differences in fundamental character: debt versus equity, domestic versus foreign, inflation sensitive versus deflation sensitive, private versus public, liquid versus illiquid. Ultimately investors attempt to group like with like, creating relatively homogeneous groups of investments that provide fundamental building blocks for the portfolio construction process.

Fixed income represents an interesting case. If investors want fixed income assets to provide a hedge against financial accidents, then only high quality, long-term, noncallable bonds satisfy the requirement. Although from a legal and structural perspective below-investment-grade bonds (a.k.a. junk bonds or high-yield bonds) belong to the fixed income family, they lack important crisis-hedging attributes. Junk bonds contain equity-like risks, as payments depend mightily on the financial health of the issuer. Even if the high-yield obligor meets contractual obligations, holders may lose bonds through a mandatory call, as lower interest rates or improved corporate health allow issuers to redeem bonds at a fixed price prior to maturity. Ironically, junk bondholders may lose if corporate prospects deteriorate or if they improve! In any case, below-investment-grade bonds provide little protection against a period of severe financial distress, since at a time of economic disruption high-yield bondholders might suffer from a corporate default.

Government bonds dominate portfolios designed to hedge against financial trauma, providing high quaility portfolio protection. Not all Treasury issues make the grade, however. Treasury Inflation-Protected Securities have no place in a properly defined fixed income portfolio. Traditional fixed income assets respond to unanticipated inflation by declining in price, as the future stream of fixed payments becomes worth less. In contrast, inflation-indexed bonds respond to unexpected price increases by providing a higher return. When two assets respond in opposite fashion to the same critically important variable, those assets belong in different asset classes.

Many investors include foreign bonds in portfolios as part of a broadly defined fixed income asset class or as a separate asset class. Neither choice makes fundamental sense. First, foreign bonds have no role in a fixed income portfolio designed to protect against deflation or financial trauma. Investors cannot know how foreign bonds might respond to a domestic financial crisis, since conditions overseas may differ from the environment at home. Moreover, foreign exchange translations influence returns in a substantial, unpredictable manner. Second, as a separate asset class, high quality foreign bonds hold little interest. The combination of low, bond-like expected returns and foreign exchange exposure negates any positive attributes associated with nondomestic fixed income. If investors pay the price (in terms of low expected returns) by buying bonds for disaster insurance, the payoff must be clear and direct.

Careful investors define asset classes in terms of function, relating security characteristics to the role expected from a particular group of investments. In the case of fixed income, introduction of credit risk, call risk, and currency risk diminish disaster-hedging attributes. Yet in reaching for return or seeking an easy way to beat the benchmark, most institutional portfolios contain disproportionate allocations to bonds lacking the purity of U.S. Treasury obligations. The net result leads to a portfolio that meets neither the goal of producing equity-like returns nor the goal of protecting against market trauma.

Judgment plays a critical role in defining and shaping asset classes. Unless the statistical analysis employed in the asset allocation process rests on reasonable asset class definitions, the resulting portfolio stands little chance of meeting institutional needs.

QUANTITATIVE AND QUALITATIVE ANALYSIS

Establishing policy asset allocation targets requires a combination of quantitative and qualitative inputs. Financial markets invite quantification. Return, risk, and correlation lend themselves to numerical measurement. Statistical methods allow analysis of possible portfolio combinations through a number of frameworks, including the capital asset pricing model (CAPM), arbitrage pricing theory (APT), and modern portfolio theory (MPT). Quantitative analysis provides essential underpinnings to the portfolio structuring process, forcing investors to take a disciplined approach to portfolio construction. Systematic specification of inputs for an asset allocation model clarifies the central issues in portfolio management.

Nobel laureates Harry Markowitz and James Tobin developed mean-variance optimization, one of the most useful and most widely used analytical frameworks. The process identifies efficient portfolios, which for a given level of risk have the highest possible return or for a given level of return have the lowest possible risk. Using inputs of expected return, expected risk, and expected correlation, the optimization process evaluates various combinations of assets, ultimately identifying superior portfolios. Those portfolios that cannot be improved represent the efficient frontier, a set of points from which rational investors will choose.

Identifying Efficient Portfolios

The mere phrase *mean-variance optimization* intimidates many investors, conjuring images of complicated quantitative methods beyond the grasp of the intelligent lay public. In fact, the optimization process rests on several basic concepts, accessible to even casual students of finance.

Mean-variance optimization identifies efficient portfolios. An efficient portfolio dominates all others producing the same return or exhibiting the same risk. In other words, for a given risk level, no other portfolio produces higher returns than the efficient portfolio. Similarly, for a given return level, no other portfolio exhibits lower risk than the efficient portfolio. Note that the definition of efficiency relates entirely to risk and return; mean-variance optimization fails to consider other asset class attributes.

Practitioners generally assume that normal, or bell-curve-shaped, distributions describe asset class returns, allowing complete specification of the distribution of returns with only a mean and a variance. Although using normal distributions facilitates implementation of mean-variance analysis, real-world security returns include significant nonnormal characteristics, limiting the value of the conclusions.

Correlations specify the manner in which returns of one asset class tend to vary with returns of other asset classes, quantifying the diversifying power of combining asset classes that respond differently to forces that drive returns. Correlation supplies a third means through which asset class characteristics influence portfolio construction, supplementing the return and risk factors.

After specifying expected returns, risks, and correlations for the set of investable asset classes, the search for efficient portfolios begins. Starting with a given risk level, the model examines portfolio after portfolio, ultimately leading to identification of a combination of assets that produces the highest return. The superior portfolio takes a place on the efficient frontier. The process then continues by identifying the highest return portfolio for a range of risk levels, with the resulting combination of superior portfolios defining the efficient frontier.

At its core, mean-variance optimization is a simple process. Employing specified capital markets characteristics, a quantitative model uses iterative techniques to search for efficient portfolios. When considering combinations of assets positioned on the efficient frontier, investors choose from a superior set of portfolios.

high return → low risk = efficiency

Limitations of Mean-Variance Analysis

Unconstrained mean-variance optimization often provides solutions unrecognizable as reasonable portfolios. Richard Michaud, in his critique of mean-variance optimization, writes "[t]he unintuitive character of many 'optimized' portfolios can be traced to the fact that mean-variance optimizers are, in a fundamental sense, 'estimation-error maximizers.' . . . Mean-variance optimization significantly overweights (underweights) those securities that have large (small) estimated returns, negative (positive) correlations and small (large) variances. These securities are, of course, the ones most likely to have large estimation errors."[2] Although Michaud's comments pertain to a portfolio of securities, his critique applies equally to a portfolio of asset classes.

Several fundamental problems limit the usefulness of mean-variance analysis. Evidence suggests that security returns do not correspond to a normal distribution, with markets exhibiting more extreme events than would be consistent with a bell curve distribution. Richard Bookstaber, author of *A Demon of Our Own Design*, states that a "general rule of thumb is that every financial market experiences one or more daily price moves of four standard deviations or more each year. And in any year, there is usually at least one market that has a daily move that is greater than ten standard deviations."[3][*] If extreme price changes occur substantially more frequently than predicted by a normal distribution, then mean-variance analysis fails to consider some extremely important information. In fact, investors care more about extraordinary situations in the tails of the distribution, such as the 1987 stock market crash, than about ordinary outcomes represented by the heart of the distribution.

The way in which asset classes relate to one another may not be stable. For example, market crises often cause otherwise distinct markets to behave in a similar fashion. In October 1987, equity markets all over the world collapsed, disappointing those portfolio managers who expected foreign diversification to cushion a drop in domestic equity prices. Although correlations among individual country stock markets before and after October 1987 measured substantially less than one, the highly correlated behavior of markets in the period immediately following the 1987 crash caused many investors to wonder what happened to the hoped-for diversification. Most investors rely heavily on historical experience in estimating quantitative inputs; yet continuous structural evolution reduces the predictive value of historical returns, risks, and correlations. Quantitative modelers face the daunting task of assigning an appropriate weight to historical data and an appropriate weight to well-considered intuitive projections.

Mean-variance optimization defines return distributions completely in terms of expected return and risk. The framework fails to consider other important attributes, such as liquidity and marketability. In fact, the inclusion of less liquid assets in a mean-variance frame-

*Normally distributed variables generate a four standard deviation event once every 15,780 trials. Based on a 250 day year, a four standard deviation event occurs once every 63 years.

work raises material issues. Most frequently, mean-variance optimization involves analysis of annual capital markets data, implicitly assuming annual rebalancing of portfolio allocations. That is, if stocks have moved above target and bonds below, then on the relevant anniversary date investors sell stocks and buy bonds in sufficient quantities to restore target allocations. Clearly, less marketable assets, such as private equity and real estate, cannot be rebalanced in a low cost, efficient manner. The inability to manage illiquid assets in a manner consistent with model assumptions reduces the applicability of mean-variance analysis.

Another problem with mean-variance optimization relates to investor time horizon. In many cases, investors care about multiple objectives that span different time horizons. For instance, endowment managers seek intermediate-term spending stability even as they pursue long-term purchasing power preservation. A mean-variance time period of three to five years might serve the spending stability criterion, while a time period spanning decades might serve the purchasing power criterion. The almost universally employed one-year time period serves neither. The rigidity of mean-variance optimization fails to accommodate real-world concerns of endowment investors.

In the final analysis, both the fundamental shortcomings and the basic attraction of quantitative methods stem from reducing a rich set of asset class attributes to a neat, compact package of precisely defined statistical characteristics. Because the process involves materially simplifying assumptions, unconstrained asset allocation point estimates produced by mean-variance optimization represent simply a starting point for further work.

Qualitative Judgments

The limitations of mean-variance analysis argue for inclusion of qualitative considerations in the asset allocation process. Judgment might be incorporated by applying reasonable constraints to particular asset class allocations. For example, an investor could express a preference for diversification by limiting any individual asset class to no more than 30 percent of assets. Such a constraint ensures that no single asset class dominates a portfolio. In addition, prospective allocations to private equity could logically be limited to a modest increase over the current allocation. Since illiquidity and lumpiness of opportunities limit prudent expansion of private equity holdings, incremental changes make sense.

Gradualism represents a virtue in and of itself. Substantial uncertainty surrounds the asset allocation process. Keynes's "dark forces of time and ignorance" cloud the future, causing even the most thoughtful estimates of capital markets characteristics to prove unreliable.[4] Deciding to make radical changes based on highly uncertain data places too much weight on a shaky foundation. Limiting asset allocation changes by constraining asset class movements represents a sensible modification of the optimization process.

Care must be taken, however, to avoid using asset class constraints simply to fashion a reasonable-looking portfolio. Taken to an extreme, placing too many constraints on the optimization process causes the model to do nothing other than to reflect the investor's original biases, resulting in the GIGO (garbage-in/garbage-out) phenomenon well known to computer scientists.

Alternatively, investors might identify superior, yet reasonable, portfolios by choosing from a set of portfolios that lay near (but perhaps not directly on) the efficient frontier. In fact, unless the current portfolio sits directly on the efficient frontier, a host of alternatives promise higher expected returns (at the same or lower risk) or lower expected risk (for the same or higher return). Some of the superior choices likely appear more reasonable than the portfolios that define the frontier, giving the investor a more comfortable, yet still superior, alternative.

Quantitative modeling proves particularly helpful in focusing investor attention on potentially rewarding asset allocation changes. By analyzing the existing portfolio using mean-variance optimization and measuring the degree to which the optimizer prefers to move in a particular direction, investors understand the relative attractiveness of prospective portfolio moves. Attractive asset classes strain at the constraints, while unattractive holdings may not even reach current allocation levels. The degree to which the optimizer "likes" a particular asset class suggests increasing or decreasing allocations, providing a starting point for qualitative assessment of the quantitative conclusion. Using informed judgment to modify and interpret mean-variance results improves the asset allocation process.

CAPITAL MARKET ASSUMPTIONS

Return and risk expectations constitute the heart of quantitative assessment of portfolio alternatives. While historical experience represents a reasonable starting point, investors seeking to create truly useful conclusions must move beyond simply plugging historical numbers into the mean-variance optimizer.

Developing a set of quantitative inputs for portfolio optimization poses some difficult issues. Most troubling may be the forward-looking nature of the estimates. While past patterns provide important input for assumptions about the future, historical data must be modified to produce a set of numbers consistent with expected market realities. Thoughtful investors strike a balance between respect for history and concern for analytical consistency.

Historical capital markets data require adjustment. Mean-reverting behavior in security prices implies that periods of abnormally high returns follow periods of abnormally low returns, and vice versa. Jeremy Grantham, a prominent money manager, believes reversion to the mean constitutes the most powerful force in financial markets.[5] If prices tend to revert to the mean, then return expectations must be adjusted to dampen expectations for recent high fliers and boost forecasts for recent poor performers.

Period-specific data frequently suggest counterintuitive conclusions. Relatively risky asset classes may show returns below those of obviously less risky investments. Assets that have little in common may move together for no apparent reason. Adjusting assumptions to reflect appropriate risk and return relationships proves critical to sensible quantitative analysis.

Structural changes in markets force analysts to weight recent data more heavily, deemphasizing numbers posted in previous, sometimes dramatically different, environments. Introduction of new classes of securities, such as the U.S. Treasury issuance of thirty-year bonds beginning in February 1977, may alter asset class characteristics in so fundamental a manner as to render earlier data far less relevant in reaching conclusions regarding future asset class behavior.

Some practitioners seem daunted by the task of fashioning precise point estimate predictions of future asset class characteristics. Comfort comes from the realization that great value stems from producing a set of forecasts with reasonable relative relationships among and between the various asset classes. Capital markets assumptions with sensible relative relationships enable identification of a set of useful portfolio alternatives. Even if point estimates of risk and return variables fail to match the subsequent reality, insofar as inputs stem from well-grounded interrelationships, the mean-variance optimization process produces valuable insight into efficient portfolio alternatives.

Unfortunately, point estimates of asset class returns remain necessary for some purposes. In evaluating the ability of various portfolio combinations to support specified spending requirements, the precise levels of forecast returns come into play. When deciding whether a portfolio can reasonably produce returns sufficient to satisfy a 4 percent, 4.5 percent, or 5 percent target rate of spending, fiduciaries face the difficult challenge of relying on forecasts of future capital markets returns. Fortunately, in the case of evaluating a portfolio's ability to support a particular level of spending, fiduciaries require reasonably accurate forecasts of long-term returns, which prove much less daunting than fashioning forecasts of short-term returns.

In mean-variance optimization, data on expected returns provide the most powerful determinant of results, demanding the greatest share of quantitative modelers' attention.[6] Forecasts of variances place second in importance, while assumptions regarding correlations prove least crucial. Fortunately, the most intuitive variables—expected returns and variances—play a more central role in the model than the less intuitive correlations.

Marketable Security Characteristics

Past returns for domestic stocks and bonds provide a sensible starting point for developing capital markets assumptions, based on the centrality of marketable securities in portfolio construction and on the availability of a lengthy series of high quality data. Choosing an appropriate time period poses interesting trade-offs. On the positive side, longer time frames provide a more robust picture of asset class returns and interrelationships with other asset classes. On the negative side, a

Table 5.1 Historical Capital Markets Data Provide a Starting Point for Quantitative Analysis

Historical Data Inflation Adjusted Using the Higher Education Price Index

	U.S. Bonds	U.S. Equity	Developed Equity	Emerging Equity	Absolute Return	Private Equity	Real Assets	Cash
Observations	80	80	36	21	17	25	25	80
Arithmetic return	2.5%	10.6%	8.3%	11.9%	9.9%	12.8%	6.2%	0.7%
Standard deviation	6.8%	22.4%	22.1%	30.0%	8.2%	23.1%	6.8%	4.0%
Growth rate	2.3%	8.2%	6.1%	8.1%	9.6%	10.9%	6.0%	0.6%

Table 5.2 Quantitative Model Inputs Rely on Modified Risk and Return Assumptions

Model Data Inflation Adjusted Using Higher Education Price Index

	U.S. Bonds	U.S. Equity	Developed Equity	Emerging Equity	Absolute Return	Private Equity	Real Assets	Cash
Expected return	2.0%	6.0%	6.0%	8.0%	6.0%	12.0%	6.0%	0.0%
Standard deviation	10.0%	20.0%	20.0%	25.0%	10.0%	30.0%	15.0%	5.0%
Expected growth	1.5%	4.1%	4.1%	5.1%	5.5%	8.1%	4.9%	-0.1%

Source: Yale University Investments Office.

trality of marketable securities in portfolio construction and on the availability of a lengthy series of high quality data. Choosing an appropriate time period poses interesting trade-offs. On the positive side, longer time frames provide a more robust picture of asset class returns and interrelationships with other asset classes. On the negative side, a long time series includes results from periods with fundamentally different structural characteristics. For instance, Jeremy Siegel's *Stocks for the Long Run* begins its study of U.S. equity and bond market returns with data from the turn of the nineteenth century. During significant portions of Siegel's study period, the United States was an emerging market, the Federal Reserve System did not exist, and long-term government bonds were not available. What relevance do stock and bond returns from the nineteenth century have to expectations for stock and bond returns today?

Recognizing the arbitrary nature of choosing any particular subset of data to use as a foundation for estimating future returns, one sensible starting point involves the landmark Ibbotson-Sinquefield study, first published in 1976.[7] Beginning at the end of 1925, the period contains a sufficient number of observations to provide a rich set of data, but encompasses a short enough span to limit the impact on markets of significant structural changes.

Using historical data (such as those contained in Table 5.1) as a foundation, sensible investors build on that base to create a coherent set of capital markets assumptions (such as those presented in Table 5.2). Since prudently managed endowments consume only post-inflation returns, all capital markets assumptions reflect an appropriate inflation adjustment.

Domestic Bonds

Domestic bond market returns provide a logical baseline for building a matrix of capital markets assumptions. Over the long sweep of time, as fixed income investors found returns eroded by spells of unanticipated inflation, bonds provided mediocre real returns of 2.5 percent per annum with risk of 6.8 percent. The October 1979 Federal Reserve decision to target monetary aggregates instead of interest rates caused bond markets to trade with greater volatility. Placing more weight on recent experience leads to an assumed expected return of 2 percent with risk of 10 percent.

Marketable Equities

Discussion of the difference in expected returns for bonds and stocks, more succinctly described as the risk premium, fills many volumes of finance journals. Even while recognizing the complexities surrounding estimation of the risk premium, asset allocators must deal with the issue explicitly or implicitly. The historical risk premium of 8.1 percent appears to be excessive, resulting in large part from the extraordinary performance of U.S. equities over the past twenty-five years. Moreover, the time series of equity and bond returns suggests that the risk premium has declined through time. Combining the tendency of a high risk premium to mean revert with the observation that the equity risk premium seems to decline secularly, justifies an assumption for U.S. equity returns of 6 percent real with standard deviation of 20 percent.

Making appropriate geographic groupings of various national equity markets poses interesting analytical questions. Approaches range from global to regional to single country. A global equity asset class fails to recognize the critical contribution that currency movements make to investment returns, while individual country asset classes create too many variables for reasonable analysis. Separating domestic equities from foreign allows investors to account for critical home country characteristics, particularly with respect to currency. A further distinction between developed and emerging markets groups assets with respect to important differentiating risk and return characteristics.

Developed economies tend to share similar economic and market fundamentals. In the long run, stock markets in Germany, Japan, and the United Kingdom ought to generate returns similar to those of the United States, while exposing investors to similar risk levels.

Assumed foreign developed market returns of 6 percent with risk of 20 percent match expectations for U.S. equities.

Relative to other marketable equities, emerging market equities expose investors to substantially greater fundamental risks, causing rational investors to expect higher rewards and higher volatility. Expected real returns of 8 percent compensate holders of emerging market equities for accepting high levels of risk, represented by a 25 percent standard deviation of returns.

Alternative Asset Characteristics

Nontraditional asset classes pose interesting challenges to the financial model builder. Unlike traditional marketable securities, alternative assets exist outside established markets. No benchmark returns guide investors seeking to model asset characteristics. Past data, limited in scope, generally describe active manager returns, with results sometimes inflated by survivorship bias. Without reliable historical information upon which to base forecasts, investors must produce estimates of expected return and risk by considering alternative asset classes from a fundamental perspective.

Absolute Return

Absolute return investing, first identified as a distinct asset class by Yale University in 1990, relies on active management for its very existence. Dedicated to exploiting inefficiencies in pricing marketable securities, absolute return managers attempt to produce equity-like returns uncorrelated to traditional marketable securities through investments in event-driven and value-driven strategies. Event-driven strategies, including merger arbitrage and distressed security investing, depend on the completion of a corporate finance transaction such as a merger or corporate restructuring. Value-driven strategies employ offsetting long and short positions to eliminate market exposure, relying on market recognition of mispricings to generate returns. Generally, absolute return investments involve transactions with relatively short time horizons, ranging from several months to a year or two.

From the perspective of the late 1980s, observers might have concluded that absolute return investing produces returns in the neighborhood of 20 percent per annum. Hedge funds had produced impressive historical records, showing high returns with low risk and with little correlation to traditional marketable securities. Yet if investors take no systematic risk, they deserve a money market rate of return. In an environment with a 4 percent cost of funds, 20 percent returns from a market neutral portfolio imply excess returns of 16 percent! The high observed returns stem from survivorship bias, a case of past performance raising the profile of successful firms and causing less successful firms to languish in obscurity. Survivorship-bias-infected data provide little help in fashioning market forecasts.

Bottom-up evaluation of value-driven absolute return investments leads to better understanding of future performance. In value-driven transactions, managers often take long and short positions in marketable equities, eliminating the impact of the market and creating two opportunities to generate excess returns. Assume a manager in the top quartile in domestic equities generates 2.6 percent excess returns.* If the manager earns the same excess return on both sides of the portfolio, long and short, gross returns total 8.9 percent, resulting from adding a 3.7 percent short-term rate of return to a 2.6 percent alpha for long positions and 2.6 percent alpha for short positions. Based on past experience, producing 2.6 percent excess returns represents a substantial achievement, suggesting that this analysis relies on aggressive assumptions. After paying management fees and incentive compensation, the investor nets approximately 6.3 percent. On a bottom-up basis, justifying return expectations of 20 percent proves difficult. In fact, the long/short investor needs to produce excess returns of more than 10 percent on both sides of the portfolio to deliver 20 percent net returns to investors. Producing such performance over extended periods of time would literally put a manager off the charts.

In the early years of an asset class, historical data suffer from extreme survivorship bias, causing forward-looking assumptions to differ dramatically from past statistics. In 1997, Yale's absolute return data, which reflected a combination of actual experience and market returns, showed a staggering 17.6 percent return with impressively low volatility of 11.8 percent. If credible, the absolute return numbers indicated returns nearly double those of domestic equities with a risk level of nearly one half. Yale responded by using a conservative approach to determine absolute return asset class characteristics,

---

*Excess return, or alpha, represents the risk-adjusted incremental return for an active strategy relative to the benchmark. For the ten years ending December 31, 2006, top quartile equity managers beat the median by 2.6 percent per year according to data compiled by Frank Russell Company. See p. 188 for a more complete discussion of value added by long/short investing.

assuming expected returns of 7 percent real with risk of 15 percent. Even with this substantial adjustment the numbers suggested that absolute return investments would generate higher returns than domestic stocks with less risk.

As asset classes mature, the issue of survivorship bias wanes. Consultants collect current returns from a critical mass of participants, reducing the impact of a few attention grabbing records. With a larger base of managers, the return inflating addition of new entrants' historical records, a.k.a. backfill bias, plays less of a role. As a result, Yale's current absolute return assumptions correspond more closely to historical experience, with equity-like real returns of 6 percent and below-equity-like risk of 10 percent.

Private Equity

Private equity includes venture capital and leveraged buyout participations, assets that respond to market influences in a manner similar to marketable equities. In fact, both venture and buyout investments resemble high-risk equity assets, raising the possibility of classifying the private assets with marketable securities.

Private managers pursuing purely financial strategies lay the weakest claim to managing a separate asset class. In the buyout arena, simply adding leverage to a company's balance sheet does little to distance the private investment from the public corporation. In the case of venture investing, a provider of late stage pre-IPO equity finance owns assets nearly identical to small-capitalization, publicly traded equity securities. Since private investments created through financial engineering strongly resemble their marketable security counterparts, the argument for segregating such private assets from public securities rests primarily on differences in liquidity.

A stronger justification for treating private equity as a distinct asset class stems from value-added management by investment principals. To the extent that venture capitalists contribute to the process of bringing a company from an idea with no revenues to a reality with tens of millions of dollars in revenues, value creation occurs independent of market activity. A buyout specialist who produces meaningful operating improvements generates similarly noncorrelated returns. Superior opportunities for value creation, combined with liquidity and structural differences, support treatment of private equity as a distinct asset class.

Historical data provide limited guidance in fashioning forward-looking capital markets assumptions. Infrequent marks-to-market cause private assets to appear less volatile than the underlying reality. Start-up companies held in a venture capitalist's partnership receive only occasional valuations, leading to relatively low levels of observed risk. Subsequent to an initial public offering, when a company begins day-to-day trading, measured volatility increases dramatically. Obviously, true risk tends to decrease as companies mature, suggesting that the observed volatility level understates risk for privately held assets. Historical data on buyout returns suffer from the same problem of unnaturally low levels of observed historical risk. The combination of infrequent reporting and market insensitive valuation policies serve to disguise true risk levels.

Guidance for specifying private equity risk and return attributes comes from the expected relationship with marketable equity investments. Illiquidity and higher risk in private assets demand a substantial premium over domestic equity's expectations of 6 percent returns with 20 percent risk. Assuming that private equity investments generate 12 percent returns with a risk level of 30 percent represents an appropriately conservative modification of the historical record of 12.8 percent returns with a 23.1 percent risk level.

Real Assets

The real assets category includes real estate, oil and gas, and timberland, which share the common characteristics of sensitivity to inflationary forces, high and visible current cash flow, and opportunity to exploit inefficiencies. Real assets provide attractive return prospects, excellent portfolio diversification, and a hedge against unanticipated inflation.

Despite important similarities, the three subasset classes differ from one another, showing only modest correlations, as supply of and demand for each depends on fundamentally different factors. For example, recent history indicates that oil and gas investments exhibit negative correlation to real estate and timber. Such diversification within real assets helps to produce steady returns through a variety of economic environments.

Real estate constitutes the core of Yale's real assets portfolio with a weight of 50 percent. Real estate markets provide dramatically cyclical returns. Looking in the rearview mirror in the late 1980s, investors rushed into real estate lured by returns that dominated those for traditional stocks and bonds. A few years later, after the market collapse, those same investors saw nothing other than dismal prospects for real estate. Poor returns nearly eliminated interest in real estate as an institutional investment asset. Reality lay somewhere between the extremes of wild enthusiasm and deep despair.

Real estate embodies characteristics of both debt and equity. Lease payments, the contractual responsibility of tenants, resemble fixed income obligations, while the property's residual value contains equity-like attributes. In extreme cases, real estate investments become nearly bond-like. For example, properties subject to long-term, triple-net leases provide cash flows that resemble bond coupon payments. In contrast, some real estate consists almost entirely of residual value. For example, hotel properties, with daily leases, provide nearly pure equity characteristics. Most real estate falls in the middle of the continuum, containing elements of debt and equity.

Oil and gas investments range from relatively conservative reserve purchases to relatively risky wildcat drilling. The real assets class focuses on acquisitions of producing properties, because in place cash flows assure inflation sensitivity. The riskier exploration activities belong in the private equity arena, at least until reserves are discovered (or not).

Oil and gas reserves generate extraordinary cash flows as production depletes reservoirs, causing investors to receive a combination of return on capital and return of capital. The reserve cash flows exhibit extremely high correlation to published energy prices, although variations in geography and quality produce differentials.

Timber investments round out the real assets trio. Although timber shares the characteristic of inflation sensitivity with real estate and oil and gas, because timber plays less of a role in the general economy, timber prices exhibit less correlation with general price levels. Financially astute timber owners manage holdings on a sustainable basis, cutting the amount of wood produced each year through biological growth. When managed on a sustainable basis, the productive capacity of the forest remains intact, preserving value across generations.

Sustainable forest management does not require lockstep harvesting of a single year's biological growth. If timber prices appear to be relatively low, the cutting program can be curtailed, deferring current year harvests to future years. In fact, the forestland owner receives a bonus in the form of an additional year's biological growth as the payment for patience. Pay for patience in the timber arena contrasts with the depletion characteristic of oil and gas investments.

Real assets returns might be expected to fall between the expected return for stocks and the expected return for bonds, consistent with the expectation that real assets' risk falls between that for stocks and that for bonds. In fact, inefficiencies in pricing of real assets argue for higher expected returns, suggesting parity in return expectations for real assets and for stocks and leading to an assumption of 6 percent real returns.

As in the case of absolute return data, historical real assets volatility numbers require modification. With marketable equity risk at 20 percent and bond risk at 10 percent, observed real assets risk of 6.8 percent seems inconsistent with the asset class's fundamental characteristics. Because real assets data come predominantly from infrequently conducted appraisals, reported returns fail to capture true economic volatility. Not only does infrequent sampling reduce opportunity to observe price fluctuations, the appraisal process tends to perpetuate whatever biases influenced past appraisals. Expected real assets risk of 15 percent lies between bond risk of 10 percent and stock risk of 20 percent. Developing capital markets assumptions by evaluating fundamental asset class characteristics allows investors to create a reasonable framework for portfolio assessment independent of cyclical market conditions.

Correlation Matrix Assumptions

The correlation matrix is the most difficult set of mean-variance optimization variables to specify. Less intuitive than either means of variances, correlations indicate the degree to which asset class returns tend to move with one another.

Considering the relationship between bond and stock returns in various economic scenarios highlights the difficulties in specifying correlations. Under normal circumstances, bond returns exhibit high positive correlation to stock returns. When interest rates fall, bond prices rise as a result of the inverse relationship between prices and yields. When interest rates decline, stock prices tend to rise as investors subject future earnings streams to lower discount rates. Strong positive correlations between stocks and bonds in normal environments produce little diversifying power.

In the case of unanticipated inflation, bonds suffer. Inflationary price increases erode purchasing power of fixed nominal bond payments, causing investors to push bond prices down. While inflation may have negative short-term consequences for stocks, in the long run stocks react positively to inflation.* With unexpected inflation,

---

*A more complete discussion of the relationship between stock returns and inflation is included in Chapter 10.

Table 5.3 Historical Correlation Matrix Provides a Starting Point for Defining the Relationship Between Asset Classes

Historical Correlation Matrix

	U.S. Equity	U.S. Bonds	Developed Equity	Emerging Equity	Absolute Return	Private Equity	Real Assets	Cash
U.S. equity	1.00							
U.S. bonds	0.01	1.00						
Developed equity	0.58	-0.04	1.00					
Emerging equity	0.40	-0.22	0.57	1.00				
Absolute return	0.69	0.11	0.49	0.53	1.00			
Private equity	0.41	-0.38	0.27	0.32	0.61	1.00		
Real assets	0.01	-0.10	0.17	0.07	-0.22	0.13	1.00	
Cash	-0.06	0.50	-0.12	-0.15	0.09	-0.18	0.06	1.00

Sources: <u>Historical Data Sources</u>: U.S. Equity: 70 percent weight on the S&P 500 (1926–2005) plus 30 percent weight on the Russell 2000 (1979–2005) or DFA Small Companies Deciles 6-10 (1926–1978). US Bonds: Lehman Brothers Government Bond Index (1973–2005) and Ibbotson Intermediate Term Government Bond Index (1926–1972). Developed Equity: MSCI EAFE Index. Emerging Equity: IFC Emerging Markets Index (1985–1997), MSCI Emerging Markets Free (1998–2003) and MSCI Emerging Markets (2004–2005). Absolute Return: Weighted Average Composite of Cambridge Associates' Data (1989–1993) and Tremont composite indexes (1994–2005). Private Equity: Cambridge Associates. Real Assets: Cambridge Associates and NCREIF.

the long-term correlation between stocks and bonds proves to be low, providing substantial diversification to the portfolio.

In a deflationary environment stocks perform poorly as economic woes cause earnings to suffer. In contrast, bonds generate handsome returns since fixed payments appear increasingly attractive as price levels decline. During periods of deflation, low or negative correlation between stocks and bonds provides strong diversification.

The fundamentally different behavior of stock returns and bond returns in environments of met and unmet inflationary expectations poses a conundrum to the financial modeler. Should the expected nondiversifying correlation apply or should the unexpected diversifying correlation apply? The fact that investors care more about the diversifying role of bonds in unexpected (particularly deflationary) circumstances magnifies the dilemma.

Data specification techniques for quantitative models evolve over time. When Yale began using mean-variance optimization in 1986, the university employed unadjusted historical data for risk, return, and

Table 5.4 Modified Correlation Matrix Reflects Assumptions About Future Interrelationships

Modified Correlation Matrix

	U.S. Equity	U.S. Bonds	Developed Equity	Emerging Equity	Absolute Return	Private Equity	Real Assets	Cash
U.S. equity	1.00							
U.S. bonds	0.40	1.00						
Developed equity	0.70	0.25	1.00					
Emerging equity	0.60	0.20	0.75	1.00				
Absolute return	0.30	0.15	0.25	0.20	1.00			
Private equity	0.70	0.15	0.60	0.25	0.20	1.00		
Real assets	0.20	0.20	0.10	0.15	0.15	0.30	1.00	
Cash	0.10	0.50	0.00	0.00	0.35	0.00	0.30	1.00

Source: Yale University Investments Office.

correlation assumptions. Calendar year 1986 returns provided a wake-up call. When the time series of data incorporated the S&P 500 return of 18.5 percent and the EAFE return of 69.9 percent, relative historical returns moved in favor of foreign equities. Recognizing the perversity of assuming that what has done well will continue to do well, in 1987 the Investments Office modified expected return data to create an internally consistent set of return assumptions. In 1988, risk levels underwent the same type of judgmental scrubbing that had been applied to return data the year before. Finally, in 1994, the Investments Office adjusted the correlation matrix to reflect the staff's informed judgments regarding expected correlations. Table 5.3 shows an unadjusted set of historical data and Table 5.4 depicts Yale's modified set of correlation assumptions. As investors accumulate experience with implementing quantitative models, the process becomes more intuitive, increasing the richness of the analysis and conclusions.

A reasonable set of capital markets assumptions serves as the basis for serious quantitative portfolio analysis. Developing sensible relative relationships produces a group of efficient portfolios, helping investors select superior asset allocation strategies. The more difficult-to-estimate specific levels of future returns provide necessary input in assessing the capacity of portfolios to support specified spending levels. A thoughtful set of capital markets assumptions contributes to a rigorous disciplined framework for the analysis of fundamental investment issues.

Misuse of Mean-Variance Optimization

Despite mean-variance optimization's potential for making a positive contribution to portfolio structuring, dangerous conclusions result from poorly considered forecasts. Some of the most egregious errors committed with mean-variance analysis involve inappropriate use of historical data. Consider allocations to real estate in the late 1980s. Real estate provided extremely strong returns during the 1980s with relatively low volatility and relatively low correlation to traditional marketable securities. Not surprisingly, naïve application of mean-variance analysis led to recommendations of extraordinary allocations to real estate.

The spring 1988 *Journal of Portfolio Management* study by Paul Firstenberg, Stephen Ross, and Randall Zisler, "Real Estate: The Whole Story" concluded that institutional allocations to real estate should be increased dramatically from the then current average of under 4 percent of portfolio assets. The authors based their conclusions on data showing government bonds with returns of 7.9 percent and risk (standard deviation) of 11.5 percent, common stocks with returns of 9.7 percent and risk of 15.4 percent, and real estate with returns of 13.9 percent and risk of 2.6 percent. Although, for purposes of their study, the authors increased real estate risk levels from historical levels to more reasonable levels, their mean variance results were anything but sensible. Efficient portfolio mixes included between 0 and 40 percent in government bonds, between 0 and 20 percent in stocks, and between 49 and 100 percent in real estate. Fortunately, the authors tempered their enthusiasm in taking the "pragmatic perspective . . . that pension funds should seek initial real estate allocations of between 15 to 20 percent."[8]

The mean-variance optimizer favored real estate because of past high returns, past low risk, and past low correlation with other asset classes. The return expectation for real estate exceeded that for stocks by 4.2 percent. Although historical real estate risk levels measured only 2.6 percent standard deviation of returns, Firstenberg used a valuation model to justify increasing risk levels to 11.3 percent, slightly below the assumed volatility of government bonds. The authors' favored real estate time series showed negative correlation with both domestic stocks (-0.26) and government bonds (-0.38). When the highest returning asset class exhibits the lowest risk and negative correlation with other asset classes, mean-variance optimizers reach the obvious conclusion.

The fundamental flaw in the Firstenberg study stems from failure to examine critically the real estate capital markets assumptions. Why should real estate be expected to return more than stocks and bonds? Why should real estate have lower risk than stocks and bonds? Why should real estate exhibit negative correlation with stocks and bonds? Real estate contains characteristics of both debt and equity. The stream of contractual lease payments resembles fixed income, while the residual value shows equity-like characteristics. Hence, return and risk expectations logically flow from and fall between those for stocks and bonds. Similarities in factors driving valuations of real estate and traditional marketable securities lead to the conclusion that correlations might be expected to be positive, albeit less than one. Instead of focusing only on adjusting the risk level of real estate, Firstenberg and his co-authors should have adjusted return and correlation levels as well.

Had an investor followed the Firstenberg advice and overweighted real estate in 1988, portfolio results would have disappointed because both stocks and bonds dramatically outperformed real estate in subsequent years. From 1988 to 1997, real estate returned an annualized 4.4 percent with stocks and bonds generating annual results of 18.0 percent and 8.3 percent, respectively. When relying on historical data, after a bull market run, asset classes appear most attractive just when future prospects prove bleakest.

Investors relying on historical data in cyclical markets invite whipsaw. In the early 1990s, after a period of disastrous real estate performance, the asset appeared less appealing as poor results were incorporated into past returns. Investors employing the Firstenberg approach increased real estate holdings in the late 1980s and avoided real estate investments in the early 1990s, buying high and selling low. In the deeply cyclical real estate market, historical data suggest high allocations at market peaks (when returns have been high and risks low) and low allocations at market troughs (when returns have been low and risks high). Past returns provide perverse signals to backward looking investors.

TESTING THE ALLOCATION

For many investors, defining the efficient frontier represents the ultimate goal of quantitative portfolio analysis. Choosing from the set of portfolios on the frontier ensures that, given the underlying assumptions, no superior portfolio exists. Unfortunately, mean-variance optimization provides little useful guidance in choosing a particular point on the efficient frontier. Academics suggest specifying a utility function and choosing the portfolio at the point of tangency with the efficient frontier. Such advice proves useful only in the unlikely event that investors find it possible to articulate a utility function in which utility relates solely to the mean and variance of expected returns.

Identifying a set of a mean-variance-efficient portfolios fails to finish the task at hand. After defining the efficient frontier, investors must determine which combination of assets best meets the goals articulated for the endowment fund. Successful portfolios must satisfy the two goals of endowment management: preservation of purchasing power and provision of substantial, sustainable support for operations. To assess the ability of a portfolio to meet these goals, creative modelers fashion quantifiable tests.

Preserving purchasing power represents a long-term goal. Endowed institutions promise donors that gifts to endowment will support designated purposes in perpetuity. Evaluating success or failure in meeting the endowment preservation goal requires a long-term measure, spanning generations. For example, Yale quantifies failure to maintain endowment value as losing one-half of purchasing power over fifty years.

Providing stable operating budget support represents an intermediate-term goal. Because university operations require stable sources of support, dramatic short-term declines in endowment income prove difficult to accommodate. Yale defines spending trauma as a 10 percent reduction in real endowment distributions over five years.

The quantitative descriptions of failure to maintain purchasing power and failure to provide spending stability necessarily vary from institution to institution. In fact, the metrics may change over time. In the late 1980s, when Yale began using quantitative tools to assess portfolio efficacy, the endowment provided approximately 10 percent of revenues. At that time, Yale defined spending trauma as a 25 percent real decline over five years. As the importance of the endowment to the budget grew, the consequences of a material decline in endowment spending grew commensurately. In 2001, when the endowment provided approximately one-third of revenues, the university redefined spending trauma as a 10 percent real decline in revenues over five years.

Unfortunately, a clear, direct trade-off exists between preserving purchasing power and supplying stable support for operations. Although obvious challenges preclude fashioning precisely equivalent measures of failure to preserve endowment assets and failure to provide stable operating budget support, obtaining rough equivalence between the two measures proves helpful in evaluating trade-offs between the two goals. The challenge for fiduciaries lies in selecting the portfolio best suited to satisfy, to the extent possible, both goals. Quantitative performance tests facilitate portfolio choice.

Simulating the Future

Once goals have been articulated and quantified, statistical simulations provide a mechanism for evaluating investment and spending policies. Investors begin with a spending policy, specifying a target rate and an averaging process. The spending policy remains constant as various investment portfolios undergo the simulation process.*

Simulations employ the capital markets assumptions developed for the mean-variance optimization. Returns for each asset class, based on assumed returns, risks, and correlations and drawn from the specified distributions, determine portfolio returns for the initial period. The spending rule dictates the amount withdrawn from endowment, leaving the residual to be invested in the second period. After rebalancing the portfolio to long-term policy weights, repeating the return generating process provides data on endowment value and spending level for the subsequent year. The process continues, creating a time series of spending and endowment values.

The simulation process described above creates one specific path, a far-from-robust test of portfolio characteristics. To increase the information content of the test, analysts conduct literally thousands of simulations, providing reams of data on future spending and endowment levels. The collective results produce a vivid picture of the future, allowing calculation of probabilities of failure to preserve assets and failure to provide stable budgetary support.

Interpreting the simulated results requires a combination of quantitative and qualitative judgment. Some portfolios fall from consideration on the basis that they are dominated by portfolios that have lower probabilities of failing to meet each of the goals. Other portfolios fail because they skew too much toward satisfying one goal at the expense of the other. Once investors eliminate clearly inferior portfolios, decision makers assess the qualitative trade-offs between reducing risk on one measure while increasing risk on another. In the final analysis,

---

*The simulation process also proves useful in evaluating spending policies. By keeping constant the investment portfolio, various spending rates and averaging processes might be tested.

portfolio selection involves careful subjective assessment of trade-offs between conflicting goals.

One significant benefit of running simulations lies in the direct link between the quantitative analysis and the goals articulated for endowment management. Mean-variance optimization, run in isolation, produces a set of efficient portfolios. The fund manager, faced with a set of efficient combinations of assets, chooses between them with little idea which portfolio might best address the fund's needs. How should investors choose between Figure 5.1's portfolio A with an expected return of 5.75 percent and standard deviation of 10.0 percent, and portfolio B with an expected return of 7.1 percent and standard deviation of 14.5 percent? Economists might suggest that a utility function be employed to identify the appropriate asset allocation. Since few market participants would have any idea how to specify such a function, this technique proves remarkably unhelpful.

In contrast, simulation data address directly the issue facing fiduciaries, describing the trade-off between the conflicting goals of endowment management. Figure 5.2 shows the set of choices identified through a program of simulations. In selecting either portfolio A with 28.4 percent probability of a disruptive spending drop and 29.6 percent probability of long-term purchasing power impairment, or portfolio B with 24.9 percent probability of a disruptive spending drop and 27.0 percent probability of purchasing power impairment,

**Figure 5.1 Mean Variance Optimization Fails
to Provide Clear Guidance to Decision-Makers**

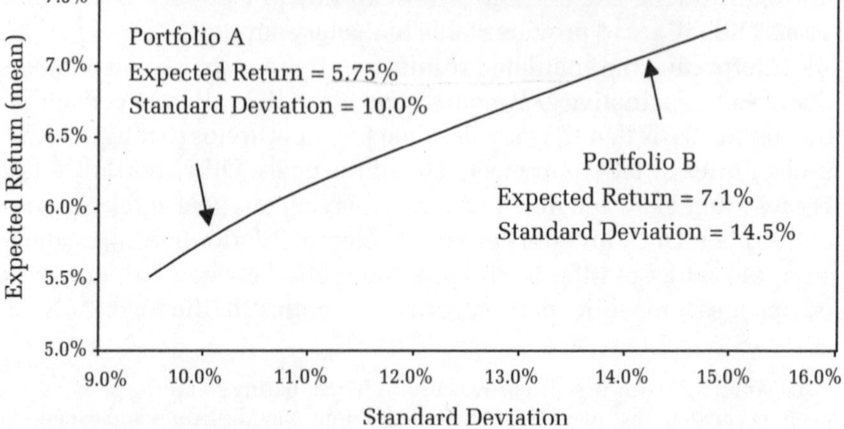

Portfolio A
Expected Return = 5.75%
Standard Deviation = 10.0%

Portfolio B
Expected Return = 7.1%
Standard Deviation = 14.5%

Expected Return (mean)

Standard Deviation

Source: Yale Investments Office

Figure 5.2 Simulations Allow Decision Makers to Understand Trade-Offs Between Critical Goals

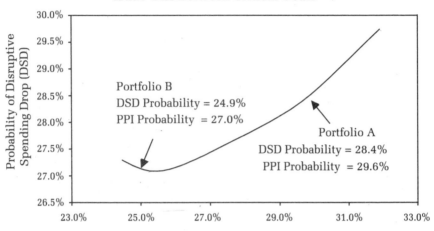

Portfolio B
DSD Probability = 24.9%
PPI Probability = 27.0%

Portfolio A
DSD Probability = 28.4%
PPI Probability = 29.6%

Probability of Purchasing Power Impairment (PPI)

Source: Yale Investments Office

investors express preferences on the trade-off between two goals central to an endowment's mission. Instead of wondering about the impact on institutional goals of a mean-variance efficient portfolio with certain expected risk and return characteristics, simulations allow investors to examine the degree to which spending and investment policies serve articulated goals. Simulations build on the foundation of mean-variance optimization, allowing direct assessment of goals identified by fund fiduciaries.

Simulations liberate mean-variance analysis from another of its practical limitations: the use of a single, frequently one-year investment period. Forward-looking simulations address the problem by allowing the use of any desired time frame. The intermediate-term issue of providing stable operating budget support can be analyzed in an intermediate-term context. The long-term issue of preserving purchasing power can be evaluated in a long-term context. By employing simulations, the mean-variance abstraction of a set of portfolios that provide the highest expected return for a given level of risk gives way to concrete measures of the degree to which portfolios meet investor goals.

Results of Disciplined Portfolio Management

The use of quantitative tools makes a difference. For example, Figure 5.3 shows the improvement in Yale's portfolio from 1985 to 2005 as the university applied quantitative asset allocation techniques to endowment management. The improvements in expected spending stability and prospective purchasing power preservation came in spite of three increases in the spending rate.

Some observers question the robustness of conclusions based on a set of institution-specific capital markets assumptions. While far from dispositive, examining the results of portfolios managed using mean-variance optimization provides some insight into the answer.

Among college and university endowments, Yale, Harvard, Princeton, and Stanford have a particularly long history of using quantitative portfolio management tools. Although minor variations in conclusions result from differences in data inputs and investment preferences among the four institutions, specific portfolio recommendations tend to be supported by all four sets of assumptions. As illustrated in Table 5.5, the independently derived sets of capital markets assumptions produce reasonably similar results.

The largest university endowments pursue asset allocation strate-

Figure 5.3 Yale Reduces Spending Volatility and Risk to Purchasing Power

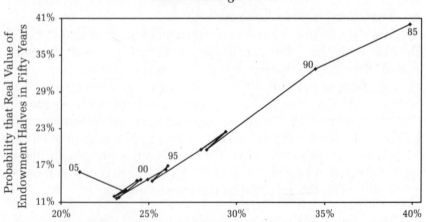

Probability of 10% Real Spending Drop Over Five-Year Period

Source: Yale University Investments Office.

Table 5.5 Large University Endowments
Pursue More Diversified Investment Approaches

Target Asset Allocation, Expected Return, and Standard Deviation of Yale,
Harvard, Princeton, and Stanford Universities, Compared to University Mean,
June 30, 2006

	Yale	Harvard	Princeton	Stanford	Mean	Endowment Mean
U.S. equity	12%	15%	12%	20%	15%	42%
U.S. bonds	4	21	7	12	11	20
Foreign equity	15	15	17	15	16	15
Absolute return	25	12	25	20	21	11
Private equity	17	13	19	10	15	4
Real assets	27	29	20	23	25	5
Cash	0	-5	0	0	-1	2
Expected return	6.9%	6.3%	6.9%	6.2%	6.6%	5.5%
Standard deviation	11.8	11.7	12.1	11.3	11.4	13.2

Source: Yale University Investments Office.

gies dramatically different from those of other educational institutions. Yale, Harvard, Princeton, and Stanford exhibit substantially greater diversification than the average endowment. Domestic equities dominate most endowment portfolios, averaging 42 percent of assets, while the better-diversified large institutional portfolios commit only 15 percent to domestic equities. Domestic bonds account for 20 percent of the average endowment's portfolio in contrast to an allocation of 11 percent by Yale, Harvard, Princeton, and Stanford. Private assets, including venture capital, leveraged buyouts, real estate, timber, and oil and gas, which barely register among the broad group of educational institutions and account for less than 10 percent of assets, play an important role for the major endowments with an allocation of 40 percent. Disciplined quantitative modeling techniques encourage investors to create well-diversified portfolios.

The largest university endowments pursue higher return strategies, causing expected returns for the funds to exceed the average by 1.1 percent, a substantial increment relative to the broader group's expected return of 5.5 percent. In spite of producing greater expected returns, large institution portfolio risk levels actually fall below risk estimates for the less well-diversified endowments. Employing rigorous quantitative portfolio analysis contributes to the construction of diversified, high-return portfolios.

CONCLUSION

Built on the philosophical principles of equity orientation and diversification, asset allocation decisions provide the framework that supports creation of effective investment portfolios. Placing policy allocation targets at the center of the investment process lends a measure of stability to funds invested in an uncertain world.

Purely statistical descriptions of various asset allocation alternatives provide little guidance for decision makers. The widely used Markowitz mean-variance optimization process produces a set of efficient portfolios, fully described by two parameters: expected return (mean) and expected risk (standard deviation). Academics identify optimal portfolios by specifying an institutional utility function that produces a point of tangency with the mean-variance efficient frontier. Even in the unlikely event the academic approach proves helpful, decision makers wonder how the chosen portfolio will interact with the institution's spending policy.

A number of problems implicit in most applications of mean-variance analysis limit its usefulness in evaluating portfolios. Incorporating sensible qualitative considerations into the asset allocation process represents a critical factor in reaching reasonable conclusions. Informed judgment plays a significant role in selecting and defining asset classes, as well as in constructing a coherent set of capital markets assumptions. Combining powerful quantitative tools and sensible qualitative decisions provides a starting point for asset allocation decisions.

The use of simulations to test portfolios created through mean-variance optimization allows assessment of the effectiveness of investment and spending policies over appropriate time horizons. Employing the same capital markets assumptions used in mean-variance analysis, the simulations allow examination of longer time frames, consideration of interaction between spending and investment policies, and translation of statistical capital market and portfolio characteristics into relevant quantitative criteria for decision makers.

Failure to achieve investment goals defines portfolio risk in the most fundamental way. Goals, and risks following therefrom, must be described in a manner allowing investment fiduciaries to understand trade-offs between various portfolios. By evaluating portfolios in terms of probabilities of maintaining purchasing power and providing stable spending streams, fiduciaries understand and choose among alternatives defined in the context of criteria directly relevant to institutional objectives.

Portfolios generated through a combination of mean-variance optimization and forward-looking simulation suffer from a number of limitations. The results depend on assumptions regarding future returns, risks, and covariances. While precise levels of return estimates are certain to be wrong, much of the power of the analysis stems from evaluating easier-to-assess relative relationships. If the quality of the capital markets return and risk assumptions represented the greatest hurdles, conclusions reached through quantitative analysis would be quite robust.

More serious problems stem from instability in the risk and covariance characteristics of asset classes. The tendency of markets for risky assets to move together in times of crisis reduces the value of diversification, at least in the short run. Questions regarding the nature of distributions of securities returns and the stability of relationships between asset classes pose serious challenges to quantitative modeling of asset allocation. Nonetheless, the process of quantifying portfolio analysis provides discipline lacking in less rigorous approaches to portfolio construction.

A systematic, quantitative portfolio construction process lies at the heart of portfolio management activity, providing a disciplined framework within which qualitative judgments inform portfolio decisions. By recognizing and affirming the centrality of policy asset allocation targets, fund managers sensibly focus on the most powerful investment management tool. Ultimately, thoughtful asset allocation work provides the basis for building a successful investment program.

6

Asset Allocation Management

The fundamental objective of portfolio management is faithful implementation of long-term asset allocation targets. If investors allow actual portfolio holdings to differ materially from asset class targets, the resulting portfolio fails to reflect the risk and return preferences determined by the asset allocation process. By holding assets in proportion to policy targets and generating asset class returns commensurate with market levels, investors achieve investment goals without slippage.

Only the most basic portfolios, consisting entirely of marketable securities, allow investors to implement investment policies precisely, holding asset classes at targeted levels and using passive investment vehicles to mirror market returns. Disciplined investors maintain targeted levels by following a systematic program of rebalancing, using proceeds from selling assets exhibiting relative strength to fund purchases of assets showing relative weakness. The use of low cost, passive investment vehicles facilitates the seamless implementation of policy asset allocation targets in marketable security portfolios. Serious pursuit of rebalancing ensures that portfolios maintain target levels, exposing the fund to the desired risk and return characteristics.

Unfortunately, for all except the simplest structures, when implementing an investment program, real world complexities drive a wedge between the clearly defined ideal and the messy reality. Investment in illiquid vehicles, pursuit of active management strategies, and use of explicit or implicit leverage cause actual performance to differ from the theoretical returns associated with the policy portfolio.

130

Less liquid asset types introduce the likelihood that actual allocations deviate from target levels. Shortfalls or surpluses in private assets require offsetting positions in more liquid assets, driving portfolio characteristics away from desired levels. Since by their very nature private holdings take substantial amounts of time to buy or sell efficiently, actual portfolios usually exhibit some functional misallocation. Dealing with the over- or underallocation resulting from illiquid positions creates challenges for thoughtful investors.

Even when actual portfolio allocations match long-term targets, active management techniques usually cause asset class returns to differ from index returns. If inefficiencies exist in the pricing of individual securities, market participants might be rewarded for uncovering attractive investment opportunities with risk-adjusted excess returns. Portfolio managers willingly accept risks associated with active management, expecting that investment skill will ultimately provide material rewards. But because the expected excess returns arrive in unpredictable fashion, if at all, the actively managed asset class might suffer from periods of material underperformance, opening a gap between a disappointing reality and the hoped-for positive active management result.

Leverage, both implicit and explicit, poses another challenge to the faithful implementation of policy asset allocation targets. By magnifying investment outcomes, both good and bad, leverage fundamentally alters the risk and return characteristics of investment portfolios. Unless fiduciaries pay close attention to investment activities, leverage exposes funds to unanticipated outcomes. Implicit leverage, often found in derivatives positions, lurks in many portfolios, coming to light only when investment disaster strikes. Explicit leverage, such as that embodied in security lending programs, contains potential to alter portfolio risk characteristics in unwelcome ways. Understanding and controlling the degree of leverage in particular policies and strategies allows investors to fashion investment portfolios appropriate to their tolerance for risk.

Many market participants treat risk with little sophistication. Portfolio managers spend enormous amounts of time, energy, and resources on asset allocation projects, implement the recommendations, and then let portfolio allocations drift with the markets. Some investors pursue active management programs by cobbling together a variety of specialist managers, without understanding the sector, size, or style bets created by the more-or-less random portfolio construction process. Other participants hire managers based on strong past performance, forgetting to evaluate the investment program, unaware of hidden leverage likely to provide volatile performance. A thoughtful portfolio management process ensures that funds accept only those risks that comport with the asset allocation targets and that promise sufficient incremental rewards.

The Greek author Palladas may have had portfolio management in mind when he wrote that "there be many a slip 'twixt the cup and the lip." Asset allocation drift and active management risk contain the potential to create outcomes measurably different from expectations based on the policy asset allocation portfolio. Moreover, exposure to implicit and explicit leverage moves portfolios to risk levels materially different from baseline expectations, dramatically altering expected investment outcomes. Disciplined implementation of asset allocation policies avoids altering the risk and return profile of an investment portfolio, allowing investors to accept only those active management risks expected to add value.

Concern about risk represents an integral part of the portfolio management process, requiring careful monitoring at the overall portfolio, asset class, and manager levels. Understanding investment and implementation risks increases the chances that an investment program will achieve its goals.   *understand*

risk

REBALANCING

Proper use of mean-variance optimization and forward looking simulations places risk considerations at the heart of the investment management process. By evaluating the likelihood that investment policies fail to meet articulated goals, investors confront directly the critical financial risks facing an institution. The asset allocation targets selected through thoughtful application of quantitative tools and informed judgment define with reasonable precision a portfolio of assets likely to satisfy institutional needs.

After establishing asset allocation policies, risk control requires regular rebalancing to policy targets. Movements in prices of financial assets inevitably cause asset class allocations to deviate from target levels. For instance, a decline in stock prices and an increase in bond prices leads stocks to be underweight and bonds to be overweight, causing the portfolio to have lower than desired expected risk and return characteristics. To restore the portfolio to target allocations, rebalancing investors purchase stocks and sell bonds.

Rebalancing facilitates reshaping of marketable security portfolios, providing an impetus to examine manager allocations. Investors improve portfolio returns by giving funds to managers expected to out-perform, and withdrawing money from those with less rosy prospects. In the absence of fundamental reasons to change manager allocations, positive results might be expected from following the strategy of with-drawing money from managers posting strong recent performance and supplying money to those with weak numbers. When in doubt, lean against the wind.

Psychology of Rebalancing

Contrarian behavior lies at the heart of many successful investment strategies. Unfortunately for investors, human nature craves the posi-tive reinforcement that comes from running with the crowd. The con-ventional attitude comes through loud and clear in the words of *Cabaret*'s Sally Bowles: "Everybody loves a winner, so nobody loved me." Contrarian investment behavior requires shunning the loved and embracing the unloved. Most people prefer the opposite.

In fact, the world of commerce (as opposed to the world of invest-ment) generally rewards following the trend. Feeding winners and killing losers leads to commercial successes. Executives who hyper-charge winners produce attractive results. Managers who starve losers conserve scarce resources. In the Darwinian world of business, success breeds success.

In the world of investments, failure sows the seeds of future suc-cess. The attractively priced, out-of-favor strategy provides much bet-ter prospective returns than the highly valued, of-the-moment alternative. The discount applied to unloved assets enhances expected returns, even as the premium assigned to favored assets reduces antic-ipated results.

Most investors find mainstream positions comfortable, in part because of the feeling of safety in numbers. The attitudes and activities of the majority create the consensus. By definition, only a minority of investors find themselves in the uncomfortable position of operating outside of the mainstream. Once a majority of players adopts a hereto-fore contrarian position, the minority view becomes the widely held perspective. Only an unusual few consistently take positions truly at odds with conventional wisdom.

Initiating and maintaining out-of-the-mainstream positions requires great conviction and substantial fortitude. Friends and acquaintances describe fundamentally different investment programs. The media push a dramatically divergent world view. Brokers urge the sale of yesterday's losers and the purchase of today's hot prospects. Advertisements proclaim a new paradigm. In the face of a seemingly overwhelming consensus, successful contrarian investors turn a deaf ear to the blandishments of the multitudes.

Establishing a contrarian position constitutes only half of the battle. Failure awaits the contrarian investor who loses nerve. Suppose an investor initially avoids the flavor of the month. Months become quarters and quarters become years. Ultimately, the weak-kneed contrarian capitulates, buying into the new-era reasoning. Of course, the buy-in comes just as the mania peaks, causing the realization of pain without the offset of gain. Taking a contrarian tack in the absence of the ability to persevere leads to poor results.

Rebalancing represents supremely rational behavior. Maintaining portfolio targets in the face of market moves dictates sale of strong relative performers and purchase of poor relative performers. Stated differently, disciplined rebalancers sell what's hot and buy what's not. Under normal circumstances, rebalancing asks for modest degrees of fortitude. When markets make extreme moves, rebalancing requires substantial amounts of courage.

Rebalancing Frequency

Investors debate the frequency with which portfolios should be rebalanced. Some follow the calendar, transacting monthly, quarterly, or annually. Others attempt to control transactions costs, setting broad limits and trading only when allocations exceed specified ranges. A small number pursue continuous rebalancing, a strategy that provides greater risk control with potentially lower costs than either the calendar or trading range approaches.

Continuous rebalancing requires daily valuation of portfolio assets. If asset class values deviate by as much as one or two tenths of a percent from target values, managers trade securities to achieve targeted levels. Trades tend to be small and accommodating to the market. Since rebalancing requires sale of assets experiencing relative price strength and purchase of assets experiencing relative price weakness, the immediacy of continuous rebalancing causes managers to sell what others are buying and buy what others are selling, thereby providing liquidity to the market. In contrast, rebalancing strategies not as responsive to the market require larger and less accommodating transactions, increasing market impact and transactions costs.

To the extent that markets exhibit excess volatility, continuous rebalancing generates excess returns. Market activity on October 27 and 28, 1997 provides a dramatic example. On October 27, a 6.9 percent drop in stock prices accompanied a rally in the bond market. The following day's reversal saw stocks rebound by 5.1 percent with bonds suffering from selling pressure. Rebalancing a 60 percent equity and a 40 percent bond portfolio on those two October days added ten basis points to returns, providing a bonus for an activity dedicated fundamentally to risk control.

Even though rebalancing profits represent a nice bonus for investors, the fundamental motivation for rebalancing concerns adherence to long-term policy targets. In the context of a carefully considered policy portfolio, rebalancing maintains the desired risk level. Thoughtful investors employ rebalancing strategies to meet policy asset allocation targets.

Rebalancing and Illiquidity

Owners of private assets face a particular challenge in rebalancing activity. At any point in time, illiquid holdings of private equity and real assets are unlikely to match targeted levels. An amount of assets equivalent to the aggregate illiquid portfolio shortfall (or surplus) must be invested in (or withdrawn from) liquid securities portfolios. Appropriate candidates for investing private asset under-allocations include shorter duration, low risk assets, since funds may be required on short notice to make investments to bring private portfolios closer to target levels. Cash, bonds, and absolute return investments provide reasonable temporary alternatives for private asset underallocations.

The strategy of investing underallocations of private assets in apparently similar marketable securities holds superficial appeal. For instance, while attempting to build a venture capital portfolio, allocation shortfalls might be invested in a portfolio of small technology stocks. Unfortunately, the strategy exposes investors to the risk that venture partnerships call funds when technology stocks trade at depressed levels, causing sales to be made at an inopportune time. In the final analysis, private assets constitute separate asset classes because they behave in a fundamentally different fashion from marketable securities, making dependence on high short-run correlation between private and public markets an internally inconsistent, potentially dangerous strategy.

When private allocations exceed target levels, as might be the case when marketable securities prices decline relative to private asset values, investors face a difficult problem. Reducing allocations to higher risk marketable securities and relying on correlations between marketable and private assets poses substantial risks. Yet, reducing allocations to lower risk assets to accommodate excessive levels of private equity further increases an already elevated portfolio risk level. Choosing the least bad alternative, investors should fund overallocations to private assets by reducing holdings of risky marketable assets, thereby controlling overall portfolio risk levels.

Using short duration, lower risk assets to substitute for generally higher return private assets decreases expected portfolio return and risk levels, while the opposite result occurs when reducing marketable security positions to accommodate a private equity overweighting. Because differences may be substantial between characteristics of target and actual portfolios, investors must analyze thoroughly the investment and spending implications of both target asset allocations and actual portfolio allocations.

The potential for material differences between actual and target asset allocation argues for gradualism in altering targets for illiquid asset classes. Keeping the reality close to the goal facilitates analysis of appropriate spending and asset management possibilities. Avoiding large differences between actual and target allocations reduces the size of the mismatch requiring temporary placement in an alternative investment vehicle, limiting the impact of a decision fraught with problems.

Rebalancing helps investors achieve the risk and return profile embodied in the policy portfolio. Institutions that follow no particular rebalancing policy engage in a peculiar form of market timing. By allowing portfolio allocations to drift with the whims of the market, portfolio risk and return characteristics change unpredictably, introducing more noise into an already highly uncertain process. In fact, over long periods of time, without rebalancing, portfolio allocations move toward the highest return asset, increasing the overall risk level of the portfolio. Ultimately, disciplined rebalancing provides risk control, increasing the likelihood that investors achieve investment goals.

ACTIVE MANAGEMENT

After establishing policy asset allocation targets, investors face individual asset class management issues. In the marketable securities arena, passive investment vehicles provide near certainty that investment results mirror market activity. To the extent that investors pursue

active strategies, actual results will likely differ from the market, causing asset class characteristics to differ from those of the market as a
whole. In the alternative asset arena, lack of passive investment vehicles inevitably causes active results to vary, sometimes dramatically,
from baseline return expectations.

Investing in passively managed vehicles representing individual
asset classes effectively eliminates variance from market results. Index
funds cost little to implement, present far fewer agency issues than do
actively managed portfolios, and promise faithful replication of market portfolios. What explains the fact that few institutional portfolios
employ passive management exclusively? Certainly, the game of active
management entices players to enter, offering the often false hope of
excess returns. Perhaps those few smart enough to recognize that passive strategies provide a superior alternative believe themselves to be
smart enough to beat the market. In any event, deviations from benchmark returns represent an important source of portfolio risk.

Investors embarking on active management strategies introduce
portfolio biases, either purposeful or inadvertent. Among the powerful
ways in which asset classes might differ from benchmarks are with
respect to size, sector, and style. Size refers to market capitalization of
securities holdings, sector concerns the nature of corporate business
activities, and style relates to the general approach taken by an active
manager (value vs. growth).

Deliberate portfolio biases create potential for significant value
added. For instance, an investor might believe that value strategies
dominate growth strategies, consciously choosing only managers with
a value orientation. Others believe that small-capitalization stocks
provide superior stock picking opportunities, moving portfolios
toward an explicit overweighting in securities of smaller companies.
Purposeful, thoughtful strategic bets might generate risk-adjusted
excess returns for the portfolio.

Portfolio biases come with potential costs. Hiring managers specializing in particular market segments sometimes skews portfolio
characteristics dramatically. Consequently, fiduciaries face the possibility of meaningful underperformance as short-term costs (poor relative performance from small stocks) overwhelm long-term
opportunities (less efficient pricing of small-capitalization securities).
Strategic portfolio biases add value only if implemented in a disciplined fashion, after thoughtful analysis, with an appropriately long
investment horizon.

Some portfolio bets result from sloppy management. If portfolio
construction simply involves collecting enough domestic equity man-

agers to fill the slots in the portfolio's roster, the resulting asset class characteristics almost certainly contain significant inadvertent biases. Unintended portfolio bets often come to light only after being directly implicated as a cause for substandard performance.

Completeness Funds and Normal Portfolios

The investment management tools of normal portfolios and completeness funds allow managers to evaluate and control portfolio biases. A normal portfolio defines the universe of securities from which a manager selects holdings. As such, a normal portfolio represents a fair benchmark for measuring manager performance. If the aggregate of the normal portfolios within an asset class matches size, style, and sector distributions of that asset class, the resulting portfolio contains no deliberate bets relative to size, style, or sector. Bets resulting from active manager decisions still influence portfolio returns, but those bets ought to be welcomed as part of a deliberate active management strategy.

If the aggregate of normal portfolios within an asset class fails to match important asset class characteristics, portfolio managers introduce biases. One way to offset inadvertent biases is through the use of completeness funds. A completeness fund simply represents the portfolio of securities, complementary to the aggregate of an asset class's normal portfolios, that causes the sum of the normal portfolios plus the completeness fund to match relevant asset class characteristics.

By offsetting gaps left by the aggregate of a fund's normal portfolios, completeness funds cause portfolio returns to be driven by deliberate choice, not inadvertently assumed residual risk. A danger in using completeness funds lies in the imprecision inherent in identifying normal portfolios. Poorly defined normal portfolios lead to poorly structured completeness funds, which may fail to fill unidentified portfolio gaps or may offset deliberate security selection bets.

Because deviations from asset class characteristics cause performance to differ from the market, fund managers must ensure that deliberate choice drives portfolio structure, not sloppy construction. Normal portfolios and completeness funds assist investors with asset class management, but precise application of these tools remains a theoretical goal, not a practical reality.

LEVERAGE

Leverage appears in portfolios explicitly and implicitly. Explicit leverage involves the use of borrowed funds for pursuit of investment opportunities, magnifying portfolio results, good and bad. When investment returns exceed borrowing costs, portfolios benefit from leverage. When investment returns match borrowing costs, no impact results. When investment returns fail to meet borrowing costs, portfolios suffer from leverage.

Implicit leverage stems from holding positions that embody greater risk than contemplated by the asset class within which they are categorized. Simply holding riskier-than-market equity securities leverages the portfolio. Unless risk levels of securities within an asset class match asset allocation risk assumptions, the portfolio either becomes leveraged from holding riskier assets or deleveraged from holding less risky assets. For example, the common practice of holding cash in portfolios of common stocks causes the equity portfolio to exhibit less risk than the market, effectively deleveraging returns.

Derivatives provide a common source of implicit leverage. Suppose an S&P 500 futures contract requires a margin deposit of 10 percent of the value of the position. If an investor holds a futures position in the domestic equity portfolio, complementing every dollar of futures with nine dollars of cash creates a position equivalent to holding the underlying equity securities directly. If, however, the investor holds five dollars of futures and five dollars of cash, the resulting implicit leverage causes the position to be five times as sensitive to market fluctuations.

Derivatives do not create risk *per se*, as they can be used to reduce risk, simply replicate cash positions, or increase risk. To continue with the S&P 500 futures example, selling futures against a portfolio of equity securities reduces risks associated with equity market exposure. Alternatively, using appropriate combinations of cash and futures creates a risk-neutral replication of the underlying securities. Finally, holding futures without risk-neutralizing cash positions increases market exposure. Responsible fiduciaries understand and control the use of derivatives in investment activity.

Leverage magnifies portfolio outcomes, containing the potential to benefit or to harm portfolio assets. In extreme cases, inconsistency between the risk profile of asset class characteristics and investment activity leads to significant losses. In less extreme cases, differences in risk profile cause portfolio attributes to vary meaningfully from targeted levels, leading to deviations from policy goals. Sensible investors employ leverage with great care, guarding against introducing material excess risk into portfolio characteristics.

Harvard University

Harvard University's endowment employs leverage in a variety of ways. Consider the university's June 2005 portfolio. By establishing an unusual asset allocation target of negative 5 percent to cash, the university hopes to enhance portfolio results by generating returns in excess of borrowing costs. Over long periods of time, Harvard's borrowing strategy promises superior results as portfolio returns should exceed leverage costs represented by the return of cash, the lowest-expected-return asset class. Of course, if returns fall below the cost of funds, results of a bad year will be made worse. In the case of Harvard's negative allocation to cash, careful disciplined analysis of portfolio considerations led to the use of leverage.

Harvard's second form of explicit leverage involves borrowing substantial amounts of funds to establish positions exploiting mispricings between securities. At June 30, 2005, the university's $29.4 billion investment pool supported long positions of $49.7 billion offset by short positions of $20.3 billion.[1] By altering fundamental asset class risk characteristics, the use of leverage magnifies security selection bets. In contrast to the asset allocation process's direct consideration of the consequences of the negative allocation to cash, by grossing up positions on the balance sheet Harvard alters portfolio risk outside of the mean-variance framework.

On top of explicit balance sheet leverage, Harvard employs implicit leverage to magnify further the impact of investment decisions. A careful reading of the footnotes to Harvard's financial statements shows off balance sheet market exposure of more than $19 billion in long positions and more than $28 billion in short positions. As a consequence of substantial explicit and implicit leverage, Harvard dramatically increases risk levels, enhancing positive and negative outcomes alike.

Many endowments use leverage shorts & longs

Sowood Capital

Harvard suffered the consequences of excessive leverage in the July 2007 collapse of Sowood Capital. Managed by former Harvard Management Company partner Jeff Larson, Sowood began operations in July 2004 with fourteen employees and $700 million of Harvard's funds. The firm's pitch book promised investors strictly market neutral, event-driven investments, quantitative-based arbitrage and value-oriented investments.[2] According to the *Wall Street Journal*, Sowood "gained around 10% annually during its first three years, often through savvy bets on debt investments," delivering on its promises to investors and growing assets to more than $3 billion.[3]

In early 2007, Jeff Larson's portfolio contained a substantial bet on the relative values of senior corporate debt and junior corporate securities. He owned the safer senior securities and sold short the riskier junior securities, establishing what he expected to be a profitable hedge against adverse market conditions.

Had Sowood simply attempted to exploit the price differential between the senior and junior securities, the firm would have avoided the attention of the *Wall Street Journal* and the *New York Times*. But because the price differential alone provided inadequate recompense, Sowood levered the portfolio by "as much as six times," hoping to transform a small price discrepancy into big returns.[4] The leverage transferred the fate for the firm from Sowood's principals to its banks.

In June, the first cracks started to appear, as the fund lost 5 percent for the month. To take advantage of the now-more-attractive opportunity, according to the *Wall Street Journal*, Sowood doubled the portfolio's leverage to twelve times.

In July, as debt markets grew increasingly unsettled, Sowood's trades should have paid off with safer positions (that Sowood owned) maintaining value and riskier positions (that Sowood sold short) losing value. Instead, perverse market forces caused the safer positions that Sowood owned to lose value without an offsetting gain from the positions that Sowood sold short.

In a July 30 letter to investors, Jeff Larson described the force that finished his fund:

> ... given the extreme market volatility, our counterparties began to severely mark down the value of the collateral that had been posted by the funds. In addition, liquidity became extremely limited for the credit portion of our portfolio making it difficult to exit positions. We, therefore, reached the conclusion over the weekend that, in the interest of preserving our investors' capital, the appropriate course of action was to sell the funds' portfolio.[5]

Leverage and a perverse market combined forces to finish Sowood Capital.

Sowood started the month of July with more than $3 billion and after suffering investment losses of more than 50 percent finished the month with approximately $1.5 billion. In the hectic final days of Sowood's life, the firm reportedly sought assistance from Harvard Management Company. Harvard refused. Sowood Capital—seeded by Harvard, staffed by Harvard, and ultimately spurned by Harvard— taught Harvard a $350 million lesson on the perils of leverage.

Too much leverage is quite dangerous

Granite Capital

Granite Capital's David Askin suffered devastating losses while pursuing an apparently sophisticated strategy of identifying, hedging, and leveraging pricing anomalies in mortgaged-backed securities derivatives. Based on a record of generating mid-teens returns with low variability, Askin attracted funds from an impressive list of investors, including the Rockefeller Foundation and McKinsey & Company. Unfortunately, explicit and implicit leverage caused the firm's entire $600 million portfolio to be wiped out in a matter of weeks.

Askin invested in collateralized mortgage obligation derivatives with exotic names such as super inverse interest only strips. As intimidating as the names might be, the securities essentially constituted pieces of pools containing ordinary home mortgages. By combining securities expected to respond in opposite ways to interest rate movements, Askin hoped to be hedged—when rates move, profits on one part of the portfolio would more or less offset losses on the other. If Askin correctly identified pricing anomalies, profits would exceed losses by a margin equal to the mispricing.

Because mispricings in fixed income markets tend to be small, investors frequently use leverage to magnify the portfolio impact of trades. At the time of his denouement, Askin employed leverage of approximately two-and-one-half times, running positions of $2 billion on $600 million of equity.

Askin's portfolio failed to weather the trauma created by the Federal Reserve's decision to increase interest rates in early 1994. What appeared to be well-hedged positions in a benign interest rate environment turned out to be wildly mismatched positions in a bearish bond market. As Askin's portfolio accumulated losses, investment banks that had loaned money to fund the positions seized the bonds, selling positions to cover their exposure. The combination of poor portfolio structure and leverage led to Askin's downfall.

Askin sustained major losses because his hedges failed to perform. And yet, had he not been leveraged, he likely would have survived the 1994 interest rate debacle. Losses of 30 percent on a leveraged $2 billion portfolio wiped out $600 million of equity. Losses of 30 percent on a $600 million unlevered portfolio would have reduced equity by a painful $180 million, but investors would live to fight another day. In fact, subsequent to Askin's demise, prices of the liquidated bonds recovered smartly. But by that time, Askin was no longer a player.*

Long-Term Capital Management

If the *Guinness Book of World Records* contained a category for hubris, the principals of Long-Term Capital Management (LTCM) would top the list. Staffed by a combination of Wall Street wizards and academic superstars (including two Nobel laureates), LTCM concocted a toxic blend of arrogance and leverage that nearly brought down the world's financial system.

LTCM's business model involved investing in a broadly diversified pool of arbitrage strategies, which attempted to exploit anomalies in the markets for equities, bonds, swaps, futures, and a broad range of other derivatives. Using sophisticated financial models to diversify overall portfolio risk, the firm believed that it had reduced risk to such a low level so as to justify an extraordinarily high level of leverage.

LTCM's use of leverage defies imagination. In January 1998, well before the firm's July collapse, LTCM's $4.8 billion of equity supported $120 billion of balance sheet positions, representing leverage of approximately twenty-five to one. In fact, the irresponsible levels of explicit leverage on the balance sheet represented only the tip of the iceberg.

LTCM's investment activities focused in large part on mispricings that could be exploited through the use of derivative contracts. In many cases, the firm could obtain the desired exposure with either

---

*Even though with an unlevered portfolio Askin may not have gone out of business, without leverage Askin never would have been in business. Leverage boosted the underlying returns on his strategy to the mid-teens level necessary to attract investment capital.

cash instruments or derivatives, but used derivatives because of the imbedded leverage. As a result, LTCM took on massive off-balance sheet positions. On a market exposure basis, combining holdings both on balance sheet and off, LTCM had a total of more than $1.4 trillion of positions supported by less than $5 billion of equity, representing leverage of more than 290 to one.

When trouble arrived in the form of Russia's financial meltdown, LTCM's staggering leverage quickly took the firm down. Even though a Wall Street bailout mitigated the damage, the fund's losses were enormous. Roger Lowenstein, in his classic *When Genius Failed*, described the ugly math:

> Through April 1998, the value of a dollar invested in Long-Term quadrupled to $4.11. By the time of the bailout, only five months later, precisely 33 cents of that total remained. After deducting the partners' fees, the results were even sorrier: each invested dollar, having grown to $2.85, shrank to a meager 23 cents. In net terms, the greatest fund ever—surely the one with the highest IQs—had lost 77 percent of its capital while the ordinary stock market investor had been more than doubling his money.[6]

LTCM produced a portfolio of generally sensible investment positions. The fatal flaw in the firm's strategy came from a nearly unimaginable degree of leverage; massive leverage magnified the positive experience on the upside and similarly exaggerated the negative experience on the downside. In contrast to LTCM, sensible investors employ leverage with great care, guarding against a degree of risk that could threaten the viability of an investment program.

Security Lending

Some types of leverage, such as negative cash positions and explicit borrowing to increase positions, exhibit themselves openly. Investment staffs prepare papers that investment committees discuss, creating awareness of the general nature and magnitude of the borrowing. Other forms of leverage remain hidden until trouble arises, causing damage to the portfolio too late for corrective action.

Most large institutional investors conduct security loan programs, which involve lending equity and debt securities to third parties, providing modest incremental income to the investor. Security borrowers, generally Wall Street financial concerns, require the loans to create short positions or cover failed trades. The security lender receives cash collateral to secure the asset on loan, making that aspect of the transaction quite safe. The lender pays a below market rate of interest on the cash collateral, expecting to reinvest the cash at a higher rate. The act of reinvestment places the entire amount of the security lending transaction at risk in an effort to generate the hoped-for spread between the below-market-rate borrowing and at-market-rate lending.

Because the security lender retains ownership of securities on loan, along with the attendant economic consequences, security lending activity produces little disruption to the portfolio. Investors find it easy to forget about security lending, relegating it to back-office status. Security lending rarely appears on investment committee agendas, treated like other functions performed by custodian banks. If considered at all, committees likely view the process as a low risk method of offsetting a portion of the bank custody fee.

Typical institutional deal structures exacerbate the unimpressive economics of security lending. Custodian banks generally run security lending programs, splitting income with investors on a seventy-thirty or sixty-forty basis, with the larger share accruing to security lenders. Such profit sharing arrangements cause banks to seek risk, since they share in returns without sharing in losses. The bank gets a good deal, earning a significant share of the profits generated by putting client assets at risk. Investors get a raw deal, earning little in return for exposing portfolio assets to meaningful downside.

The Common Fund

The Common Fund, an organization providing investment services to educational institutions, learned in 1995 that its security lending program managed by First Capital Strategists had incurred estimated losses of $128 million.[7] Transgressions by a rogue trader, Kent Ahrens, caused the losses that later calculations showed to be nearly $138 million. According to Ahrens, in early 1992 he lost $250,000 on an equity index "arbitrage" trade. Instead of closing out the position, he tried to offset the loss with speculative trading. After more than three years of deception and fraud, Ahrens's cumulative losses reached a staggering level.

The Common Fund security lending debacle hurt the firm in meaningful ways, tarnishing its sterling reputation and causing large numbers of client defections. At June 30, 1995, the Common Fund had

$18.1 billion of marketable equity and fixed income assets under management. One year later, assets amounted to $15.5 billion, a dramatic $5.2 billion, or 25 percent, less than would have been expected had asset levels simply kept pace with markets.

The First Capital Strategists story tells much more than the tale of a rogue trader. It illustrates the risks in pursuing investment strategies with poor payoff structures, highlights problems of monitoring certain types of trading activity, and shows dangers of inventive schemes inappropriate for the nature of the investment activity.

Security lending activity at its best involves "make a little, make a little, make a little . . ." as investors earn small positive spreads on security loans. Unfortunately, to "make a little" an investor exposes a lot creating the possibility of "make a little, make a little, make a little, lose a lot." This negatively skewed return pattern exhibits limited upside (make a little) with substantial downside (lose a lot), representing an unattractive distribution of outcomes for investors.

Decades ago, security lending exhibited more favorable characteristics. In the 1970s, when security lenders paid no interest on cash collateral, extremely handsome returns resulted from the activity. Since cash collateral secured the value of the asset on loan and the collateral could be reinvested in U.S. Treasury bills, security lending participants faced essentially no risk. "Make something, make something, make something" described the activity, while "lose a lot" failed to register.

Structural changes and increased competition forced security lenders to pay interest on cash collateral, ultimately causing reinvestment risk to enter the equation. When security lenders could no longer create positive spreads by simply investing collateral in Treasury bills, generating returns required accepting credit risk, interest rate risk, or even more exotic risks.

The Common Fund, through its relationship with First Capital Strategists, accepted these risks with enthusiasm. Table 6.1 lists the wide range of authorized collateral reinvestment strategies that the Common Fund employed beginning in the early 1980s. Alternatives ranged from extremely conservative to quite aggressive. Equity index arbitrage, properly implemented, poses little risk to invested assets. On the other end of the spectrum, Mexican broker repurchase agreements embody substantial risks.

By following standard Wall Street practice of referring to many reinvestment strategies as "arbitrages," the Common Fund promoted a false sense of security. Webster's Dictionary defines arbitrage as "the often simultaneous purchase and sale of the same or equivalent secu-

**Table 6.1 The Common Fund Exposed Participant Assets
to Material Risk**

Approved Investment Strategies, 1994

Equity index arbitrage

Fixed income arbitrage

OTC option arbitrage

Treasury/Eurodollar (TED) spread arbitrage

Dividend reinvestment arbitrage

Corporate restructuring arbitrage (risk arbitrage)

Forward and reversible equity arbitrage

Convertible security arbitrage

Warrant arbitrage

Equity and corporate bond repurchase agreements

Repurchase agreements with Mexican brokers collateralized with Mexican
government securities

Matched positions

Triparty repurchase agreements

Interest rate and cross currency swaps

Fixed income securities called for redemption

---

rity (as in different markets) in order to profit from price discrepancies." In today's security markets, occasional mispricings of futures contracts for stocks and bonds relative to cash markets provide true (albeit fleeting) arbitrage opportunities. Other so-called arbitrages do not involve "the same or equivalent security," thereby exposing assets to much more substantial risk.

For example, convertible arbitrage involves owning a convertible bond and selling short the stock of the issuing company to exploit perceived mispricings between relatively cheap bonds and relatively expensive stock. Implementing convertible arbitrage requires dynamic hedging, which may or may not be feasible, and assumption of unhedged residual interest rate and credit risks. Under certain circumstances, convertible arbitrage offers attractive risk reward relationships. Under no circumstance does convertible arbitrage create riskless returns.

At best, referring to risky strategies as arbitrages is a Wall Street conceit, an attempt to create an aura of mystery and sophistication surrounding the investment process. At worst, the practice constitutes deceptive advertising, an effort to lessen investor concerns surrounding fundamentally risky activities.

A further problem with security lending activity concerns the high level of trading required. Monitoring high levels of activity poses considerable challenges to the trading organization, outside investors, and other responsible professionals, such as lawyers and accountants. When investment positions turn over several times daily, supervisors can only trust that traders faithfully implement strategies and follow guidelines. Investors can only trust that supervisors monitor the process carefully. High levels of trading activity create difficult control issues.

In contrast, long-term investment activity raises fewer monitoring issues. Security positions held for months or years generate far less control risk than positions held for minutes or hours. Moreover, the temptation to hide losing trade tickets in a drawer or to violate guidelines to trade out of losses seems more consistent with the speculative mindset of a trader than with the temperate attitude of an investor. In fact, many of the 1990s' most sensational losses resulted from the activity of rogue traders such as Nicholas Leeson, who brought down Barings PLC; Toshihide Igushi, who caused Daiwa Bank to be exiled from the United States; and Robert Citron, who forced Orange County into bankruptcy. While avoiding trading strategies provides no guarantee against fraud, pursuing longer term investment programs lessens control risks for fiduciaries.

Poor deal structure contributed to the dangers of the Common Fund's security lending program. First Capital Strategists earned between 25 percent and 33 percent of profits generated by putting the Common Fund member institutions' funds at risk. In essence, First Capital flipped coins in a "heads I win, tails you lose" game. Since the firm did not share in losses, employees had strong incentive to recommend and pursue risky strategies.

Poor incentives provide only a partial explanation of the problem. The Common Fund knowingly participated in First Capital Strategists' risk-seeking activity. Prior to the Kent Ahrens debacle, two events brought the risky nature of the reinvestment vehicles to the fore. In August 1987, First Capital incurred a loss of $2.5 million by speculating on an aborted hostile takeover of Caesar's World. While First Capital reimbursed the Common Fund for the loss, the transaction highlighted risks involved in corporate restructuring "arbitrage." Later, beginning in September 1989, First Capital accumulated a position in the ill-fated employee-led attempt to take over United Airlines. Ultimately liquidated at a loss of $2.6 million to the Common Fund, the trade caused security lending for fiscal year 1990 to show a loss of $577,600. The Caesar's World and United Airlines incidents forced trustees of the Common Fund to be acutely aware of the risks associated with the firm's security lending program.

In essence, the Common Fund leveraged its assets by participating in security lending, borrowing funds (the cash collateral), and securing the loans with Common Fund member institution stocks and bonds. First Capital invested proceeds from the loans in risky vehicles, hoping to generate positive returns. While dangers inherent in trading activities and problems associated with poor deal structure provide the most visible contribution to the Common Fund's disaster, the root of the problem originates with the inappropriate use of the leverage implicit in the security lending program.

CONCLUSION

Placing asset allocation targets at the center of the portfolio management process increases the likelihood of investment success. Disciplined rebalancing techniques produce portfolios that reflect articulated risk and return characteristics. Less rigorous approaches to portfolio management almost guarantee that actual asset allocation differs from desired levels, leading to outcomes less likely to satisfy institutional goals.

Attractive investment opportunities frequently contain elements of illiquidity, introducing some rigidities into a portfolio's asset allocation. By inducing investors to hold positions inconsistent with targeted levels, illiquid assets cause overall portfolio characteristics to deviate from desired levels, creating challenges for disciplined rebalancing activity.

Pursuit of active management introduces friction between investment results and benchmark returns. Sensible investors take great care in identifying portfolio biases, ensuring that differences result from deliberate choices, not inadvertent consequences of portfolio construction. Normal portfolios and completeness funds assist managers in understanding and controlling active management bets.

While successful active management programs eventually create value, investors face the interim possibility of experiencing periods of underperformance. Many sensible investment strategies require time horizons of three to five years, introducing the likelihood that even ultimately correct decisions appear foolish in the short run. When market prices move against already established positions, investors with strong hands add to holdings, increasing the benefit from active management. Conversely, sensible investors trim winning positions, preventing excessive exposure to recently successful strategies. Leaning against the wind proves to be an effective risk control measure.

Leverage contains the potential to add substantial value and create great harm, posing particular danger to investors pursuing long-term strategies. Keynes warns that ". . . an investor who proposes to ignore market fluctuations . . . must not operate on so large a scale, if at all, with borrowed money."[8] Fiduciaries strive to identify and assess sources of explicit and implicit portfolio leverage, seeking to ensure that the leverage influences the portfolio in an acceptable manner.

Many high profile investment disasters of recent years stem from leverage lurking beneath the superficial portfolio characteristics. The Common Fund made explicit use of leverage in its risk-seeking security lending program, exposing educational institution assets to high levels of risk in exchange for modest expected returns. David Askin employed explicit leverage on top of the implicit leverage inherent in his mortgage-backed securities derivatives positions, turning an otherwise serious impairment of value into a total wipeout. Avoiding headline grabbing disaster requires thorough understanding of the sources and magnitude of exposure to leverage.

Serving institutional goals requires disciplined implementation of asset allocation policies, centered on regular rebalancing to ensure that portfolio characteristics match targeted levels. Many activities pursued by institutional fund managers create frictions that cause portfolio results to differ from expectations. Illiquid investments often provide attractive active management opportunities, while posing significant challenges to the rebalancing process. Investors employing active management strategies expose funds to the impact of performance differentials relative to benchmark results. Use of leverage magnifies investment results, potentially altering portfolio characteristics in a manner unanticipated by asset allocation analyses. Sensible investors rebalance regularly, carefully consider active management, and limit leverage.

illiquid investments
bck in your cash
hard for
rebalancing

7

Traditional Asset Classes

The definition of an asset class employs both art and science in an attempt to combine like with like, seeking as an end result a relatively homogenous collection of investment opportunities. Appropriately defined asset classes include groups of positions that collectively provide a coherent contribution to an investor's portfolio.

Traditional asset classes share a number of critical attributes. First, traditional asset classes contribute basic, valuable, differentiable characteristics to an investment portfolio. Second, traditional holdings rely fundamentally on market-generated returns, not on active management of portfolios. Third, traditional asset classes derive from broad, deep, investable markets.

The basic, valuable, differentiable characteristics contributed by traditional asset classes range from provision of substantial expected returns to protection against financial crises. Careful investors define asset class exposures narrowly enough to ensure that the investment vehicle accomplishes its expected task, but broadly enough to encompass a critical mass of assets.

Traditional asset classes rely fundamentally on market-generated returns, providing reasonable certainty that various portfolio constituents fulfill their appointed missions. In those cases where active management proves essential to the success of a particular asset class, the investor relies on unusual ability or good fortune to produce results. If an active manager exhibits poor skill or experiences bad luck, the investor suffers as the asset class fails to achieve its goals.

Because traditional asset classes depend on market-driven returns, investors need not rely on serendipity or the supposed expertise of market players.

Traditional holdings trade in broad, deep, investable markets. Market breadth promises an extensive array of choices. Market depth implies a substantial volume of offerings for individual positions. Market investability assures access by investors to investment opportunities. Traditional asset classes occupy well-established, enduring marketplaces.

Traditional asset classes encompass stocks and bonds. Asset classes that investors employ to drive portfolio returns include domestic equity, foreign developed market equity, and emerging market equity. Equity exposure can be diversified by holdings of U.S. Treasury bonds, which promise protection from financial catastrophe. Traditional asset classes provide several of the basic building blocks required by investors to create a well-diversified portfolio.

Descriptions of traditional asset classes help investors understand the role that various investment vehicles play in a portfolio. By assessing an asset class's expected returns and risks, likely response to inflation, and anticipated interaction with other asset classes, investors develop the knowledge required to build a portfolio. An outline of issues surrounding alignment of interests between issuers of securities and owners of securities illustrates the potential pitfalls and possible benefits of participating in certain asset categories.

DOMESTIC EQUITY

Investment in domestic equities represents ownership of a piece of corporate America. Holdings of U.S. stocks constitute the core of most institutional and individual portfolios, causing Wall Street's ups and downs to drive investment results for many investors. While a large number of market participants rely far too heavily on marketable equities, U.S. stocks deserve a prominent position in investment portfolios.

Domestic stocks play a central role in investment portfolios for good theoretical and practical reasons. The expected return characteristics of equity instruments match nicely with the need to generate substantial portfolio growth over the sweep of time. To the extent that history provides a guide, long-term returns encourage investors to own stocks. Jeremy Siegel's 203 years of data show U.S. stocks earning 8.4 percent per annum, while Roger Ibbotson's eighty years of data show stocks earning 11.1 percent per annum.* No other asset class possesses such an impressive record of long-term performance.

The long-term success of equity-dominated portfolios matches expectations formed from fundamental financial principles. Equity investments promise higher returns than bond investments, although in the short run the prospect of higher returns sometimes remains unfulfilled. Not surprisingly, the historical record of generally strong equity market returns contains several extended periods that remind investors of the downside of equity ownership. In the corporate capital structure, equity represents a residual interest that exhibits value only after accounting for all other claims against the company. The higher risk of equity positions leads rational investors to demand higher expected returns.

Stocks exhibit a number of attractive characteristics that stimulate investor interest. Interests of shareholders and corporate management tend to be aligned, allowing outside owners of shares some measure of comfort that corporate actions will benefit both shareholders and management. Stocks generally provide protection against unexpected increases in inflation, although the protection proves notoriously unreliable in the short run. Finally, stocks trade in broad, deep, liquid markets, affording investors access to an impressive range of opportunities. Equity investments deserve a thorough discussion, since in many respects they represent the standard against which market observers evaluate all other investment alternatives.

Equity Risk Premium

The equity risk premium, defined as the incremental return to equity holders for accepting risk above the level inherent in bond investments, represents one of the investment world's most critically important variables. Like all forward-looking metrics, the expected risk premium stands shrouded in the uncertainties of the future. To obtain clues about what tomorrow may have in store, thoughtful investors examine the characteristics of the past.

Yale School of Management Professor Roger Ibbotson produces a widely used set of capital market statistics that reflect an eighty-year stock-and-bond return differential of 5.7 percent per annum.[1] Wharton

---

*The 203-year history reflects the 200 years of data in Siegel's *Stocks for the Long Run*, grown by the three years of subsequent returns in Ibbotson's data set.

Professor Jeremy Siegel's 203 years of data show a risk premium of 3.0 percent per annum.[2] Regardless of the precise number, historical risk premia indicate that equity owners enjoyed a substantial return advantage over bondholders.*

The size of the risk premium proves critically important in the asset allocation decision. While history provides a guide, careful investors interpret past results with care. Work on survivorship bias by Phillipe Jorion and William Goetzmann demonstrates the unusual nature of the U.S. equity market experience. The authors examine the experience of thirty-nine markets over a seventy-five-year period, noting that "(m)ajor disruptions have afflicted nearly all of the markets in our sample, with the exception of a few such as the United States."[3]

The more-or-less uninterrupted operation of the U.S. stock market in the nineteenth and twentieth centuries contributed to superior results. Jorion and Goetzmann find that the U.S. market produced 4.3 percent annualized real capital appreciation from 1921 to 1996. In contrast, the other countries, many of which experienced economic and military trauma, posted a median real appreciation of only 0.8 percent per year. Thoughtful market observers place the exceptional experience of the U.S. equity markets in a broader, less-compelling context.

Even if investors accept U.S. market history as definitive, reasons exist to doubt the value of the past as a guide to the future. Consider stock market performance over the past two hundred years. The returns consist of a combination of dividends, inflation, real growth in dividends, and rising valuation levels. According to an April 2003 study by Robert Arnott, aptly titled "Dividends and the Three Dwarfs," dividends provide the greatest portion of long-term equity returns. Of the Arnott study's two-hundred-year 7.9 percent annualized total return from equities, fully 5.0 percentage points come from dividends. Inflation accounts for 1.4 percentage points, real dividend growth accounts for 0.8 percentage points, and rising evaluation accounts for 0.6 percentage points. Arnott points out that the overwhelming importance of dividends to historical returns "is wildly at odds with conventional wisdom, which suggests that . . . stocks provide growth first and income second."[4]

Arnott uses his historical observations to draw some inferences for the future. He concludes, with dividend yields below 2.0 percent (in April 2003), that unless real growth in dividends accelerates or equity market valuations rise, investors face a future far less remunerative than the past. (Note that in August 2007 the dividend yield of the S&P

*See pages 55–58 for Ibbotson's and Siegel's stock and bond return data.

500 stood at 1.75 percent). Observing that real dividends showed no growth from 1965 to 2002, Arnott holds out little hope of dividend increases driving future equity returns. The alternative of relying on increases in valuations assigned to corporate earnings for future equity market growth serves as a thin reed upon which to build a portfolio.

Simple extrapolation of past returns into the future assumes implicitly that past valuation changes will persist in the future. In the specific case of the U.S. stock market, expectations that history provides a guide to the future suggest that dividends will grow at unprecedented rates or ever-higher valuations will be assigned to corporate earnings. Investors relying on such forecasts depend not only on the fundamental earning power of corporations, but also on the stock market's continued willingness to increase the price paid for corporate profits.

As illogical as it seems, one popular bull market tome published in 1999 espoused the view that equity valuation would continue to increase unabated, arguing for a zero equity risk premium. Advancing the notion that over long periods of time equities always outperform bonds, in *Dow 36,000: The New Strategy for Profiting from the Coming Rise in the Stock Market*, James Glassman and Kevin Hassett conclude that equities exhibit no more risk than bonds.[5] The authors ignore the intrinsic differences between stocks and bonds that clearly point to greater risk in stocks. The authors fail to consider experiences outside of the United States where equity markets have on occasion disappeared, leading to questions about the inevitability of superior results from long-term equity investment. Perhaps most important, the authors overestimate the number of investors that operate with twenty- or thirty-year time horizons and underestimate the number of investors that fail to stay the course when equity markets falter.

Finance theory and capital markets history provide analytical and practical underpinnings to the notion of a risk premium. Without expectations of superior returns for risky assets, the financial world would be turned on its head. In the absence of higher expected returns for fundamentally riskier stocks, market participants would shun equities. For example, in a world where bonds and stocks share identical expected returns, rational investors would opt for the equal-expected-return, lower-risk bonds. No investor would hold equal-expected-return, higher-risk stocks. The risk premium must exist for capital markets to function effectively.

While an expected risk premium proves necessary for well-functioning markets, Jorion and Goetzmann highlight the influence of survivorship bias on perceptions of the magnitude of the risk premium.

Arnott's deconstruction of equity returns and analysis of historical trends suggest a diminished prospective return advantage for stocks over bonds. Regardless of the future of the risk premium, sensible investors prepare for a future that differs from the past, with diversification providing the most powerful protection against errors in forecasts of expected asset class attributes.

past not always a good predictor of future

Stock Prices and Inflation

Stocks tend to offer long-term protection against generalized price inflation. A simple, yet elegant, means of understanding stock prices developed by Nobel laureate James Tobin compares the replacement cost of corporate assets to the market value of those assets. In equilibrium, Tobin argued that the ratio of replacement-cost-to-market value, which he named "q," should equal one. If replacement cost exceeds market value, economic actors find it cheaper to buy assets on the stock exchange than in the real economy. Conversely, if market value exceeds replacement cost, economic actors generate profits by building companies and floating shares on the stock exchange. Clearly, in rational markets, the value of corporate assets on a stock exchange should equal the real world replacement cost of those selfsame assets.

To the extent that general price inflation increases the replacement cost of corporate assets, that inflation should be reflected in increasing stock prices. If inflation did not result in higher equity prices, the newly inflated replacement cost of assets would exceed market value, allowing investors to purchase companies on the stock exchange at below intrinsic value. Until and unless stock prices reflect price inflation, publicly traded companies represent bargain basement merchandise.

In spite of the clear theoretical link between stock prices and inflation, the stock market presents a mixed record on incorporating inflation into equity prices. The 1970s provide a dramatic example of equity market failure to reflect rising price levels in stock prices. In 1973 and 1974, inflation eroded purchasing power by 37 percent and stock prices decreased by a total of 22 percent, hitting equity investors with a double whammy that caused losses of 51 percent in inflation-adjusted terms.

Jeremy Siegel observes that stock prices "provide excellent long-run hedges against inflation" and weak short-term protection against rising prices.[6] Presumably, the positive long-term relationship between inflation and stock prices stems from rational behavior, as market participants weigh the costs of acquiring assets in the real economy against the costs of acquiring similar assets on the financial exchanges. Possibly, the negative short-term relationship between inflation and stock prices results from irrational behavior, as investors respond to unanticipated inflation by increasing the discount rate applied to future cash flows without adjusting those future flows for the increases in inflation. While capital markets history supports Siegel's observation, the difference in short-run and long-run responses by equity prices to inflation creates a paradox. Because the long run consists of a series of short runs, no theory explains both the poor short-term record and the strong long-term record of stock price protection against price increases. In any event, investors seeking short-term shelter from inflation need to look beyond holdings of marketable equities.

Alignment of Interests

Stocks exhibit a number of characteristics that tend to serve investor goals. The general alignment of interests between corporate managers and shareholders bodes well for stock investors. In most instances, company executives benefit from enhancing shareholder value, serving the financial aspirations of management and investor alike. For example, corporate managers often share in gains associated with greater corporate profitability, indirectly through increased compensation and directly through increased values for personal shareholdings.

Unfortunately, the separation of ownership (by shareholders) and control (by management) in publicly traded companies introduces agency problems that occur when managements (the agents) benefit at the expense of shareholders (the principals). The most common wedge between interests of shareholders and management stems from compensation arrangements for management. High levels of salary and benefits accrue to management regardless of the level of underlying company achievement. Because larger companies provide larger compensation packages than smaller enterprises, corporate managers pursue corporate growth simply to achieve higher levels of personal earnings regardless of the impact of corporate size on enterprise profitability.

Managements divert funds to purposes that satisfy personal preferences at the expense of corporate performance. Company art collections, business jets, lavish offices, and corporate apartments confer benefits on senior managers at the expense of legitimate company goals. Investors cringe upon reading stories regarding WorldCom chief executive Bernard Ebbers's receipt of more than $400 million of personal loans from the company and Tyco chief executive Dennis Kozlowski's diversion of $600 million of company assets for personal purposes, including the purchase of a $6,000 shower curtain. Outsized financial and nonfinancial rewards for management, whether legitimate or otherwise, come directly from the pockets of company shareholders.

Yet, the most troubling scandal lies not with the chief executives that crossed the line, but with those that feathered their beds while following the rules. Former General Electric chief executive Jack Welch brought shame on himself and his company with a retirement package filled with personal perquisites. Beginning with lifetime use of a $15 million apartment bought by General Electric, the list includes access to the company's Boeing 737 jets, corporate helicopters, and a car and driver for him and his wife. No doubt worried that the hundreds of millions of dollars paid to Mr. Welch during his tenure at General Electric proved inadequate to support his retirement, the company provided "wine, flowers, cook, housekeeper and other amenities," including tickets to "top sporting events and the opera," to cater to the former chief executive's needs.[7] Even the reliably business-friendly editorial pages of the *Wall Street Journal* characterized Mr. Welch's retirement package as "the playthings of corporate opulence."[8]

The compensation excess exemplified by Ebbers, Kozlowski, and Welch represents the tip of the iceberg. The deeper problem, as described by William McDonough, president of the Federal Reserve Bank of New York, lies in the fact that rapid increases in chief executive compensation in the past two decades represent "terribly bad social policy and perhaps even bad morals." McDonough suggested that corporate boards "should simply reach the conclusion that corporate pay is excessive and adjust it to more reasonable and justifiable levels."[9]

Stock Options

The use of stock options to reward corporate management produces a subtle disconnect between the interests of management and shareholders. Options-based compensation schemes work effectively when company share prices increase, as both management and shareholders gain. The alignment of interests breaks down when share prices decrease, as management loses only the opportunity to benefit from stock price increases. In fact, management fails to suffer at all when corporate boards reset option prices to reflect the newly diminished stock price. In sharp contrast to management's loss of a mere opportunity, when share prices decrease shareholders lose cold, hard cash.

Options-based compensation schemes represent a no-lose game for management of publicly traded companies.

Microsoft provides a textbook example of using option grants to insulate employees from share price declines. In April 2000, Chief Executive Steve Ballmer faced a problem of low morale among employees concerned about the consequences of the Justice Department's antitrust activity and a four-month, 44 percent stock price decline. To boost spirits, Ballmer awarded more than 34,000 Microsoft employees stock options priced at the then current stock price. The chief executive wrote in an email to employees that "we know stock options are an important part of our compensation." Even while asserting that preexisting options "will have value long run," Ballmer expressed his hope that "these new grants will let people see returns much sooner."[10] By setting the option strike price near the stock's fifty-two week low, the company effectively insulated employees from the dramatic decline in Microsoft's shares. The company provided no such succor to shareholders.

In response to the all-too-numerous abuses of trust in the late 1990s, many corporations began to review options-based compensation. In a particularly notable move, in July 2003, Microsoft announced plans to eliminate its options program and substitute a program of restricted stock awards. Unlike the asymmetric option payoff, restricted stock produces a congruence of outcomes in which management and shareholders profit and suffer together. Chief Executive Steve Ballmer remarked, "whether it's dividend policy or how much risk to take, it's always good to have the employees thinking as much like the shareholders as possible."[11] If substantial numbers of corporations follow Microsoft's lead, corporate management will likely better serve shareholder interests in the future.

In spite of a general alignment of interests between shareholders and company managers, too many abuses exist. Excessive executive compensation, whether in the direct form of inflated salaries or the indirect form of unreasonable corporate perquisites, lines the pockets of corporate managers at the expense of shareholders. Sometimes, as in the case of options-based compensation, a disconnect exists between management and shareholders. One sure way to reduce the conflict between the owners of shares and the managers of companies involves ownership of stock by corporate management. Savvy investors seek companies with high levels of insider ownership.

Market Characteristics

At December 31, 2006, the U.S. stock market boasted assets in excess of $18.2 trillion, making it the largest liquid capital market in the world. More than 6,190 securities constituted the market, as defined by the (misnamed) Wilshire 5000. The enormous size of the U.S. stock market prompts many participants to divide the whole into any number of parts. Typical categories include size of market capitalization (small, medium, and large), character of security (growth or value), and nature of business (utility, technology, and health care, for example). At year-end 2006, the U.S. stock market traded at a dividend yield of 1.7 percent, a price-earnings ratio* of 19.5 and a price-book ratio† of 2.5.[12]

Summary

U.S. domestic equities represent the asset of choice for many long-term investors. Finance theory predicts and practical experience demonstrates that stocks provide superior returns over reasonably long holding periods. The general alignment of interests between shareholders and management serves both the goals of outside owners and the aspirations of inside managers. Holdings of equities provide protection against inflation in the intermediate and long run. Attractive characteristics of equity holdings argue for a significant role in most portfolios.

Yet investors must guard against relying on equities to exhibit their general characteristics in any specific time frame or allowing equities to account for too large a portion of the target portfolio. History may overstate the attractiveness of U.S. stocks. Returns of bonds and cash may exceed returns of stocks for years on end. For example, from the market peak in October 1929, it took stock investors fully twenty-one years and three months to match returns generated by bond investors.[13] Alignment of interests between shareholders and management breaks down with distressing frequency. Stock prices often fail to reflect underlying price inflation, at times for extended

*A price-earnings ratio measures valuation by comparing a company's stock price per share to its earnings per share.
†A price-book ratio measures valuation by comparing a company's stock price per share to its book value (assets minus liabilities) per share.

periods. Although equity markets do not deliver returns in a steady, stable, inflation-hedging fashion and corporate managements sometimes fail to serve shareholder interests, equity investments remain a central part of thoughtfully assembled, long-term-oriented investment portfolios.

U.S. TREASURY BONDS

Purchasers of U.S. Treasury bonds own a portion of the public debt of the United States government. Holdings of government bonds play a prominent role in well-structured fixed income portfolios, reflecting the attractive investment characteristics of full-faith-and-credit obligations of the government and the significant volume of debt securities issued by the government.

Because U.S. Treasury bonds enjoy the full-faith-and-credit backing of the U.S. government, bondholders face no risk of default. Holders of government debt sleep secure in the knowledge that interest and principal payments will be made in full and in a timely manner. Lack of default risk does not, however, liberate bondholders from exposure to price fluctuations. When interest rates rise, bond prices fall, as purchasers of existing assets need an adjustment to reflect the now-higher rates available on newly issued debt. When interest rates fall, bonds prices rise, as sellers of existing assets require greater compensation for their now-more-attractive fixed stream of future payments. Of all risky investments, investors expect the lowest returns from U.S. Treasury bonds, due to the high degree of security intrinsic in obligations of the U.S. government.

Interest Rate Risk

Bonds confuse investors. The inverse relationship between interest rates and bond prices (rates up, prices down and vice versa) proves central to understanding the role of fixed income in an investment portfolio. Yet surveys show that a large majority of investors fail to grasp even the most basic elements of bond math. Even highly respected market observers sometimes get it wrong. An article in the *New York Times* business section ironically entitled "Better Understanding of Bonds" asserted that "duration and bond prices move in lockstep with interest rates. A bond with a duration of seven years would gain 7 percent of its price when interest rates moved up one percentage point. The same bond would lose 7 percent when rates moved down that amount."[14] Of course, the *Times* described the relationship between prices and yields in perfectly perverse prose. Increases in interest rates cause price declines, not price increases. If a highly regarded, financially sophisticated *New York Times* business reporter cannot get it right, what chance does an ordinary investor have?

Duration measures the effective maturity of a bond, considering the timing and present value of individual cash flows received over the term of the instrument.* Longer duration bonds exhibit greater sensitivity to interest rate changes than do shorter duration bonds. By increasing a portfolio's duration, investors gain greater exposure to interest rate moves, creating a roughly equivalent choice between more assets with lower duration and fewer assets with higher duration. Portfolio managers wishing to reduce the opportunity costs of holding fixed income assets might rely on a small allocation to a long duration portfolio, in essence buying the diversifying power of bonds on the cheap.

In the realm of U.S. Treasury bond investing, risk relates primarily to time horizon. An investor with a six-month time horizon finds six-month Treasury bills riskless, as no doubt exists about the timely payment of the face value of the bill at maturity. That same six-month-time-horizon investor finds ten-year Treasury notes quite risky. As interest rates change, the value of the note might vary materially, even over a six-month holding period. An increase in rates leaves the investor with a loss, while a decline in rates provides the investor with an unexpected windfall.

Similarly, an investor with a ten-year time horizon faces significant risk with six-month Treasury bill investments. The six-month bills must be rolled over nineteen times to generate a ten-year holding period return. At the outset, the investor knows the rate only on the first six-month bill. The nineteen future rollover rates hold considerable uncertainty. Unless investors match holding period with maturity, price changes or rate changes may cause returns to diverge from expected levels.

---

*The term duration was first used in 1938 by Macaulay, who developed a formula to measure the average economic life of a security. Duration constitutes a weighted average of the proportions of the present value of the expected cash flows from a bond, with each payment weighted by the period in which the payment is expected to be received.

Diversifying Power

U.S. Treasury securities provide a unique form of diversification for investor portfolios, protecting against financial crisis and economic distress. In the stock market collapse of October 1987, when the U.S. stock market plummeted more than 20 percent in a single day, investors sought the safe haven of U.S. Treasury obligations. Even as stock prices fell off of a cliff, Treasury bonds staged an impressive rally. During the economic distress surrounding the confluence of the 1998 Asian, Russian, and American capital markets crises, investors engaged in a "flight to quality," favoring the security of U.S. Treasury obligations. Similarly, amid the credit crunch of August 2007, Treasury bill yields dropped two full percentage points in a matter of days to an intraday low of 2.5 percent. At that time, the spread between LIBOR and Treasury bills amounted to a stunning three percentage points, fully four times the average spread that prevailed for the month of June 2007. In times of crisis, government securities provide the greatest degree of protection to investor portfolios.

The protection to portfolio values provided by government bonds comes at a high price. Expected returns for fixed income instruments fall short of expected returns for equity-oriented investments. Some investors attempt to mitigate the opportunity costs of owning government bonds by holding higher-yielding corporate paper. Unfortunately, nongovernment bonds exhibit characteristics such as credit risk, illiquidity, and optionality that reduce effectiveness as a hedge against financial distress. The purity of noncallable, long-term, default-free Treasury bonds provides the most powerful diversification to investor portfolios.

Panic of 1998

In the summer and early fall of 1998, the Asian financial crisis painted a bleak backdrop for securities markets. A mid-July slump in equity markets accelerated in August when devaluation and default in Russia contributed to investor anxiety. The near collapse in September of the insanely levered Long-Term Capital Management hedge fund fueled bearish sentiment, causing market participants to demand immediate liquidity and safety.

During the worldwide collapse in equity prices, as shown in Figure 7.1, the broad-based Wilshire 5000 declined 22 percent from its all time peak on July 17th to the market bottom on October 8th. Reflecting a strong preference for quality and size, large-capitalization stocks outperformed small securities in dramatic fashion with the S&P 500 outpacing the Russell 2000 by a margin of 14 percent, or -19 percent to -33 percent. Developed foreign and emerging equity returns provided little solace for diversified portfolios, with the markets falling 21 percent and 27 percent, respectively.

Amid the market tumult, long-term Treasuries posted solid gains, returning 8 percent and besting the results of every major asset class. Credit risk and optionality dampened the performance of high quality corporate bonds and mortgages, limiting returns to 5 percent and 2 percent, respectively. Junk bonds and emerging debt produced losses, reflecting the high degree of equity exposure implicit in risky bond positions. High yield posted a -7 percent return and emerging markets generated a dismal -24 percent result over the period.

Asset class performance surrounding the 1998 market panic illustrates the superior diversifying power of pure fixed income—long-term, noncallable, default-free. Under normal circumstances, credit exposure and option risk increase returns; in times of crisis, U.S. Treasury bonds provide the protection that investors require.

Treasury bonds act as a cushion

Figure 7.1 Treasury Bonds Protect Portfolios in Turbulent Markets

Various Asset Class Returns, July 17, 1998 to October 8, 1998

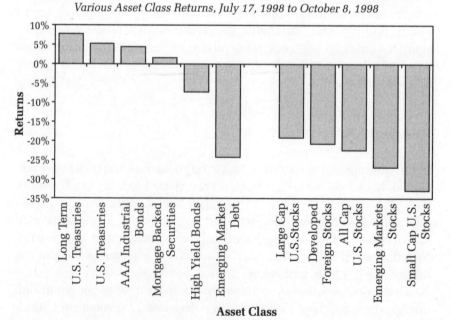

Bond Prices and Inflation

To add a further measure of complexity to the world of bond investing, investors in traditional U.S. Treasury bonds observe only nominal returns. In some instances, investors care primarily about nominal returns. For example, if a debtor desires to pay off a fixed obligation, the debtor requires only the amount of the debt, nothing more and nothing less. Nominally denominated investments, like Treasury bonds, match nominal liabilities nicely. If, on the other hand, an institution hopes to maintain the purchasing power of endowment assets, that institution needs to keep pace with inflation. Inflation-sensitive investments, unlike Treasury bonds, fulfill inflation-sensitive requirements. For holders of traditional Treasury debt securities, changes in inflation rates influence after-inflation returns in unpredictable ways, leading to potential variation between anticipated and actual outcomes.

Investors price fixed income instruments to generate positive inflation-adjusted rates of return. When the inflation rates experienced by investors more or less match the expectations formed at the beginning of the holding period, bondholders receive the anticipated after-inflation return. When inflation rates exceed expectations, the unanticipated inflation erodes the purchasing power of the promised stream of fixed payments, causing investors to receive disappointing after-inflation returns. When inflation rates fall short of expectations, the lower rate of general price inflation provides investors with a purchasing power boost. Deviations between original inflationary expectations and actual experience contain the potential to cause dramatic changes in real returns for fixed income investors.

When inflationary expectations fail to match actual experience, bonds tend to behave differently from other financial assets. Unanticipated inflation crushes bonds, while ultimately benefiting equities. Unanticipated deflation boosts bonds, while undermining stocks. Bonds provide the greatest diversification relative to equities in cases where actual inflation differs dramatically from expected levels.

Alignment of Interests

Interests of Treasury bond investors and the U.S. government prove to be better aligned than interests of corporate bond investors and corporate issuers. The government sees little reason to disfavor bondholders. In essence, action taken to reduce the value of government bonds

[handwritten: Treasury bonds weather the storm]

represents a transfer from bondholders to non-bondholders. In fact, if all debt were held domestically, advantages or disadvantages accruing to the government from changes in bond values would balance equal-and-offsetting disadvantages or advantages accruing to bondholders, leading to transfers from one group of citizens (taxpayers or bondholders) to another group of citizens (bondholders or taxpayers). Moreover, were the government to disadvantage bond investors, future access to credit markets might be impaired. Worry over misalignment of interests causes little lost sleep for owners of Treasury bonds.

Investors in Treasury bonds generally perceive the government as a neutral player in the debt management process. Unlike corporate debtholders, who sit squarely across the table from the issuers of corporate obligations, government bondholders expect fair treatment. Consider the fact that from 1975 to 1984, the U.S. Treasury offered a dozen issues of thirty-year bonds that contained call provisions for the final five years of the issue's life. A call provision allows the debt issuer to redeem a debt issue at a fixed price. Economically motivated issuers exercise call provisions only when the fixed-call price stands below the value of the bond calculated in absence of a call provision. Exercise of a call provision eliminates debt with high coupons relative to current market levels, benefiting the issuer and hurting the investor.

Because of the special nature of the government's role in debt markets, bond market participants debated whether the government would employ the call option for debt management purposes or for economic refundings. If the government used the call option for debt management, then bondholders faced an idiosyncratic risk as likely to provide a benefit as a cost. If the government used the call option for economic refundings, then bondholders faced a risk of economic loss.

Government bondholders received the answer to the question of how the Treasury would behave on January 14, 2000 when the Treasury "announced the call for redemption at par on May 15, 2000 of the 8-¼% Treasury Bonds of 2000–05." [15] The government responded to economic incentives, calling high-interest debt to reduce financing charges.

In later refundings, the U.S. Treasury explicitly cited an economic motivation for calling bonds. In the unimaginatively titled January 15, 2004 *Public Debt News* release, "Treasury Calls 9-⅛ Percent Bonds of 2004–09," the government noted that "these bonds are being called to reduce the cost of debt financing. The 9-⅛ percent interest rate is significantly above the current cost of securing financing for the five years remaining to their maturity. In current market conditions, Treasury estimates that interest savings from the call and refinancing will be about $544 million."[16] In other words, the ability to refinance the 9-percent-plus-coupon bonds at an interest cost of between 3 percent and 4 percent resulted in substantial interest savings for the government.

Even though the government acted in an economic fashion by exercising the call provision on the 9-⅛s Treasury bonds of 2004–09, the fact that investors debated whether the government would exercise the call provision to generate interest savings signifies the unusual relationship between the government and its creditors. In fact, the program of callable Treasury issuance lasted a mere ten years and involved a relatively small portion of overall government bond issuance. Moreover, the call provisions affected only the last five years of the thirty-year bond's life, in contrast to the much more aggressive call provisions typically included in issues of long-term corporate debt. Perhaps the U.S. Treasury stopped selling callable bonds to improve the character of securities offered to government bond market participants. In any event, of all debt issuers, the government promotes the greatest alignment of interests with its creditors.

At December 31, 2006, roughly 31 percent of U.S. government bond issues represented debt issued by government-sponsored enterprises (GSEs). (The Government National Mortgage Association, known as "Ginnie Mae," the Federal Home Loan and Mortgage Corporation, known as "Freddie Mac," and the Federal National Mortgage Association, known as "Fannie Mae," constitute the largest GSEs.) Many market participants treat debt issued by GSEs as close substitutes for U.S. Treasury obligations. In fact, credit quality of GSEs ranges from the full-faith-and-credit status enjoyed by Ginnie Mae to the less exalted status of Fannie Mae and Freddie Mac. Many GSEs operate in a nether land between the certainty of government guarantees and the uncertainty of corporate promises to pay. While chances of default by GSEs seem quite low to most market observers, many GSE obligations contain options that may disadvantage bondholders.

Investors seeking the purity of U.S. Treasury debt face a surprisingly daunting task. Many high quality bond investment vehicles hold large quantities of GSE debt, as fund managers pursue the time-honored investment practice of hoping to get something for nothing in the form of incremental yield on GSE paper (the something) without exposing the portfolio to additional risk (the nothing). The twin possibilities of credit deterioration and exercise of options by the GSEs carry the potential to harm bondholder interests. Investors seeking high quality fixed income exposure avoid GSE debt and opt for the purity of U.S. Treasury bonds, the full-faith-and-credit obligations of the U.S. government.

Cash

Investors frequently divide fixed income assets into cash and bonds, with the former consisting of instruments maturing within one year, and the latter including instruments with more than a year to maturity. For investors with short investment horizons, cash represents the riskless asset as market participants know nominal and real returns with reasonable certainty. Certainty of return comes with a high price as returns over the eighty-one years through December 31, 2006 amount to a mere 3.7 percent per annum for cash, which falls to a paltry 0.7 percent per year after adjustment for inflation.

Because investors frequently employ one-year horizons when conducting portfolio analysis, cash naturally enters the matrix of capital markets returns, causing many long-term investors to misidentify cash holdings as a riskless asset. If investors conducted analysis over periods consistent with an appropriate investment horizon, cash would appear as a substantially riskier asset.

Some investors argue that cash provides necessary liquidity for endowment funds, ignoring the massive amounts of liquidity resident in institutional portfolios. Interest income, dividend payments, and rental streams provide liquid cash flows, facilitating the ability of the investment fund to meet spending distribution requirements. Natural turnover of assets provides another source of funds. Bonds mature, companies merge, and private assets become liquid, serving as sources of cash flow. Manager sell decisions create yet another set of liquidity events. Finally, if income flows, natural asset turnover and manager sales create insufficient liquidity to meet spending requirements, investors retain the ability to direct sales of assets to provide for current consumption. The modest transactions costs incurred in selling assets pale in comparison to the drag on returns created by holding cash as a standard part of an institutional portfolio. Based on delivery of poor real returns and failure to serve as a riskless asset for long-term investors, cash plays no significant role in a well-constructed endowment portfolio.

Market Characteristics

At December 31, 2006, U.S. government bonds totaled $3.2 trillion, of which $2.2 trillion represented full-faith-and-credit obligations of the U.S. Treasury and $1.0 trillion represented debt of government spon-

sored enterprises. U.S. Treasury bonds trade in the deepest, most efficient market in the world.

The universe of Treasury bonds sported a yield to maturity* of 4.9
percent at year-end 2006 with an average maturity of 6.9 years and a
duration of 5.0 years. Agency issues promised a yield of 5.1 percent
with a 5.1-year average maturity and 3.5-year duration.

Summary

U.S. Treasury bonds provide a unique form of portfolio diversification,
serving as a hedge against financial accidents and unanticipated deflation. No other asset type comes close to matching the diversifying
power created by long-term, noncallable, default-free, full-faith-and-
credit obligations of the U.S. government.

Investors pay a price for the diversifying power of Treasury bonds.
The ironclad security of Treasury debt causes investors to expect (and
deserve) low returns relative to those expected from riskier assets.
While holders of long-term Treasury bonds stand to benefit from
declining price inflation, in an environment of unanticipated inflation
Treasury bondholders lose. Treasury bonds' modest expected returns
and adverse reaction to inflation argue for modest allocations to the
asset class by long-term investors.

FOREIGN DEVELOPED EQUITY

Investments in developed economy equity markets provide the same
expected returns as U.S. equity investments. But overseas investments
exhibit two critical differentiating characteristics relative to domestic
holdings. First, markets in different regions respond to different economic forces, causing returns to behave differently from one region of
the world to the next. Second, investment in non-U.S. markets
exposes investors to foreign currency fluctuations, adding another
variable to the investment equation.

Developed economy equity markets share similar levels of
expected return. Comparability in economic infrastructure, commonality in drivers of economic performance, and secular liberalization in
flows of labor, goods, and services across national boundaries combine

*Yield to maturity represents the rate of return anticipated by holding a bond to
its maturity date.

to cause investors to expect similar long-run results from investments in developed equity markets. Although investor enthusiasm for individual countries waxes and wanes along with strong or weak recent market performance, over reasonably long periods of time, investors might expect the developed markets in North America, Europe, and Asia to produce roughly comparable returns.

In fact, in the thirty-seven years since the 1970 inception of the Morgan Stanley Capital International (MSCI) Europe, Australasia and Far East (EAFE) Index that tracks non-U.S. equity market performance, EAFE countries generated 10.8 percent per annum returns relative to 11.2 percent per annum returns for the U.S. dominated S&P 500 Index. While the domestic and international results fall in the same neighborhood, the United States enjoys a slight margin of superiority. Because such market performance comparisons exhibit a high degree of sensitivity to beginning and ending dates, the most reasonable conclusion supports the assumption of approximate equivalence between expected returns for domestic and international equities.

Diversifying Power

The lack of correlation between foreign markets and the U.S. market provides valuable diversification to investors. Some observers speculate that the process of global economic integration has caused individual country equity markets to behave increasingly one like the other, leading to less prospective diversification. As evidence of increasing correlation between markets, diversification skeptics point to the behavior of equity markets in the crash of 1987 and in the financial dislocations during the crisis of 1998. In both instances, stock markets worldwide exhibited similar, extraordinary declines. Yet, market declines in 1987 and 1998 constituted short-term events in which market players expressed extreme preferences for liquidity and quality. After brief periods during which many developed equity markets moved in concert, individual country markets reverted to fluctuation in response to country-specific drivers of local market performance.

Consider the relative returns of equity markets in the United States and Japan. In the 1980s, Japan dominated all other world stock markets, returning 28.4 percent per annum versus 16.5 percent per annum for other non-U.S. markets and 17.4 percent per annum for the U.S. equity markets. Near the end of the extraordinary bull run in Japanese stocks, Japan boasted the largest market capitalization in the world, surpassing even the massive U.S. market in size.

In the 1990s, Japan's fortunes reversed. During the last decade of the twentieth century, Japan's economy collapsed, contributing to a market decline of 0.9 percent per annum for the decade. In contrast, other non-U.S. markets returned 13.5 percent per annum and the United States market produced an astonishing 18.2 percent return per annum. As Japan's stock market declined, the country lost its dominant equity market position, falling so far behind the United States that at one point Japan's equity market capitalization amounted to less than one-fifth of the U.S.'s market capitalization. Clearly, investments in individual equity markets behave differently, generating returns that differ one from the other, thereby providing diversification to portfolio holdings.

Foreign Currency Exposure

Investors in foreign equities assume foreign exchange risk as an unavoidable part of overseas equity exposure. Realistic investors expect foreign currency translation neither to add to nor to subtract from investment results. Even though much ink spills and many trees fall in the service of market prognosticators who fill reams of pages in attempts to divine the future of foreign exchange rates, no one really knows where currencies will go. Sensible investors avoid speculating on currencies.

Some observers suggest that holders of foreign equities should routinely hedge foreign exchange exposure. Unfortunately, hedges prove difficult to fashion as foreign equity managers face uncertain holding periods and unknowable future position sizes, creating issues regarding the appropriate term and magnitude of the hedge. As a result, foreign equity investors necessarily assume at least some foreign exchange risk along with commitments to the asset class.

Fortunately, finance theorists conclude that some measure of foreign exchange exposure adds to portfolio diversification. Unless foreign currency positions constitute more than 20 percent or 25 percent of portfolio assets, currency exposure serves to reduce overall portfolio risk. Beyond 20 percent to 25 percent of portfolio assets, the currency exposure constitutes a source of incremental risk, suggesting consideration of some corrective action.

Performance Chasing

Investors tend to seek diversification when the core portfolio asset disappoints, either in absolute or in relative terms. For instance, from 1998 to 2003, a period during which foreign markets underperformed, returning a cumulative -18.5 percent relative to a cumulative -6.4 percent for the broad U.S. market, college endowments maintained a relatively stable allocation to non-U.S. equities. The fact that foreign stock allocations fell in a narrow range of between 12.5 percent and 13.8 percent for the period indicates that investors were engaged in rational rebalancing activity. In contrast to the rational rebalancing in the face of poor relative performance, as foreign markets took off in 2004, allocations to foreign equities took off, too. In the three years from 2004 to 2006, non-U.S. equities posted returns of 23.9 percent per annum and emerging markets generated returns of 35.8 percent per annum, completely dominating the U.S. market returns of 13.1 percent per annum. In response, college endowment managers chased performance, boosting foreign equity allocations from 13.8 percent in 2003 to 15.6 percent in 2004 to 17.4 percent in 2005 and finally to 20.1 percent in 2006. Momentum strategies generally end badly.

Strong relative performance of foreign equities caused endowment managers to dramatically increase non-U.S. equity holdings, with investors frequently citing diversification as the rationale for boosting foreign allocations. Disappointing performance from the diversifying asset may cause investors to reduce allocations at an inopportune time. Sensible investors pursue diversification as a policy to reduce risk, not as a tactic to chase performance. By following a disciplined policy of maintaining a well-diversified set of portfolio exposures, regardless of market zigs and zags, investors establish the conditions for long-run success. In fact, when taking market conditions into account, investors increase the odds of success by diversifying into asset classes after they suffer poor performance. In any case, foreign equities provide an important tool for reducing portfolio risk without sacrificing expected returns.

Foreign Equity Prices and Inflation

Investors in domestic equities face an inflationary paradox—stocks appear to provide good long-term protection against inflation, while they seem to offer poor short-term protection. Foreign stock investors encounter no such conundrum. The tenuous link between (a) domestic inflation and (b) the returns of foreign stocks translated into dollars proves so remote as to render foreign equities useless as a hedge against inflation.

Alignment of Interests

As a first approximation, alignment of interests between U.S. investors and foreign corporations resembles the relationship between U.S. investors and U.S. corporations. Generally speaking, both domestically and overseas, equity investors expect corporate management to look after shareholder interests.

Even though the corporate scandals at Enron and WorldCom, among others, highlighted the shortcomings of American corporate governance, the fact remains that in the United States a strong coincidence of interest exists between shareholders and management. As a broad generalization, elsewhere in the world corporate managements focus less single-mindedly on profit generation. In some countries, cultural norms lead to greater concern for the needs of other stakeholders, including workers, lenders, and the broader community. In other countries, poor governance structures allow controlling shareholders to divert resources from minority shareholders. While a lesser coincidence of interests between overseas managements and their shareholders constitutes a disadvantage to owners of foreign shares, the advantages of increasing the investment opportunity set argue for inclusion of non-U.S. securities in individual investor portfolios.

Market Characteristics

At December 31, 2006, developed foreign markets totaled $23.8 trillion, as measured by Morgan Stanley Capital International. The sum of the twenty-two countries included by MSCI in the non-U.S. developed world exceeded the market capitalization of the U.S. market, which stood at $18.2 trillion as of year-end 2006. Japan led the non-U.S. world with $5.0 trillion in assets. Other large markets include the United Kingdom ($3.8 trillion), France ($2.4 trillion), Canada ($1.8 trillion), and Germany ($1.6 trillion). Europe accounted for 63 percent of the non-U.S. world, Asia for 26 percent, Canada for 7 percent and Australia/New Zealand for 5 percent.

Overall, foreign developed equity markets sported a dividend yield of 2.4 percent, a price-earnings ratio of 16.0, and a price-book ratio of 2.7. Regional variations matter. Europe yielded 2.7 percent at year-end 2006 relative to 1.1 percent for Japan, while European securities posted a price-earnings ratio of 14.5 and a price-book ratio of 2.6 relative to respective ratios of 21.2 and 2.1 for Japan.

Summary

Since expected returns from foreign developed markets roughly approximate expected returns from U.S. markets, investors establish positions in foreign developed equity markets primarily to provide portfolio diversification. The most important source of diversification stems from the fact that forces driving returns in equity markets outside of the United States differ from forces driving returns in the United States. Foreign currency exposure adds a further measure of diversification to investor portfolios.

Sensible investors invest in foreign equity markets through thick and thin, regardless of recent past performance. All too often, market players seek the diversification promised by foreign stocks following a period of strong relative foreign market returns. When the diversifying strategies fail to produce returns superior to domestic market results, investors abandon the disappointing diversifying assets. Performance-chasing players use international equities to whipsaw portfolios, locking in poor relative returns and damaging investment results.

EMERGING MARKETS EQUITY

Emerging markets represent a high-risk, high-expected-return segment of the marketable equities universe. Defined as a group of countries with economies in an intermediate stage of development, neither undeveloped nor developed, emerging markets present a formidable array of fundamental risks for investors. On a macro level, investors concern themselves with the development of the overall economy and the maturation of the securities markets' infrastructure. On a micro level, investors worry about quality of management and profit orientation of nascent enterprises.

Market observers frequently confuse strong economic growth with strong equity market prospects. Consider the extreme case of a command economy with resource allocation rules that operate without the benefit of securities markets. Clearly, economic growth occurs without any impact on stock prices, as equity securities do not exist. In the less extreme case of market-oriented economies with poor resource allocation, providers of equity capital might receive consistently poor returns. Corporate revenues may accrue disproportionately to corporate management (through salaries), to labor (through wages), or to government entities (through taxes), leaving inadequate recompense for capital. In well-functioning economies, prices and returns adjust to reflect financial market conditions. Not all emerging market economies function well. Profitable equity market investments require profitable enterprises, for investors ultimately share in corporate earnings. Therein lies the primary microeconomic risk for emerging market investors. In emerging markets, as elsewhere, economic growth may not lead to corporate profitability, which in turn translates into stock market success.

Economic history contains many examples of emerging markets that submerged. In an article dramatically entitled "Survival," Stephen Brown, William Goetzmann, and Stephen Ross identify thirty-six stock exchanges operating at the beginning of the twentieth century. Of the thirty-six, "more than half suffered at least one major hiatus in trading . . . usually due to nationalizations or war." More distressingly to investors who believe in the inevitability of progress, of the thirty-six markets that operated in 1900, fully fifteen remained classified as emerging markets more than 100 years later. One market, located in Serbia's Belgrade, fails even to make the twenty-first century list of emerging markets. The authors dryly note that "in fact, the very term 'emerging markets' admits the possibility that these markets might fail."[17]

In recent years, investors enjoyed the opportunity to invest in an ever-expanding set of developing markets. Morgan Stanley Capital International, the leading constructor of non-U.S. market indices, began tracking emerging markets in 1988 with an index of eight countries ranging from Mexico to Jordan to Thailand. Five years later, the population stood at nineteen with notable additions of India, Korea, and Portugal. By 1998, the total reached twenty-eight as South Africa, Russia, and a number of central European countries joined MSCI's coverage universe. In 2001, Egypt and Morocco joined the index, while Sri Lanka departed. Because of investment restrictions and lack of liquidity, Venezuela left the index in 2006, bringing the emerging market country population to twenty-five.

On occasion, countries move out of the emerging world to the developed world. In 1997 Portugal made the leap, and in 2001 Greece followed. As emerging economies make progress, more countries will advance to the ranks of the developed world.

The Bull Case for Emerging Markets

Antoine van Agtmael, longtime investor in emerging markets, articulates a bullish perspective on emerging markets in his excellent book, *The Emerging Markets Century*.

> As we enter the Emerging Markets Century, the time has come to rethink what we mean by "risk." Gazing back in the rearview mirror, we once regarded emerging markets as crisis-prone, volatile, desperately poor, small in the global economy to the point of irrelevancy, dependent on Western consumer markets, and heavily protected. Stock markets were poorly regulated and prone to manipulation; a lack of participation by institutional investors and pension funds left much room for speculation and insider trading; corporate disclosure was notoriously poor.
>
> More developed markets, in contrast, led in economic stability, technology, market size, and transparency. A better legal framework and corporate governance protected investors while domestic pension funds and a large mutual funds industry were ready buyers of stocks and bonds. And, of course, a huge gap remained in the size, sophistication, and quality of companies between the West and "the Rest."
>
> Today, the case for emerging market investing is different precisely because (1) these markets themselves are *less* different and more global than before and (2) a growing number of companies are becoming world-class. While emerging markets were until fairly recently regarded as a small yet risky niche, the increasing importance of these countries and the importance of these companies has propelled emerging markets from being the spice of an investment portfolio to a more central role that is more mainstream and less of a gamble. The practical implications of this broad-based shift both in real and perceived risk are that emerging markets should be a core component of investors' portfolios rather than an afterthought but that they will also be less exciting going forward.[18]

While Antoine van Agtmael's work supports the role of emerging markets equities as a core asset class, their relatively immature regulatory environments argue for special care on the part of investment managers. Emerging markets may be "less exciting going forward," but they will continue to be exciting.

Emerging Market Equity Prices and Inflation

The link between inflation in the United States and emerging market stock returns suffers from the same issues as the link between U.S. inflation and foreign developed stock returns. That said, basic commodities play an important role in a number of emerging markets economies. To the extent that the U.S. suffers commodity-price-induced inflationary pressures, investments in emerging markets stocks may provide partial protection against the inflation.

Alignment of Interests

Development of market infrastructure in emerging economies proceeds in fits and starts as legislators, regulators, and corporate managements learn the rules of the game. Investors accustomed to the protections afforded in the United States find most emerging markets quite inhospitable. Quality of securities legislation ranges from poor to good, enforcement of regulations varies from inadequate to adequate, and fidelity of managements to shareholders' interests falls all over the lot. *Caveat emptor.*

Government policies sometimes interfere with investor interests, occasionally in dramatic fashion. In 1998, during the Asian crisis, Malaysia restricted the convertibility of the ringgit, effectively prohibiting foreign investors from repatriating funds. Because of bad behavior regarding capital controls, MSCI removed Malaysia from one of the firm's emerging market indices. Not until Malaysia removed capital controls in late 1999 did the country reestablish its credentials as a full-fledged member of the MSCI roster.

In emerging markets, corporate actions resemble, at times, the Wild West. One market observer suggested that Russian equity investors put money in enterprises where management attempts grand theft and avoid commitments to companies where management engages in petty larceny. The rationale for the superficially contradictory advice lay in the notion that managements of truly valuable enterprises attempted to steal the entire entity, while managements of less valuable enterprises simply sought to pilfer small pieces.

The inferior alignment of interests facing investors in emerging markets represents one of the critical risk factors that cause investors to demand higher rates of return for emerging markets equity investments. Since investors operate in an environment with less-evolved frameworks for the definition and resolution of legal and regulatory issues, the resulting uncertainty forces sensible investors to seek premium returns.

Emerging markets governments occasionally drive wedges between the interests of shareholders and managements. Controls on the ownership and voting rights of local shares sometimes lead to the creation of two classes of share owners, with attendant problems for the second-class foreign investor. Capital controls, although infrequently imposed, interfere with the ability of foreign investors to transfer funds freely. Government regulation in the emerging markets contains the potential to harm foreign investor interests.

In other instances, corporate managements fail to act in shareholder interests. A particularly prevalent problem in many Asian countries involves family-controlled companies satisfying family desires at the expense of external minority shareholder wishes. An absence of transparency compounds the problem as outside investors often lack the information required to identify and address insider-dealing issues.

As emerging markets mature and as global capital markets liberalize, structural problems with misalignment of interests become less severe. Nonetheless, rational investors require a substantial return premium to expose assets to companies that operate in the less-than-ideal emerging markets legal and regulatory framework.

Market Characteristics

At December 31, 2006, emerging markets equities totaled $7.2 trillion according to MSCI. Ranging from India ($824 billion) and China ($816 billion), which by market-capitalization would rank in the middle of the developed market cohort, to the much smaller markets of Peru ($38 billion) and Jordan ($30 billion), the emerging markets universe encompasses a broad range of countries. Asia accounts for 53 percent of emerging market equity assets, Latin America for 20 percent, Europe for 16 percent, and Africa and the Middle East for 12 percent.

Emerging market valuations trumped those of the United States at year-end 2006 (at least for investors seeking value). The emerging markets dividend yield amounted to 2.1 percent relative to 1.7 percent for the United States. The price-earnings ratio stood at 15.6, representing a substantial discount to the U.S. market level of 19.5. Emerging markets traded at a price-book ratio of 2.5, identical to the U.S. level.

Summary

Investors in emerging markets equities require substantial expected returns to compensate for the high level of fundamental investment risk. During the period for which good data exist, investors received inadequate compensation for risks incurred. From 1985, when the World Bank's International Finance Corporation began measuring emerging markets equity returns, to December 2006, emerging markets equities produced 12.0 percent per annum returns (as measured by the IFC Global Composite) relative to 13.1 percent for the S&P 500 and 12.4 percent for EAFE. The deficit relative to developed market returns indicates that emerging market investors accepted higher fundamental risks than developed market investors without earning excess returns. Investors in emerging markets hope the future treats them better than the past.

Because of macroeconomic and microeconomic concerns, emerging markets equities promise high expected returns with commensurately high levels of risk. An allocation to emerging markets stocks contains the potential to enhance the risk and return characteristics of well-structured investment portfolios.

CONCLUSION

Investors find a number of essential components of a well-diversified, equity-oriented portfolio in the traditional asset classes of domestic equity, U.S. Treasury bonds, foreign developed market equity, and foreign emerging market equity. Domestic and foreign equities drive portfolio returns, while Treasury bonds provide diversifying power. By employing traditional asset classes in a well-diversified portfolio, investors build a strong foundation for investment success.

In the course of providing basic, valuable, differentiable characteristics to investor portfolios, traditional asset classes rely on market-generated returns. By investing in asset classes in which market forces drive returns, investors achieve a high level of confidence that the various asset classes will produce the expected long-term results, dramatically reducing the risk of active-management slippage between hoped-for asset class performance and actual outcomes.

Traditional asset classes trade in broad, deep, investable markets, ensuring substantial levels of commitment by a range of Wall Street firms. The resulting competition leads to market transparency and efficiency, increasing the likelihood that investors transact on fair terms.

Investors without active management expertise rely primarily on traditional asset classes for portfolio construction, perhaps, adding exposure to Treasury Inflation-Protected Securities and an index of real estate investment trusts to round out the portfolio. Investors with active management expertise not only enjoy the possibility of producing market-beating returns for domestic and foreign equities, but also benefit from the inclusion of asset classes that depend on active management, including absolute return, real assets, and private equity.

8
Alternative Asset Classes

Alternative asset classes—absolute return, real assets, and private equity—contribute to the portfolio construction process by pushing back the efficient frontier, allowing creation of portfolios with higher returns for a given level of risk or with lower risk for a given level of return. Investors who employ alternative assets as legitimate tools in the portfolio allocation process reduce dependence on traditional marketable securities, facilitating the structuring of truly diversified portfolios.

As separate asset classes, each alternative investment category adds something distinctive and important to portfolio characteristics. Absolute return and real assets provide diversification, generating returns driven by factors materially different from those determining results of other asset classes. In contrast, private equity returns depend on many factors common to the determination of marketable equity returns. Although private investments provide little diversification, well-selected private holdings contain the potential to make a dramatic contribution to portfolio returns.

Prices for many alternative assets lack the efficiency typical of prices for traditional marketable securities, leading to opportunities for astute managers to add substantial value in the investment process. In fact, investors in alternative asset classes must pursue active management since market returns do not exist in the sense of an investable passive option. Even if investors could purchase the median result in an alternative asset class, the results would likely disappoint. Longer term median historical returns have lagged comparable marketable security results, both in absolute and risk-adjusted terms. Only by generating superior active returns do investors realize the promise of investing in alternative assets.

ABSOLUTE RETURN

Absolute return investing consists of inefficiency-exploiting marketable securities positions that exhibit little or no correlation to traditional stock and bond investments. Well-structured absolute return portfolios provide equity-like returns with powerful diversifying characteristics.

Absolute return managers reduce market risk by investing in event-driven or value-driven situations expected to behave independently of market forces. Event-driven positions depend on the completion of a specific corporate finance transaction such as the consummation of a merger or the emergence of a company from bankruptcy. Value-driven strategies employ hedged portfolios in which short positions offset long positions, dramatically reducing the investor's systematic risk. Absolute return managers seek to generate high levels of returns, independent of market results, in contrast to the relative benchmark-beating returns sought by active marketable security managers.

The short duration of absolute return strategies makes the short-term cost of funds a fair starting point for evaluating manager performance. The basic math of hedged positions implies that (in the absence of skill and fees) investors deserve a money market rate of return.* If managers add value, returns will exceed short-term rates. If managers fail to add value, returns will fall short of money market rates.

Without active management, absolute return does not exist. The fundamental notion of absolute return investing rests on identification

---

*Absolute return strategies that employ offsetting long and short positions (merger arbitrage and long/short investing) earn money market returns in the absence of manager value added (or subtracted). On one side of the portfolio, assume a manager invests contributed funds in long positions. On the other side of the portfolio, assume a manager executes a short sale. Upon consummating a short sale, the manager receives cash proceeds from the transaction. Even though the cash must be posted as collateral with the lender of the security, the short seller earns a "rebate," or money market rate, on the proceeds. If the long position and short position both track the market precisely, gains (losses) from the long match losses (gains) from the short, eliminating the systematic market factors from performance. Under such circumstances, the investor earns the money-market-like short rebate on invested assets.

and successful exploitation of inefficiencies in pricing marketable securities. In the absence of value added by active managers, investors receive money market rates of return, appropriate compensation for creating positions without material market exposure.

[handwritten: find pricing inefficiencies exploit them and]

Event-driven Investing

Event-driven opportunities exist because of the complexities inherent in business combinations and corporate reorganizations. Mainstream portfolio managers recognize that the determinants of the merger endgame and the bankruptcy resolution differ materially from the factors that predominate in day-to-day security valuation. The legal and regulatory environment changes upon announcement of a proposed combination or reorganization, giving the informed specialist an advantage over the competent generalist. Superior analytical skills create a meaningful edge for active event-driven investors.

The opportunity exploited by event-driven investors stems in part from sales of securities by investors unwilling to commit the resources to develop a thorough understanding of the circumstances surrounding complex corporate finance transactions. In the case of distressed securities, selling pressure comes from investors unable or unwilling to hold securities of failing or failed companies. The sometimes massive supply of securities from holders uncomfortable with positions in companies undergoing basic structural change allows event-driven investors to establish positions with attractive embedded returns.

Merger arbitrage represents a typical event-driven absolute return strategy, with results related to the manager's ability to predict the probability that a deal will close, the likely timing and the expected consideration for the transaction. Upon announcement of a stock-for-stock deal, the price of the target company's stock generally rises to a level somewhat below the acquirer's offer, creating an opportunity for the merger arbitrageur to profit. Uncertainty regarding the ultimate outcome of the transaction causes many holders to sell, motivated by the concern that gains stimulated by the merger offer might disappear for any of a number of reasons. After careful assessment of deal-specific factors, merger arbitrage investors buy the stock of the target company and sell shares of the acquiring company, hoping to profit from the elimination of the spread when the transaction closes. Because the arbitrageur holds long positions offset by short positions, the direction of the overall market plays little role in determining the position's returns. Instead, results depend on the merger arbitrageur's ability to assess correctly the factors relevant to the ultimate conclusion of the transaction.

Newell Rubbermaid Merger Arbitrage

The March 1999 combination of Newell and Rubbermaid illustrates some of the market dynamics underpinning event-driven investment opportunities. After the October 1998 announcement of the proposed merger, Rubbermaid shares responded by rising nearly 25 percent as shown in Figure 8.1. Trading volumes increased more than ten-fold, from an average of 566,000 shares per day in the week prior to the announcement to 5,960,000 shares per day in the week following. Taking advantage of the merger induced price rise, traditional long-only investors exited the stock and created an opportunity for merger arbitrageurs to establish positions.

The terms of the definitive agreement called for a tax-free exchange of shares in which holders of Rubbermaid would receive 0.7883 shares of Newell upon closing, expected in early 1999. By buying a share of Rubbermaid at the post announcement price of $31.81

Figure 8.1 Merger Arbitrage Spread Narrows as Closing Date Nears

Merger Between Newell and Rubbermaid

October 12, 1998–March 15, 1999

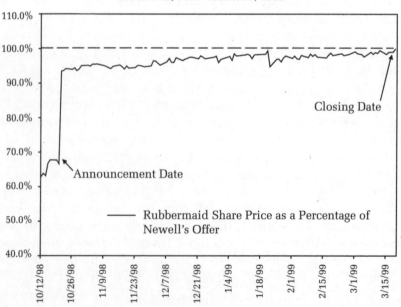

and selling 0.7883 of a share of Newell at $43.25, arbitrageurs generated net proceeds of $2.28 per share. If the companies were to complete the transaction on the originally proposed terms, arbitrageurs would have equivalent value positions at the closing. Upon consummation of the deal, merger arbitrageurs would close out positions by delivering Newell shares received from the Rubbermaid exchange to cover the original Newell short sale.

Back-of-the-envelope calculations illustrate the return characteristics of the transaction. When the deal closed on March 24, 1999, merger arbitrageurs earned the $2.28 post announcement spread between the two stocks and a short rebate of about $0.57 for a total of approximately $2.85. Cash flow yield played essentially no role in the return calculation since the dividends earned on the Rubbermaid shares offset the dividends paid on the Newell shares. Based on an initial capital commitment of $31.81 per share, the position delivered a gross return of about 9 percent over a five month period, equivalent to an annualized return in the low 20 percent range.[1]

The Newell Rubbermaid combination proceeded without a hitch, as the spread between Rubbermaid and Newell shares narrowed week-by-week until the scheduled closing. Not all merger arbitrage transactions proceed as smoothly. The September 1998 combination of WorldCom and MCI Communications began in November 1996 as a proposal by British Telecommunications plc to acquire MCI in the largest cross border transaction ever. Between the initiation of merger discussions and the ultimate resolution, merger arbitrageurs wrestled with a laundry list of problems, including antitrust concerns, regulatory approvals, changes in company business strategy, corporate operating difficulties, international political issues, and competition from competing bidders.* Regardless of whether deals take a simple path from inception to resolution or follow a convoluted route, the returns to merger arbitrage investors depend far more on the specific event than on the general direction of the market.

In the distressed securities area, event-driven investors look for opportunity in securities of companies undergoing reorganization. Because

---

*The story of Farallon Capital Management's handling of the MCI Communications/WorldCom combination appears in Harvard Business Case N9-299-020, "Farallon Capital Management: Risk Arbitrage," written by Robert Howard and Andre Perold in February 1999. The case study describes the ultimately successful efforts of Tom Steyer, David Cohen, and Bill Duhamel in navigating the complexities of an extraordinary merger transaction.

of the complexity of the issues surrounding bankruptcy, many market participants sell positions regardless of price, creating an opportunity for hard working investors to profit. By assessing the timing of the company's emergence from bankruptcy and valuing the expected package of securities, players in the distressed securities arena generate returns more dependent on events important to the bankruptcy process than on the level of the overall stock market.

Event-driven strategies lack the power to insulate investors completely from financial market moves. In the case of merger arbitrage, factors influencing the stock market or the financing market may alter the likelihood either that a particular merger will be completed or that mergers in general will move forward, causing a commonality of influence. In the case of distressed investing, to the extent that investors receive equity interests as part of a package of securities distributed upon a company's reorganization, the market exerts direct influence on the ultimate return to a distressed securities investment. In spite of identifiable links between event-driven investing and market moves, under a wide range of circumstances event-driven strategies provide meaningful portfolio diversification.

In times of financial crisis, the correlation between event-driven strategies and market activity increases to uncomfortable levels. During the stock market crash in October 1987, merger arbitrage positions fell in step with the general market, providing little protection in the short run against the dramatic market decline. As time passed, investors recognized that companies continued to meet contractual obligations, ultimately completing all merger deals previously announced. The return of confidence improved merger arbitrage results, providing handsome returns relative to the market.

Results of two prominent merger arbitrage firms, which later formed the base for Yale's absolute return portfolio, illustrate the importance of evaluating performance over reasonable time horizons. Pursuing the conservative approach of investing only in announced deals, the two firms reported combined results of -17.9 percent for the fourth quarter of 1987, somewhat ahead of the S&P 500 return of -22.5 percent but well behind expectations for event-driven strategies. Even though no merger deals "broke," the market turmoil caused investors to demand higher compensation for merger arbitrage risk, resulting in a dramatic widening of spreads. In the first quarter of 1988 the arbitrage managers rebounded, posting results of 16.3 percent, far ahead of the S&P 500 returns of 5.7 percent. Viewed in isolation, the last quarter of 1987 provided disappointing double digit losses coincident with the stock market crash, failing to protect the portfolio during the period of crisis. Viewed as a package, the fourth quarter of 1987 with the worst results ever for both firms and the first quarter of 1988 with the best results ever for both firms, essentially preserved assets and provided meaningful diversification relative to the equity market's losses.

Not all periods of financial trauma end as happily as the aftermath of the crash of October 1987. In August 2007, an extraordinary credit crisis called into question the viability of an estimated $400 billion of merger-related financing. As a result, prospective returns on the First Data and TXU merger arbitrage deals skyrocketed from low double digit levels in June 2007 to more than 70 percent in mid-August 2007. Both First Data and TXU closed, providing handsome returns to intrepid investors who made late summer bets on the deals. In contrast to the 1987 experience, however, a number of 2007 vintage deals failed to close. The link, however unusual, between markets and merger deals lessens the diversifying power of merger arbitrage. That said, even though diversifying financial assets, including absolute return strategies, may show high correlation to marketable securities for short time periods, over reasonable investment horizons assets driven by fundamentally different factors produce fundamentally different patterns of returns.

Because event-driven investors strive to hit singles and doubles, creating a broadly diversified portfolio makes sense. In an environment without huge potential winners to offset inevitable costly mistakes, careful investors limit the costs that any one position might impose on the portfolio.

Event-driven portfolios benefit from engaging managers with a broad set of investment tools. Hiring a specialist focused only on one aspect of the business, say merger arbitrage, forces investors to ride a return rollercoaster. When opportunities abound, investors reap attractive returns from the niche strategy. If high returns attract capital to the activity, or if the supply of investment opportunities wanes, specialized investors continue to commit funds to their sole area of expertise, ultimately reaping poor returns from funds invested at inopportune times.

In contrast, if a manager develops expertise in more than one event-driven strategy, when returns appear sparse in one segment funds flow naturally to more attractive segments. The ability to target areas of relative opportunity dampens the inevitable fluctuations experienced by focused funds and creates the possibility of structuring higher return, lower risk portfolios.

Value-Driven Investing

Value-driven absolute return strategies rest on the manager's ability to identify undervalued and overvalued securities, establish positions, and reduce market exposure through hedging activity. If an investor purchases a portfolio of attractively priced stocks and sells short an equivalent amount of expensively priced stocks, the offsetting long and short positions eliminate systematic exposure to the equity market. Results depend entirely on stock-picking ability, with the long/short investor enjoying the opportunity to add value with both long ideas and short ideas. Skillful value-driven managers win on both sides of the portfolio.

While value-driven and event-driven strategies share a lack of correlation with traditional marketable securities, value-driven portfolios require a longer time horizon than do event-driven portfolios. Expected holding periods for merger arbitrage and distressed securities correspond to the anticipated date of corporate combination or bankruptcy resolution, implying a reasonably short duration for event-driven strategies. In contrast, value-driven positions lack the clear triggers present in event-driven investing. To the consternation of fund managers, undervalued stocks frequently decline, while overvalued positions often rise, leading to poor near-term performance relative to expectations. Even without adverse price moves in the short run, mispricings identified by long/short investors may take years to resolve.

Value-driven managers share much in common with active managers of traditional marketable securities. On the long side, concentrated portfolios of thoroughly researched securities provide the underpinnings for investment success. On the short side, the same bottom-up techniques of fundamental analysis used to evaluate long positions provide the basis for identifying overvalued securities. Adding the flexibility to exploit overvalued positions—through short sales—doubles the opportunity for a manager to add value. While short selling shares a common foundation with long investing, a successful short portfolio represents more than a richly priced inverse of a long portfolio.

Short Selling Challenges

Management of the short side of the portfolio poses several challenges peculiar to selling securities short. First, investors frequently underestimate the resilience of corporate management. Even when the facts and figures indicate that a company deserves classification as one of the "living dead," managers frequently find a way to escape the seemingly inevitable consequences of their circumstances. Second, the portfolio management implications of adverse price movements require greater diversification of short positions. If a stock moves against a short seller by increasing in price, the position increases in size. To take advantage of the now more attractively priced short opportunity the investor faces the uncomfortable prospect of further increasing the position. Starting with a modest allocation to a particular short idea allows an increase in position size without creating an uncomfortable concentration in a single stock. Contrast the dynamics of a losing short position with the behavior of a losing long position. As the long's price declines it becomes a smaller portion of the portfolio, reducing its impact on returns and facilitating new purchases at the newly discounted, relatively more attractive price. The simple math of price behavior argues for running reasonably diversified portfolios of short positions. Short sellers face challenges from success, as well as from failure. When the stock price of a fundamentally troubled company crashes, the short seller benefits, but the size of the short position declines dramatically, requiring identification of attractive replacement candidates. While long managers often run with successful investments for years, short managers hope to operate on a treadmill, with frequent turnover of holdings caused by the exit of winning positions from the portfolio. The price dynamics of short selling cause successful short managers to follow and hold a large number of securities.

Aside from a peculiar set of investment challenges, short sellers face some unusual technical problems in managing portfolio positions. To execute trades, short sellers borrow securities to deliver to the buyer on the other side of the transaction. (Buyers purchasing shares, whether from a short seller or a natural seller, expect to receive securities on the trade's settlement date.) As long as short sellers maintain the borrow, the position remains intact. If the short seller loses the borrow because the security lender recalls the security, the short seller must replace the borrow or lose the position. When the market for borrowing a particular security becomes tight, short sellers face a short squeeze. Security borrowers tend to have most trouble with small, less liquid companies, exactly the type of security likely to present interesting short opportunities.

The unusual set of problems confronting short sellers places an effective limit on portfolio size, forcing managers to constrain the level of assets under management. A reasonable portfolio size constitutes a necessary precondition for the potential to add value, as excessive levels of assets amount to a nearly insurmountable barrier to success. Even though the aggressive assumption that value-driven managers might outperform the market by as much as several percentage points each on the long and short sides seems to fly in the face of traditional active manager experience, limits on portfolio size provide hope for significant outperformance by long/short managers.

Return Expectations

Hedge fund managers who attempt to produce truly independent returns generally articulate reasonably modest goals. Consider a fund manager with a portfolio consisting of equal measures of long positions and short positions. From a market perspective, the longs offset the shorts. In a rising market, losses from the shorts offset gains from the longs. In a falling market, losses from the longs offset gains from the shorts. Balanced long/short investing takes the market out of the equation.

Security selection represents the primary source of return for disciplined long/short investors. To the extent that managers identify undervalued long positions and overvalued short positions, the portfolio stands to benefit from twice the security selection power available to long-only managers.

A secondary source of returns for long/short managers comes from the rebate earned from establishing short positions. Short sales generate cash proceeds that earn close to a money-market rate of interest. While the short rebate adds to the return of the long/short investor, a short rebate proves insufficient in and of itself to justify pursuing a long/short investment strategy. If an investor wishes to earn a money-market return, buying a money-market fund provides a more direct, less costly, and less risky route to generating cash returns.

Suppose long/short fund managers exhibit security selection skill consistent with top-quartile, long-only domestic equity managers. For the ten years ending December 31, 2006, one widely used universe of active managers showed top quartile returns of 2.6 percent per annum above the market.* If a long/short manager produces top quartile results on each of the long and short sides of the portfolio, security selection generates a return of 5.2 percent. The expected magnitude of

*Russell/Mellon Analytical Services produces the manager data used in this section. The Russell 3000 provides the passive benchmark employed to measure relative performance.

gains available from astute security selection falls far short of double digits.

Adding a short-term interest rate (reflecting the short rebate) to the value added from security selection produces the gross return for long/short investing. Over the ten years ending December 31, 2006, short-term interest rates averaged 3.7 percent per annum. Combining the top-quartile security selection return of 5.2 percent with the money-market return yields a total return of 8.9 percent, before fees.

Fees create a substantial burden for hedge fund investors. A management fee of one percent and a profits interest of 20 percent combine to subtract 2.6 percent from the gross return, leaving a net return of 6.3 percent for the investor.* Even with substantial active management success (as defined by two top-quartile results), net returns to long/short hedge fund investors show only a modest increment over money-market rates.

In cases where long/short managers exhibit mediocre stock picking skill, results disappoint. Consider the results of the median equity manager. For the ten years ending December 31, 2006, the median active domestic equity manager produced gross returns of 1.1 percent per annum above the market return. Doubling the median active management return produces a 2.2 percent return for security selection. Incorporating the cash return of 3.7 percent generates a gross return of 5.9 percent. The fee burden shaves the net return to 3.9 percent, a result disturbingly close to the 3.7 percent return of simply holding cash!

Finally, contemplate the poor position of an underperforming manager. Over the ten years ending December 31, 2006, third-quartile managers underperformed the market by 0.1 percent before fees. With an active management deficit, long/short investors earned 3.5 percent, which falls short of the return for holding cash. Fees take the gross return to a 2.0 percent net result, bringing the misery of below-cash returns to investors suffering the consequences of poor active management.

Even though average and below-average investment results sting investors, the investment manager makes out nicely in all cases. Regardless of performance, the manager collects a one percent fee, representing more-or-less standard compensation for traditional long-only money management. Adding the profits interest allows the skillful top-quartile manager to earn 2.6 percent, a hefty load on a sin-

---

*Begin with a gross return of 8.9 percent. Subtract the 1.0 percent management fee, leaving a 7.9 percent return. Take a 20 percent profits interest (0.2 x 7.9 = 1.6) from the remaining return, producing a 6.3 percent net result.

gle-digit return. Total fees for median stock pickers amount to 2.0 percent. Even in instances where net returns to investors fail to reach the returns available on cash, the manager profits handsomely. Fees for third-quartile performers total 1.5 percent, adding the insult of excessive fees to the injury of poor performance.

The example of balanced long/short equity management provides a powerful illustration of the central role that active management plays in absolute return investing. In the absence of superior active results, investors face certain disappointment. Long/short equity managers must consistently produce better than top-quartile returns to justify the fee structure accepted by hedge fund investors. Investors unable to identify the best of the best should pursue passive investment strategies.

Yale's absolute return portfolio provides an example of the potential of the asset class and conforms to the expectations generated by considering the fundamental investment attributes of absolute return strategies. Established as a separate asset class in 1990, the pioneering portfolio produced 13.2 percent per annum returns for the seventeen years ending June 30, 2007. With a remarkably low risk level of 5.7 percent standard deviation of returns, the risk/reward relationship indicates that managers exploited some rewarding market anomalies.* The absolute return portfolio's diversifying power exceeded expectations, showing essentially no correlation to domestic equities (0.02 vs. the Wilshire 5000 Index) and domestic fixed income (0.02 vs. the Lehman Brothers Government Corporate Index).

Survivorship Bias and Backfill Bias

Like other alternative assets, absolute return investments lack an investable benchmark, forcing investors to look elsewhere for defining characteristics of the asset class. Because of absolute return's limited institutional history, understanding its quantitative attributes proves more difficult than understanding those of real estate, leveraged buyouts, and venture capital. Students of more longstanding alternative investment approaches enjoy the benefit of more than three decades of data on active manager results that describe the experience of institu-

---

*The Sharpe ratio, a measure of excess return generated per unit of risk, for Yale's absolute return portfolio amounted to 1.8 over its seventeen-year life. In contrast, passive investments in domestic equities and fixed income posted Sharpe ratios of 0.9 and 0.7, respectively, over equivalent periods.

tional investors and provide intriguing clues about the character of fund performance. The paucity of data regarding absolute return strategies requires investors to seek alternative methods for estimating asset class attributes.

Survivorship bias and backfill bias present a serious problem for investors in marketable securities. Liquidity facilitates the hiring and firing of stock and bond managers, leading to churning in the population of active managers. Poor performers leave (survivorship bias) and strong firms enter (backfill bias), constantly altering the character of the standards implicit in the collection of returns used for assessing active managers.

Manager churn presents less of a problem for investors in illiquid assets. Managers of private assets taint the data pool with considerably less frequency than their marketable security counterparts. Institutions tend to select real estate, venture capital, and leveraged buyout funds from a reasonably well-defined list of acceptable alternatives, leading to a fairly coherent definition of any given year's institutional cohort. The partnership vehicles through which investors conduct most private investing preclude easy departure from the business. Private investing results—good, bad, or indifferent—play out over the term of the partnership regardless of the degree of confidence investors express in the fund managers.

Absolute return suffers from particularly acute forms of survivorship bias and backfill bias, related to the combination of fairly high liquidity and relative immaturity. As large numbers of new (and not-so-new) entrants fail, the firms and their mediocre records disappear. Immaturity suggests a substantial amount of flux, as managers posting attractive risk-adjusted returns enter the realm of institutional acceptability, adding sometimes eye-popping records to the store of absolute return information. Liquidity allows easy entry and exit, creating instability beneath the surface of the pool used to evaluate manager returns.

Statistics on past performance of hedge funds fail to provide much insight into the character of this relatively new segment of the investment world. Survivorship bias presents a pervasive problem for gatherers of historical return data. The fact that poorly performing firms fail at higher rates than well-performing firms causes data on manager returns to overstate past results, since compilations of data at any point in time from the current group of managers inevitably lack complete performance numbers from firms that failed in the past. In the well-established, comprehensively documented world of traditional marketable securities, survivorship bias presents a significant, albeit quantifiable problem. In the less-well-established, less comprehensively documented arena of hedge fund investing, survivorship bias creates a much more substantial informational challenge.

Even when database managers attempt to include results from failed firms, the history of returns often lacks completeness. Because most compilers of data rely on self-reporting of results by hedge funds, the integrity of the history depends on the fidelity of the hedge funds. As struggling hedge funds fight to stay in business, reporting of results to third-party database providers takes a back burner to the day-to-day challenges of crisis management.

Consider the record of Long-Term Capital Management (LTCM), the infamous hedge fund that nearly brought down the world's financial system. According to the *New York Times*, the database of Tremont Capital Management, a leading purveyor of hedge fund data, contains LTCM's performance only through October 1997, nearly a year prior to the firm's collapse.

Inception-to-date-of-reporting-cessation performance (March 1994 through October 1997) for LTCM stood at 32.4 percent per year net to investors, representing an impressive return on a large amount of capital. Obviously, Long-Term Capital's early record inflated the hedge fund industry's aggregate results. From the point in October 1997 when Long-Term Capital stopped reporting results to the point of the firm's October 1998 demise, returns (if they can be called returns) amounted to -91.8 percent. The staggering loss appears nowhere in Tremont's treasure trove of data.

The yawning chasm between Tremont's reported 32.4 percent per annum and LTCM's actual -27.0 percent per annum produces a staggering gap between perception and reality. The statistical omission of the implosion of LTCM inflates history in a manner that fundamentally misleads investors regarding the true character of hedge fund investing.

Statistical descriptions of hedge fund returns frequently suffer not only from survivorship bias, but also from backfill bias. As hedge funds became popular in the 1990s, only those funds with successful track records rose above the fray, attracting attention from market observers and money from investors. Funds with mediocre records languished in obscurity. Funds with strong returns garnered assets and acclaim, entering the consultants' manager universes and generating a substantial positive spin on the reported returns. In many instances, the keepers of the numbers added the past results of newly found strong performers to the ranks of the reporting managers, providing an unrepresentative boost to past performance data. Backfill bias causes data on hedge fund performance to overstate the realities of the hedge fund marketplace.

Academic studies that analyze the impact of survivorship bias and backfill bias come to some stunning conclusions. In a study of 3,500 hedge funds over more than ten years, Roger Ibbotson of the Yale School of Management concluded that survivorship bias added 2.9 percent annually to returns and backfill bias added an additional 4.6 percent annually to returns.[2] In aggregate, data-gathering errors inflated reported returns by fully 7.5 percent per annum, an enormous increment in a world where the difference between success and failure often depends on a few tenths of a percentage point. Burton Malkiel of Princeton University, in examining a well-known database, observed that of 331 hedge funds that reported results in 1996, more than 75 percent disappeared by 2004.[3] As expected, the returns of the live funds exceeded the returns of the dead funds. Perhaps not so expected was the 7.4 percent annual return differential between the two groups of funds. For the eight-year period, Malkiel estimates survivorship bias inflated returns by an average of 4.4 percent per annum and backfill bias boosted results by an average of 7.3 percent per annum. Ibbotson and Malkiel's studies call into question the usefulness of hedge fund databases. Survivorship bias and backfill bias matter.

Hedge Funds with Market-Related Risk

Consider two broad categories of hedge funds—those that avoid market risk and those that accept market risk. In cases where funds steer clear of market risk, investors without skill deserve to earn only money-market levels of return. The argument that supports a cash-like return for investors who do not accept market risk depends on the line of reasoning underpinning the analysis of long/short manager returns: those hedge fund strategies that do not expose assets to systematic market risk depend solely on strong active results to achieve gross results in excess of cash returns.

Many hedge fund strategies expose assets to various types of systematic risk. In fact, Goldman Sachs and Merrill Lynch each created and marketed synthetic hedge funds to mimic the systematic risk components of the hedge fund world. Merrill Lynch's Factor Index, which employs the S&P 500, Russell 2000, MSCI Emerging Markets, U.S. Dollar Index, and One-Month LIBOR, weights each of the components to produce returns similar to those of the Hedge Fund Research Weighted Composite Index (HFRI). Merrill Lynch touts the strong relationship between the Factor Index and HFRI, noting a 95 percent correlation between June 2003 and June 2006. In marketing materials, the investment bank suggests that the Factor Index produces hedge fund exposure "in a less expensive, more transparent and more liquid manner."[4]

The notion of a passive hedge fund investment turns logic on its head. Hedge funds rest on the premise of hedging, or offsetting, market exposure. The idea that hedge fund returns could be explained and replicated by a collection of passive market indices suggests that managers are not doing their job and that investors are being sold a bill of goods. If investors really want to vary exposure to Merrill Lynch's Factor Index components, they should simply alter their allocations to the S&P 500, Russell 2000, et al. The oxymoron of passive hedge fund exposure belongs in no serious investor's portfolio.

Perhaps the most blatant example of hedge fund exposure to market forces lies in the long-only manager that simply establishes a private partnership, calls it a hedge fund, and charges a 20 percent profits interest. In such situations, the manager receives 20 percent of the market's return, an egregiously high fee for a factor over which the manager exerts no control. Fair fee structures reward managers for adding value by manipulating variables under the managers' control. In the case of a fully invested, long-only equity fund, a manager might be reasonably rewarded with 20 percent of the incremental return over an appropriate market benchmark, such as the S&P 500 for a large-capitalization domestic equity manager or EAFE for a foreign-stock specialist. In situations where managers receive a portion of gains over and above a fair benchmark, the managers receive a reward for adding value. Unfortunately, hedge fund structures almost universally pay managers a share of the profits after returning capital, equivalent to no hurdle at all. Without a market-sensitive hurdle rate, managers receive a percentage of the gains generated by market exposure. The substantial toll imposed by typical hedge fund fee structures causes the overwhelming number of hedge funds to fail to serve investor interests.

Evaluating the returns of market-sensitive hedge funds poses nearly insurmountable problems, challenging to even the most sophisticated of investors. Separating the impact of the wind at the back (or the wind in the face) contributed by market forces from the influence of the skill (or lack thereof) exhibited in security selection proves incredibly difficult, particularly in instances where the manager invests in a broad range of markets and frequently adjusts market exposure. Regardless of the insight garnered by investors investigating market-sensitive hedge funds, the investment manager with an industry-standard deal structure receives a share of the returns generated by market action, representing unreasonable compensation for gains over which the manager exercises no control.

Absolute Return and Inflation

Since short duration characterizes absolute return investments, well-structured absolute return portfolios exhibit high sensitivity to the short-term cost of money. In event-driven merger arbitrage and distressed security transactions, investors generally expect resolution within months, with longer term deals extending to no more than a year or two. Since event-driven investors factor the cost of funds into the investment equation, as investors enter new deals the calculations reflect the then-current cost of funds. Similarly, the short rebate earned by the value-driven long/short investor represents a short-term cost of money. Just as money market rates tend to track inflation rates, so does the short-duration, cost-of-funds-sensitive absolute return portfolio.

Alignment of Interests

The profits interest typically paid by investors in hedge fund structures creates an option for managers that threatens investor interests. In the event of hedge fund gains, the manager shares in a substantial portion of profits. In the event of hedge fund losses, the investor bears the burden alone. The asymmetry of the profits-interest structure clearly favors the fund manager.

Significant co-investment on the part of the manager works to reduce, if not eliminate, the dysfunction of the incentive-compensation option. In the case where the hedge fund experiences good performance, the manager reaps rewards both from the co-investment and from the profits interest. In the case where the fund loses money, the manager's co-investment causes a sharing of the investor's pain. A meaningful side-by-side commitment of investment manager capital substantially reduces the misalignment of manager and investor interests.

Market Characteristics

At December 31, 2006, the hedge fund industry contained an estimated 12,500 firms, controlling more than $1.5 trillion in equity capital.[5] Moreover, because many hedge funds employ significant leverage, their actual buying power exceeds their equity capital. Of the $1.5 trillion in capital, approximately $880 billion in assets pursue strategies that might be classified as absolute return.

Summary

Absolute return strategies require active management, since without accepting market risk or identifying security mispricings investors expect to earn only the risk-free rate. Since the very definition of absolute return rests on lack of correlation with traditional marketable securities, exploitation of individual security valuation anomalies forms the basis of the asset class. Event-driven managers generate returns by conducting thorough research in complex corners of the investment opportunity set, an area often avoided by mainstream analysts. Value-driven managers attempt to add value by identifying undervalued and overvalued securities, creating portfolios with roughly offsetting long and short market exposures. Well-managed absolute return portfolios provide a high return, low risk source of diversification.

Absolute return investing appeals to investors who believe that providing funds to superior managers operating with few constraints will lead to impressive investment results regardless of the upswings and downswings of traditional marketable securities. Indeed, the experience of a number of sophisticated institutional investors indicates that well-structured absolute return portfolios produce high, uncorrelated returns with low risk, adding an extremely valuable diversifying stream of returns to investor portfolios. Of course, successful absolute return investors devote an extraordinary amount of resources to identifying, engaging, and managing high quaility managers.

Purveyors of hedge fund statistics paint a rosy picture wildly at odds with reality. Academic studies show that survivorship bias and backfill bias combine to inflate reported returns by anywhere from high single digits to low double digits. A clear view of hedge fund returns would discourage many thoughtful investors from entering the hedge fund arena.

On top of the enormous difficulties in identifying a group of genuinely skilled investment managers and overcoming the obstacle of extremely rich fee arrangements, investors confront a fundamental misalignment of interests created by the option-like payoff embedded in most hedge fund fee arrangements. Investors find coincidence of interests only in those situations where the absolute return manager invests substantial personal assets side-by-side with investor monies.

Casual approaches to fund selection lead to almost certain disappointment. Absolute return investing belongs in the domain of sophisticated investors who commit significant resources to the manager evaluation process. While the promise of hedge funds proves attractive to many market participants, those investors who fail to identify truly superior active managers face a dismal reality. In the absence of superior security selection, investment strategies that avoid market exposure deliver money-market-like expected returns. The hefty fee arrangements typical of absolute return funds erode the already low cash-like return to a truly unacceptable level, especially after adjusting for risk. Absolute return investors find generating risk-adjusted excess returns a daunting task.

REAL ASSETS

Real assets consist of ownership interests in investment vehicles that exhibit a high correlation to inflation. Many investors, including educational endowments, seek protection against inflation in order to offset inflation-sensitive liabilities. Real assets include Treasury Inflation-Protected Securities, real estate, timber, and oil and gas.

The strength of inflation protection varies with the type of real asset. Treasury Inflation-Protected Securities (TIPS, also known as Treasury Inflation-Indexed Securities) track inflation precisely, at least as the Consumer Price Index measures inflation. Oil and gas reserves change in value in direct response to changes in energy prices, which represent a substantial component of broad inflation gauges. Timber products bear a similar relationship to price indices, although timber plays a far less important role than does energy in overall price inflation. Real estate holdings correlate with inflation less directly than primary inputs like energy and timber, although when property markets operate in equilibrium a strong link exists between real estate and inflation.

Aside from protecting portfolios against inflation, real assets produce high levels of current cash flow and (in most cases) attractive expected total returns. Unlike commodity indices, which give investors simple price exposure, well-chosen and well-structured real assets investments provide price exposure plus an intrinsic rate of return. For example, oil and gas reserve purchases in the past two decades generated low double-digit rates of return above and beyond the return from holding period increases in energy prices. Price exposure plus an intrinsic rate of return trumps price exposure alone.

In the future, the population of real assets alternatives might expand beyond the conservative investments of TIPS and the high-return alternatives of real estate, oil and gas, and timber. Pure commodity price exposure holds little interest to sensible investors, as long-term returns approximately equal inflation rates. TIPS provide inflation-like returns with substantially less risk than commodity investments. Oil and gas reserve purchases and timber investments provide investors with commodity price exposure and an intrinsic rate of return, thereby dominating price exposure alone. If markets provide other commodity-based opportunities to gain price exposure and to earn an intrinsic rate of return, then those assets could join the rank of sensible real assets alternatives.

Real assets play an important role in portfolios, particularly for investors who seek to satisfy inflation-sensitive liabilities. The diversifying power derived from correlation with inflation and the intrinsic rate of return generated above simple price exposure argues for a significant allocation to real assets.

Inflation-Linked Bonds

In January 1997, the U.S. Treasury began issuing TIPS, creating an important new tool for U.S.-dollar-based investors. TIPS protect investors from increases in the general level of prices by adjusting the principal amount of the security for inflation. Since the fixed coupon rate on TIPS applies to the inflation-adjusted principal of the bonds, both interest and principal payments reflect changes in inflation rates.

The combination of extraordinary credit quality and precise protection against inflation causes TIPS to produce modest real returns. During the period that Lehman Brothers tracked TIPS' real yields, inflation adjusted returns ranged from 1.3 percent to 2.5 percent, averaging 1.9 percent.* Investors pay a high price in the form of low expected returns from the double-barreled conservatism of TIPS.

Just as standard U.S. Treasury bonds provide a riskless instrument for investors wishing to generate certain nominal returns, TIPS provide a riskless instrument for investors wishing to generate certain real returns. Based on commonality of issuer, default-free status, and structural similarities in payment of interest and principal, many market observers group standard U.S. Treasury bonds with TIPS. In fact, when the U.S. Treasury began issuing TIPS, Lehman Brothers, architect of the most widely used debt market indices, placed TIPS in a cohort that included regular-issue Treasury bonds.

The error of grouping regular Treasuries with TIPS lies in the fundamentally different response of the two types of bonds to unantici-

*Data cover the period from May 2004 to December 2006.

pated changes in the price level. Unanticipated inflation harms regular bonds by reducing the purchasing power of the fixed stream of payments. In contrast, unanticipated inflation benefits TIPS in the form of higher returns as payments adjust for increases in the price level. Unexpected deflation helps regular bonds by increasing the purchasing power of the fixed stream of payments. In contrast, unexpected deflation hurts TIPS by reducing the stream of periodic interest payments, even though deflation fails to reduce the final principal payment. TIPS, far from belonging with standard bonds, belong in the real assets category.

A comparison of a traditional U.S. Treasury note and a TIPS security illustrates critical differences in the two instruments. Consider the U.S. Treasury 4.25 percent Note due January 15, 2011 and the U.S. Treasury Inflation-Indexed Security 3.5 percent Note due January 15, 2011. At year-end 2006, the straight bond and the inflation-protected bond boasted yields to maturity of 4.7 percent and 2.4 percent, respectively. Because the bonds share identical credit characteristics and identical maturity dates, the difference in yields stems solely from inflation expectations. The 2.3 percent difference between the straight bond yield and the inflation-protected bond yield represents the market's best estimate of inflation over the bonds' term. If inflation exceeds 2.3 percent, the TIPS holder wins. If inflation falls short of 2.3 percent, the straight bond owner wins.

At maturity, TIPS investors receive a possible bonus, as the bonds pay the greater of the inflation-adjusted principal or the original face value. In a deflationary world, investors benefit from the payment of the nondiscounted par amount of the bonds. In an environment of general price inflation, the right to receive par for the TIPS at maturity carries the greatest value at the time of issuance. In concert with price increases, the indexed value of the bond's principal increases, creating a surplus over the par value of the bond. Were deflationary conditions to develop, the accumulated surplus would deplete before the par protection kicked in. Investors wishing to enjoy the maximum protection of the par put constantly roll holdings of TIPS into the most recently issued securities.

Some foreign governments issue inflation-protected securities. As with standard bond issues, U.S.-domiciled investors approach non-U.S. Treasury debt with caution. The United Kingdom, Canada, Sweden, France, Italy, Germany, Greece, Japan, Australia, and New Zealand boast substantial programs of inflation-indexed bond issuance. Because foreign government bonds generally make payments in the currency of the realm, U.S. investors face foreign exchange risk.

The combination of divergent future domestic and foreign inflation rates and unknown future foreign exchange translations serve to render non-U.S. government inflation-indexed bonds useless as a hedge against U.S. inflation.

U.S. corporate issuance of inflation-protected securities poses a different set of issues. As is the case with straight corporate debt, inflation-indexed corporate securities generally suffer from credit risk, illiquidity, and unattractive call provisions. In addition, investors might consider the implications of holding corporate inflation-protected securities in a high-inflation environment. Just when the protection against price increases proves most valuable, the ability of a corporation to make good on its promises to pay might prove least likely.

TIPS and Inflation

TIPS produce the perfect hedge against inflation, because bond-payment mathematics dictate direct correspondence between returns and changes in inflation rates. The combination of the default-free character of full-faith-and-credit obligations of the U.S. government and the mathematically certain protection against inflation provide investors with a powerful portfolio tool.

Alignment of Interests

TIPS share with standard-issue Treasury offerings a balance in alignment of interests between creditor and debtor. Unlike relationships between private borrowers and lenders, in which the borrower seeks gains at the lender's expense, the government attempts to fashion a fair deal for parties on both sides of the borrowing transaction.

In promoting TIPS, the Department of the Treasury highlights advantages to both the creditor and the debtor. From the creditor's perspective, TIPS "provide a distinctive contribution to any diversified portfolio." From the debtor's perspective, TIPS "allow Treasury to broaden its investor base and diversify its funding risks."[6] The even-handed approach to debtor and creditor separates the U.S. government from profit-seeking private-sector borrowers.

Market Characteristics

At December 31, 2006, outstanding issues of TIPS amounted to only $369 billion. First issued by the U.S. Treasury in January 1997, the program provides a valuable, diversifying alternative for investors. At year-end 2006, TIPS promised a real (after-inflation) yield of 2.4 percent with an average maturity of 9.6 years and a duration of 6.4 years.

Summary

Although TIPS amount to only around 17 percent of the value of standard Treasury bonds, inflation-sensitive TIPS constitute a compelling addition to the tool set available to investors. Bolstered by the default-free, full-faith-and-credit backing of the U.S. government, TIPS serve as a benchmark against which to measure other inflation-sensitive investments.

Real Estate

Investments in real estate provide investors with exposure to the benefits and risks of owning office properties, apartment complexes, industrial warehouses, and retail establishments. High quality real estate holdings produce significant levels of current cash flow generated by long-term, in-place lease arrangements with creditworthy tenants. Properties that produce sustained levels of high cash flow exhibit stable valuations, as a substantial portion of asset value stems from relatively predictable cash flows. In contrast, properties that produce uncertain cash flows, as in the case where leases approach expiration and owners face re-leasing risk, show near-term variability in residual value. In the extreme case of properties that produce no cash flow, real estate takes on a speculative aura as valuation depends entirely on prospective leasing activity.

Real estate assets combine characteristics of fixed income and equity. Fixed income attributes stem from the contractual obligation of tenants to make regular payments as specified in the lease contract between tenant and landlord. Properties encumbered by long-term lease obligations exhibit predominantly bond-like qualities. Equity attributes stem from the residual value associated with leases expected to be executed for currently vacant space or for anticipated future vacancies. Properties without tenants or with tenants on short leases exhibit predominantly equity-like qualities.

Archetypal real estate investments consist of well-located, well-leased, high quality properties that allow investors to anticipate regular receipt of rental income from leased space and to expect income within a reasonable time frame from vacant space. Real estate with a significant operating component fails to meet the set of core investment criteria, as the operational attributes largely determine the investment outcome, creating an equity-like investment play. Core investments do not include raw land, ground-up development activity and hotel operations, primarily because these investments rely substantially on operating expertise to produce cash flows.

Risk and Return Characteristics

Real estate returns and risks fall between those of bonds and equities. With bond-like rental streams and equity-like residual values, investors expect real estate to produce results somewhere between the results of the bond market and the stock market. Ibbotson Associates data for the past eighty years indicate that stocks returned 10.4 percent annually and government bonds 5.4 percent annually. Splitting the difference suggests that real estate investors might realistically expect returns in the neighborhood of 2.5 percent per annum above bonds.

Nearly two decades of data confirm the notion that real estate returns fall between stocks and bonds. Returns covering 1987 to 2006 for a broad-based index of real estate holdings stand at 8.4 percent per annum, poised between the 11.8 percent per annum return for the S&P 500 and the 6.5 percent per annum return for intermediate-term U.S. Treasury bonds.[7] Capital markets history confirms expectations regarding relative returns for real estate.

Valuation of real estate poses less of a challenge than does valuation of many other risky assets. Consider the fact that, with markets in equilibrium, replacement cost for existing assets constitutes an important determinant of market value. In fact, the real estate market provides a powerful example of the efficacy of Tobin's "q," the ratio between market value and replacement cost of an asset. If the market value of a particular real estate asset exceeds replacement cost, nearby real estate development of a similar product type makes economic sense. Clearly, under such circumstances, the income yield expressed as a percentage of cost of a newly constructed building would exceed the income yield on the more highly valued existing asset, creating incentives to build new, high-yielding buildings. Conversely, if replacement cost exceeds market value, real estate development makes no economic sense. In such a situation, the income yield on cost falls short of the income yield on less highly valued existing assets. Instead of building new buildings, rational market participants buy existing properties, thereby driving market values toward replacement cost.

Tobin's "q" proves particularly useful in the real estate market, because replacement cost constitutes a readily determinable, easily observable variable. While in the stock market Tobin's "q" produces insight into valuation of individual companies, broad market sectors, and even the entire equity market, the challenges of determining replacement cost of today's complex, far-flung corporate entities proves daunting. In contrast, assessing the cost of constructing a suburban retail mall or a downtown office building proves far more manageable. In fact, many knowledgeable investors assess an asset's cost of replication and then use discount to replacement cost as an important investment criterion when making real estate acquisitions.

Public versus Private Holdings

Real estate investments hold the unusual distinction of offering large numbers of investment vehicles in both publicly traded and privately held categories. The distinction between public and private positions in real estate lies in form, not substance. Both public and private holdings of real estate assets expose investors to the benefits and perils of property positions.

Many investors in real estate benefit from an unusual investment vehicle, the real estate investment trust, or REIT. A REIT, unlike a typical corporate entity, pays no income taxes as long as the REIT distributes at least 90 percent of its taxable income and generates at least 75 percent of that income from rents, mortgages, and sales of property.[8] REITs serve as a pass-through structure in which income passes through the security, without being taxed, to the security holders who take responsibility for the tax liability, if any. REITs exist in both publicly traded and privately held forms.

Even though both publicly traded and privately held real estate vehicles expose investors to real estate assets, public-market securities frequently trade at prices that deviate from fair value. Green Street Advisors, a highly regarded research firm that concentrates on publicly traded real estate securities, routinely examines discrepancies between market price and fair value. The results give short-term investors pause. At one point in 1990, by Green Street's estimate, real estate securities traded at more than a 36 percent discount to fair value. By 1993, the stock market reversed itself, valuing real-estate-related holdings at a 28 percent premium to fair value. The yin and yang continued. In late 1994, the discount reached 9 percent, while in 1997, stock market investors paid more than a 33 percent premium to fair value. In the late 1990s, a poor market for real estate securities (that coincided with a wonderful market for most other securities) brought valuations to a deficit of more than 20 percent, a level reached in early 2000. As the non-real-estate portion of the stock market entered bear territory, real estate securities took on bullish characteristics, leading to a greater-than-22-percent premium to fair value in early 2004. At year-end 2006, security prices stood at a not-too-hot and not-too-cold 2 percent premium over fair value.[9] The wide swings between price and fair value in the public securities arena produced low correlation between returns of publicly traded and privately held real estate assets.[10]

Discrepancies between price and fair value disturb careless short-term players, because any premium paid on purchases and any deficit incurred on sales loom large in damaging holding-period returns. For canny investors, deviations between price and fair value allow purchases at a discount and sales at a premium, buying low and selling high to enhance portfolio returns. Longer term investors face fewer issues regarding differences between price and fair value, because over longer investment horizons the short-term noise in the price/fair-value relationship matters less. Careful investors either exploit price/fair-value differences or employ dollar-cost averaging to enter and exit markets that deviate measurably from fair value.

Although exceptions exist, publicly traded real estate securities generally provide reasonably low-cost exposure to relatively high quaility pools of real estate assets. Discrepancies between market price and fair value create opportunities for investors to build portfolios using relatively attractively priced assets. When REITs fall from favor, research analysts explain why the publicly traded shares deserve a permanent discount to privately held assets, with justifications ranging from illiquidity, management ineptitude, and high overhead costs, to the inflexibility of REIT structures. When REITs ride high, the same analysts argue that public vehicles command a premium for good reasons, including liquidity, management expertise, economies of scale, and advantages of the REIT format. Regardless of the idea of the moment, sensible investors favor REITs when portfolios trade at a discount to private market value and avoid REITs when shares trade at a premium.

Active Management

Inefficiencies in the pricing and operation of real estate assets create opportunity for active management. Investors increase return and lower risk by exercising careful judgment in selecting assets and by using diligence in managing properties.

Real estate lends itself to active management because mispricings create opportunities for nimble investors to take advantage of market anomalies. The task of identifying underpriced and overpriced properties poses surmountable hurdles, since valuations depend largely on readily observed variables. Calculation of replacement cost for an asset provides important information on the value of a well-located property. Information on leases in place, combined with projections of future lease rates and an estimate of residual value, produce an easily analyzed stream of cash flows. Sales of comparable properties provide hard numbers reflecting the willingness of investors to pay for bricks and mortar or a stream of expected cash flows. Active management decisions for real estate rest on the fundamental characteristics of replacement cost, discounted cash flows, and sales of similar assets, providing clear reference points unavailable for most other asset types.

Sony Building Acquisition Douglas Emmett's 1993 acquisition of the Sony Building in Burbank, California illustrates some important valuation tools. Los Angeles ranked among the hardest hit markets in the real estate debacle of the early 1990s, with vacancy rates reaching a staggering 24 percent for Class A office space in the metropolitan market. As a result, prices for office buildings declined dramatically. In a signature transaction, Sam Zell, the famed "grave dancer," bought Two California Plaza for $100 million, approximately one quarter of what it cost to build a few years earlier.

Nearby Burbank, a distinctly different market with substantially stronger underlying fundamentals, experienced sympathetic price declines, suffering by association with Los Angeles. Amid the tumult, as part of a corporate rationalization program, Coca Cola decided to sell the Burbank property housing its former subsidiary, Sony Pictures. The sales price of $83 million compared favorably to the building's construction cost of more than $120 million, providing the purchaser a 30 percent discount to replacement cost.

Cash flow from lease payments further supported the acquisition. One hundred percent of the space was leased to Sony, at the time a credit rated single A by Standard & Poor's. If the investor received only those payments guaranteed by Sony, all invested capital would be repaid along with sufficient excess cash flow to generate annual returns of 12.3 percent. This low double digit return included no estimate of residual value for the building upon expiration of the lease. With reasonable assumptions regarding lease renewals and residual value, returns jumped to the 20 percent to 25 percent range. In an interest rate environment where comparable maturity U.S. Treasury Notes yielded about 6.5 percent, the relatively high quality Sony payment stream represented a handsome baseline return for a deal with substantial upside and little downside.

Comparable sales data tell less about the attractiveness of the Sony acquisition than about the timing. The lack of bids for the Sony Building and other properties in the area signaled a contrarian opportunity to buy deeply out-of-favor assets, not a lack of value. Fortified by substantial discounts to replacement cost and high levels of investment grade cash flow, investors move forward with confidence in the face of dismal market conditions. When the tone of the market improves to the point that real estate players pronounce that asset irreplacability justifies paying a meaningful premium to replacement cost and that a tight leasing environment presages transformation of low current cash yields into higher future cash flows, contrarian investors offer properties for sale.

The striking Sony building, with its handsome tenant finishes, promised a more-than-satisfactory baseline return with the protection of a purchase price substantially below replacement cost.* The limited downside of the Sony Building along with substantial potential upside created a positively skewed distribution of outcomes, providing extremely attractive investment characteristics.

In fact, the Sony Building's appealing acquisition characteristics translated into an equally appealing investment outcome. When Douglas Emmett converted the firm's pool of real estate assets into a REIT in October 2006, each of the assets received a third party appraisal to support the valuation and allocation of REIT shares. Based on the appraised value, the Sony building (now called Studio Plaza) gener-

---

*Peter Guber and Jon Peters, the former co-chairmen of Sony Pictures Entertainment, had lavishly appointed offices on the top two floors of the building. Rumored to have cost hundreds of dollars per square foot, the improvements were included as part of the purchase price.

ated a holding period return in excess of 20 percent per annum. Ultimately, Douglas Emmett's investors reaped rich rewards for the firm's contrarian instincts and real estate management expertise.

Manager Specialization Investors generally benefit from engaging specialists to manage a fund's commitment to real estate. Experts in a particular geography and a particular property type—office, retail, residential, industrial—enjoy a substantial edge over generalist managers, who suffer from spreading resources an inch deep and a mile wide. Specialization leads to greater understanding of the particular dynamics of different markets, allowing one manager to focus on the relatively static mass of central business district office buildings and another manager to focus on the ever-changing inventory of suburban office properties. Similarly, one manager might specialize in massive department store anchored malls and another might specialize in smaller infill community retail centers. By concentrating management resources on a fairly narrowly defined market segment, fund managers make better buys, better sales, and better day-to-day asset management decisions.

Investors choosing to select a group of valuation-driven specialist managers create more powerful portfolios, albeit at the price of a loss of diversification. By pursuing attractive investment opportunities, selected on a bottom-up basis, funds develop concentrations in the most out-of-favor asset types. For instance, prompted by relative valuations, investors may at times hold outsized positions in California retail properties or Southeastern suburban office buildings, creating a profile with dramatic deviations from the characteristics of any broad-based real estate index. Even though idiosyncratic portfolios tend to exhibit substantial tracking error relative to the market, a carefully chosen group of niche managers contains the potential to produce outstanding investment results.

Real Estate Prices and Inflation

The strong relationship between replacement cost and market value leads to one of real estate's most attractive investment attributes, a high correlation with inflation. Since the labor and materials used to construct buildings rise in cost along with inflation, the replacement cost of real estate tracks inflation closely. Yet even though replacement cost responds to changes in the general price level, the nature of an asset's lease structure influences the rate of response of changes in market value to inflationary pressures. For example, a property subject to long-term, fixed-rate leases shows little near-term correlation to inflation. Only as lease expiration nears will inflation influence asset valuation. Alternatively, properties with shorter-term leases exhibit much greater inflation sensitivity. Moreover, some leases explicitly allow landlords to pass through inflationary increases in expenses or, in the case of retail properties, contractually entitle landlords to receive a percentage of sales. Such inflation-responsive lease structures cause asset values to reflect inflationary moves.

The importance of replacement cost both in valuation analysis and in inflation sensitivity relies on markets reflecting reasonable equilibrium between supply and demand. In cases where supply of real estate space fails to match demand, prices respond to the disequilibrium, not to the expected relationship with replacement cost or with inflation. In the late 1980s, investor enthusiasm for owning commercial real estate and federal tax incentives for developing properties combined to create a vast oversupply of commercial office buildings. The excesses in the real estate market contributed to the savings and loan crisis, as many thrifts suffered from the burden of underperforming or non-performing real estate loans. High quality, albeit poorly leased, properties traded at steep discounts to replacement cost. Prices responded to the disconnect between supply and demand, failing to track inflation. Similarly, in the early 2000s, a post-Internet-bubble decline in demand for office space led to widespread vacancies and a decline in real estate prices, resulting in a disequilibrium that decoupled falling real estate prices from consistently positive levels of inflation. Unless markets operate in reasonable equilibrium, the relationship between real estate prices and inflation breaks down. Yet when markets exhibit equilibrium, sensitivity to changes in the general price level represents a particularly attractive characteristic of real estate.

Alignment of Interests

In the realm of publicly traded REITs, investors face the same set of questions about alignment of interests that apply to other publicly traded equities. Just as in the broader universe of marketable stocks, interests of shareholders and managements generally, but imperfectly, coincide.

In the world of private real estate vehicles, investors face a range of investment structures. On one end of the continuum, high quality managers receive budgeted fees that reflect reasonable costs of running an investment firm, receive profits interests only on returns in excess of the opportunity cost of capital, and invest substantial assets side-by-side with investors. On the other end of the continuum, low quality managers charge high fees on large pools of assets, extract profits interests on returns in excess of investor capital contributions and invest O.P.M., other people's money.

Market Characteristics

Real estate investors face significant investment opportunities in both public and private markets. At December 31, 2006, the National Association of Real Estate Investment Trusts tracked a universe of real estate securities that totaled $436 billion. The REIT population posted a dividend yield of 3.3 percent and traded at a 2.2 percent premium over fair value.

At December 31, 2006, the NCREIF National Property Index included unleveraged real estate assets valued at an aggregate of $247 billion. The privately held real estate cohort paid a dividend yield of 6.2 percent, which represented a premium 1.5 percent over the ten-year U.S. Treasury yield.

Summary

In terms of risk and return, real estate falls between higher risk equity and lower risk debt. The hybrid nature of the expected investment characteristics matches the hybrid nature of the fundamental traits of real estate investments. With its inflation-sensitive nature, real estate provides powerful diversification to investor portfolios.

Real estate investors enjoy the opportunity to choose between publicly traded and privately held investment vehicles. While sensible alternatives exist in both public and private forms, careful investors pay close attention to fee arrangements and look hard at manager quality.

Oil and Gas

Oil and gas investments provide claims on future streams of inflation-sensitive income, supplying protection against unanticipated inflation and playing an important role in portfolio diversification. In addition to furnishing attractive diversifying characteristics, oil and gas assets present opportunities for superior managers to add value.

Market participants gain exposure to energy assets either by acquiring futures contracts or by purchasing oil and gas reserves; whether through futures positions or reserve acquisitions, investors seek price-driven returns. In order to gain commodity exposure without betting exclusively on prices, savvy investors structure portfolios around value-added purchases of well-defined energy reserves operated by superior management teams.

Oil and gas reserve purchases boast a number of advantages over the simple price exposure provided by futures contracts. First, reserve acquisitions tend to produce high, equity-like expected returns. Over the past two decades, well-structured investments in low-risk producing reserves typically generated low double-digit unleveraged returns, without considering price movements. Second, superior active managers add value in the process of acquiring, developing, financing, operating, and liquidating assets. Expertise and discipline create more value in the complex physical world of natural resources than in the highly efficient financial world of commodities markets. Finally, long duration energy reserves provide a long-term hedge against sustained periods of high energy prices.

Public versus Private Holdings

Ironically, diversified portfolios of public securities produce less transparent and less effective exposure to energy prices than do focused private acquisitions of energy reserves. In the realm of publicly traded energy companies, investors face questions regarding the degree to which integrated oil companies consume oil and gas (as inputs to the refining process, for example) and the degree to which companies produce oil and gas (as outputs of the exploration process, for example). Even if investors successfully determine the net corporate exposure to energy prices, the question of company hedging policies remains. Broadly diversified, publicly traded companies provide uncertain exposure to energy prices, leading real assets investors to prefer pure private reserve acquisition plays.

Active Management

Purchases of oil and gas reserves by high quality active managers provide investors with the opportunity to gain exposure to energy prices and to earn a significant baseline rate of return. Merit Energy Company, founded in 1989 by Bill Gayden, a former colleague of Ross Perot, successfully delivered on the twin promises of handsome returns from disciplined underwriting and substantial portfolio diversification from energy price exposure.

Merit typically acquires low-risk oil and gas reserves using assumptions that produce a 12 percent to 14 percent return without assuming energy price appreciation or depreciation. In a remarkable coincidence between acquisition assumptions and subsequent reality, from 1990 to 2005, Merit produced net returns of 19.2 percent per annum, which consisted of 12.2 percent from acquisition economics, 2.1 percent from improved operations and development, and 4.9 percent from price appreciation.

Presumably, investors in energy price futures would have obtained only the roughly 5 percent per annum price appreciation. Investors in reserve purchase programs received double-digit returns above and beyond the price movement, dominating the results of the commodity futures investors.

Energy Prices and Inflation

Energy investments belong in the real assets portfolio because of their strong correlation with inflation. Energy constitutes roughly nine percent of the Consumer Price Index (CPI), creating a direct link to inflation. Unsurprisingly, an Ibbotson Associates study found a positive correlation between direct energy production investments and CPI, using data for the period from 1970 to 1998.[11] In contrast, Ibbotson found a negative correlation between direct energy investments and a variety of marketable securities, including domestic stocks, foreign stocks, Treasury bonds, and Treasury bills. Both statistics and common sense support the idea of energy investments as a hedge against inflation.

Alignment of Interests

The old saw—that sensible investors never back an energy partnership touted on Wall Street, because all the good deals come together in Houston—contains some truth. Poorly structured oil and gas partnerships abound. Unscrupulous operators gain advantage over naïve investors by exploiting the complexities of industry-specific concepts such as net profits interests, overriding royalty interests, working interests, net revenue interests, and operating interests. That said, by following sensible deal structuring principles, including a high level of co-investment by the deal's promoter, investors create the opportunity to enjoy the significant benefits of investments in producing oil and gas reserves.

Market Characteristics

Oil and gas investors confront a broad tableau, including marketable energy equities of $4.6 trillion, representing 10 percent of global equities as of December 31, 2006. Institutional private investments amounted to $28 billion on December 31, 2006, according to Cambridge Associates, of which $20 billion pursued energy reserve purchases.

Summary

Energy investments provide dramatic diversification to institutional portfolios, as energy prices show negative correlation to traditional securities over many time periods. Pure price exposure, as obtained through the purchase of energy futures contracts, comes at a high price in the form of low expected return. Sensible investors opt for reserve purchase programs that promise price exposure (along with the accompanying diversification) and returns in the low double-digit range. Perhaps more than in any other investment activity, investors must be wary of low quality operators with opaque, egregious deal structures.

Timber

Timberland offers strong return potential, steady cash flow, inflation protection, and portfolio diversification. Investment returns stem from several sources, the most important being the value of timber harvested and changes in the value of residual timber and land. Timber values, which relate to the biological growth of trees and changes in timber prices, can be influenced by sound silvicultural practices. The sale of conservation easements and land parcels for "higher and better use" (HBU) provide the potential to boost returns. Finally, incremental revenue can be generated through other activities, including leasing of land for the exploitation of mineral deposits, recreational pastimes, and alternative energy uses.

Historically, timber has performed well as an investment, although accurate data are difficult to obtain. The most frequently cited series, first created by Hancock Timber Resource Group, combines known timber prices with assumptions about forest growth and value to generate a timberland return series beginning in 1960.* Hancock/NCREIF estimates that U.S. timberland returned 12.7 percent per annum from 1960 through 2005, or roughly 8.1 percent per annum after inflation. Since 1987, the NCREIF Timberland Property Index produced a cash yield of approximately 6 percent per annum.

In addition to generating strong returns, timberland provides diversification relative to securities markets: the Hancock/NCREIF index exhibited a correlation of -0.17 with the S&P 500. In part, low correlation stems from the consistent return to timberland from biological growth. While the S&P 500 produced a calendar loss eleven times since 1960, the timberland index generated a loss in only one of those eleven years and losses on only three years overall. Like other real assets, timberland serves as a hedge against unanticipated inflation. Because timber is a basic production input for a number of end products, changes in timber prices correlate strongly with inflation.

Timberland Ownership

The U.S. Forest Service classifies approximately 22 percent of the United States as timberland, or land capable of producing industrial

---

*For the period from 1960 to 1986, Hancock estimates the index return based on known price data and assumptions about forest growth and characteristics. Index returns from 1987 onward are calculated by NCREIF based on the performance of actual timberland properties. The return series beginning in 1987 is officially called the NCREIF Timberland Property Index. Performance in early years depends on critical assumptions about forest characteristics. The more recent property-based index reflects the returns on a limited number of properties.

wood.* Federal, state, and local governments own nearly 30 percent of U.S. timberland, with a higher ownership percentage in the Pacific Northwest and a lower percentage in the South. Nonindustrial users hold approximately 80 percent of privately owned timberland, much of it not suitable for institutional investment. The Hancock Group estimates the investable universe is only 20 percent to 30 percent of nonindustrial private timberland, with the remainder consisting of small, low quality or poorly located tracts. Combining industrial timberland with investable nonindustrial private timberland gives a total U.S. investable timberland base of approximately $125 billion. By comparison, the value of investable real estate in the United States is approximately $3.5 trillion.†

In recent years, ownership of timberland in the United States shifted from forest products companies to institutional investors. At one time, companies viewed timberland ownership as essential, providing mills with a captive, dependable source of raw materials. Over time, the inefficiencies in ownership and management of forestry assets became apparent as trees were cut without regard to economic value to keep a steady supply of wood arriving at the mill. Several large companies that separated the mill operations and timber operations into independent entities saw dramatic bottom-line improvements in both segments.

Once companies viewed timberland assets as distinct from the core wood processing business, companies became less attached to holding massive wood inventories and more focused on the benefits of selling timberlands. First, timberland sales offered a means of raising capital to modernize mills, streamline operations, or pay down debt. Second, timberland sales offered the opportunity to boost stock prices through the realization of hidden value and by raising returns on capital. Finally, some companies divested U.S. holdings to move into lower cost, higher productivity timberlands in other regions of the world.

Over the past decade, approximately 33 million acres of timberland traded in the United States with annual sales averaging 2.6 percent of the investable timberland universe. Most timberland on the selling block ended up in the hands of newly created timberland

---

*One third of the United States is classified as forestland. Two thirds of forestland is classified as timberland.
†Estimated by PricewaterhouseCoopers and the Urban Land Institute in 2005. The $3.5 trillion figure excludes single family and owner-occupied residences, as well as corporate, nonprofit, and government real estate.

REITs or newly interested institutional investors. The new owners often did not own mill assets, allowing them to focus exclusively on maximizing the value of the timberlands. As a result, the new owners adopted more sophisticated financially driven silvicultural techniques, more extensive merchandising operations, and more aggressive monetization strategies for nontimber values.

Timber Pricing

As with any other product, the locus of supply and demand drives timber prices. Local, national, and global dynamics all influence the price a landowner receives for logs.

At a local level, the supply of timber depends on everything from weather conditions to the availability of loggers. Timber demand at a local level derives from mills which purchase delivered logs or buy stumpage from timberland owners.* Because of the high costs of transporting logs, proximity to a mill influences the price a timberland owner receives for logs. Mill closures diminish local demand for logs, pushing prices lower. On the flip side, new mills and mill modernization programs drive prices higher.

Ultimately, end product demand supports timber prices. Industries important to timber demand include construction (both new home construction and renovations), paper and packaging, and furnishings. Lumber and wood panel products, for example, which are heavily used in construction and remodeling make up over 50 percent of U.S. wood product production. Strong levels of new home construction, home renovations, and GDP growth translate into strong demand for lumber. The inverse holds true, as weak end product demand leads to mill closures and weak timber prices.

Over short time horizons, timber prices experience swings driven by end product demand cyclicality. Over a longer time horizon, timber prices benefit from increasing global demand for forest products. However, secular demand trends for certain products do not support increased demand for certain types of timber. For example, in recent years, increased use of electronic media led to reduced growth in demand for paper, paperboard, and newsprint. However, many other timber end products have less obvious or cost effective substitutes. Lumber, for example, remains a cheap and efficient construction material, with no serious substitutes on the horizon.

*Stumpage is the right to cut standing timber.

Differences in end product demand drive variations in prices for different timber species and grades. Determinants of prices for small, low-quality trees used for pulp differ from those that influence prices for large, high quality trees used in furniture production. In addition, changing technologies create relative price differentials among types of timber. For example, the development of oriented strand board (OSB), a panel of material made from stacked sheets of narrow wood strips, has led to a decrease in demand for plywood and the large diameter logs required to make plywood.

International dynamics affect timber supply and demand, as imports and exports of wood products play a significant role in determining timber prices. While approximately 11 percent of the U.S. harvest is exported, imports, primarily from Canada, account for nearly 25 percent of U.S. forest products consumption. U.S. dollar–Canadian dollar currency fluctuations strongly influence U.S. forest product and timber prices.

Active Management

Investments in timberland follow two principles that underlie attractive real assets investments. First, discounted pricing contributes to high risk-adjusted returns. In the case of timber, investors seek substantial discounts to the metric of standing timber value. Second, opportunities to create value independent of market or commodity price fluctuations add to the attractiveness of timber investments.

Active management plays a somewhat less critical role in real estate, energy, and timber investments than it does in illiquid investments in leveraged buyouts and venture capital. Because the assets themselves drive a substantial portion of real estate, energy, and timber returns, investors receive the asset-based returns even in the absence of stellar active management. In contrast, without superb active management, investments in venture capital make no sense at all.

Timber Prices and Inflation

Timberland shines during periods of high inflation and market turmoil. In the inflationary years of 1973 and 1974, for example, the S&P 500 returned an annualized -20.8 percent. After adjusting for inflation of 10.5 percent per year, the S&P generated an annualized return of an even more dismal -28.3 percent. Over those same two years, however, timberland returned a nominal 36.6 percent per year, equating to an annualized real return of 23.7 percent. That said, because links to inflation require that markets operate in reasonable equilibrium, secular trends that influence end-product demand might overwhelm short-term inflation sensitivity, disappointing the inflation hedging aspirations of timberland investors.

Alignment of Interests

Timber investment management organizations (TIMOs) provide a vehicle through which investors might participate in timberland investments. In the 1990s, when institutional investors began to show interest in timber, the existing TIMOs exhibited a variety of problems. Many were owned by large banks or insurance companies, creating the potential for conflicts between the interests of the financial conglomerate and the interests of the institutional timberland investor. Further limiting the set of attractive alternatives, a number of TIMOs employed unappealing allocation models, either allocating investments to specific investors on a first-come, first-served basis or on a subjective assessment of client needs and preferences. Few TIMOs sported sensible structures.

Today, a number of TIMOs meet reasonable institutional standards, with independent organizations offering well-structured commingled funds that contain fair deal terms. Even so, investors must continue to look out for and avoid the structural deficits that plagued the timber management industry in the 1990s.

Market Characteristics

According to Cambridge Associates, as of December 31, 2006, thirty TIMOs managed a total of $5.9 billion in commingled funds. Separate institutional accounts managed by those same TIMOs amount to an additional $14.0 billion. Timber REITs provide a further $11.9 billion of investment opportunity.

Summary

Timber offers institutional portfolios an opportunity to realize high risk-adjusted returns and a degree of protection against unanticipated inflation. Along with real estate and energy investments, timber provides a hedge against inflation without the significant opportunity costs of investment in TIPS.

Sustainable harvests of timberland produce substantial cash flows, similar to the high income levels characteristic of other real assets investments. The inefficiencies in the illiquid markets for timber create opportunities for high quality managers to add substantial value. Timber represents a valuable addition to the set of institutional investment alternatives.

PRIVATE EQUITY

Properly selected investments in leveraged buyouts and venture capital generate high returns relative to other equity alternatives, enhancing overall portfolio results. Superior private equity returns come at the price of higher risk levels, as investors expose assets to greater financial leverage (in the case of buyouts) and more substantial operating uncertainty (in the case of venture capital). Because of the strong fundamental links between private equity investments and marketable equities, private equity provides limited diversification to investors.

Private equity investments overcome the problems associated with divergence of interests between shareholders and management evident in many of today's publicly traded companies. Separation of ownership (by shareholders) and control (by management) results in a substantial gap between the interests of shareholders and the actions of management, since without significant equity interests managers often pursue a wide range of activities designed to improve their lot at the expense of outside owners. Over-the-top offices, excessive salaries, bloated fleets of airplanes, and other unjustified managerial perquisites rarely enter the picture in profit-oriented private investments. Private company managements operate with longer time horizons and lower risk aversion, aggressively pursuing strategies that promote creation of enterprise value. Because private deals generally require management to take material ownership stakes, interests of outside owners and operating management align.

In the venture capital world, entrepreneurial start-ups engage individuals who exhibit a single-minded focus on building successful companies. In the realm of buyouts, companies attract management devoted to improving the operation's bottom line, addressing the challenges of a highly leveraged capital structure with the goal of achieving a profitable exit. Managements in buyout and venture deals share the goals and objectives of owners.

In spite of differences between the technology orientation of traditional venture capital and the mature business bias of the leveraged buyout arena, discussions of private equity generally include both venture and buyout investments. In addition to the shared characteristics of illiquidity and high return potential, venture and buyout investing embrace a scope of activities that share important attributes with marketable equities.

Leveraged buyouts respond to many of the same factors that influence marketable securities. In fact, in transactions driven solely by financial engineering, buyouts simply represent turbo-charged equity, with leverage magnifying the results—good or bad—produced by a particular company. For example, when Warburg Pincus took Bausch & Lomb private in a 2007 leveraged buyout transaction, the fundamental nature of the company's consumer products business remained the same. Bausch & Lomb continued as the self-described "eye health company dedicated to perfecting vision and enhancing life for consumers around the world."[12] Corporate valuation continued to respond to changes in consumer demand, commodity prices, production efficiency, and regulatory activity. The underlying similarity between the publicly traded Bausch & Lomb and the privately held Bausch & Lomb suggests that investors should expect high levels of correlation between marketable securities and leveraged buyouts.

Although early stage venture capital lacks strong links with marketable equities, later stage venture investing depends significantly on the stock market. Later stage venture investments provide capital for companies ready to go public or to be sold, buying the company time to wait for a ready public market or an attractive corporate suitor. Market action influences the price at which later stage venture investors enter an investment and plays an even more critical role in the price at which investors exit successful positions.

Even early stage valuations respond somewhat to equity market conditions. When entrepreneurs start companies in an industry favored by the equity markets, venture capitalists pay premium prices to participate. Conversely, less highly desired enterprises command lower entry valuations, providing investors with relatively attractive starting points. As companies mature, equity market conditions increasingly influence venture capital valuations.

In their most basic form, venture and buyout investing represent a riskier means of obtaining equity exposure. The high leverage inherent in buyout transactions and the corporate immaturity intrinsic to venture investments cause investors to experience greater fundamental risk and to expect materially higher investment returns.

Strangely, historical results generally fail to reflect the hoped-for enhanced returns, while both correlation measures and risk levels fall below expectations. Unfortunately, poor returns for private investing probably reflect reality while the lower-than-expected correlation and lower-than-expected risk constitute a statistical artifact. Illiquidity masks the relationship between fundamental drivers of company value and changes in market price, causing private equity's diversifying power to appear artificially high. If two otherwise identical companies differ only in the form of organization—one private, the other public—the infrequently and less aggressively valued private company appears much more stable than the frequently valued publicly traded company, particularly in a world where securities markets exhibit excess volatility. Even though both companies react in identical fashion to fundamental drivers of corporate value, the less volatile private entity boasts superior risk characteristics, based solely on mismeasurement of the company's true underlying volatility. Not only does lack of day-to-day valuation information reduce reported risk levels, the private company gains spurious diversifying characteristics based solely on lack of co-movement with the more frequently valued public company.

While a fair portion of the observed "diversification" provided by private equity stems from the infrequent valuations accorded illiquid assets, some lack of correlation between marketable and private assets results from value-added strategies pursued by private firms. Consider the case of an idea, a garage and an entrepreneur financed with venture capital. As the company develops its product, initiates sales and becomes profitable, value creation takes place independent of the action on the floor of the stock exchange. Because results from company building activities loom large relative to results from the original corporate base, venture investments provide diversification relative to traditional marketable securities.

Similar value-added possibilities exist in the leveraged buyout arena, allowing adept private investors to enhance returns by achieving operating improvements in portfolio companies. Because buyout transactions generally involve companies with a reasonably substantial corporate base, market influences play the primary role in valuation, with firm-specific value-added opportunities playing a secondary role. Even though when compared to venture capital investments the more mature buyout companies offer less dramatic opportunities for business growth, value-added strategies contain the potential to offer a source of uncorrelated returns.

Pure financial engineering holds little interest for serious private equity investors, since providing financing represents a commodity-like activity with low barriers to entry. In the leveraged buyout business, simply adding leverage to a company increases expected returns and boosts risk levels, doing nothing to promote the goal of achieving risk-adjusted returns. In the venture capital arena, later stage investors supply little more than cash, hoping to benefit from the work of early stage investors and the prospect of achieving rapid liquidity through an initial public offering or sale. Private investors offering only capital operate in an extremely competitive market with reasonably efficient pricing mechanisms and little opportunity to demonstrate an investment edge.

Private equity opportunities become compelling only when managers pursue well-considered value-added strategies. By seeking to improve corporate operations in the context of an appropriate financial structure, investors increase the scope of return-generating activity, allowing realization of superior results less dependent on the whims of the market.

Leveraged Buyouts

Leveraged buyout transactions involve private ownership of mature corporate entities with greater-than-usual levels of debt on their balance sheets. The high levels of leverage produce a correspondingly high degree of variability in outcomes, both good and bad. Leveraged buyout investments, in the absence of value-adding activities by the transaction sponsor, simply increase the risk profile of the company.

The increase in risk generally comes at a high price. Buyout partnerships charge substantial management fees (often ranging between 1.5 percent and 2.5 percent of committed funds), a significant profits interest (usually 20 percent), and a variety of transactions and monitoring fees. The general partners of many buyout funds suggest that they engage in more than simple financial engineering, arguing that they bring special value-creation skills to the table. While the value added by operationally oriented buyout partnerships may, in certain instances, overcome the burden imposed by the typical buyout fund's generous fee structure, in aggregate buyout investments fail to match public market alternatives. After adjusting for the higher level of risk and the greater degree of illiquidity in buyout transactions, publicly traded equity securities gain a clear advantage.

Performance and Buyout Funds

In the private equity world, active management success goes hand-in-glove with investment success. In asset classes such as domestic equity and fixed income, which contain passive investment alternatives, investors can buy the market. By owning a marketable security index fund, investors reap market returns in a cost-efficient, reliable manner. In the inefficient private equity world, investors cannot buy the market, as no investable index exists. Even if a leveraged buyout index existed, based on past performance, index-like results would fail to satisfy investor desires for superior risk-adjusted returns. In fact, only top-quartile or top-decile funds produce returns sufficient to compensate for private equity's greater illiquidity and higher risk. In the absence of truly superior fund selection skills (or extraordinary luck), investors should stay far, far away from private equity investments.

Consider two decades of buyout partnership returns. For funds formed beginning in 1985, limited partners received a disappointing 7.3 percent median return. In contrast, the S&P 500 delivered 11.9 percent returns. First quartile buyout results reach double digits with a 16.1 percent per annum result, while third quartile performance falls into negative territory at -1.4 percent per annum. The median buyout result compares unfavorably to the marketable security alternative which produced higher returns with less risk.[13]

Academic research backs up the notion that private equity produces generally mediocre results. Steven Kaplan of the University of Chicago Graduate School of Business and Antoinette Schoar of the Sloan School of Management at MIT, in an August 2005 study on private equity performance, conclude that "LBO fund returns net of fees are slightly less than those of the S&P 500."[14] The study covers the period from 1980 to 2001. Kaplan and Schoar's results should dismay prospective private equity investors. Because the authors make no adjustment for leverage, the failure of LBO funds to match stock market returns adds the insult of higher risk to the injury of poor performance.

Investors in buyout partnerships received miserable risk-adjusted returns over the past two decades. Since the only material differences between privately owned buyouts and publicly traded companies lie in the nature of ownership (private vs. public) and character of capital structure (highly leveraged vs. less highly leveraged), comparing buyout returns to public market returns makes sense as a starting point. But, because the riskier, more-leveraged buyout positions ought to generate higher returns, sensible investors recoil at the buyout industry's deficit relative to public market alternatives. On a risk-adjusted basis, marketable equities win in a landslide.

A Yale Investments Office study provides insight into the additional return required to compensate for the risk in leveraged buyout transactions. Examination of 542 buyout deals initiated and concluded between 1987 and 1998 showed gross returns of 48 percent per annum, significantly above the 17 percent return that would have resulted from comparably timed and comparably sized investments in the S&P 500. On the surface, buyouts beat stocks by a wide margin. Adjustment for management fees and general partners' profit participation bring the estimated buyout result to 36 percent per year, still comfortably ahead of the marketable security alternative. Note the extreme positive bias of the buyout sample. Long-term studies show that median buyout returns fall in the neighborhood of those produced by the S&P 500. In the sample of deals presented to Yale, buyouts crush marketable securities.*

Because buyout transactions by their very nature involve higher-than-market levels of leverage, the basic buyout-fund-to-marketable-security comparison fails the apples-to-apples standard. To produce a risk-neutral comparison, consider the impact of applying leverage to public market investments. Comparably timed, comparably sized, and comparably leveraged investments in the S&P 500 produced an astonishing 86 percent annual return. The risk-adjusted marketable security result exceeded the buyout result of 36 percent per year by an astounding 50 percentage points per year.

Some part of the failure of buyout managers to produce attractive risk-adjusted returns stems from an inappropriate fee structure. Buyout investors generally pay 20 percent of profits to the investment firm's partners. Because the incentive compensation fails to consider the investor's cost of capital, buyout partnerships capture 20 percent of returns generated by the favorable wind at the long-term equity investor's back. Of course, in the case of transactions that employ

---

*The sample for the buyout study contains extraordinary survivorship bias. The data employed came from offering memoranda provided to the Yale Investments Office by firms hoping to attract Yale as an investor. Needless to say, only firms with successful track records came calling on the university, hoping to attract funds. A further potential source of bias stems from consideration of only completed transactions, since more successful deals might achieve early liquidity while the walking wounded might linger in buyout portfolios for years. Lacking reasonable valuations for private companies remaining in fund partnerships necessarily limits the study to those investments that exited with a sale or public offering and those that departed with a bankruptcy or liquidation.

greater-than-market levels of leverage, the investor's cost of capital increases along with the degree of leverage. Pure financial engineering represents a commodity, easily available to marketable securities investors through margin accounts and futures markets. Buyout managers deserve scant incremental compensation for adding debt to corporate balance sheets. By paying buyout partnership sponsors 20 percent of all gains, the fund investors compensate the fund managers with a significant portion of leveraged market gains over which the fund manager exercises no control and for which the fund managers deserves no credit. The large majority of buyout funds fail to add sufficient value to overcome a grossly unreasonable fee structure.

Another part of the industry-wide problem of poor returns relates to misalignment of incentives in large funds. Buyout firms generally begin with modest amounts of assets under management, totaling in the hundreds of millions of dollars. Management fees cover overhead and incentive fees reward superior performance. Successful buyout funds almost invariably increase fund size, for example, moving from $250 million for Fund I to $500 million for Fund II to $1 billion for Fund III to $2 billion for Fund IV and ever more for funds of increasing numerals. As fund size increases, management fees as a percentage of assets remain relatively constant, resulting in a dramatic increase in the dollar value of fee income. The change in compensation structure alters general partner motivation.

The partners of newer, smaller funds focus predominantly on generating investment returns. Since modest levels of fees cover reasonable operating expenses, strong investment returns define the only path to wealth. Not only do superior returns lead to large profits interests, strong results allow the general partners to raise subsequent, ever larger funds.

Eventually, as fund size increases, fee income becomes an increasingly significant profit center. As fee income grows, general partner behavior changes, focusing on protecting the firm's franchise and maintaining the annuity-like character of the stream of fees. Larger buyout funds pursue less risky deals, employing lower levels of leverage. Mega funds often exploit their franchises by expanding into other (fee-generating) lines of business, including real estate, fixed income, and hedge fund management. The big partnerships devote more time to cultivating and nourishing limited partner relationships, the source of the funds (and fees). Less time remains for investment activity. Returns suffer.

Past return data provide dramatic support for the notion that larger funds produce inferior results. For the ten years ending December 31,

Larger funds take on less risky investments

2005, buyout funds with more than $1 billion of committed capital produced returns of 9.3 percent per year, falling short of both the overall buyout industry return of 9.7 percent per year and the $500 million to $1 billion cohort return of 10.3 percent. Buyouts in the range of $250 million to $500 million performed even better, posting results of 11.4 percent per annum.[15] Large size correlates with lower returns.

Academic work supports the negative relationship between size and performance. Josh Lerner of Harvard Business School and Antoinette Schoar of MIT's Sloan School found "a strong relationship between fund growth and returns—the more dramatic the increase between two funds, the sharper the decline in return between the funds."[16] Increases in fund size benefit the general partner at the limited partners' expense.

Casual observers might draw the superficial conclusion that the key to success in buyout investing involves concentrating on smaller buyout funds. While smaller funds undoubtedly offer greater alignment of interests between the general partners and the passive providers of funds, a policy of simply choosing to invest in smaller funds may not lead to satisfactory results.

First, after adjusting the returns of smaller buyout funds to account for higher levels of risk, excess returns may disappear. Smaller buyout funds invest in smaller companies, which necessarily carry higher levels of operational risk. Adding greater operational risk to higher financial risk creates a substantial risk-adjusted hurdle for the small-company-buyout investor. Investors must receive material compensation for the heightened risk and additional illiquidity in small company buyout investing.

Second, an investor backing smaller buyout funds solely based on historical performance makes the mistake of investing while looking through the rearview mirror. Superior absolute, if not risk-adjusted, returns attract flows of capital. As market participants conclude that small buyouts outperform large buyouts, the market responds by creating large numbers of partnerships devoted to pursuing middle-market buyout transactions. Any excess returns that may have existed will be threatened by the influx of new capital and new participants. Be wary of the market's ability to eliminate sources of superior risk-adjusted returns.

Yale's Experience Yale's buyout portfolio returns provide a ray of hope to investors seeking risk-adjusted excess returns. The university attempts to invest only with firms that place central importance on enhancing the effectiveness of corporate operations. Company building strategies permit buyout fund managers to add value beyond the increase in returns expected from adopting higher risk capital structures. By identifying managers that implement operationally oriented strategies, Yale creates the possibility of winning in a tough arena.

Consider the data in the study of buyout transactions presented to Yale between 1987 and 1998, as shown in Table 8.1. Yale participated in 118 of 542 transactions in the sample, generating gross returns of 63 percent relative to a risk equivalent benchmark of 41 percent. If the risk adjustment appropriately captures the return expected from financial engineering, the premium return earned by Yale represents value added by the fund manager. Even though fund manager fees take an estimated 15 percentage points of annual return, the university's net returns of 48 percent still comfortably exceed the risk-adjusted marketable securities bogey.

Yale's buyout results rely far less on leverage than do the results of the broad pool of buyout transactions. Contrast the broad pool's nearly 70 percentage point difference between the unlevered S&P return and the risk-adjusted benchmark with Yale's 21 percentage point difference. Less reliance on leverage and more attention to operations lead to superior risk-adjusted results. By employing an approach that emphasizes operating improvements and employs lower leverage, Yale's buyout portfolio manages to produce handsome absolute and risk-adjusted returns.

Table 8.1 Buyout Managers Fail to Create Excess Returns
Completed Deals, 1987–1998

| | **Entire Sample** | | **Yale's Portfolio** | |
	Return	Debt/Equity Ratio	Return	Debt/Equity Ratio
Buyout return	48%	5.2	63%	2.8
Risk-equivalent marketable security benchmark	86%	5.2	41%	2.8
S&P 500 benchmark	17%	0.8	20%	0.7
Number of deals	542		118	

Source: Yale University Investments Office.

Active Management

No sensible investor manages private assets passively. Even if participation in a broadly diversified market alternative were available,
investors would face nearly certain disappointment. Burdened by
staggering fees and characterized by well above marketable equity
risk levels, a broad collection of private funds would likely produce
returns far from sufficient to compensate for the risk incurred. Investors
justify the inclusion of private equity in portfolios only by selecting top
quality managers pursuing value-added strategies with appropriate
deal structures.

Due Diligence The character of a private equity fund's investment
principals constitutes the single most important criterion in evaluating
the merits of an investment. Driven, intelligent, ethical individuals
operating in a cohesive partnership possess an edge likely to translate
into superior investment results. On the other end of the spectrum,
individuals willing to cut corners, operationally, intellectually, or eth-
ically, place an investor's funds and reputation at risk.

The central importance of choosing strong investment partners
places enormous weight on the due diligence process. Concluding
that a private equity firm consists of credible, professionally qualified
individuals in pursuit of interesting investment opportunities serves
merely as a starting point. Before making a commitment, careful
investors determine that the fund's principals exhibit the characteristics necessary to justify entrusting institutional assets to their care.
Because of the long-term nature of private equity contracts, investors
ultimately rely on the good faith of fund managers to behave in the best
interests of the limited partners. While negotiating appropriate deal
terms remains important, contractual arrangements almost invariably
fail to deal with all of the important issues that ultimately arise in the
general partner/limited partner relationship. Good people can overcome bad contracts, but good contracts cannot overcome bad people.

Comprehensive due diligence requires substantial effort. Personal
and professional references provided by prospective fund managers
provide an initial set of contacts. Because of the inevitable selection
bias in a hand-picked reference list, sensible investors seek candid,
confidential assessments from other individuals, including both business colleagues and personal acquaintances. Over time, investors
develop networks that facilitate reference checking and increase the
quality of decision making. Careful investors make skeptical calls,

actively looking for potential issues. Going through the motions by conducting superficial checks adds nothing to the due diligence process.

Careful investors evaluate the fund manager's investment operation by spending sufficient time at the firm's offices to assess the character of the workplace. Firms exhibit distinct personalities that influence the quality of operations in fundamental ways, suggesting that investors favor those groups deemed a good personality fit. Spending time in informal, social settings further enhances the information set used to evaluate the decision makers. Selecting individuals driven to produce superior results in a high quality manner constitutes the central challenge of manager selection.

In spite of the enormous importance of conducting thorough due diligence, many investors fail to devote the time and energy necessary to make well-informed judgments. In 1999, one of the principals of a $2 billion buyout fund reported that only one investor took the time to meet the firm's full team before committing funds. By foregoing the opportunity to assess the quality of an investment operation's personnel, prospective investors fail to execute the most important task.

Long-Term Commitments Private investment addresses Keynes's notion that the job of investment might be done better if decisions were "permanent and indissoluble, like marriage, except by reason of death or other grave cause . . ."[17] While falling somewhat short of the gravity of the decision to marry, funding a private equity firm represents a long-term commitment. In contrast to the termination of a marketable securities manager where the vestiges of any relationship quickly disappear, evidence from terminated private investment funds remains on the books for years to come. Knowledge that private investment decisions represent long-term commitments forces sensible investors to establish high hurdles for initiating investment relationships.

The illiquid nature of private investing allows private equity managers to make the longer term decisions necessary to pursue successful investment strategies. Marketable securities managers know that clients possess little patience for performance shortfall, pulling the trigger quickly when the numbers fail to meet expectations. As a result, stock jockeys learn to overdiversify portfolios, holding small positions in securities selected as much to avoid disappointment as to generate exciting returns. In contrast, private fund managers "lock in" assets for long periods of time, with partnership terms that often span a decade or more. While the typical fundraising cycle of two to three years might pressure managers to shorten investment time frames, investors frequently accept the argument that "it's too early to judge the most recent fund," allowing private asset managers to make truly long-term decisions.

In fact, when evaluating private funds, investors face little choice but to focus on changes in corporate operations, not minute-by-minute fluctuations in market value. By emphasizing an investment's intrinsic value, investors assess factors under the manager's control, liberating private fund managers from the frequently fickle judgments of the equity markets and allowing pursuit of sensible investment strategies.

Strong private equity groups use the long investment horizon to pursue strategies that add substantial value to corporate activities. Fund managers providing only capital operate at a competitive disadvantage to groups that improve company operations in a fundamental way. In the leveraged buyout arena, supplying money to purchase a well-run company constitutes a commodity, as all major investment funds boast the financial skills necessary to complete plain vanilla transactions. Low barriers to entry allow former investment bankers to respond to mid-career crises by abandoning the life of an agent and embracing the glories of an investment principal, flooding the market with capital to pursue "clean" deals. In contrast, buyout firms that demonstrate the ability to deal with substantial operating issues carve out a special transactional niche, creating the potential for less competitive, proprietary deal flow. The combination of less competition for operationally oriented transactions and potential benefits from addressing operational issues provides a compelling investment opportunity.

Clayton, Dubilier & Rice and WESCO Clayton, Dubilier & Rice (CDR), a firm with a long distinguished track record, focuses its efforts on "messy" deals—transactions that require a high degree of intervention by the principals. The firm implements its value-added investment strategy by bringing individuals with operating backgrounds into the partnership. These partners provide valuable perspective during the due diligence process, identifying acquisition candidates that might benefit from the firm's unusual skills. Once CDR acquires a company, operating partners take a "hands on" approach to improving corporate operations. One subclass of transactions that CDR pursues involves corporate divestitures. Frequently, the divested subsidiary lacks basic corporate organizational structure, having relied on the parent company to provide a variety of essential business services. Value creation results as CDR uses its combination of operational and financial expertise to create a stand-alone company from the erstwhile corporate division.

In February 1993, CDR principals began evaluating a spin-off of WESCO, Westinghouse's electrical equipment and supplies distribution arm. Within a short time, the buyout firm identified several major business issues: (1) transition from corporate subsidiary to a market-driven business; (2) improvement of inventory and logistics management; and (3) reduction of corporate overhead. More than one-half of WESCO's 250 branches posted losses in 1993, contributing to firm-wide red ink totaling more than $3 million on a revenue base of $1.6 billion.

On top of material business issues, WESCO suffered from sleepy management that let the company drift. The company required a more aggressive team to instill a sense of corporate mission, repair damaged morale, and improve lackluster performance.

management is key

After Westinghouse rejected CDR's initial bid as inadequate, the firm continued to work on the project. Operating partner Chuck Ames drove the process, identifying a management plan and preparing to run the company, if necessary. By February 1994, when Westinghouse came back to CDR, Ames had identified a chief executive, Roy Haley, with the ability to create and manage the new company.

When CDR acquired WESCO for $330 million, the company lacked basic corporate infrastructure. Creating information technology, finance, and internal control divisions from scratch provided the basic building blocks necessary for corporate existence. Implementing the operating plan crafted prior to acquisition created substantial additional value, moving the company from losses to meaningful profits.

By 1997, when a financial buyer purchased WESCO, the firm generated $90 million of operating income on $2.7 billion of revenue. The turnaround in performance produced great results for CDR. The buyout firm's original $83 million of equity generated proceeds of $511 million, providing annual returns of nearly 47 percent to the firm's limited partners. The extraordinary results stem from one measure of financial engineering and several measures of operating improvement.

Few firms possess the skill set required to address the severe operating problems and company building challenges found at WESCO. By combining operational and financial skills, CDR exemplifies the potential for unusual value creation.

synergy

Buyouts and Inflation

Because buyout valuations correlate strongly with marketable equity valuations, buyouts tend to exhibit the poor short-term inflation hedging characteristics typical of marketable equities. That said, since a buyout's more highly leveraged balance sheet contains substantial levels of fixed rate liabilities, which lose value in an environment of unanticipated inflation, buyouts may perform somewhat better than less levered companies in an inflationary period.

Alignment of Interests

Investors in buyout funds benefit from structural forces that serve to align the interests of corporate management and providers of capital. High degrees of balance sheet leverage force company managers to manage assets efficiently, with energies focused on generating cash flows to satisfy debt service obligations. The lure of shareholder-unfriendly corporate perquisites pales in comparison to the specter of default and the grail of profit participation. Buyout transactions serve to align interests of managers and investors.

Unfortunately, investors in buyout partnerships face the same set of issues that confront investors in any scheme where the sponsor receives a profits interest. Profit-sharing arrangements create options that may lead to behavior that benefits the fund operator and disadvantages the provider of funds. To offset the optionality of the profits interest, substantial levels of co-investment by the sponsor of the buyout partnership create a symmetry regarding gains and losses that goes a long way toward keeping interests aligned.

In the ideal world, management fees cover reasonable firm overhead while profits interests provide attractive incentive compensation. In the real world, excessive management fees, a particularly acute problem for larger buyout funds, drive a wedge between the interests of the general partners and the limited partners. Deal fees, which many funds charge upon successful consummation of a transaction, represent an egregious means by which fund managers enrich themselves at the expense of their capital-contributing partners. The rationale for deal fees mystifies thoughtful investors. Since investors pay management fees to compensate the fund managers for day-to-day work on the fund, what role do transaction fees play? Monitoring fees represent a similarly superfluous charge. Why do buyout firms assess a fee for monitoring investments when they already collect a more than adequate management fee? In fact, buyout funds, particularly large funds that produce fees of hundreds of millions of dollars, represent an unfortunate example of misalignment of interests between fund managers and investors.

Academic research on fees gives buyout investors pause. Using data on terms for 144 buyout funds formed between 1992 and 2006, Andrew Metrick and Ayako Yasuda of the University of Pennsylvania's Wharton School estimate that the present value of fees consumes an average of nearly $20 of every $100 under management. Little wonder that limited partners so often fail to achieve reasonable returns!

The researchers examine the absolute level and relative size of fixed revenues (management fees and entry transaction fees) and variable revenues (carried interest, monitoring fees, and exit transaction fees). The mix between fixed revenues, which buyout mavens pocket simply for showing up, and variable revenues, which depend on investment performance, further discourages thoughtful investors. Fully 62 percent of revenues come from fixed fees, leaving only 38 percent to reward performance. In fact, a portion of fees classified as variable by Metrick and Yasuda, namely monitoring fees and the exit transaction fee (on the amount for the original investment), accrue to the general partner in the instance of no investment performance, painting a dismal picture indeed.[18]

Market Characteristics

At December 31, 2006, the U.S. leveraged buyout industry controlled approximately $342 billion in capital, of which approximately 57 percent was invested in companies with the remainder committed by investors, but undrawn. More than 360 buyout partnerships were active in the United States at the end of 2006.[19]

Summary

Buyout funds constitute a poor investment for casual investors. The underlying company investments in buyout funds differ from their public market counterparts only in degree of balance sheet risk and liquidity. The higher debt and lower liquidity of buyout deals demand higher compensation in the form of superior returns to investors. Unfortunately for private equity investors, in recent decades buyout funds delivered lower returns than comparable marketable securities positions, even before adjusting for risk.

Fees create a hurdle that proves extremely difficult for buyout investors to clear. Aside from substantial year-to-year management fees, buyout funds command a significant share of deal profits, usually equal to one-fifth of the total. On top of the management fee and incentive compensation, buyout managers typically charge deal fees and often charge monitoring fees. The cornucopia of compensation ensures a feast for the buyout manager, while the buyout investor hopes at best for a hearty serving of leftovers.

As with other forms of investment that depend on superior active management, sensible investors look at buyout partnerships with a high degree of skepticism. Unless investors identify top-quartile, or even top-decile managers, results almost certainly fail to compensate for the degree of risk incurred.

Venture Capital

Venture capital partnerships provide financing and company building skills to start-up operations with the goal of developing companies into substantial, profitable enterprises. Providers of funds to venture capital partnerships respond to multiple sources of attraction: driving an important element of the capitalist system, savoring the glitz surrounding the celebrity of the venture capital industry, and garnering a share of the gains generated by entrepreneurial activity.

Part of the attraction of venture capital investing lies in the option-like character of individual investments. Downside losses cannot exceed the amount invested. Upside gains can multiply the original stake many fold. The combination of limited downside and substantial upside produces an investor-friendly, positively skewed distribution of outcomes.

Unfortunately for investors, the promise of venture capital exceeds the reality. Over reasonably long periods of time, aggregate venture returns more or less match marketable equity returns, indicating that providers of capital fail to receive compensation for the substantial risks inherent in start-up investing.

Aside from the dismal picture provided by historical experience, all but the most longstanding investors in venture partnerships face a problem in adverse selection. The highest quality, top-tier venture firms generally refuse to accept new investors and ration capacity even among existing providers of funds. Venture firms willing and able to accept money from new sources frequently represent relatively unattractive, second-tier (or worse) investment opportunities.

Prior to the technology bubble of the late 1990s, investors in venture partnerships received returns inadequate to compensate for the risks incurred. In a few glorious years, the Internet mania allowed venture investors to share in a staggering flood of riches. Yet the bubble-induced enthusiasm for private technology investing produced an unanticipated problem for venture investors. Indiscriminate demand allowed the managing partners of venture funds to increase the flow of management fees and take a greater share of profits. After the post-bubble collapse, venture capital partnerships maintained their newly fashioned investor-unfriendly terms, creating an even higher hurdle for investment success.

Although investing in venture capital partnerships promises participation in the substance and glamor of backing start-up enterprises, investors providing capital to the venture industry receive returns inadequate to compensate for the high degree of risk. Only if investors generate top-quartile, or even top-decile, results do returns suffice to compensate for the risks incurred.

The Glamorous Appeal of Venture Capital

In September 1995, Pierre Omidyar, a French-born Iranian immigrant, started an online auction site, ostensibly to help his girlfriend sell her collection of Pez dispensers. Even though by late 1996, the business expanded nicely and produced solid profits, the company's founder decided to seek outside assistance. Two years after the humble beginnings of the company now named eBay, Omidyar invited venture capital provider Benchmark Capital to make an investment and join the board. The then-recently-formed Silicon Valley venture firm made a $6.7 million investment in Omidyar's eBay, valuing the company at $20 million.

After Benchmark's investment, eBay's growth continued apace, fueled by the engagement of a new management team headed by the impressive Meg Whitman. The company soon proved ready for prime-time, as the September 1998 launch of eBay's initial public offering powered the company's valuation to $700 million. The IPO pricing proved fleeting, as investor interest drove the first day's price from the offering level of $18 per share to $47 per share, representing the "fifth-highest first-day gain in the market's history."[20] At the close of trading on September 23, 1998 the market valued eBay at more than $2 billion. Benchmark's $6.7 million investment exploded to more than $400 million, a breathtaking sixty-fold increase in a little more than a year.

The eBay rocket ship had barely begun its journey. In April 1999, with the stock trading at $175 per share, the company's market value totaled in excess of $21 billion. Looking to lock in some of the firm's extraordinary gains, Benchmark Capital distributed a portion of its position to the limited partners. With Benchmark's $6.7 million investment worth $6.7 billion, the investment multiple of 1,000 times qualified eBay as "the Valley's best-performing venture investment ever."[21]

Far from a flash in the pan, eBay continued to mature, becoming a standard-bearer among Internet companies. On July 22, 2002, boasting a market capitalization of $15.7 billion, eBay joined the ranks of the S&P 500, taking the 104th place, just ahead of the venerable BB&T Corporation, a North Carolina based financial services concern with a storied past that dated to the Civil War. On the last day of trading in 2007, eBay's valuation stood at $45 billion, representing a 2,250 multiple of the valuation assigned to the firm by Benchmark Capital's original investment.

Everyone made money. Pierre Omidyar, eBay's founder, created wealth beyond imagination. Meg Whitman, along with the rest of eBay's management and employees, received a huge payday. Venture capitalists and their financial backers posted staggering investment gains. Even public shareholders generated significant holding period returns. Venture capital ruled.

Although eBay stands apart, the venture capital world's other successes, companies such as Cisco, Genentech, Amazon.com, Starbucks, and Intel, produced enormous gains for entrepreneurs and investors alike. Even start-ups that ultimately failed, such as @home and Excite.com, provided opportunities for financial backers to profit as company valuations soared to multi-billion-dollar levels, before plummeting back to earth.

The Harsh Reality of Venture Capital Performance

Unfortunately for investors, gains from high profile venture-backed successes prove insufficient to produce acceptable returns on an industry-wide basis. Over long periods of time, venture investors receive no more than market-like returns with demonstrably higher levels of risk. The promise of venture capital fails to deliver.

Venture capital partnerships produced a surprisingly low median return of 3.1 percent for the twenty years beginning in 1985. In contrast, the S&P 500 returned 11.9 percent per annum. Venture results exhibited a wide dispersion, ranging from 721 percent to -100 percent, with a standard deviation of 51.1 percent. First quartile results of 16.9 percent provided much better than median results, while third quartile returns of -6.7 percent significantly impaired investor capital.[22]

Venture capital returns proved disappointing, even when measured at the peak of one of the greatest speculative manias. The *2001 Invest-ment Benchmarks Report* reported that a sample of nearly 950 venture capital funds produced a 19.6 percent rate of return for the twenty-year period ending December 31, 2000. In absolute terms, the nearly 20 per-cent per year over twenty years appears handsome indeed.

Consider, however, if instead of making venture capital invest-ments, investors made equivalent investments, in timing and in size, in the S&P 500. The marketable security result of 20.2 percent per annum outpaces the composite venture capital return. Even at the point of maximum return for venture capital, investors in plain-old-large-capitalization common stocks enjoyed higher returns with lower risks.   *S&P 500 had greater returns than VC*

Aside from the intuitive conclusion that investors in privately held start-up companies face materially higher risk than investors in publicly traded large-capitalization corporations, more rigorous defini-tion of the risk differential proves difficult. Suffice it to say that ven-ture investors must achieve top-quartile or top-decile results to begin to argue that they achieved superior risk-adjusted returns.

high margins for VC

Franchise Firms

Atop the hierarchy of venture capital partnerships stand a relatively small number of venture firms that occupy an extraordinary position. This group of eight or ten firms enjoys a substantial edge over less-exalted practitioners. Top-tier venture capitalists benefit from extraor-dinary deal flow, a stronger negotiating position, and superior access to capital markets. In short, participants in the venture capital process, from the entrepreneur to the investment banker, prefer dealing with this small set of franchise firms.

In no other area of the capital markets does the identity of the source of funds matter in the way that it does in the venture capital world. Consider the bond markets. Do the issuers of government or corporate debt care about the identity of the bondholders? Consider the equity markets. Do the managements of publicly traded companies care about the identity of the stockholders? While in certain unusual circumstances, such as in a contested change in corporate control, issuers of securities may care about the identity of their holders, gen-erally the name, rank, and serial number of security owners prove of little interest to security issuers. Consider the real assets markets. Do managers of office buildings, operators of oil wells, or caretakers of timberlands care about the identity of the owners? Overwhelmingly, the source of funds for investment purchases matters little or nothing to the individuals responsible for managing assets.

In contrast, managers of venture-capital-backed enterprises care enormously about the source of funds. A disproportionate share of entrepreneurs seeking start-up financing seek out venture firms with strong franchises, in the belief that funding from a top-tier firm increases the odds of ultimate success. General partners of franchise venture firms constitute a truly extraordinary group, bringing exceptional judgment and unequaled company-building skills to the board table. Start-up firms benefit from the franchise venture capitalists' accumulated wisdom, well-established connections, and hard-won investment insights. Thoughtful entrepreneurs often willingly and knowingly accept a discounted valuation to cement a deal with a venture capitalist of choice. The reputation of the venture capital elite creates a virtuous circle in which investment success begets investment success.

Academic research supports the notion of franchise firm performance persistence in the venture capital arena. Steven Kaplan of the University of Chicago Graduate School of Business and Antoinette Schoar of MIT's Sloan School of Management find substantial persistence of fund performance, suggesting that "[g]eneral partners whose funds outperform the industry in one fund are likely to outperform in the next and vice versa." The authors note that their "findings are markedly different from the results for mutual funds, where persistence has been difficult to detect."[23] While Kaplan and Schoar identify some persistence in buyout returns, they find "a statistically and economically strong amount of persistence" particularly in venture funds.[24]

Recent entrants to the arena of venture investing, as well as longer-term players with run-of-the-mill portfolios, face a challenge unique to the venture industry. All of the top-tier venture capital partnerships limit assets under management and none of the top-tier partnerships currently accept new investors. Consequently, outsiders remain outside, limiting the available set of choices for new investors hoping to enter and existing investors hoping to upgrade.

New participants in the venture market must consider the return prospects of venture firms available for new-money investment. Obviously, industry-wide returns suffer with the removal of the records of relatively longstanding, relatively large, relatively high performing funds. Since the available opportunities for the overwhelming number of investors exclude the top-tier venture firms, return expectations require a commensurate downward adjustment. In the context of an industry that historically produced returns similar to marketable equity returns, even a moderate downward adjustment spells trouble.

The inability to access the venture elite drives the final nail in the coffin of prospective venture investor aspirations.

Venture Capital and Inflation

As with any corporate entity, the venture capital investor's claim on the nominal value of company assets ought to provide a positive correlation to inflation. As with other assets that exhibit some link to marketable equity prices, the poor short-term relationship between marketable equities and inflation calls into question the inflation-hedging ability of venture capital.

Alignment of Interests

Venture funds share with buyout funds and hedge funds the incentive compensation scheme that creates option-like payoffs for the general partner. A high level of co-investment by the general partner represents a sure way to align investor interests, creating a salutary symmetry in general partners' attitudes toward gains and losses. Unfortunately, in the broader venture world, significant general partner co-investment represents the exception, not the rule. Interestingly, however, a fair number of the venture capital elite invest substantial amounts of personal funds side-by-side with their limited partners.

Investment success allows fund sponsors to move the terms of trade in the general partners' favor. The technology bubble of the late 1990s provides a case in point. Inspired by enormous investor demand, venture firms raised bubble-era funds in the neighborhood of ten times the size of funds raised only a decade earlier, moving from a typical 1990-vintage fund size of $100 million to $150 million to a 2000-vintage fund size of $1 billion to $1.5 billion. Along with the increase in fund size came an increase in fee income that far outpaced the growth in the size of the professional staff. The dramatic rise in asset-based income transformed fees from an overhead recovery mechanism to a partnership profit center.

More distressing to limited partners, venture partnerships used the huge increase in investor interest in all things technological to extract a greater share of fund profits. Prior to the technology mania, venture firms operated in a well-defined hierarchy that gave most firms a 20 percent share of profits, a handful of demonstrably superior firms a 25 percent share of profits, and Kleiner Perkins Caufield & Byers—the dean of the industry—a 30 percent share of profits. Elite firms double dipped by creating larger profits and keeping a greater share.

During the Internet bubble, greed prevailed. Seemingly limitless demand for venture capital investments allowed the rank and file to move their profits interest from 20 percent to 25 percent and the superior firms to move from 25 percent to 30 percent. In an extraordinary act of selflessness and generosity, Kleiner Perkins, which could have moved its share of profits to 40 percent or even 50 percent, kept its profit share at 30 percent. The general partners of Kleiner Perkins, while acutely aware of their market power, no doubt decided to leave the firm's profit share at 30 percent to benefit the institutional missions of the firm's endowment and foundation investors.

Faced with an opportunity to skew deal terms in the general partner's favor, in spite of the industry's mediocre record of adding value, venture capitalists reacted with aplomb. In the aftermath of the bubble, a number of firms reduced fund sizes to more rational levels, mitigating the negative impact of excessive fees, but instances of funds reducing the profits interest have yet to come to light. In spite of dismal post-mania venture investment performance, the ratchet in profits interest appears to work in one direction only.

Market Characteristics

At December 31, 2006, the U.S. venture capital industry controlled approximately $131 billion in capital, of which approximately 62 percent was invested in companies, with the remainder committed by investors, but undrawn. More than 870 venture partnerships were active in the United States at the end of 2006.[25]

Summary

Venture capital investments appeal to a wide range of market participants motivated by the prospects of participating in a fundamental driver of the capitalist system, reveling in the glamor of high profile start-up successes and benefiting from outsized investment returns. As illustrated by the case of eBay, venture investing sometimes produces truly breathtaking results.

Unfortunately, eBay's corporate achievements and stock market success stand far apart from the usual venture investment results. In aggregate, venture investors fare about as well as their marketable equity counterparts. After adjustment for risk, the overwhelming majority of venture capital fails to produce acceptable risk-adjusted returns.

The new entrant to the world of private entrepreneurial finance faces an obstacle quite apart from the barriers hampering investment success in other asset classes. The top tier of venture partnerships, essentially closed to new money, enjoy superior access to deals, entrepreneurs, and capital markets. Exclusion from the venture capital elite disadvantages all but the most longstanding, most successful limited partners.

CONCLUSION

Nontraditional asset classes provide powerful tools for investors who seek to reduce risk by constructing well-diversified portfolios and to augment returns by pursuing profitable active management opportunities. Absolute return strategies and real assets holdings add diversifying power, while private equity investments enhance portfolio return prospects.

Absolute return investments consist of event-driven and value-driven strategies that exploit mispricings in marketable securities. By offsetting market exposure with hedges, investors reduce systematic risk and cause results to depend on manager skill. Event-driven positions rely on evaluation of events associated with corporate mergers and bankruptcies, while value-driven positions depend on identification of misvalued securities. Because absolute return strategies generate equity-like returns largely independent of market movements, the asset class contributes extremely attractive return and diversification characteristics to portfolios.

Yale pioneered the use of absolute return as an asset class, first employing it in 1990. As of June 30, 2007, inception-to-date returns clocked in at 13.2 percent per annum, with a standard deviation of only 4.9 percent (relative to the Wilshire 5000's 11.2 percent return and 14.0 percent standard deviation). Absolute return fulfilled its mission of producing uncorrelated returns, showing monthly correlations of an identical 0.02 with both stocks and bonds.

Real assets protect investment portfolios against unanticipated increases in inflation, with investors paying a price for real assets' diversifying power by accepting expected returns below those of marketable equities. Under normal circumstances, high levels of current cash flow provide a stabilizing influence, reducing the volatility of portfolio fluctuations. From both a risk and a return perspective, Yale's real assets portfolio succeeded, posting a 17.8 percent per annum return from inception in July 1978 to June 2007.

Private equity positions enhance portfolio returns at the price of meaningfully increasing portfolio risk, while producing little in terms of diversifying power. Investor experience over the past two decades failed to live up to expectations, as funds generally delivered below marketable equity returns at above marketable equity risk levels. Burdened by extraordinary fees in the form of substantial profit-sharing arrangements, investors face the difficult task of selecting top decile funds to realize the promise of private investing.

Strong alignment of interests marks most private equity arrangements, creating an appropriate set of incentives for fund managers. Significant co-investment by partners of buyout and venture funds moves investment decisions toward a principal orientation and away from a potentially damaging agency perspective. Side-by-side commitment of general partners' dollars causes all parties to share in the gains and losses, forcing decision makers to consider the downside—as well as the upside—of corporate actions. The show of confidence inherent in a significant general partner co-investment sends a strong signal to potential investors.

Strategies for adding value to corporate operations make private equity an interesting investment activity, creating the possibility of exploiting less competitive deal-sourcing environments and identifying operations-enhancing opportunities. To the extent that private asset managers increase corporate value in a substantial way, investment results exhibit independence from the forces that drive valuation of marketable equities. Only by adding significant increments of value do private fund managers begin to earn the extraordinary fees associated with private equity deals. Strong active management—at the investor level, the fund level, and the company level—forms the basis for successful private equity programs.

By selecting high quality partnerships that pursue value-adding strategies, Yale University achieved rates of return in excess of 30 percent per annum on private equity investments over the thirty years from 1978 to 2007, highlighting the potential contribution to portfolio results from a well-managed private equity program. Even after adjusting for the higher risk inherent in venture capital and leveraged buyout participations, Yale's results stack up well relative to other investment alternatives.

Successful investors in nontraditional asset classes engage in active management, seeking to identify the highest quality people to manage investment funds. In selecting partners, due diligence efforts center on assessing the competence and character of the individuals responsible for portfolio decisions. Developing partnerships with extraordinary people represents the single most important element of alternative investment success.

9
Asset Class Management

Active managers compete in an extremely tough arena, since markets tend to price assets accurately. Enormous sums of money deployed by highly motivated investors seek to exploit perceived mispricings at a moment's notice. Winning at the game of active management requires great skill and, perhaps, more than a little good fortune. Serious investors consider carefully the certain results of low cost passive management before opting for the uncertain returns of high cost active management.

Significant costs raise the hurdle for active strategies. Identifying a portfolio that merely beats the market fails to define success, as managers must build portfolios that beat the market by a sufficient margin to cover management fees, transactions costs, and market impact. Because of the leakage of fees and costs from the system, a staggeringly large percentage of money invested in marketable securities falls short of producing index-like returns. Overcoming the costs of active management presents a formidable challenge.

In the context of an extraordinary complex, difficult investing environment, fiduciaries tend to be surprisingly accepting of active manager pitches. Institutions all too often pursue the glamorous, exciting (and ultimately costly) hope of market-beating strategies at the expense of the reliable, mundane certainty of passive management. Instead of examining critically the factors that drove past performance, investors frequently simply associate superior historical results with investment acumen.

Because of the nearly insurmountable hurdles in beating the market, prudent investors approach active strategies with great skepticism. Beginning with the presumption that markets price assets correctly places the burden of proof on the manager who promises risk-adjusted excess returns. Only when compelling evidence suggests that a strategy possesses clear potential to beat the market should investors abandon the passive alternative.

Active managers worth hiring possess personal attributes that create reasonable expectations of superior performance. In selecting external managers, investors must identify individuals committed to placing institutional client goals ahead of personal self-interest. Alignment of interests occurs most frequently in independent investment management firms run in an entrepreneurial fashion by energetic, intelligent, ethical professionals. Engaging investment advisors involves consequences beyond issues of financial returns, as fiduciaries entrust both the institution's assets and reputation to the external management firm.

Even after identifying a promising investment management firm, the job remains uncompleted until the investor and advisor negotiate satisfactory deal terms. The fundamental goal in establishing contractual arrangements consists of aligning interests to encourage investment advisory agents to behave as institutional fiduciary principals. Slippage between what the investor wishes and what the advisor does imposes substantial costs on institutions, reducing the likelihood of meeting basic investment goals and objectives.

THE GAME OF ACTIVE MANAGEMENT

The thrill of the chase clouds objectivity in assessing active management opportunities. Playing the game provides psychic rewards, generating grist for the mill of cocktail party conversation. Keynes likens active investment to children's entertainment: "For it is, so to speak, a game of Snap, of Old Maid, of Musical Chairs—a pastime in which he is the victor who says *snap* neither too soon nor too late, who passes the Old Maid to his neighbor before the game is over, who secures a chair for himself when the music stops. These games can be played with zest and enjoyment, though all the players know that it is the Old Maid which is circulating, or that when the music stops some of the players will find themselves unseated."[1] Fiduciaries must ensure that active management leads to higher expected portfolio returns, not just higher investment manager job satisfaction.

The willingness to believe that superior performance comes from intelligent hard work clouds clear judgment. The investment world worships success, deifying the market seer du jour. Instead of wondering whether a manager at the top of the performance charts made a series of lucky picks, observers presume that good results stem from skill. Conversely, in public perception, poor results follow from lack of ability. Market participants rarely wonder whether high returns came from accepting greater than market risk, or whether low returns resulted from lower than market risk. The investment community's lack of skepticism regarding the source and character of superior returns causes strange characters to be elevated to market guru status.

Joe Granville

Of all the individuals who moved markets with their predictions, Joe Granville may be among the strangest. In the late 1970s and early 1980s, the technical analyst made a series of "on the money" predictions. Strikingly, on April 21, 1980 when the market fell to a two-year low of 759, Granville issued a buy signal, anticipating a powerful rally that took the average over 1000 within three months. In January 1981, Granville's next major market call, a sell signal, prompted "waves of selling," causing markets to decline sharply on record volume. The next day his picture appeared on the front page of the *New York Times*, while *Washington Post* headlines read "One Forecaster Spurs Hysteria— Markets Sink in Panic Selling." Granville predicted he would win the Nobel Prize, crowing that he had "solved the 100-year enigma, calling every market top and bottom."

Granville's technically driven forecasts came replete with costumes and props. His routine included dressing as Moses to deliver the Ten Commandments of investing, dropping his trousers to read stock quotations from his boxers, and appearing on stage in a coffin filled with ticker tape.

Such antics did nothing to diminish his following. In late 1981, markets fell worldwide, sometimes in apparent response to Granville's calls. According to Rhoda Bramner of *Barron's*: "while Granville strutted across the investment stage, the market pretty much followed his bearish script."[2]

Unfortunately for Granville, he missed the turn of the market in 1982. Stubborn bearishness kept his followers out of the early stages of one of history's greatest bull markets. In a cruel twist of fate, Granville turned "wildly bullish" prior to the 1987 crash. As a result, a 1992 study by Hulbert's *Financial Digest* concluded that Granville ranked last among an undistinguished group of investment newsletter writers, down 93 percent over the twelve-year period.

Joe Granville's one-time prominence in the investment world provides evidence of the investing public's association of superior returns with investment skill. Granville's methodology relied on technical factors with absolutely no predictive power. Yet he moved markets, fooling large numbers of people into following his absurd predictions.

The Beardstown Ladies

In the early 1990s, the Beardstown Ladies captured the investing public's attention. Based on an impressive historical record of beating the S&P 500 by 8.5 percent per year for the ten years ending in 1993, the matrons of Beardstown parlayed their success into a lucrative writing and lecturing career. Their first book, *The Beardstown Ladies Common-Sense Investment Guide: How We Beat the Stock Market—And How You Can Too*, sold more than 800,000 copies. The group followed with four more books, *The Beardstown Ladies' Pocketbook Guide to Picking Stocks; The Beardstown Ladies' Guide to Smart Spending for Big Savings: How to Save for a Rainy Day Without Sacrificing Your Lifestyle; The Beardstown Ladies' Stitch-in-Time Guide to Growing Your Nest Egg: Step-by-Step Planning for a Comfortable Future*; and *Cookin' Up Profits on Wall Street*. The Beardstown empire, which in addition to books included lectures, videos, and cassettes, rested on the public's belief in the solid foundation of the Beardstown Ladies' extraordinary investment success.

All of the hoopla surrounding the Beardstown Ladies met with relatively little skepticism. Assertions of superior performance provided *prima facie* evidence of the efficacy of their investment approach. No further analysis needed.

Unfortunately, the Beardstown Ladies possessed so little analytical ability that calculating investment returns challenged their capabilities. Because the investment club's treasurer erred when using a computer program, she reported a two-year return as applying to a ten-year period. In fact, upon critical examination, the extended record of reported strong relative performance turned out to be worse than mediocre. Figures compiled by Price Waterhouse concluded that the Beardstown Ladies produced returns of only 9.1 percent per annum, falling short of the S&P 500 return by 5.8 percent per year and failing to meet previously reported results by a staggering 14.3 percent per year. In short, the investment record merits not even a modest magazine article.

The fundamental lesson from the Beardstown Ladies' saga relates to the attitude investors take toward performance records. Markets price securities efficiently enough that when presented with a superior performance record, the initial reaction ought to be that strong performance most likely resulted from a series of favorable draws from the distribution of potential outcomes. Only when managers articulate a compelling, coherent investment philosophy should fiduciaries begin to consider the active management opportunity.

Jim Cramer

Jim Cramer deserves a prominent place in the pantheon of investment anti-heroes. Educated at Harvard College and Harvard Law School, Cramer squanders his extraordinary credentials and shamelessly promotes stunningly inappropriate investment advice to an all-too-gullible audience.

Cramer made a name as an unabashed cheerleader for tech stocks during the Internet bubble. He rationalized the purchase of absurdly valued securities by asserting that the professionals "got it wrong" and the public is "much, much smarter than you realize."[3] Near the peak of the market in January 2000, Cramer articulated six "commonsensical rules" that allow the "average individual" to "routinely beat the professionals." Included in his list of rules were "buy stocks of companies you like," "buy expensive stocks," and "buy stocks that move in chunks."[4] Cramer's inane rules proved perfectly timed to inflict the maximum damage to his readers' portfolios.

Cramer never minces words. He described the "momentum/growth camp" as a group of investors that "would rather buy stocks that have both earnings and technical momentum, regardless of price. In other words, it doesn't matter how expensive they are, as long as they execute."[5] Not content simply to promote an irresponsible momentum strategy amid a market bubble, Cramer took the then long-suffering value managers to task. He registered palpable contempt for the "value/contrarian camp," contending that "denial is the basis of the value thesis." He accused value investors of exhibiting "systematic blindness to all things tech," chiding Warren Buffett for his "preposterous" preference for "Coke over Microsoft."[6]

In February 2000, Cramer wrote about the arrogance of value mutual fund managers, lamenting that "[n]ot only do they have the guts to tell us that we are wrong to own our Ciscos and our Yahoo!s, they also insist that they are the only authority on what to buy."

Cramer asserted that value managers holding Philip Morris "should have to answer to their dereliction of duty" and added that "the worst are the managers who bought the Cokes and Pepsis . . ." He followed with a piece of advice for mutual fund investors in "growth-turned-value stories": "Take control. Fire these guys."[7]

Of course, Cramer's advice missed the mark by a wide margin. In the year following the publication of his anti-value rant, Coke gained 10 percent, Pepsi, 36 percent and Philip Morris, a stunning 171 percent. Meanwhile, Cramer's favorites collapsed, with Cisco down 57 percent and Yahoo! declining by a staggering 84 percent.

If Cramer's early 2000 preference for Cisco and Yahoo! over Philip Morris and Coke laid waste to his adherents' portfolios, his calls on the grocery business destroyed even more value. In February 2000, Cramer suggested that "the death knell for value investing may very well be sounding right now because of technological innovation." He asserted that old economy grocer Albertsons was "being hit by a fundamental paradigm shift," which "will only get worse as Urban Fetch, Kozmo and Webvan expand."[8] Cramer unequivocally placed his bet on Internet-era firms.

Nine months after Cramer's prognostication, Fetch discontinued its consumer delivery business. Even though Kozmo never executed its hoped-for public offering (sparing Cramer's readers an opportunity to lose money), the firm managed to muddle through until April 2000 when it ceased operations. Webvan, which boasted a market capitalization of more than $5 billion at the time of Cramer's February 2000 call, filed for bankruptcy in July 2001. Meanwhile, Albertsons, the dinosaur doomed to extinction, posted profits of more than $500 million on nearly $38 billion of 2001 revenues. Ultimately, on May 30, 2006 Albertsons succumbed to a takeover by a group led by SuperValu. Scorekeepers note that from the time of Cramer's misguided, top-of-the-market advice to the date of merger consummation, Albertsons returned an annualized 0.5 percent per annum, beating the S&P 500's 0.2 percent per annum and trouncing the NASDAQ's −9.1 percent per annum.

In spite of Jim Cramer's massively misguided top-of-the-market advice, in March 2005, CNBC gave him his own TV show, *Mad Money*. On *Mad Money*, Cramer makes a mockery of the investment process, throwing chairs, shoving toy bears in meat grinders, wearing sombreros, and decapitating bobble-head dolls (made in his own likeness).[9] Betwixt and between his sophomoric antics, Cramer throws out hundreds of stock recommendations. In fact, according to an August 2007 *Barron's* article, a database covering six months of Cramer's picks contained an astounding 3,458 stocks. *Barron's* concludes that "the credible evidence suggests that the telestockmeister's picks aren't beating the market. Did you really expect more from a call-in host who makes 7,000 stock picks a year?" To make a dismal story worse, Cramer failed to beat the market in spite of a post-broadcast surge of an average of 2 percent for his picks. *Barron's* negative assessment would be even more dire were transaction costs and taxes included.

Aside from Cramer's unsurprising inability to choose thousands of stock market winners in any given year, he seems to have admitted to market manipulation when he ran a hedge fund in the late 1990s. In a December 23, 2006 interview with *Wall Street Confidential*, Cramer flat out said ". . . a lot of times when I was short at my hedge fund . . . I would create a level of activity beforehand that could drive the futures." He further noted that "it doesn't take much money. . . ." In the interview he goes on to describe ways to manipulate the prices of individual stocks.[10] According to *Barron's*, Cramer later "said he'd only been talking hypothetically."[11] Surely the Harvard-educated Cramer, who served a stint as editor in chief of the *Harvard Crimson*, knows that there is nothing hypothetical in the clause "when I was short at my hedge fund." Does Jim Cramer need a lesson in the subjunctive?

Joe Granville, the Beardstown Ladies, and Jim Cramer provide compelling evidence that market participants frequently and uncritically accept simple prominence as proof of sound underlying investment strategy. The falls from grace suffered by Joe Granville and the Beardstown Ladies (and perhaps a future fall from grace for Jim Cramer) should encourage investors to adopt skeptical attitudes when evaluating active management opportunities.

PERSONAL CHARACTERISTICS

Real estate investors invoke the mantra "location, location, location." Sensible investors seeking to engage an active manager focus on "people, people, people." Nothing matters more than working with high quality partners.

Integrity tops the list of qualifications. Aside from the fact that moral behavior represents a fundamentally important standard for human interaction, working with ethical advisors increases the likelihood of investment success. Choosing external advisors of high integrity reduces the gap between the actions of the advisors and the interests of an institutional fund.

Inevitable differences exist between the interests of an endowment and an outside money manager. The more profound issues might include differences in financial goals, time horizon, tax status, and various forms of business risk. Regardless of the structure of contractual arrangements, external advisors tend to respond to personal incentives. Employing individuals with high moral standards reduces the severity of conflicts of interest, as ethical managers consider seriously the goals of the institutional client when resolving conflicts.

Loyalty plays an important part in investment management relationships, allowing longer term thinking to dominate decision making. In the best of circumstances, the interdependence of institutional investors and external advisors creates a spirit of partnership, enhancing opportunities to create successful, lasting relationships.

Loyalty flows both ways. Investors owe external advisors the opportunity to pursue investment activities within a reasonable time frame. Firing a poorly performing manager simply to remove an embarrassing line item from a quarterly investment report fails to meet the test of reasonableness. Likewise, an investment advisor abandoning reliable partners simply to pursue a lower cost source of capital follows a short-sighted strategy.

Obviously, loyalty does not require permanent maintenance of the status quo. Relationships between fiduciaries and external managers come to an end for a variety of compelling reasons. Far too frequently, however, investors abandon good partners for trivial reasons, imposing unnecessary costs and needlessly disrupting portfolio management activities. Investment advisors and institutional fund managers operating with a presumption of loyalty enhance opportunities for long-term success.

Top-notch managers invest with a passion, working to beat the market with a nearly obsessive focus. Many extraordinary investors spend an enormous amount of time investigating investment opportunities, working long after rational professionals would have concluded a job well done. Great investors tend to have a "screw loose," pursuing the game not for profit, but for sport. Markets fascinate successful investors.

The best investors care about risk. Diligence and hard work take an investment manager only so far, as even the most carefully researched decisions ultimately face the vicissitudes of market forces. Because so much lies beyond a portfolio manager's control, superior investors seek to know as much as can be known, limiting uncertainty to the irreducible minimum. Well-researched investment ideas tend to be the least risky, since, as Yale's great economist Irving Fisher observed, "risk varies inversely with knowledge."[12]

Money provides an obvious motivation, bringing enormous wealth to successful investment advisors. Yet money managers seeking to maximize income constitute a poor group from which to choose. Profit maximizing business plans involve unbridled asset growth and unimaginative benchmark hugging strategies, factors at odds with investment success. Appealing money managers limit assets under management and make aggressive, unconventional security choices, incurring substantial risks for their money management business with the hope of generating superior investment returns.

Warren Buffett produced his own set of desirable money manager characteristics in a March 2007 announcement of the search for his successor as Berkshire Hathaway's chief investment officer:

> Picking the right person(s) will not be an easy task. It's not hard, of course, to find smart people, among them individuals who have impressive investment records. But there is far more to successful long-term investing than brains and performance that has recently been good.
>
> Over time, markets will do extraordinary, even bizarre, things. A single, big mistake could wipe out a long string of successes. We therefore need someone genetically programmed to recognize and avoid serious risks, including those never before encountered. Certain perils that lurk in investment strategies cannot be spotted by use of the models commonly employed today by financial institutions.
>
> Temperament is also important. Independent thinking, emotional stability, and a keen understanding of both human and institutional behavior is vital to long-term investment success. I've seen a lot of very smart people who have lacked these virtues.
>
> Finally, we have a special problem to consider: our ability to keep the person we hire. Being able to list Berkshire on a resume would materially enhance the marketability of an investment manager. We will need, therefore, to be sure we can retain our choice, even though he or she could leave and make much more money elsewhere.[13]

Even Warren Buffett worries about losing a colleague to a better economic opportunity!

Due diligence on the principals of an investment management organization provides critical input into the manager selection process. Spending time with manager candidates, both in business and social settings, allows assessment of whether the manager exhibits characteristics of a good partner. Questioning individuals on manager-supplied reference lists confirms or negates impressions gathered in the due diligence process. Contacting people not included on an official reference list, including past and present colleagues, competitors, and others, provides opportunities to evaluate the quality of a prospective manager's business dealings and integrity level.

In the intensely competitive investment management arena, only a small percentage of managers overcome the enormous burden of fees to post market-beating records. Identifying members of the small group that will prove to be successful requires an intense focus on personal characteristics. Only the best of the best will succeed.

ORGANIZATIONAL CHARACTERISTICS

The right people tend to create the right organization, reinforcing the centrality of selecting strong partners. However, finding great people, while necessary, marks only a starting point in the search for a money manager, for strong people in a poorly structured organization face the markets with a significant, unnecessary handicap. In a world rich with alternatives, compromising on structural issues makes little sense.

Attractive investment management organizations encourage decisions directed toward creating investment returns, not toward generating fee income. Such principal-oriented advisors tend to be small, entrepreneurial, and independent.

Size and Client Base

Appropriate size depends on the nature of the investment opportunity. In general, smaller tends to be better. Market size matters little when trading highly liquid securities such as U.S. Treasury bonds and large-capitalization domestic equities. Of course, such markets provide few opportunities to generate excess returns. Interesting active management situations reside in smaller, less liquid markets, requiring managers to exercise discipline in limiting assets under management.

Constraints related to the number of clients limit rational firm growth as severely as do constraints related to asset size. While routine communication might be conducted through broad-based mailings or by client service personnel, informed clients inevitably require meaningful amounts of an investment principal's time and energy. An investment advisor opting for less involved, less burdensome clients makes a potentially serious mistake. First, high quality clients occasionally provide useful input into the investment process. Second, in the event that the firm experiences an explicable stretch of poor performance, high quality clients continue to support the manager's activities. Less sophisticated clients control unreliable money, oftentimes exhibiting pro-cyclical tendencies, buying high, selling low, and introducing instability into the investment management operation.

A strong client base creates advantages for both the investment advisor and the clients themselves. If a money management firm's client roster contains "weak hands," temporary poor relative performance might cause substantial asset withdrawals. Such withdrawals harm other clients directly, in the case of transactions costs spread among participants in commingled funds, and indirectly, in the case of client defections leading to poor firm morale.

In contrast, intelligently supportive clients contribute financial and emotional support to investment managers experiencing a rough stretch of performance. By adding assets to an underperforming manager's account, the client stands to profit from a future reversal of fortune, while the manager benefits from the client's vote of confidence.

Entrepreneurial Attitude

Small, independent firms operate on the opposite end of the spectrum from large subsidiaries of financial services conglomerates. Appropriate firm size and sensible ownership structures contribute to superior investment results. The tendency of smaller, principal-oriented firms to behave in an entrepreneurial fashion provides critical context to the investment management process. Entrepreneurial environments emphasize people, putting them ahead of bureaucracy and structure. By placing people first, investment organizations increase chances for success.

In entrepreneurial organizations, individuals drive decisions, placing great importance on selecting partners with attractive behavioral characteristics. Great people provide the core of a strong entrepreneurial operation, according to venture capitalist Len Baker, because they "execute better, respond better to surprise, and attract other great people." He suggests that managers "be out there, be obsessive, and be bottom up." [14]

Entrepreneurial capitalism rests on three driving forces: innovation, ownership, and adaptation. Each characteristic contributes to successful money management organizations.

Innovation

According to Schumpeter, innovators "see things which only subsequently prove to be true."[15] By building an investment process that promotes foresight, investment advisors lay the groundwork for success. Excess returns stem from out-of-the-mainstream positions that subsequently achieve recognition, often in startling surprise to ordinary market observers. By identifying the unexpected consequence before the fact, successful investment managers realize superior returns from exploiting superior insights. Without creative portfolio choices, investment managers face dismal prospects, since the old combination represents the consensus view. Market efficiency drives returns on market-like portfolios to the average, causing conventional portfolios with conventional ideas to produce conventional results, a poor outcome for active investment managers.

In efforts to innovate, entrepreneurs encourage experimentation, accepting occasional shortfalls as the price paid for potential gains. Repeated failure precedes success in many entrepreneurial endeavors, requiring an organizational culture that encourages experimentation and accepts mistakes. By explicitly permitting failure, but holding down its costs, investment organizations create an environment allowing managers to construct truly novel, high-potential investment portfolios.

Ownership

Financial and psychic ownership leads to superior results. Strong investment management firms reward contributions monetarily while engaging the hearts and minds of staff members. Widely distributed ownership enhances organizational stability, facilitating long-term thinking. Carefully structured financial incentives elicit appropriate behavior from investment personnel, discouraging fee-driven activity and encouraging return-generating behavior. Psychic ownership provides a powerful complement to financial rewards. By causing investors to "buy in" to the process, interests of manager and client come together.

Adaptation

Adaptation involves careful selection, amplifying the strong and eliminating the weak. In choosing a portfolio of attractive positions from a large universe of potential opportunities, successful investors express unusual insights ahead of the herd. Strong ideas command meaningful portions of assets, magnifying the impact of high conviction positions, while weak positions disappear. When circumstances change, managers reconfigure portfolios to reflect new realities. Not only does adaptation influence the tactics of security selection, but as markets evolve, adaptation may lead to new investment strategies. If inefficiencies disappear in a particular niche, the entrepreneur leaves the unattractive market and seeks new mispricings to exploit. Both tactically and strategically, adaptation plays an important role in money management.

Contrast the flexibility of entrepreneurial organizations with bureaucracies. Bureaucratic structures deal effectively with repetitive, regular, slow-to-change environments. Control-oriented processes emphasize structure, subordinating the role of people. Bureaucracies employ conventional wisdom and seek consensus, punishing failure quickly and ruthlessly. By pursuing safety and avoiding controversy, bureaucratic structures systematically screen out the market opportunities likely to yield superior returns. Bureaucracies deal poorly with constantly changing market environments and fail to address even elementary active investment management problems.

Many bureaucratic functionaries pursue investment with "name brand" money managers, reducing career risk by choosing widely recognized firms blessed by an external consultant. Large, process-driven entities that produce consistent results provide a safe haven for the timid client. Well-respected firms develop franchises, using their good name to attract and retain assets. In the realm of marketable investments, the franchise provides no benefit to the portfolio management process. The value of the franchise lies solely in the comfort level provided to clients.

Comfortable investment decisions fail to generate exciting results. Discomfort represents a necessary, albeit not sufficient, condition of success. Because entrepreneurial firms tend to be newer and smaller, track records may be harder to define and interpret. Less process-driven strategies depend heavily on individuals, reducing the fiduciary's ability to rely on the franchise for results. While backing an entrepreneurial group takes more courage than serving up a "name brand" recommendation, investment success may require backing managers without standard institutional credentials.

Unfortunately, once-attractive investment partners sometimes mature into unattractive bureaucracies. Schumpeter's concept of creative destruction takes hold, as organizations evolve from small entrepreneurial "craft shops" to large enterprises with characteristics that undermine the premise that supported forming the firm in the first place. As the organization grows, mutation ". . . incessantly revolutionizes the economic structure *from within*, incessantly destroying the old one, incessantly creating a new one."[16] Institutional acceptability threatens the very characteristics that made the firm interesting in the first place. As time and size erode the entrepreneurial enthusiasm that brought initial success to the firm, the fund manager needs to reject the old partners and seek new partners to provide superior management capabilities. The process of creative destruction, which Schumpeter concludes is "the essential fact about capitalism," poses challenges for investment management organizations.[17]

Investment Guerrillas

Miles Morland, formerly general partner of Blakeney Management, captured the essence of the strengths of an entrepreneurial investment management organization in a letter describing why he did not proceed with a contemplated joint venture involving a much larger financial services conglomerate. Blakeney manages assets in Africa and the Middle East.

> I am afraid we are not going to go ahead with our merger. . . . Blakeney is a small group of guerrillas. Our success comes from our ability to fight and forage in places too small and too risky for people with more to lose. That is also what makes it such an exhilarating place to work. We are focused completely on getting and doing business with no thought for our supply lines or on whose territory we are trespassing. [Your firm] is a big and powerful uniformed army. Thanks to you it has retained its entrepreneurial spirit more than any other large American firm but that is like saying that the parachute troops are more entrepreneurial than the tank battalions. Big firms by their nature need disciplines and chains of command. Their sheer size means that when they venture overseas they build

complex relationships with other powers in other lands who speak the same language. . . .

Guerrillas cannot be integrated into the regular army without losing what it is that makes them effective. All the professionals at Blakeney have previously been officers in the regular army and have deserted to join the guerrillas. It is the thought that you personally are a guerrilla at heart that has made us go on with the negotiations despite the warning signs. If we ask ourselves how will this deal help us do more and better business, and how will it make our lives more interesting and more fun, we cannot find an answer. Everything points in the opposite direction. This is no criticism of [your firm] or the excellent people we have gotten to know there. It is the reality of forming an affiliation with someone as big as you. Even if we don't have to put on uniforms we will have to run our business in a way that acknowledges the rules that are imposed on you and when we go foraging for business we will have to respect your existing alliances. We are rustlers by nature not herders. We want to make lightning raids in Zimbabwe and Ghana and Egypt while your partners . . . are holding meetings to decide . . . about how and where they are going to deploy their mighty troops. When they arrive we hope they will find a few of the local cattle are missing.

. . . I hope we can continue to do things together. All this only started because of the respect I have for you personally. I bear the blame for not realizing sooner what the implications of the deal were. At the end of the day, we might have been the majority shareholder and you the minority one, but if a majority mouse lies down with a minority elephant it is not the elephant who is going to end up as a pancake.

By selecting investment managers with an entrepreneurial orientation, fiduciaries improve the chances for investment success. Large, multiproduct, process-driven firms face the daunting hurdle of overcoming bureaucratic obstacles. Small, focused, independent firms with excellent people provide the highest likelihood of identifying the contrarian path to excellent investment results.

Independent Organizations

Investors increase the degree of coincidence of interests with fund managers by choosing to work with focused, independent firms. Particularly severe conflicts between investor goals and money manager actions arise in "financial supermarkets"—large, bureaucratic organizations that offer a variety of investment management options. Employees at financial conglomerates turn over at substantially greater rates than at independent firms. Compensation explains part of the reason. The investment management subsidiary's revenues flow to the financial supermarket, which takes some as profit and returns some as salary to the subsidiary's principals. Successful portfolio managers employed by supermarkets have the option of simply moving across the street, opening up shop, and garnering 100 percent of the revenues associated with their efforts. The profit objective of the financial supermarket creates instability at the investment management subsidiary, opening a gap between the interests of the firm and the client. A desire for independence explains another part of the reason for high employee turnover. The opportunity to operate without interference from bureaucrats intent on serving corporate interests appeals to the best investment minds. Ill-informed, outside intervention in the decision-making process, however well-intentioned, creates the potential for suboptimal outcomes and provides incentive to establish an independent firm. A final motivation comes from a sense of ownership. Owner operators simply work harder and better than rank-and-file employees. Small, independent, entrepreneurial organizations provide greater coincidence of interest between firm and client.

Investment focus improves the chances of satisfying client objectives. A narrow product line forces managers to live and die by investment results, creating an enormous incentive to produce superior returns. In contrast, a firm with a broad product line anticipates that hoped-for gains on winning products more than offset inevitable losses on losing strategies, reducing the cost of any single product failure. Even worse, in seeking steady streams of income, financial supermarket managers fashion broadly diversified portfolios, tracking market benchmarks closely enough to avoid termination and too closely to achieve excellence. Investors prefer that fund managers place all their eggs in one basket, and watch that basket with great care. By selecting concentrated, focused managers, investors increase chances for success.

In pursuing stable flows of revenues, financial conglomerates seek income growth at the expense of investment performance. Investment managers soon recognize that rewards come primarily from attracting new cash flows, not generating superior investment returns. Since size is the enemy of performance, asset gatherers win at their clients' expense.

Public ownership of an investment management organization introduces another set of issues for the firm's clients. While the goals of a privately held financial supermarket differ materially from the interests of the money management clients, in the case of a publicly owned money manager the introduction of outside shareholders further exacerbates the conflicts of interest. The most obvious, and perhaps the most severe, problem concerns the conflict of interest between money management clients and external shareholders.

Fortress Investment Group

When an independent investment management firm files to go public, the offering documents contain clues regarding the consequences for owners of the firm, their clients, and the public shareholders-to-be. But, offering documents frequently fail to address head-on the fundamental conflict that arises from introducing public shareholders into the mix. In the context of a private firm, the investment manager accepts the responsibility to provide superior investment results to clients that entrust assets to the investment manager's care. In the context of a public firm, the investment manager retains the responsibility to serve the clients' interests and adds a responsibility to public shareholders. The interests of the clients and the public shareholders often conflict.

The public offering of shares in the Fortress Investment Group, a $26 billion manager of private equity partnerships, hedge funds, and publicly traded alternative investment vehicles, highlights the issues confronting a publicly traded firm's clients. Take the case of dividends. The November 2006 registration statement proudly notes that "unlike many publicly traded asset managers, we intend to pay out a significant portion . . . of our annual distributable earnings in the form of quarterly dividends."[18] Substantial dividends clearly benefit shareholders. In contrast, investors in Fortress's asset management products suffer from the firm's dividend policy.

Consider the source of funds for dividend payments. The most reliable income stream comes from the management fees that Fortress charges for asset management services. Higher fees and increased assets under management benefit the public shareholder. Neither higher fees nor increased assets benefit the clients of the Fortress funds. In fact, both factors produce lower investment returns. To add insult to injury, some portion of the fees paid by Fortress's clients go not to the principals making the investment decisions, but to faceless public shareholders. The issue of dividend payments highlights the conflict between clients and shareholders.

In an attempt to justify the public offering, the offering statement includes a helpful section entitled "Why We Are Going Public," that contains the headers People, Permanence, Capital, and Currency. With respect to "People," Fortress suggests that publicly traded shares would "increase our ability to provide financial incentives to our existing and future employees."[19] The Fortress statement ignores the obvious fact that public shareholders claim a portion of the funds that otherwise would have been available for distribution to the firm's investment professionals. A public offering diminishes the size of the compensation pool, making Fortress's claim disingenuous at best.

Regarding "Permanence," Fortress expects to benefit from an increase in the proportion of capital that institutions and individuals allocate to the firm. No evidence exists that capital providers prefer publicly traded firms to privately held firms. In fact, if capital providers seek high risk-adjusted returns, the fundamentals support the opposite conclusion.

As to "Capital" and "Currency", Fortress suggests that publicly traded shares facilitate the firm's ability to grow, create new investment products, and finance future strategic acquisitions. Increases in assets and numbers of products may well benefit Fortress principals and public shareholders, but do nothing to serve the interests of the clients of Fortress funds.

Strangely absent from the list of reasons to go public is "Greed." Just prior to the IPO, on December 18, 2006 the Fortress principals (five in number) sold 15 percent of the firm to Japanese securities firm Nomura "for approximately $888 million, all of the proceeds of which went to the Principals."[20] Moreover, between September 30, 2006 and the consummation of the IPO, the Fortress S-1 registration statement noted that "we distributed $528.5 million to our principals."[21] In addition, careful readers who make it to page 80 of the offering circular note that shortly prior to the initial public offering, the principals of Fortress entered into a $750 million credit agreement, which provided funds for refinancing a prior $175 million credit facility and for "investment in various existing and new Fortress Funds, and to make a one-time $250 million distribution of capital to our principals."[22] Finally, in a tangle of complexity that only a lawyer could love, the registration statement describes a "tax receivable agreement," which might produce payments to the principals that "could be material in amount."[23]

Between the $888 million Nomura windfall, the $528.5 million of pre-IPO distributions, and the $250 million loan distribution, the five principals of Fortress cashed in to the tune of $1,666.5 million. Finding the three elements of the Fortress principals' paydays required careful reading of pages and pages of legalistic prose in the company's disclosure documents. In a straightforward world, the section entitled "Why We Are Going Public" would contain one header, "Greed," that transparently outlined the $1.7 billion of payments to the fortunate few.

The Fortress IPO clearly benefits the senior principals of the firm and just as clearly imposes costs on both the junior Fortress professionals and the firm's clients. By giving a piece of the pie to outside shareholders and by cashing out themselves, the senior principals leave far less to compensate their subordinates. By introducing a responsibility to serve the interests of public shareholders, Fortress creates a conflict with their fiduciary obligation to clients. Public offerings of money management firms benefit the few at the expense of many.

[handwritten margin note: IPO's benefit Shareholders at the top]

United Asset Management

United Asset Management (UAM), a once-acquisitive conglomerate of investment advisors, illustrates the problems with external ownership of investment managers. At the end of 1998, with equity interests in forty-five firms and managing in excess of $200 billion, UAM ranked among the world's largest owners of investment management firms. While the firm boasted an impressive level of assets under management, UAM operated with a fundamentally flawed strategy.

The UAM investment manager roster included a number of well-known, highly regarded groups, including Acadian Asset Management and Murray Johnstone Limited. While superior historical performance created UAM manager reputations, their acquisition by UAM dimmed prospects for future excess returns. The emphasis on asset gathering, loss of entrepreneurial drive, and diversion of revenues to passive shareholders created conditions that led to investment mediocrity.

Even though UAM's 1997 annual report lists the name, address, and investment strategy of each of the firm's affiliated managers, no performance data appear. Net client withdrawals of $16.0 billion in 1997, representing 9.4 percent of assets at the beginning of the year, pointed to the conclusion that managers produced generally unsatisfactory performance. The few textual references to investment performance do little to confuse the annual report's clear message: manager rewards stem from increasing assets under management, not from generating superior investment returns.

Board chairman Norton Reamer addresses the leakage of assets by identifying "improving our firms' net client cash flow [as] our top priority in 1998. . . ."[24] The report later outlines incentive programs to reach the goal, "which is clearly a function of improved client service and retention as well as product development and marketing." Where is the reference to investment returns? The annual report indicates that new acquisitions will "concentrate on firms with the highest growth potential," not on firms most likely to provide superior performance.

In spite of a roaring bull market, UAM failed to increase "net client cash flow." Throughout 1998, nearly $20 billion in assets left the money management firms under UAM's umbrella. While UAM continued to articulate a goal of increasing assets through improved client servicing, the firm announced several investment-oriented initiatives designed to improve performance.

The performance improvement initiatives evidently failed, as 1999 proved no more successful than 1998. UAM's annual report noted that assets under management increased a scant $1.2 billion during the bull-market year; investment gains of $22.5 billion only slightly surpassed client outflows of $21.1 billion.*

On June 16, 2000, UAM threw in the towel, entering into an agreement to sell the firm to Old Mutual. The *Wall Street Journal* noted that the purchase price, which amounted to about 1.2 percent of assets under management, stood at the low end of the "going rate of 1%-to-5% of assets," reflecting "some of the restructuring work that lies ahead."[25] Trevor Moss, a London-based securities analyst, observed that UAM had "about the same level of assets under management that it had about five years ago," a dismal showing in the context of the U.S. equity market's nearly threefold increase.[26]

UAM fizzled for a variety of reasons. External ownership of investment firms inevitably alters the institutional culture, diminishing the entrepreneurial spirit so critical to successful money management organizations. When senior professionals "cash out," the single-minded focus on generating strong results dissipates, sapping the vitality of the

---

*The sale of an affiliate reduced assets under management by $200 million.

firm. After the sale of a firm, junior professionals face a less rosy future. According to UAM disclosure documents, after a typical acquisition, only 50 percent to 70 percent of revenues remain with the investment management firm. The diversion of resources to passive external shareholders reduces the size of the pie available for distribution to investment professionals, creating instability. Employees of professional services firms with substantial outside ownership enjoy the option of moving across the street, setting up shop and garnering a greater share of the newly formed independent firm's profits.

In October 2007, Old Mutual's president and chief executive officer Scott Powers acknowledged the challenge of external ownership, noting that "[i]t's taken us a while to figure out the right mix of short-term and long-term incentives." Five years after the UAM purchase, Old Mutual "largely completed" the process of changing revenue sharing agreements into profit sharing arrangements, a step that reduces incentives to gather assets. In 2007, Powers articulated a longer term goal "to get equity into the hands of our affiliates." While providing equity ownership to the principals of investment management subsidiaries moves the organizational structure in the right direction, the ultimate sharing of equity necessarily falls short of the 100 percent ownership characteristic of an independent investment manager.[27]

Pursuit of investment excellence in the context of a conglomerate of investment managers proves futile, as the goals of external owners fail to coincide with the aspirations of investors. Asset gathering creates diseconomies of scale for investors, decreasing the possibility of achieving superior performance. The transformation of senior managers from owners to employees creates changes in firm culture that disadvantage investors. Finally, compensation for external shareholders impairs the money management firm's ability to pay portfolio managers at competitive levels, leading to turnover among personnel and posing risks to investor assets. Significant external ownership of asset management firms creates barriers to investment success.

Investment Banks and Investment Management

Conflicts of interest abound in the financial world, with large, complex organizations facing the widest range of issues. Investment banks frequently sponsor private equity funds, using access to proprietary deal flow as a selling point. Unfortunately, deals originated by the investment banking network come with built-in conflicts. When a company engages an investment bank to sell a division, alarm bells should ring when the banker suggests that the investment bank's private equity fund purchase the division. Is the investment bank serving the interest of a good corporate client by paying a rich price for the division? Or, is the investment bank serving the interest of the private equity fund by paying a low price? Under such circumstances, fairness opinions notwithstanding, no fair price exists.

Less subtle conflicts permeate the process. Investment banks sometimes put themselves in untenable positions, advising companies at the same time as they provide financing. In August 2007, Lehman Brothers found itself horribly conflicted when its Home Depot Supply transaction floundered amid the LBO debt crunch. As reported in the *International Herald Tribune*, Lehman "advised Home Depot on the sale at the same time it was also providing financing to the buying group. Suddenly, Lehman was turning around and threatening to scuttle a deal it had advised one of its most important clients to accept."[28] Ultimately, Goldman Sachs replaced Lehman as an advisor and Lehman retraded the deal, obtaining more lucrative terms for its financing. Advisory and financing roles always conflict; the stresses of the LBO funding crisis brought the conflict into high relief.

After deals close, investment banks often continue to provide financial advisory and capital markets services to portfolio companies. In an unusual public description of the bonanza created by captive private equity funds, the December 14, 1990 *Wall Street Journal* detailed fees generated by Morgan Stanley's investment in Burlington Industries.

Morgan Stanley and Burlington Industries

In 1987, Morgan Stanley's leveraged buyout fund invested $46 million of equity in the $2.2 billion purchase of Burlington Industries. Over the next three years, the investment bank charged the company more than $120 million in fees for services ranging from underwriting to advising on divestitures. Because Morgan Stanley controlled the board of Burlington Industries, decisions regarding financing and divestitures were neither arm's length nor exposed to market forces. At best, all transactions benefited the company, with Morgan Stanley compensated at market rates for services rendered. At worst, unnecessary transactions generated above-market fees, disadvantaging the company and Morgan Stanley fund investors. When a fund sponsor profits by charging advisory fees at the direct expense of investors, serious conflicts of interest ensue.

Noting that "nearly every time Burlington needed advice, Morgan Stanley turned on the meter," *Wall Street Journal* reporter George Anders suggests that "the story of Burlington Industries raises troubling questions about Wall Street's foray into merchant banking."[29] Fees generated by Morgan Stanley "for everything from underwriting Burlington's high yield debt to overseeing a blizzard of divestitures" dwarf the equity investment made by the partners of Morgan Stanley in the Burlington transaction, providing handsome returns to the investment bank irrespective of the returns delivered to the firm's private equity investors.[30]

Goldman Sachs and the Water Street Corporate Recovery Fund

Goldman Sachs created an even more extensive web of conflicts when in 1990 it established the Water Street Corporate Recovery Fund, a $783 million "vulture fund" set up to make concentrated investments in distressed securities. Hoping to be viewed as a savior of bankrupt companies, instead Goldman stirred up a hornet's nest of conflicts.

One set of conflicts existed between Goldman's financial restructuring advisory business and control investing in distressed situations. Investment banks generally rely on "Chinese walls" to contain sensitive data supplied by clients in the course of advisory assignments, keeping inside information away from securities analysts and traders. The term Chinese wall may be employed because such walls are easily removed at an assignment's end. A cynic (or realist) might argue that paper-thin permeability more aptly describes Chinese walls. Because Goldman partner Mikael Salovaara both ran the Water Street Fund and continued to advise clients on restructuring, any shred of separation between the business disappeared, causing "traders at other firms (to joke) that Mr. Salovaara had a 'Chinese wall' in the middle of his brain."[31]

The Water Street Fund investment in distressed bonds of toymaker Tonka illustrates several strands of the web of conflicts. After accumulating a position in Tonka's debt securities, Salovaara competed for an assignment to advise Mattel on a possible acquisition of Tonka, in the process, perhaps, picking up potentially valuable non-public information regarding the value and salability of Tonka's bonds. Goldman's advantage infuriated junk bond investors not privy to the information, causing several to complain publicly and to suggest they would reduce activity with Goldman's trading desk.[32]

Ultimately, Tonka agreed to be acquired by Hasbro, creating yet

Goldman selfish with bond position

another problem for Goldman. The Water Street Fund owned more than half of Tonka's bonds, having acquired the position at less than 50 percent of face value.[33] Even though Tonka's board of directors wished to sell the company to Hasbro, Goldman played hardball, holding out for more money for the firm's bond position. While such tactics raise few eyebrows in the rough and tumble world of distressed debt, some clients saw Goldman's actions as inconsistent with the firm's avowal to avoid any participation in hostile merger activity. Ultimately, the investment bank's tactics worked, increasing payments received for the Tonka bond position by reducing the value of other participants' Tonka and Hasbro shareholdings. Goldman's investment returns came at great expense, tarnishing the firm's reputation for putting clients first.

A final strand in the conflict web relates to Goldman's junk bond trading activity. To avoid competition, the firm limited the high yield trading desk's activity in bonds that interested the Water Street Fund. Goldman's trading clients, already concerned about the firm's possible informational advantages, faced market makers less able to take positions.

Goldman's advisory conflict troubles went beyond the Tonka case. According to an article in the June 4, 1991 *Wall Street Journal*, "nine of twenty-one companies that the Water Street Fund selected for 'restructuring' are or were Goldman clients."[34] Perceptions mounted that Goldman invested the Water Street Fund with an unfair advantage.

Faced with a storm of controversy, Goldman shut down the fund in May 1991, several years ahead of schedule. Even though the Water Street Fund generated handsome returns during its abbreviated life, the fund's enduring legacy may be its rich series of lessons on conflicts of interest.

Goldman Sachs and the Global Equity Opportunities Fund

In mid August 2007, Goldman Sachs faced unprecedented carnage in its hedge fund portfolio. The firm's flagship $7.5 billion Global Alpha Fund, managed by Mark Carhart and Raymond Iwanowski, posted a stunning year-to-date decline of 27 percent.[35] The lower profile North American Equity Opportunities Fund dropped 25 percent in the first seven and a half months of the year. And, for good measure, the Global Equity Opportunities Fund lost a stunning 30 percent of its value in the second week of August alone.[36] In aggregate, the net value of the three funds managed by Carhart and Iwanowski declined by an impressive $4.7 billion during the first eight months of the calendar year.

Goldman had no skin in the game. The firm's chief financial officer David Viniar characterized Goldman's investments as "nothing substantial; very immaterial, if at all." Goldman simply collected fees for mismanaging the hedge funds; the losses belonged to the firm's investors. Yet, presented with an extreme market dislocation, Goldman chose to become a principal.

In response to the dramatic price declines, Goldman Sachs arranged a $3 billion injection into the Global Equity Opportunities Fund, of which approximately $2 billion came from Goldman Sachs itself. On a conference call explaining the move, David Viniar asserted the infusion of capital benefited Goldman Sachs and "the current investors in the fund, giving them the firepower to take advantage of the opportunities in the market today." In reality, Goldman used the bulk of the infusion to play defense. The fund managers employed the cash contribution to bring the fund's leverage down from an irresponsible level of approximately 6 to 1 to a still high (but more defensible) level of around 3.5 to 1.[37]

Goldman's move raises a number of questions. If, indeed, the move benefited existing clients by reducing leverage and providing firepower, why did Goldman choose to benefit only clients of the Global Equity Opportunities Fund? What of the fiduciary responsibility of Goldman Sachs to clients invested in the Global Alpha Fund and the North American Equity Opportunities Fund? Goldman Sachs's David Viniar noted that the fund managers were reducing risk and reducing leverage in both Global Alpha and North American Equity Opportunities. Why should Global Equity Opportunities receive a so-called benefit from Goldman in the form of a cash contribution that presumably allowed low-cost deleveraging, while the unfavored funds faced the market-related costs of selling assets in a hostile trading environment?

The timing of Goldman's investment raises questions about the firm's favored access to what senior management characterized as "a good investment opportunity." Instead of providing the opportunity to existing clients of the Global Equity Opportunities Fund, Goldman took the lion's share for itself and reached out to a select group of investors for the rest, ultimately raising $1 billion from the likes of Eli Broad, C.V. Starr (Maurice "Hank" Greenberg), and Perry Capital.[38] As a fiduciary for the investors in Global Equity Opportunities Fund, should not Goldman first offer the chance to take advantage of the fund's opportunities to the existing investors?

Viewed from another perspective, Goldman's investment in Global

Equity Opportunities might actually harm the fund's clients, in contrast to the benefit that Goldman claims. Goldman and the firm's favored co-investors enjoyed the opportunity to invest $3 billion in the Global Equity Opportunities Fund at net asset value on the day of their choosing. Goldman got a sweet deal. Had the $3 billion been invested in the securities that comprise the fund, the market impact of the sizable trades would no doubt force prices up, increasing Goldman's cost basis. Instead, by using the contributed assets to reduce leverage, Goldman bought in at a price that otherwise would have been impossible to achieve. Existing investors suffered dilution of their position.

Finally, Goldman Sachs provided the cherry-picking investors better deal terms than those accorded the existing Global Equity Opportunities Fund investors. In an analyst conference call, Goldman Sachs president and co-chief operating officer Gary Cohen noted that the firm's cash infusion put Goldman in an "equal position to all the existing investors." In fact, the new money pays no management fee, pays a reduced carry of 10 percent, and benefits from a hurdle rate of 10 percent. Because Goldman and the other favored investors received preferential terms on their investment, their actions certainly disadvantaged the existing fund investors.

In any event, Goldman picked an opportune time to make its commitment to the Global Equity Opportunities Fund. Bloomberg reported that in the week following the cash infusion, the fund rose 12 percent. A September 20th AP release noted that Goldman's investment had appreciated 16 percent in little more than a month. At least in the short run, Goldman made out well. Global Equity Opportunities Fund clients shared in the rebound, but by dint of Goldman's investment, in an attenuated fashion. Presented with an attractive investment opportunity, Goldman became a principal, riding roughshod over the interests of the firm's hedge fund clients and enriching itself in the process.

While investors cannot avoid conflicts entirely, fewer differences in interest exist when investing with independent investment management organizations. Avoiding affiliates and subsidiaries of financial services firms does little to reduce the rich set of investment manager alternatives.

DEAL STRUCTURE

Appropriate deal terms play an important role in producing satisfactory investment results. After identifying an attractive investment management firm, investors face the issue of evaluating (or negotiating) compensation arrangements. The degree of efficiency in asset pricing determines in part the nature of the compensation scheme, with passive management of efficiently priced securities demanding different treatment from active exploitation of anomalously priced assets. All aspects of investment management fee structures contain potential for conflict between the interests of investors and investment managers, forcing fiduciaries to pay close attention to explicit and implicit incentives embodied in management contracts.

Co-investment

Co-investment provides a powerful means of aligning fiduciary and fund manager interests. To the extent that a manager becomes a principal, issues regarding agency behavior diminish. Unfortunately, along with substantial co-investment, issues arise regarding possible differences in goals between mortal, taxpaying money managers and immortal, tax-exempt institutional investors. That said, co-investment reduces the incentive for investment advisors to profit at the expense of clients.

While any level of co-investment encourages fund managers to act like principals, the larger the personal commitment of funds the greater the focus on generating superior investment returns. Managers cease to benefit from attracting new capital at the point where the return diminution on the manager's personal stake caused by increasing assets under management exceeds the opportunity costs of fees foregone by limiting asset growth. Because the easily measured level of fees foregone generally eclipses the fuzzy estimate of size-induced performance drag, only the wealthiest managers confront a clear trade-off favoring asset growth limitations. Even though the numbers might favor asset-gathering strategies for most managers, substantial levels of co-investment send strong signals to investors regarding the principal orientation of fund managers. The idea that a fund manager believes strongly enough in the investment product to put a substantial personal stake in the fund suggests that the manager shares the investor's orientation.

Investment of personal assets side-by-side with client capital creates a powerful alignment of interests. While profit participations focus manager attention on the investor goal of generating handsome investment returns, a profit sharing arrangement in which managers share only in gains creates an option that encourages risk-seeking behavior. By making a substantial co-investment, managers participate directly in gains and losses, leading to more balanced assessment of investment opportunities. To realize the hoped-for behavioral outcome, the co-investment commitment must be large relative to the manager's net worth, even though the amount might be modest in absolute terms. When writing a check representing a material portion of personal assets, the investment manager steps into the role of a principal.

While co-investment generally improves the investor's position by aligning investment interests, differences in goals bear careful scrutiny. Taxpaying fund managers in partnership with tax-exempt institutional investors face different after-tax return scenarios. Mortal decision makers operate with shorter time horizons than appropriate for an enduring organization's permanent funds. Individuals with large fund investments frequently desire greater diversification than required by most institutions, which hold an already well-diversified collection of assets. Even though differences in tax status, time horizon, and risk tolerance drive wedges between the interests of individual fund managers and the goals of institutional investors, the benefits of substantial co-investment far outweigh the likely costs.

co-investment very profitable

Compensation Arrangements for Marketable Securities

The character of sensible compensation arrangements for investment managers varies with the degree of efficiency in asset pricing. Passive management of government bonds demands fee arrangements different from those appropriate for active management of private equity. For most asset classes investors face well-entrenched fee arrangements, ranging from asset-based fees for relatively efficiently priced marketable securities to a combination of asset-based fees and incentive payments for less efficiently priced asset types. Because marketplace practices frequently deviate from ideal compensation structures, price-taking investors generally take the pragmatic approach of choosing the best option from a set of bad alternatives.

Passive Strategies

Passive asset management differs fundamentally from active asset management. Size, the enemy of active investors, works in favor of index fund managers. For example, passive funds with large numbers of investors and sizable pools of assets frequently offer crossing opportunities, in which some portion of exiting investor demand for funds matches entering investor supply of funds, allowing nearly costless exit from and entrance to the investment pool.* Scale improves tracking of benchmarks, as large size facilitates full replication of the investment universe, reducing the need for tracking-error-inducing sampling procedures. Experience shows that funds with billions of dollars track benchmarks with little or no slippage.

Barclays Global Investors, one of the world's largest index fund managers, offers a wide variety of products designed to mirror various marketable security benchmarks, segregated into distinct pools for different types of investors. The largest pool of assets, designed to track the S&P 500, contained $127 billion on December 31, 2006. Before fees the fund returned 8.46 percent for the trailing ten years relative to 8.42 percent for the S&P 500 index. The much smaller bond pool, with $1.6 billion on December 31, 2006, showed similarly impressive results, with ten-year returns of 6.33 percent relative to 6.26 percent for the Lehman Brothers Government Corporate Index.

The commodity-like nature of passive investing commands commodity-like compensation. Index fund managers compete with the alternative of internally managed passive portfolios, forcing fees to a paltry two basis points per year for large accounts.** By choosing passive alternatives for efficiently priced assets, investors expect predictable results at a bargain price.

While strong arguments support passive management for all marketable securities, two factors argue strongly for passive management of bond portfolios in particular. First, to satisfy the deflation hedging role of fixed income, investors must hold long-term, high quality, noncallable bonds, suggesting the creation of stable duration government bond portfolios. Second, the extraordinary efficiency in the pricing of government bonds makes active security selection decisions a costly exercise in futility. The need for a stable maturity structure and the futility of individual security bets require that investors manage bond portfolios passively.

While domestic equity investors enjoy more flexibility in structuring portfolios than bond investors, the difficulty of identifying mate-

---

*Barclays Global Investors estimates that in recent years 60 percent to 70 percent of the firm's S&P 500 equity index fund transactions represented crossing trades. Such internal trades create no market impact and require no commission payments.

**Barclays Global Investors' fee schedule for the S&P 500 Index Fund starts at 7 basis points on the first $50 million, moves to 5 basis points on the next $50 million, and ends up at 2 basis points for amounts over $100 million. A basis point is ¹⁄₁₀₀ of 1 percent.

rial mispricings in the stock market, particularly among large-capitalization securities, leads many investors to index common stocks. By
avoiding high fees and substantial transactions costs, index funds provide long-term results that represent a formidable hurdle for investors
hoping to outperform. Yet, in spite of the clear difficulties in producing risk-adjusted excess returns, most investors pursue active management strategies.

Active Strategies

Careful active investors pay close attention to fee arrangements, recognizing that fees represent a substantial obstacle to market-beating performance. Active managers of marketable securities generally receive
asset-based fees in exchange for portfolio management services. On one
level, interests coincide. To the extent that a manager increases assets
through superior investment performance, both the manager and the
investor win as the manager's income increases and the investor's
return pleases. On other levels, interests conflict. The manager may pursue a "staying in business" strategy to protect fee income by closet
indexing, holding a market-like portfolio unlikely to produce results
that would lead to termination. Perhaps even more damaging, the
manager may conclude that gathering assets provides greater fee income
than generating superior returns.

    In growing assets, managers simply respond to economic incentives.
With asset-based fees, income increases as assets under management
increase. Frequently, managers find it easier to add assets by attracting
new accounts than by creating excess returns. With distressingly few
exceptions, fund managers aggressively pursue marketing activities,
attempting to gather as many assets as possible. Retaining assets
requires avoiding disastrous performance, causing money managers to
create market-like portfolios that all but eliminate the chance for superior performance. Investment management represents, at best, a secondary consideration for most institutional fund managers.

    Creating appropriate deal structures allows investors to mitigate
many of the conflicts inherent in the investment advisory relationship.
Sensible fee arrangements contain two elements: base compensation
that covers reimbursement of reasonable overhead costs and incentive
compensation that rewards a manager's value added. The incentive
compensation, or profits interest, represents a share of the returns
generated in excess of a benchmark appropriate to the investment

activity. For example, large-capitalization domestic marketable equity managers might be rewarded for returns generated in excess of the S&P 500, while foreign equity managers might receive a profits interest in returns above the Morgan Stanley Capital International EAFE Index. Fair deal structures, rare in the investment management arena, encourage appropriate behavior on the part of money managers.

Unfortunately, the overwhelming majority of marketable security managers employ asset-based fee schemes, causing market gains or losses and portfolio inflows or outflows to overwhelm the impact of manager skill. Even though a number of managers offer superficially attractive incentive compensation arrangements, three factors diminish the appeal of most schemes. First, the vast bulk of marketable security funds generate profits primarily from asset-based fees, encouraging managers to emphasize increasing asset totals. In other words, even when firms offer incentive arrangements, those incentive arrangements fail to influence fund manager behavior because investment firms continue to rely on fee income expressed as a percentage of assets under management. Second, investment managers tend to offer terms on incentive schemes that involve modest levels of risk to the firm's existing income flows. Instead of taking a "blank slate" approach that sets baseline fees at a level that covers reasonable overhead, money managers try to structure incentive arrangements that ensure continued income flows even with mediocre performance, protecting the profit margins implicit in existing fee structures. Finally, investors choosing between a traditional asset-based fee and an alternative incentive-oriented structure encounter cognitive dissonance, as the performance expectations implicit in hiring an active manager cause expected costs of incentive compensation to exceed anticipated payments from a traditional asset-based fee arrangement. While the concept of incentive compensation structures for active managers of marketable securities carries a great deal of theoretical appeal, the limitations of real-world arrangements reduce the effectiveness of incentive schemes in causing fund managers to behave as principals.

Investment management fees, whether asset-based or incentive-oriented, represent a heavily scrutinized term in most contract negotiations, with investors seeking the lowest possible fee burden along with a "most-favored-client" clause ensuring advantageous treatment in the future. Beneath the open, honest discussion concerning marketable equity fee arrangements lie hidden soft dollar payments, representing old-fashioned kickbacks designed to increase investment advisor cash flow at the direct expense of investor clients.

Soft Dollars

The history of soft dollars provides a worrisome tale. Prior to May 1, 1975, Wall Street operated under a system of fixed commissions that set rates far above the costs of executing trades. Competitive forces caused brokerage firms to circumvent the fixed prices, by providing rebates to favored customers in the form of soft dollars. Soft dollars, in essence a kickback from broker to trader, funded the purchase of both investment-related and noninvestment-related goods and services.

Think about the implications of soft-dollar trades for investors. Paying inflated commissions to trade securities, for whatever purpose, reduces investment returns. The reduction in return comes straight from the investor's pocket. The benefit, in the form of goods and services, accrues directly to the fund manager. Because the costs of soft-dollar goods and services would otherwise have come from the fund's management fee, soft dollars represent nothing other than a well-disguised increase in management fees. Wall Street benefits at the investor's expense.

A T. Rowe Price disclosure document, dated March 1, 2004, describes the soft-dollar game. "[U]nder certain conditions, higher brokerage commissions may be paid in return for brokerage and research services. . . . [S]uch services may include computers and related hardware. T. Rowe Price also allocates brokerage for research services which are available for cash. . . . [T]he expenses of T. Rowe Price could be materially increased if it attempted to generate additional information through its own staff. To the extent that research services of value are provided by brokers or dealers, T. Rowe Price is relieved of expenses it might otherwise bear." Investors learn of T. Rowe Price's soft-dollar policies through carefully constructed, legally correct prose buried on pages 90 and 91 of an infrequently read disclosure document. Even though T. Rowe Price presumably satisfies legal requirements with its disclosure, the firm compromises investor interests with its soft-dollar usage.

After May Day 1975, when the SEC abolished the system of fixed commissions, the *raison d'être* for soft dollars vanished. Price competition would set brokerage commission rates. Under-the-table kickbacks could disappear. Unfortunately for investors, fund managers realized that soft dollars transferred research-related expenses from their account (management fee income) to the investors' account (trading expenses). As a result, the money management industry enthusiastically defended the use of soft dollars.

Instead of banning soft dollars, in 1975 Congress created a safe harbor for their use under Section 28(e) of the Securities Exchange Act of 1934. Perverting a piece of legislation originally designed to protect the investing public, Congress bowed to pressure from Wall Street and explicitly allowed fund managers to deplete investor assets, legitimizing soft dollars by instructing the SEC to define appropriate use. Why do market participants tolerate the inefficiencies involved in paying inflated prices for trading securities and then receiving rebates in the form of goods and services? The answer lies in the lack of transparency of the process, which allows money managers to profit in an opaque manner. Were the soft-dollar charges as transparent as the highly visible management fees, the investment management industry would have no use for soft dollars.

When the Securities and Exchange Commission examined the soft-dollar issue in the mid 1980s, the commission not only missed an opportunity to eliminate the scourge of soft dollars, it actually expanded the epidemic. In wonderfully bureaucratic prose, the SEC noted that its 1986 release addressed "[i]ndustry difficulty in applying the restrictive standards" on soft-dollar usage by "adopting a broader definition of 'brokerage and research services.'" In other words, if the restrictions bind, loosen the constraints. The SEC's 1986 soft-dollar regulations favored the advisor over the advisee.

SEC Chairman Arthur Levitt described soft dollar conflicts in a February 15, 1995 *Wall Street Journal* article: "Soft-dollar arrangements can create substantial conflicts of interest between an advisor and its clients. For example, advisors may cause their clients to pay excessive commission rates, or may overtrade their clients' accounts simply to satisfy soft-dollar obligations. Soft-dollar arrangements may also result in inferior executions when advisors direct trades to the wrong broker to satisfy a soft-dollar obligation." [39]

To ameliorate conflicts surrounding brokerage activity, in February 1995, the SEC proposed a new rule under the Investment Advisors Act of 1940 that would require investment managers to disclose the services they receive for brokerage commissions. The report would list the twenty brokers to which the advisor directed the largest amounts of commissions during the previous year, the top three execution-only brokers, the aggregate amount of commissions directed by the advisor to each broker, and the average commission rate paid to each broker. The disclosure would permit a client to assess the costs and benefits of the soft-dollar services that the advisor receives, and, consequently, whether the client should attempt to limit the advisor's use of soft-dollar brokers. Unfortunately, no action resulted from the 1995 SEC rule proposal.

In spite of Chairman Levitt's public concerns about soft dollars, the SEC again failed to protect mutual-fund investors in 1998. The regulator's *Inspection Report* dryly notes "the widespread use of soft dollars," as "almost all advisors obtain products and services other than pure execution from broker-dealers and use client commissions to pay for those products and services." The report recognizes that "advisors using soft dollars face a conflict of interest between their need to obtain research and their clients' interest in paying the lowest commission rate available and obtaining the best possible execution." The report details instance after instance of questionable use and outright abuse of soft dollars, including payment "for office rent and equipment, cellular phone services and personal expenses, employee salaries, marketing expenses, legal fees, hotels and car rental costs." Wall Street's definition of research bears little correspondence to Merriam-Webster's.

In spite of the fundamental, irreconcilable conflict of interest in soft-dollar use and in spite of the long litany of soft-dollar abuse, the 1998 *Inspection Report* concludes only that the SEC "should reiterate and provide additional guidance, consider adopting recordkeeping requirements, require more meaningful disclosure and encourage firms to adopt internal controls." Instead of protecting investor interests, the SEC defended Wall Street's gravy train.

While the substance of the 1998 *Inspection Report* argued for abolition, the SEC wimped out. Faced with a concerted lobbying effort by interested parties—including investment managers, Wall Street firms, and the normally sensible trade association of research analysts—and a lack of pressure from individual investors, the self-styled "investor's advocate" opted to tighten regulation instead of taking the high road of total eradication. A cynic might argue that the SEC acts on highly visible, easy-to-understand investor protection issues, while allowing low-profile, difficult-to-comprehend abuses to remain.

One of the most outrageous "legitimate" uses of soft dollars involves payoffs made by investment advisors to consulting firms. According to the 1998 SEC report, performance attribution services constitute "a significant portion of the total commission dollars used in soft dollar transactions."[40] Obviously, any competent investment manager develops internal capabilities to understand sources of investment returns, creating evaluation mechanisms specific to the firm's particular approach to markets. Purchasing performance attribution from consultants serves simply to line the pockets of the consulting firm at the expense of the investment manager's clients. Presumably, the consulting firm receiving the payoff places the investment management firm in a favored position when making manager recommendations. While investment advisors may wish to improve their standing by purchasing useless information from consulting firms, using client assets for the purpose turns inanity to ignominy.

Some investment managers need so much assistance in evaluating performance that they purchase reports from a variety of consultants. The SEC study cites a large institutional advisor that "directed $882,000 in client commissions to pay for 13 separate performance analyses." According to a report in *Pensions and Investments*, J&W Seligman & Co., a money management firm with $24.3 billion under management, engaged seven consulting firms to provide performance attribution reports, using client assets to fund the purchase through soft dollars.[41] By paying substantial sums to Callan Associates ($79,000), Evaluation Associates ($100,000), Frank Russell ($26,789), Madison Portfolio Consultants ($17,500), SEI Corporation ($10,000), Wellesley Group ($52,500), and Yanni-Bilkey Investment Consulting ($25,000), J&W Seligman no doubt expects favorable treatment in the next search conducted by the compromised consultants. Payoffs dishonor everyone involved.

Beyond the "legitimate" use of soft dollars to "curry favor with the consultant in his rankings and recommendations of advisors," nearly 30 percent of investment advisors employ soft dollars for "non-research products and services." The purchases, which fall outside of the safe harbor, include use of soft dollars for office rent, equipment, marketing expenses, phone services, and salaries. The SEC observed that "virtually all of the advisors that obtained non research products and services had failed to provide meaningful disclosure of such practices to their clients."[42] Aside from using an illegitimate source of funds for legitimate business expenses, many advisors stepped over another line by diverting funds for personal use, including purchase of travel, entertainment, theatre tickets, limousine services, interior design, Internet website design and construction, and computer hardware and software. In the most flagrant abuse of soft dollars, investment advisors defrauded clients by directing "funds ostensibly for verbal 'regional research' and 'strategic planning' to family members of the advisor's principal," by transferring soft dollars through a daisy chain of companies controlled by the advisor's president, and by paying "round trip airfare to Hong Kong for the principal's son." Even though soft dollars did not cause the theft, the opacity of the arrangement facilitated the crimes.

Some clients benefit from a different aspect of the current system of commission-related activity, taking advantage of the murky character of directed brokerage. With directed brokerage, plan sponsors cause trades to be executed by specified brokers, paying higher than market commission rates. A portion of the above-market rate flows back to the plan sponsor in the form of cash rebates or investment-related goods and services. Two factors drive directed-brokerage activity—directed-brokerage investors gain an advantage at the expense of clients not directing brokerage, and fund sponsors use rebates from directed brokerage to purchase goods and services unavailable through normal procurement channels.

Investment advisors commonly aggregate trades for a number of separate account clients, allocating shares to accounts on a pro rata basis. If one client requests that brokerage be directed to a particular securities firm, in order to receive a cash rebate, that client accrues an unfair benefit relative to other clients. In fact, the client who "steps out" of the aggregated trade likely benefits implicitly from *all* of the brokerage conducted by the investment advisor at the designated firm. Such arrangements exist only as long as they remain hidden from view. If disclosed, disadvantaged clients would demand fair and equitable treatment.

Some investors, particularly in political or corporate environments, fail to obtain sufficient direct support for investment management operations. To augment direct appropriations, investments staff sometimes employ directed-brokerage and soft-dollar programs, generating resources outside regular appropriations or operational channels.

Appearing before a Department of Labor Working Group on Soft Dollars and Commission Recapture, the former director of the New Jersey Division of Investment openly testified that "he utilizes soft dollars to pay for needed administrative expenses," since "he does not receive sufficient funding from the New Jersey State Legislature." In fact, the former director urged that "the current interpretation of 'research' should be expanded to include travel and hotel expenses."[43] Soft dollars provide a convenient mechanism for the New Jersey Division of Investment to circumvent constraints imposed by the state legislature, allowing the investment operation to thwart the intent of New Jersey's elected representatives.

In April 2007, SEC Chairman Christopher Cox added his voice to the chorus calling for soft-dollar reform. In a speech to the Mutual Fund Directors Forum, Cox asserted that:

Soft dollars can serve as an incentive for fund managers to disregard their best execution obligations, and also to trade portfolio securities inappropriately in order to earn credits for research and brokerage. Soft dollars also represent a lot of investors' hard cash, even though it isn't reported that way. The total of soft dollars runs into the billions each year for all investment funds in the United States.

An agency focused on ensuring full disclosure to investors has to be very concerned about this, because soft dollars make it more difficult for investors to understand what's going on with their money. Hard dollars eventually end up being reported as part of the management fee the fund charges its investors. But soft dollars provide a way for funds to lower their apparent fees—even though, in the end, investors pay for the expense anyway.

The very concept of soft dollars may be at odds with clarity in describing fees and costs to investors. The 30-year-old statutory safe harbor, in Section 28(e) of the Exchange Act, was probably thought to be a useful legislative compromise when it was packaged with the abolition of fixed commissions. But surely in enacting Section 28(e) Congress meant to promote competition in research, not to create conflicts of interest by permitting commission dollars to be spent in ways that benefit investment managers instead of their investor clients.[44]

In May 2007, SEC Chairman Cox called for repeal or substantial revision of the safe harbor that protects soft-dollar arrangements between broker dealers and money managers. Cox noted the current system produced a "witch's brew of hidden fees, conflicts of interest and complexity in application that is at odds with investors' best interests."[45]

While the SEC attempts to reform soft-dollar practices, the question remains—why do soft dollars exist? Powerful market participants in the brokerage community benefit from the inherent murkiness of soft-dollar transactions. Third party providers of soft-dollar-eligible goods and services maintain a strong vested interest in supporting the current system. Investment advisors employing soft dollars increase net income by transferring a portion of investment management costs to clients.

Soft-dollar activity flies in the face of reasonable governance. Investment advisors employ soft dollars to pay off consulting firms and increase investment management revenues, relying on the technique's opacity to hide from view. Fund managers incur frictional costs to pursue initiatives with directed commissions for which "hard" dollars are unavailable, frustrating the intentions of fund fiduciaries. Soft dollars and directed brokerage, the slimy underbelly of the brokerage world, ought to be banned.

Compensation Arrangements for Nontraditional Assets

Fee arrangements in the nontraditional asset arena typically include some form of profits interest. In spite of important limitations, when compared to typical marketable security deal terms, alternative asset deal structures better align interests of fund managers and fund providers, as the profits interest focuses manager attention on generating investment gains. Large co-investment by managers provides the strongest force for creating parallel interests, causing the manager to share in investment losses as well as in investment gains. Forcing managers to pay attention to the downside of an investment mitigates concerns about the one-way nature of profit sharing options.

Without substantial levels of co-investment, deal structures in the alternative arena encourage investment managers to expose investor assets to risk, as the managers typically receive compensation in the form of an option-like profits interest. Facing a "heads I win, tails you lose" arrangement, managers respond by adopting an agent's perspective, focusing on achieving personal gains that may or may not correspond to generating risk-adjusted investment returns for the providers of capital.

A particularly troublesome problem results from granting investment managers a profits interest without specifying an appropriate benchmark or hurdle rate. By paying 20 percent of gains after return of capital, investors give asset managers a windfall in the form of a profit participation in market-generated gains over which the manager exercises no control. In creating structures without a reasonable measure of the opportunity cost of funds, investors diminish the likelihood of realizing superior risk-adjusted returns.

Alternative asset compensation arrangements consist of fee income, generally calculated on portfolio value or committed capital, and incentive schemes, generally calculated as a portion of investment gains. In the rarely achieved ideal world, fees offset ordinary costs of pursuing the investment business, while profits interests create incentives for adding value to the process. All too frequently, fees exceed the level required to cover costs, becoming a profit center, and profit participations cover more than value added, rewarding (or penalizing) managers for results beyond their control.

Fee Income

Reasonable fee income provides sufficient revenue to cover a firm's overhead, allowing investors to run the business comfortably. Investment principals deserve fair salaries, nicely appointed offices, and sufficient resources to structure and manage the portfolio. Ideally, investors would discuss with fund managers the level of resources required to operate the firm, setting a budget sufficient to meet the agreed-upon needs. In practice, few firms take a budgeted approach to setting fees. Most firms maintain industry-standard fee percentages as fund sizes grow and generate enormous cash flows simply from raising ever larger funds.

Deal fees, paid to private fund managers upon consummation of an acquisition, serve to line the pockets of fund managers at the direct expense of investors. Typically found in the leveraged buyout arena, such fees motivate firms to do deals and provide an unnecessary addition to the more-than-generous compensation package represented by management fees and carried interests. Fees in excess of those required to run the business drive a wedge between the interests of investors and fund managers, subtly shifting the manager's focus to maintaining fees at the expense of generating returns.

Profits Interests

Incentive compensation in the form of a share of gains generated by fund investments provides a powerful tool to motivate fund managers. A fair and effective arrangement splits the value added by the fund manager between the manager and the investor. Both parties deserve to share in incremental gains, since without the manager's work there would be no value added, while without the investor's capital there would be no deal. Achieving a hurdle rate that reflects the investor's opportunity cost of capital represents the point at which a fund manager begins to add value. Unfortunately, in much of the private equity world, hurdles do not exist. By providing profits interests after return of capital, investors compensate fund managers inappropriately. Incentive compensation in the form of sharing value added causes managers to pursue the active investor's goal of creating risk-adjusted excess returns.

A particularly egregious deal structure causes investors to pay incentive compensation to fund managers before the return of invested capital. Under some private equity arrangements, the investor's capital account declines by the amount of management fees paid. If "gains" are calculated off of the reduced base, fund managers may receive a profits interest on a fund that fails to return investor capital. At the very least, fund managers ought to return investor capital before reaping the significant rewards of incentive compensation.

Fairness demands that investors earn hard hurdles before profit sharing begins. Hard hurdles represent rates of return that investors realize before fund managers participate in gains, with only profits above the hurdle rate subject to sharing. Soft hurdles, a popular marketing scheme, allow fund managers to "catch up" after exceeding the hurdle rate, providing little value for investors (except in the case where a manager produces truly miserable returns).

Identifying an appropriate hurdle rate poses a tricky problem, since alternative markets lack a ready benchmark such as the S&P 500 for marketable domestic equities. In the case of absolute return, the cost of funds as expressed by a one-year interest rate provides a reasonable starting point. Since absolute return managers generally take short duration positions, measuring investment success relative to short-term interest rates makes sense. In the case of real assets, where expected returns fall between bonds (representing a lower risk measure of an institution's opportunity cost of funds) and stocks (representing a higher risk measure of opportunity cost), intermediate-term fixed income returns plus a small premium might give us an appropriate hurdle. When forming new funds, investors and fund managers revisit the question of an appropriate hurdle rate in light of changes in market conditions. For instance, as interest rates moved downward throughout the 1990s, appropriate real assets hurdle rates declined from high single digits to mid single digits.

In contrast to reasonable deal structures sometimes available to investors in absolute return and real assets, investors in venture capital and leveraged buyouts face generally unattractive partnership terms. By compensating private equity managers with 20 percent, 25 percent, or 30 percent of every dollar generated after return of capital, standard profit sharing arrangements fail to consider the opportunity cost of capital. At the very least, private managers ought to return a money market rate before collecting a profits interest. The long-term return on a marketable equity benchmark provides a hurdle rate more appropriate to the risk of private equity. In fact, the higher risk inherent in venture capital and leveraged buyout investments suggests using a multiple of long-term equity returns as a threshold for benchmarking private equity funds.

Risk-adjusted marketable security hurdle rates for private investments avoid the problem of compensating (or penalizing) fund managers for market moves that they cannot control. In the bull market of the 1980s and 1990s, buyout managers "earned" 20 percent of the profits on gains attributable to stock-market-induced valuation increases. In a reasonable world, investors might compensate private managers with a profits interest in returns exceeding some premium over long-run historical results from marketable equity investments, implying a mid-teens hurdle rate.

Fair incentive compensation schemes for alternative asset managers face nearly insurmountable obstacles. Under the current conditions of overwhelming demand for high quality groups, investors lack power to influence terms, facing the choice of accepting the standard deal or walking away. Investors hoping to encourage fund managers to behave as principals look to other aspects of deal structure.

Absolute Return Investment Vehicles

Absolute return managers, operating in a marketable securities environment, generally allow investors to withdraw assets and to make contributions on a reasonably frequent basis. Although partnership terms generally restrict the timing and size of inflows and outflows, stable investors face the possibility of incurring costs created by other investors' cash moving in and out. Cash contributions to an existing partnership dilute the interest of existing investors. By buying into an existing commingled fund, new investors participate in an established portfolio without paying transactions costs to establish positions. Cash withdrawals pose the same free rider problem as departing monies fail to bear the full burden of trading costs required to raise the cash necessary to compensate departing investors.

A more significant problem arises when cash outflows disrupt a manager's investment strategy. During the market panic in late 1998, many hedge fund managers worried about the magnitude of year-end withdrawals. The threat of potentially large withdrawals posed a dilemma, as on the one hand managers needed to prepare to accommodate departing investor demands while on the other hand asset sales at depressed prices harm the portfolio. The confluence of tough market conditions and concern regarding client withdrawals caused many managers to raise cash by selling assets trading at temporarily depressed prices, impairing results for the manager and steadfast investors alike.

Fund managers solve the free rider problem by allocating costs appropriately to entering and exiting investors. In the case of easily measured transactions costs, managers simply assess entry and exit fees, resulting in a fair allocation of costs. To meet the objective of distributing costs fairly, fees must be paid to the fund, not to the manager, as the fees offset costs incurred by the fund. More complicated procedures address the issue of allocating less predictable costs, particularly charges from transactions conducted in markets with poor liquidity. A rough approximation of fairness results from segregating new investor contributions, investing the funds, and contributing the resulting assets to the general portfolio at cost. Even though the package of securities purchased by the entering investor may not bear precisely the same level of transactions costs as would trades in existing portfolio securities, if the manager makes new purchases in markets similar to the existing holdings the new entrant bears a fair burden. Upon exit, the departing investor receives a pro rata share of the general portfolio in a segregated account, incurring the transactions costs associated with the liquidation process and insulating continuing investors from any adverse impact. By causing entering and exiting investors to absorb costs related to purchases and sales, fund managers avoid unfair treatment of existing investors. Most importantly, the process allows managers to invest assets without regard to concerns regarding extraordinary withdrawal requests, since departing investors simply receive the proceeds of their proportionate share of the fund.

Private Equity Investment Vehicles

Private equity managers best serve investor interests by focusing undivided attention on a single investment vehicle. With only one place to conduct business, managers avoid the inevitable conflicts that arise when managing multiple funds with non-coincident goals.

For example, if a buyout firm manages an equity pool and a mezzanine debt pool, tensions arise in pricing transactions. Better pricing on the mezzanine debt leads to worse results for the equity holders, and vice versa. Some firms attempt to deal with pricing issues by creating a formula for determining the terms of mezzanine finance. By pre-specifying the relationship between the mezzanine coupon level and U.S. Treasury rates, as well as pre-identifying the size of the equity kicker for the bondholders, fund managers hope to avoid the tricky issues involved in dividing expected returns between competing sets of investors.

Because dynamic market conditions constantly alter terms of trade for various investment tools, formulaic approaches inevitably fail to reflect the current market. If the formula determines worse-than-market terms for mezzanine debt, fund managers fail to discharge fiduciary duties to mezzanine investors. If the formula results in a better-than-market deal, equity investors suffer. The convenience of controlling a captive mezzanine fund comes at the cost of a serious conflict between the interests of lenders and owners. In the event of financial distress, problems become even more painfully obvious with some members of the firm wearing mezzanine hats and others wearing equity hats. If equity owners seek forbearance from lenders, fund managers find themselves in a hopelessly conflicted position. The best course for bondholders frequently differs from the path preferred by equity owners, posing a dilemma for even the best intentioned fund manager. In the case of bankruptcy, the problems worsen as interests clash in the zero-sum game of allocating value to debt and equity. By creating and managing multiple funds, managers invite exposure to the crossways pull of competing interests.

While debt and equity funds provide a dramatic example of tensions arising from management of multiple funds, complementary activities create similar types of issues. Criteria that determine which fund receives a particular transaction, carefully delineated in the fund offering documents, frequently fail to address subsequent realities, creating messy allocation issues for fund managers. Perhaps even more important, the fund manager faces the daily problem of deciding which particular activity will receive the manager's time and attention. Because multiple funds contain different sets of investors with different interests, in choosing which activities to pursue the fund manager decides which set of investors to serve.

Fund manager investment outside of investment pools deserves careful scrutiny. Investment principals must avoid doing private deals for their own account, even if the transactions seem too small, too funky, or otherwise inappropriate for the institutional fund. Investors deserve the complete dedication of fund manager investment efforts. Undiluted focus of all professional energies on the management of a single investment pool forms an important starting point in serving investment client needs.

KKR's Deal Structure Flaws

Poorly structured private investment deals often produce dramatically misaligned interests. The well known buyout firm, Kohlberg,

Kravis, & Roberts (KKR), negotiated partnership terms in its 1993 fund that enriched the principals regardless of the results for the limited partners. Like managers of most private equity funds, KKR received a carried interest of 20 percent of the partnership's profits. Unlike most funds, KKR did not aggregate investments when calculating the profits interest. That is, KKR collected 20 percent of the profits on successful deals, with no offset for losses incurred in failed transactions, creating an incentive to roll the dice. KKR owned a share of the profits of big wins, but suffered none of the pain of big losses. In essence, the deal structure encouraged the firm to take enormous risk by creating option-like payoffs for the general partners through use of extreme financial or operating leverage.

KKR's agreement with the limited partners called for a management fee of 1.5 percent of assets, typical of leveraged buyout partnerships. Such management fees, designed to cover the cost of running a buyout fund's business, became a profit center for KKR because of the enormous size of funds under supervision. Not satisfied with excessive management fees, KKR collected deal fees for consummating transactions, monitoring fees for managing positions and investment banking fees for subsequent capital market transactions. The overly generous management fees, deal fees, monitoring fees, and investment banking fees drive a wedge between the interests of the general partners (more is better) and the limited partners (less is more). Contrast this with the terms of Warren Buffett's original partnership, in which he charged no management fee, believing that he should only profit if his co-investors profited![46]

KKR's August 1995 purchase of Bruno's illustrates the misaligned interests. The $1.2 billion transaction, which included an equity investment of $250 million, involved the acquisition of a chain of supermarkets headquartered in Mississippi. KKR charged an acquisition fee of $15 million, which exceeded the general partners' investment by a significant margin. Pro-rated management fees, charged on committed capital, amounted to $3.75 million on an annual basis. The monitoring fee consumed an additional $1 million annually. Moreover, in 1997 KKR charged Bruno's investment banking fees of $800,000. In exchange for financing the purchase and paying tens of millions of dollars of fees, in February 1998, the limited partners lost their entire investment when Bruno's declared bankruptcy, filing for Chapter XI.

Properly structured deals cause general partners and limited partners to share in both profits and losses. If a managing agent shares only in profits, incentives to take risk abound. Management fee income that covers only overhead forces investors to perform before receiving extraordinary profits. Fees above the basic overhead level represent an undeserved transfer from limited partners to general partners. The combination of high levels of fee income and option-like payoff structure allowed KKR to profit unreasonably on the Bruno's deal, while the firm's investors wrote off the transaction.

Some aspects of the unusually egregious fee structure employed by KKR disappeared in 1996, when the firm raised a then-market-leading $5.7 billion fund. Pressured by substantial institutional investors, the buyout firm agreed to aggregate the results of all deals in the fund, offsetting deficits from losers before taking profits on winners. While KKR's investors expect to benefit from the pooling of transaction results, the firm continues to benefit from extraordinary levels of fee income, ensuring general partner success regardless of limited partner investment results.

KKR's fee income in 2006 illustrates the role of fees in the stunning transfer of wealth from limited partners to general partners. According to the July 3, 2007 preliminary S-1 filed with the SEC to facilitate KKR's proposed IPO, in 2006 the firm received $67 million in monitoring fees and $273 million in transaction fees. Harvard Business School Professor Josh Lerner estimates that fund management fees in 2006 amounted to approximately $350 million.[47] KKR's senior professionals, who reportedly numbered twenty-five, collected an estimated $690 million in fees simply for showing up, turning on the lights, and going about their day-to-day business.

In spite of KKR's 1996 removal of the deal-by-deal incentive compensation clause, investors generally exercise little influence over deal terms, as investment managers hew to an industry standard scale that provides higher levels of income at lower risk than would a fair compensation structure. Consider an environment where managers receive base fees to cover reasonable overhead and earn a portion of excess returns to provide incentive. Since a majority of market participants fail to beat a fair risk-adjusted benchmark, most fund managers would face a substantial decline in income under a fair deal structure.

Because profits interests begin to accrue after return of capital, private managers collect incentive compensation after investors receive a zero rate of return. If private managers received a profits interest in gains only above a risk-adjusted benchmark, based on historical results the overwhelming number of managers would fail to earn incentive compensation. Because the investment management industry receives compensation far in excess of levels justified by the degree of value created, investors encounter enormous resistance to institution of reasonable deal structures.

Unfortunately, when altering the terms of the trade, investors face the challenge of making industry-wide changes, since manager-by-manager change introduces the potential for instability. If a single private equity manager promoted a fair deal structure, compensation for that firm's principals would fall far short of industry standards. Personnel at the firm could cross the street, work for a private fund operating under the unfair profit sharing regime, thereby increasing personal income dramatically. The innovative private fund, offering a fair deal, retains only those principals without other alternatives.

Investors find terms of trade in the private equity arena moving away from fairness. Fees on multibillion-dollar buyout funds generate tens of millions of dollars per annum, far in excess of amounts necessary to fund reasonable levels of partnership operating expenses. Buyout fund profits interests take 20 percent of returns created by the stock market's upward bias, not to mention 20 percent of returns produced by highly leveraged capital structures. After adjusting for fees, profits interests, and the risk, no excess return remains for the overwhelming number of capital providers.

Venture capital investors fare little better. In the past, the venture community fell into a neat three-tier structure with Kleiner Perkins atop the hierarchy earning a 30 percent profits interest, a handful of superb firms receiving a 25 percent carry, and the rest of the industry taking home 20 percent of gains. The late 1990s Internet mania turned many solid venture capitalists into bull market geniuses, causing them to demand an increase in compensation from 20 percent of profits to 25 percent or even 30 percent. While a few making the move deserve inclusion in the elite ranks of the industry, most simply say "it's the market" or "we need to do it for competitive reasons." Such top-of-the-market increases in compensation persisted through the subsequent period of weak venture returns, creating a pattern of one-way ratcheting of deal terms against investor interests.

A recent study by two Wharton School academics, Andrew Metrick and Ayako Yasuda, produced some startling results regarding the relationship between fee income and profits interests. The authors examined detailed records of 238 funds raised between 1992 and 2006. Based on their modeling of the partnership characteristics, "about 60 percent of expected revenue comes from fixed-revenue components which are not sensitive to performance."[48] The conclusion that the majority of general partner compensation takes the form of fee income calls in question the basic private equity partnership structure.

Michael Jensen, professor emeritus at the Harvard Business School, expressed concerns about private equity compensation schemes in a

September 2007 interview with the *New York Times*'s Gretchen Morgenson. Jensen, "the man whom many consider to be the intellectual father of private equity," "deplores the newfangled fees that private equity firms are levying on their clients." Jensen said, "I can predict without a shred of doubt that these fees are going to end up reducing the productivity of the model. And it creates another wedge between the outsiders and insiders, which is very, very serious. People are doing this out of some short-run focus on increasing revenues, and not paying attention to what the strengths of the model are."[49] Investors in private equity fare best with smaller, more entrepreneurial fund managers that benefit less from fees and more from profit participation.

Negotiating Change

While long established practices limit the ability of investors to negotiate fair deal terms, in the early 1990s the real estate industry presented an opportunity for radical restructuring. After recklessly throwing staggering amounts of capital into real estate in the 1980s, institutions withdrew almost completely from the market after the turn-of-the-decade collapse in prices. Those few investors interested in committing funds faced a host of unattractive investment management alternatives.

Large fee-driven advisors dominated institutional real estate activity in the 1980s. Firms such as AEW, Copley, Heitman, JMB, LaSalle, RREEF, and TCW amassed billions of dollars in assets, driven by the steady stream of acquisition fees, management fees, and disposition fees. Not surprisingly, the real estate advisory community adopted a laser-like focus on initiating, maintaining and enhancing flows of fee income, often neglecting even to consider the notion of generating investment returns for clients.

JMB's Fee Bonanza

Headquartered in Chicago and named for Robert Judelson, Judd Malkin, and Neil Bluhm, JMB typified the fee orientation of the 1980s advisory crowd. Not content to collect flows of income based on the fair value of client assets, the firm went to extraordinary lengths to collect its fees even as portfolio assets withered in the 1990s real estate collapse.

Exhibiting nearly unbelievable greed, JMB retained underwater positions simply to collect fees from clients. In July 1986, the firm acquired Argyle Village Square, a retail property in Jacksonville, Florida, for $22 million as part of a portfolio of properties held in a commingled fund, Endowment and Foundation Realty—JMB II. Encumbered by a mortgage of $12.4 million, the property generated fees for JMB of 1.25 percent on the gross value of the asset, equivalent to nearly 2.3 percent on the original equity investment.

By 1992, Argyle Village Square declined in value to the extent that the property's mortgage exceeded its market price. The anchor tenant, discount department store Zayre's, vacated its space, dramatically impairing the property's future prospects. Instead of turning the shopping center over to the lender, JMB held the asset on its books at zero equity value, continuing to collect fees from investors based on the gross value of the property. With a cash return of 1.1 percent (after debt service and before fees), Argyle Village Square's fee of 1.25 percent exceeded the property's income. To add injury to insult, JMB used investor cash flow from other assets to make up the difference, ensuring the continued flow of the full level of fees to the firm. In spite of repeated requests from investors to dispose of Argyle Village and stop the diversion of portfolio cash flow to pay fees, JMB retained the shopping center and piggily fed at the trough of investor assets.

In the "largest real estate acquisition ever," JMB's 1987 purchase of Cadillac Fairview, a collection of Canadian retailing properties, generated a fee bonanza for the firm on a stupendous scale.[50] Continuing its practice of assessing fees on the gross value of transactions, JMB's initial fee amounted to one percent of the C$6.8 billion deal, representing a load of 3.4 percent on original equity contributions of approximately C$2.0 billion. JMB included in the gross transaction value a portfolio of assets worth approximately C$560 million already under contract for sale, causing the firm to "earn" C$5.6 million for acquiring and immediately selling assets with absolutely no potential to benefit investors.

JMB's "feeing" frenzy continued with annual asset management fees of 0.5 percent per year on gross fair market value (equivalent to 1.7 percent of initial equity), participation fees of 1.75 percent per year on cash flow and capital proceeds, and disposition fees of 1.0 percent on gross proceeds (with a parenthetical reminder in the Offering Memorandum that gross proceeds "includes indebtedness," in case the investor forgot).

In addition to initial fees, annual fees, participation fees, and disposition fees, JMB retained the right to provide property management, leasing, insurance brokerage, and other services with compensation negotiated on an "arms-length" basis. Not satisfied with the staggering array of fee-generating opportunities, JMB contracted to receive incentive fees of 15 percent of profits after providing a 9 percent simple annual return to investors.

Unfortunately for JMB and its co-investors in Cadillac Fairview, in the tough environment of the early 1990s, the overpriced, overleveraged buyout suffered. Notwithstanding an additional 1992 equity contribution of C$700 million, by 1994 interests representing the C$2.7 billion of equity contributed by investors traded at 20 cents to 25 cents on the dollar. As pension investors from California, Massachusetts, Illinois, and Iowa watched the relentless decline in asset value, JMB continued to collect its management fees.

Responding to outrage over the real estate advisor's insulation from the failure of the Canadian mega-deal, JMB voluntarily reduced its annual fee from $30 million to $25 million, while noting that the fee compensated the firm for advising Cadillac Fairview, not the investors! Judd Malkin highlighted the lack of coincidence of interest with his investors, observing that "[i]f I cut my fees by one-half, it still doesn't change their return." [51]

Succumbing to the inevitable consequence of too much debt and too little cash flow, in December 1994, Cadillac Fairview filed for protection from creditors in Canadian bankruptcy court. In spite of the failure of the company and massive losses by its investors, JMB aggressively sought to retain the gravy train, suing Cadillac Fairview for C$225 million, of which C$180 million represented the future stream of fees for advising the company on its Canadian properties. JMB settled the fee claim for C$22.5 million in 1995.

In spite of the massive failure of Cadillac Fairview and JMB's outrageous treatment of investors, Neil Bluhm raised another institutional fund, Walton Street Capital, in 1997. The original fund paved the way for a series of funds, which as of 2007 boasted $3.5 billion of aggregate equity commitments. Bluhm's asset-gathering ability and fee-charging acumen created a net worth sufficient to merit a rank of 215 on the 2006 Forbes' list of the 400 wealthiest Americans. [52]

While JMB may represent the worst of the fee-driven excesses, in the 1980s all major real estate advisors focused on collecting fees, not generating investment returns. Institutions hoping to exploit real estate opportunities in the early 1990s faced a collection of discredited advisors operating with fundamentally flawed deal structures. Fortunately, an almost total withdrawal of capital from the real estate market provided substantial negotiating leverage to investors willing to commit funds to the cash-starved asset class.

•   •   •

The capital drought of the early 1990s placed investors and real estate fund managers on equal footing, allowing negotiation of fair deal terms. Providers of funds negotiated management fees sufficient to cover overhead, but insufficient to create a profit center. Investors obtained a hard hurdle, forcing managers to provide a fair return before earning a profits interest. In cases where real estate managers enjoyed a substantial net worth, general partner commitments to funds amounted to tens of millions of dollars, often exceeding the contributions made by many of the limited partners. When managers exhibited more modest means, recourse loans from the partnership provided funds for the manager's co-investment.

The dearth of capital in the early 1990s created an unusual opportunity for investors to alter the compensation arrangements for real estate investing. Moving from the dysfunctional fee-driven agency structure of the 1980s to a well-aligned investment-return-oriented principal structure in the 1990s promoted the interests of investors and fund managers alike.

While the return of capital to real estate investing in the late 1990s eroded some of the deal structure gains, many managers chose to continue employing principal-oriented structures even when presented with rich fee-driven opportunities. Aside from purely economic considerations, the loyalty engendered by previous successful pursuit of mutually rewarding investment activities contributed materially to the decision to continue working with the existing structure. The dislocations in the real estate markets contributed to long lasting changes in institutional deal terms.

CONCLUSION

Market efficiency creates substantial hurdles for investors pursuing active management strategies, causing most to fail even to match results of market benchmarks. Although trying to beat the market proves tough and costly, fiduciaries frequently accept active manager claims at face value, attribute investment success to skill (not luck), and fail to adjust results for risk. In the face of active management obstacles, market players respond to the thrills and excitement generated by playing a game with scores tallied in the millions, and even billions, explaining the nearly universal pursuit of active strategies by institutional investors.

Thoughtful investors approach active management opportunities with great skepticism, starting with the presumption that managers exhibit no skill. Historical performance numbers deserve careful scrutiny, with astute observers mindful of the part good fortune plays in successful track records. Odds of winning the active management game increase when committing funds to managers possessing an "edge" likely to produce superior performance in extremely competitive markets.

Selecting the right people to manage assets poses the single biggest challenge to fiduciaries, since integrity, intelligence, and energy influence portfolio outcomes in the most fundamental manner. The actions of external managers contribute not only to investment performance, but also to the reputation and public perception of the institution itself, forcing fiduciaries to embrace extremely high standards in manager selection.

Appropriate organizational structure plays a part in successful execution of investment programs by ensuring sufficient alignment of interest between the institutional fund and the external advisor. Independent investment advisors with carefully structured economic incentives stand the greatest chance of producing high risk-adjusted returns, as appropriate incentives cause managers to place institutional goals ahead of personal agendas. While thoughtful deal terms and sensible organizational attributes contribute to the likelihood of success, even the most carefully constructed arrangements fail when implemented by the wrong people.

Entrepreneurial firms provide the greatest likelihood of dealing successfully with ever changing market dynamics, ultimately increasing the chances of delivering superior investment returns. Unfortunately, successful firms contain the seeds of their own destruction, as size inhibits performance and age saps energy. Vigilant fiduciaries stand ready to cull the old and tired, while identifying the new and energetic.

Deal structure plays a critical role in shaping the behavior of investment managers and determining the fairness of investment gain and loss allocations. By encouraging asset managers to behave as principals, appropriate deal terms cause investors to seek investment gains and de-emphasize return-reducing streams of fee income.

Typical compensation arrangements cause asset manager income to depend on factors beyond the investment advisor's control. As bull market gains inflate marketable security portfolios and increase private fund assets, managers benefit through enhanced management fees and profits interests. Bear market losses impose costs unrelated to manager actions. In the case of both marketable and private deal structures, investment advisors' compensation waxes and wanes with the market's fortunes, resulting in earnings streams not directly tied to the level of value created.

By operating under asset-based compensation arrangements that fail to consider value-added measures, investment managers lose focus on return generation, emphasizing instead a stay-in-business strategy designed to protect streams of fee income. Partly as a consequence of poor deal structure, standard compensation arrangements allocate investment gains and losses unfairly, frequently enriching the investment manager while generating substandard risk-adjusted returns to providers of funds.

Appropriate deal terms serve to encourage fund managers to behave as principals, causing them to pursue gains while avoiding losses. Structural characteristics that play an important role in aligning investment manager and investor interests include the nature of the investment vehicle, level of fees, form of incentive compensation, and size of manager co-investment. By seeking investment arrangements that motivate managers to pursue high levels of risk-adjusted portfolio gains, investors encourage a focus on generating satisfactory investment results.

Investors hoping to beat the odds by playing the game of active management face daunting obstacles ranging from the efficiency in pricing of most marketable securities to the burden of extraordinary fees in most alternative asset investment vehicles. Only by identifying extremely high quality people operating in an appropriately structured organization do active investors create an opportunity to add value to the investment process. Painstaking identification, careful structuring, and patient implementation of investment management relationships provide essential underpinnings to an active management program.

10
Investment Process

Structuring a portfolio consistent with fundamental investment tenets requires a governance process that produces an appropriate policy portfolio, avoids counterproductive market timing, and identifies effective investment management relationships. One of the most critical portfolio management decisions concerns the choice between (a) developing an organization with the capability of selecting high quality active managers, and (b) deploying a strategy with an emphasis on bare bones passive vehicles. While choosing an active approach broadens the asset class opportunity set and holds the promise of market-beating returns, active strategies demand a significant commitment of resources. Those institutions that engage in active management without proper support face the unpalatable prospect of generating disappointing results for themselves and creating opportunities for better prepared investors.

Two important tenets of investment management—contrarian thinking and long-term orientation—pose challenges for governance of endowment funds. Because large bureaucratic organizations invariably use groups of people (investment committees) to oversee other groups of people (investment staff), consensus-building behavior permeates the investment process. Unless carefully managed, group dynamics frequently thwart contrarian activities and impose shorter than optimal time horizons. Creating a governance process that encourages long-term, independent, contrarian thinking represents a critical undertaking for endowed institutions.

John Maynard Keynes, in *The General Theory*, describes the difficulties inherent in group investment decision making: "Finally it is the long-term investor, he who most promotes the public interest, who will in practice come in for most criticism, wherever investment funds are managed by committees or boards or banks. For it is the essence of his behavior that he should be eccentric, unconventional, and rash in the eyes of average opinion. If he is successful, that will only confirm the general belief in his rashness; and if in the short run he is unsuccessful, which is very likely, he will not receive much mercy. Worldly wisdom teaches that it is better for reputation to fail conventionally than to succeed unconventionally."[1] The challenges facing an institution attempting to structure effective governance processes center on exercising appropriate fiduciary oversight, while encouraging "eccentric, unconventional, and rash" behavior.

balance between beating the market and following market

ACTIVE versus PASSIVE MANAGEMENT

Perhaps, the most important distinguishing characteristic of an investor concerns the ability (or lack thereof) to make high quality active management decisions. Skillful active investors sensibly employ a broader set of asset class alternatives, enriching opportunities for portfolio diversification. Adept active investors pursue market-beating strategies in marketable securities, potentially enhancing asset class returns. The active investor enjoys the greatest opportunity to create and implement portfolios with high potential returns and low prospective risks.

The surest path to making effective active management decisions comes from engaging a highly qualified staff of professionals committed to serving the interests of the investment fund. A dedicated staff supplies the resources necessary to identify the exceedingly rare group of managers able to add value in the investment process. In addition, hiring a group of individuals to manage a particular investment fund reduces the severity of the principal-agent conflicts that pervade the money management industry, as the staff serves as a strong advocate for the institution's interests.

Investors without the resources to make well-informed active management judgments sensibly limit portfolio choices to passively managed, broad-based asset classes of marketable securities, including domestic equity, foreign developed equity, emerging market equity, real estate investment trusts, U.S. Treasury bonds and U.S. Treasury Inflation-Protected Securities. The intensely competitive investment world inevitably punishes casual attempts to beat the market, leading the rational resource-constrained investor to employ a manageable set of low-cost passive alternatives.*

Certain asset classes require active management skills if the investor hopes to realize an attractive risk-adjusted outcome: absolute return, real assets, and private equity. In each case, no market exists for the investor to buy; active management proves critical to producing acceptable results. In each case, fee arrangements—the combination of an asset-based management fee and a profits interest—create a substantial hurdle for investment success and provide dramatic punishment for investors who fail. In each case, in large part because of the generous fee arrangements, median asset class returns fail to provide satisfactory risk-adjusted returns to providers of capital. In each case, identifying managers with substantial potential involves a broad range of qualitative and quantitative skills. Success in absolute return, real assets, and private equity depends critically on high quality active management decisions.

Aside from allowing investors to effectively use a broader set of asset classes, a high quality team of professionals enables an institution to seek market-beating results in the relatively efficiently priced marketable securities arena. Even though low cost, passive alternatives provide a high hurdle for active managers, with diligent investigation and a sufficiently long time horizon, top-notch investment professionals face reasonable prospects of producing superior active management records.

The role of active management takes center stage in deliberations regarding the structure of the investment organization and governance of the investment process. Institutions that create well-staffed, high quaility investment organizations with effective committee oversight enjoy the opportunity to employ a broader range of asset classes and exploit an intriguing set of market inefficiencies. Institutions without substantial staff resources sensibly follow a strategy limited to passively managed portfolios. The choice between the active and the passive approaches to portfolio management carries implications for nearly every aspect of the investment process.

---

*My 2005 book, *Unconventional Success: A Fundamental Approach to Personal Investment*, covers the investment issues faced by investors without the resources to pursue active management programs.

OPERATING ENVIRONMENT

To produce a high quaility, actively managed portfolio, investment management organizations require a strong staff overseen by a well-functioning investment committee. Effective investment committees provide appropriate oversight while taking care not to impinge on staff responsibilities. Limiting committee meetings to four per year prevents trustees from becoming too involved in day-to-day portfolio management decisions, yet allows staff to receive appropriate guidance from the committee. By presuming that initiatives come from staff, not from committee members, responsibility for the nature and direction of the investment program rests squarely on the shoulders of the investment office. In short, the investment committee should play the role of a board of directors for the fund management operation.

Investment Committee

A strong investment committee brings discipline to the endowment management process. By thoroughly and thoughtfully vetting investment recommendations, the committee inspires staff to produce ever more carefully considered proposals. Ideally, committees rarely exercise the power to reject staff recommendations. If a committee frequently turns down or revises investment proposals, the staff encounters difficulty in managing the portfolio. Investment opportunities often require negotiation of commitments subject to board approval. If the board withholds approval with any degree of regularity, staff loses credibility in the eyes of the investment management community. That said, the committee must provide more than a rubber stamp for staff recommendations. In a well run organization, committee discussion of investment proposals influences the direction and nature of future staff initiatives. Effective portfolio management requires striking a balance between respect for the ultimate authority of the investment committee and delegation of reasonable responsibility to the investment staff.

Committee members often provide assistance between meetings, providing feedback on past actions and suggesting strategies for the future. Informed give and take elevates the investment dialog, challenging staff and committee to improve the quality of investment decision making.

Investment committee members should be selected primarily for good judgment. While no particular background qualifies an individual to serve on the committee, broad understanding of financial markets proves useful in overseeing the investment process. Aggregating a collection of investment specialists occasionally poses dangers, particularly when committee members attempt to manage the portfolio, not the process. Successful executives bring a valuable perspective to the table provided they suspend their natural inclination to reward success and punish failure. The sometimes deep rooted corporate instinct to pursue winners and avoid losers pushes portfolios toward fundamentally risky momentum-driven strategies and away from potentially profitable contrarian opportunities. The most effective investment committee members understand the responsibility to oversee the investment process and to provide support for the investment staff, while avoiding actual management of the portfolio.

Investment Staff

Strong investment staffs drive the portfolio management process. Whether dealing with broad issues of asset allocation and spending policy or specific issues of portfolio management and manager selection, the staff needs to make a rigorous, compelling case for adopting a particular course of action. Advocacy must not compromise disclosure, as actual and potential weaknesses need to be fully described and discussed. Intellectual dishonesty ultimately proves fatal to the investment process.

Without a disciplined process for articulating investment recommendations, decision making tends to become informal, even casual. In the case of asset allocation decisions, effective staff analysis establishes and articulates a coherent, intellectual framework from which well-grounded recommendations flow. In the case of individual manager decisions, a rigorous evaluation of all aspects of the investment opportunity, including thorough due diligence on the quality of the investment principals, serves as an essential precondition to committing investment funds.

Written recommendations provide a particularly useful means of communicating investment ideas. The process of drafting memos often exposes logical flaws or gaps in knowledge. Awareness that a critical audience of colleagues and committee members will review investment memos stimulates careful, logical exposition of proposals. Comprehensive written treatments of investment issues provide a common background for staff and committee members, supporting high quality discussion at meetings.

Better decisions come from small internal decision-making groups consisting of no more than three or four people. As the number of people involved in a decision increases, the likelihood of a conventional, compromising consensus increases. Obviously, with a large staff, the same small group of people need not make all decisions. For example, different groups might make recommendations for different asset classes, preserving the principle of small group decision making while allowing organizations to engage the staff resources necessary to deal with growing portfolio complexity and increasing asset levels.

Investment organizations benefit from the constant renewal provided by the addition of young professionals. Their energy, enthusiasm, and fresh perspective prevent dry rot from taking hold. The apprenticeship training process benefits both the trained and the trainer, as the process of teaching benefits both the student and the teacher. As Yale economist James Tobin observed, "I never fail to learn, from the students themselves and from the discipline of presenting ideas clearly to them." In a well-structured organization, new hires make an early impact. Pushing responsibility down in an organization improves performance and enhances satisfaction.

Organizational Characteristics

Strong investment management groups share a number of characteristics, with great people constituting the single most important element. In October 1987, Treasury Secretary Henry Paulson, then a senior executive at Goldman Sachs, speaking at Yale's School of Management, articulated a compelling case that high quality individuals gravitate toward entities that operate on the cutting edge, that embrace a global strategy, that provide opportunities to benefit from focused mentorship, and that encourage early acceptance of significant responsibility.

Organizations on the cutting edge choose from a broader opportunity set. By examining nontraditional asset allocations, investors improve the chances of finding a portfolio mix well-suited to the institution's needs. By considering alternatives outside of the mainstream, investors increase the likelihood of discovering the next big winner well before it becomes the next big bust. By evaluating managers without the requisite check-the-box institutional characteristics, investors boost the odds of uncovering a highly motivated, attractive group of partners. Operating on the periphery of standard institutional norms increases opportunity for success.

A global perspective facilitates understanding of investment alternatives, providing valuable context for consideration of even the most parochial domestic opportunity. Aside from improving an investor's decision-making framework, global reach increases the scope of investment choices, enhancing the possibility of identifying superior options. Obviously, along with the expanded range of possibilities comes the increased potential for failure. Overseas commitments entail inherently higher levels of risk as availability of information and depth of understanding almost invariably compare unfavorably to knowledge of domestic market alternatives.

Focused mentorship provides essential training for new staff as individuals assimilate investment management principles primarily through experience. While academic training provides a necessary foundation, aspiring investors learn best through serving an apprenticeship, benefiting from day-to-day exposure to the thoughts and actions of experienced colleagues.

Giving junior members of the team early responsibility challenges all members of an investment organization to spread critical skills throughout the group. Transmitting key principles to younger colleagues magnifies the impact of more senior players, broadening the scope of an organization's reach and the range of its accomplishments. As a corollary benefit, the training process reinforces and freshens the commitment of all participants to the group's core investment beliefs.

While both organizations and individuals benefit from Paulson's paradigm of a cutting edge, globally oriented institution that provides focused mentorship and early responsibility, successful investment organizations require an additional dimension. Most operations thrive by taking a conventional, middle-of-the-road approach to management. Success in investment management requires an unconventional, out-of-the-mainstream understanding of markets.

Independent thinking contributes to strong investment decision making. Large, bureaucratic plan sponsors provide an example of counterproductive practices where standard investment manager search techniques exclude nearly all interesting managers from consideration. By circulating "requests for proposals" that require vast quantities of detailed information to complete, the bureaucrats encourage the wrong sort of manager to apply. The seemingly endless questionnaires—that include criteria for minimum historical performance levels, asset size, and years of experience—ensure conventionally unimaginative and ultimately unsuccessful management. While the bureaucratic process practically guarantees poor results, the bureaucrat's job proves secure, as massive stacks of paper protect every investment decision. Bureaucracies lack the imagination and courage to pursue nonconventional paths that prove essential to building a successful investment program.

Self awareness plays a critical role in investment analysis. Understanding and exploiting strengths makes an obvious contribution to performance. Recognizing and dealing effectively with weaknesses represents a less obvious factor. Ruthlessly honest evaluation of absolute and comparative advantages and disadvantages increases the likelihood of backing winners and avoiding losers.

Frank, open discussions of failures and successes provide essential feedback for improved decision making. By understanding failures, investors create the opportunity to avoid making the same mistake in the future. Analysis of winners provides keys for unlocking future successes. In contrast, assigning blame engenders an atmosphere that discourages risk taking, impairing the investment process in a fundamental fashion. Stated differently, successful investment cultures encourage professionals to find new mistakes to make, instead of simply repeating old errors.

Providing an environment with low costs of failure encourages experimentation, allowing investors to take well-considered, intelligent risks knowing that losses do not threaten careers. The type of unconventional behavior necessary for meaningful investment success produces its share of shortcomings.

Consider the record of the Yale investments team responsible for the university's stellar record over the past two decades. In every instance where Yale launched a major investment initiative (e.g., absolute return, real estate, timber, oil and gas, buyouts, venture capital, international private equity, active domestic equity, and active foreign equity), the crack investment team initially backed a manager that failed to stand the test of time. Yet, in every instance, the initiatives (implemented by an improved set of managers) contributed enormously to Yale's investment success. Encouraging experimentation and tolerating failure represent necessary preconditions for developing winning strategies.

Collegiality plays a critical role in creating and sustaining an appropriate investment environment. Supportive co-workers lessen the lonely contrarian's feelings of vulnerability that stem from the frequent failures that mark even the most successful investment programs. Understanding colleagues take some of the sting out of mistakes, facilitating continued pursuit of risky investment opportunities.

Successful investors operate outside of the mainstream. In institutional settings which prize conformity, pursuit of potentially rewarding investment opportunities requires strong intellectual leadership.

Without strong leadership, investment management decisions fail to rise above normal bureaucratic standards and produce predictably mediocre results. By establishing a decision-making framework that encourages unconventional, controversial actions, an effective leader provides the foundation for a successful investment program.

ORGANIZATIONAL STRUCTURE

The nature of the not-for-profit investment governance process has changed dramatically over time. Decades ago, trustees generally chose individual securities at regularly scheduled quarterly meetings. Simple portfolios contained relatively few positions, allowing full review in a period of several hours. Finance committees populated by "titans of industry" frequently contributed direct, useful knowledge regarding individual security holdings.

In the 1960s and 1970s, the standard portfolio management structure involved a handful of external managers who typically pursued balanced mandates and placed modest demands on fiduciaries. Governance issues remained similar to those confronting trustees managing portfolios "out of their back pockets." Instead of monitoring dozens of individual securities, investment committee members tracked and evaluated a limited group of outside managers. Because the managers invested largely in familiar securities and home markets, the process proved comfortable for trustees and staff alike.

In recent decades, demands placed on investment staff and trustees have multiplied along with the increase in the number of institutional asset classes and the corresponding explosion in the number of specialty investment managers. Even as trustees deal with the greater complexity of the investment world, they have encountered dramatic increases in the breadth and seriousness of issues facing nonprofit institutions. As a consequence, many institutions have devoted adequate time and attention to investment management.

The structure of investment organizations often failed to keep pace with changes in the external world. In many cases, institutions remained rooted in the past, devoting insufficient resources to financial asset management. Endowment management suffered in the not uncommon circumstance where the treasurer spent only a fraction of the work week supervising hundreds of millions of dollars. Failing to provide adequate staff support falls in the category of penny wise and pound foolish. For every additional one percent per annum added to investment returns, a half billion dollar endowment generates an incremental five million dollars annually. The costs of a high quality investment organization pale in comparison to the value of improved results.

Attracting and compensating qualified investment professionals poses challenges for nonprofit institutions. In the private sector, financial services professionals earn staggering amounts of money. In contrast, as is the case for most employees in not-for-profits, nonprofit investment professionals earn substantially less than their for-profit counterparts. The combination of a below market nonprofit pay scale and extraordinary private sector compensation creates potential for divisive tension regarding compensation issues in the nonprofit community.

Separate Management Companies

To deal with compensation issues, a number of universities established distinct management companies to invest endowment assets. The fundamental problem with this organizational (and in some cases, physical) separation concerns the tendency to treat the management company solely as an investment entity. Proper stewardship of endowment assets requires consideration of both spending and investment policies, with particular attention to the ways in which they interact. The job is not likely to be well done if the management company takes responsibility for investment decisions while others determine spending policies.

In fact, stewardship of endowment assets improves when the investment operation becomes part of the fabric of the institution. The greater the degree of professional interaction between endowment managers and the rest of the educational enterprise, the more credibility investment professionals have in discussing and recommending spending policies. At universities, common avenues of interaction include teaching by investment staff, seeking portfolio advice from faculty, working with development office staff, and contributing to the analysis of noninvestment financial issues. Aside from enhancing the overall contribution of the investment operation to the wider organization, interacting with other parts of the institution increases professional fulfillment for investment staff.

Ironically, establishing separate investment management companies to facilitate increased compensation for professionals sometimes exacerbates the problem. Greater separation leads to less identification with the institution, reducing the psychic income garnered from supporting the not-for-profit's eleemosynary mission. Psychic income foregone must be replaced with hard cash, further straining the bond between the management company and the rest of the institution.

Stanford Management Company

The 2006 travails of Stanford Management Company illustrate in high relief the issues surrounding compensation of investment professionals in an academic institution. In the 1990s, Stanford established its endowment management operation as an organization both physically and psychologically separate from the campus. The investment team occupied some of the most expensive real estate in the world on Sand Hill Road adjacent to the offices of Kleiner Perkins Caufield & Byers. For most of the 1990s, Laurie Hoagland ably led the Stanford investment operation which produced consistently superior results. Mike McCaffrey, former chief executive of investment bank Robertson Stephens, took over the management of Stanford's portfolio in September 2000, building on Hoagland's base and running the portfolio effectively in the difficult period following the collapse of the Internet bubble in March 2000.

Yet, McCaffrey found it difficult to deal with the compensation constraints of the not-for-profit world. He found that his employees faced a constant barrage of offers from the private sector. Frustrated by staff turnover, he sought a means to increase his staff's compensation in order to improve retention. He hit upon the idea of using Stanford Management Company to manage external assets which would provide a revenue stream he could use to enhance his colleagues' pay.

McCaffrey structured a proposal for the Stanford board. The plan made substantial progress, gathering initial support from the trustees and indications of interest from both individual and institutional investors. At the eleventh hour, however, McCaffrey decided not to move forward based on an insufficient level of enthusiasm from Stanford.

Paul Allen, co-founder of Microsoft, was one of the interested parties who hoped to invest a portion of his considerable wealth with the Stanford team. Undeterred by Stanford's lack of enthusiasm, McCaffrey and Allen formed a new venture, Makena Capital, to pursue the asset management business as an independent entity. Two senior Stanford Management professionals joined McCaffrey at Makena, gutting the leadership ranks of the university's investment organization. Makena raised $7 billion in short order, including $1.5 billion from Paul Allen, a stunning accomplishment for a start-up organization.

Among the troubling issues raised by the departure of Stanford's senior investment team, the most important issue concerns organizational culture. By operating less like a not-for-profit and more like an investment bank where pay matters above all else, Stanford Management failed to select employees who identified with Stanford's institutional mission. Instead of finding individuals who wished to earn handsome compensation and support one of the world's great educational institutions, Stanford attracted investment professionals who were in it for the money. Inevitably, the not-for-profit pay discount led to high turnover among those who wanted Wall Street compensation.

A stable, cohesive team brings enormous strengths to the investment process. Aside from the obvious benefits of continuity to portfolio management, investment professionals who identify with the organization's mission and who become part of the fabric of the place ultimately serve institutional needs in a superior fashion. Stanford Management Company's failure to create a culture consistent with the university's mission ultimately imposed significant costs on one of the world's great educational institutions.

Institutions need not establish separate investment companies to address compensation issues. Exceptions to standard policies can be made to pay reasonably competitive salaries, including the use of incentive-based compensation, without the radical break implied by creation of a separate legal entity. Dealing with the trade-offs within the context of the university, while difficult, lessens the magnitude of the problems associated with complete separation of the investment management organization.

While the desire to create separate compensation schemes for university investment professionals appears to drive the establishment of separate management companies, hopes for improved governance may also contribute to the decision. As the breadth and complexity of investment alternatives increase, so do the demands on trustees responsible for overseeing investment operations. Establishing an independent management company allows the institution to look beyond the existing group of trustees when selecting fiduciaries to oversee endowment assets.

Yet governance issues can be addressed without creating a separate management company. Since its establishment in 1975, Yale's Investment Committee included nontrustee advisors to assist in governance. The use of outside advisors, who bring valuable insight and perspective to the process, obviates the need to establish a separate investment company to draw from a broader pool of governance talent. As an added bonus, service by outside advisors on the investment committee gives an institution the opportunity to get a close look at an interesting group of institutional supporters. In fact, at Yale, a number of investment committee members have gone on to serve on the university's governing board.

Establishing appropriate governance and compensation structures for endowment management organizations poses a difficult set of issues as radical differences between private sector and nonprofit compensation levels create inevitable tensions. While establishing distinct subsidiaries to manage endowment funds addresses oversight and pay issues, the accompanying physical and psychological separation imposes significant costs on the broader organization. Addressing compensation and governance concerns within the context of the entire institution provides a solution more likely to produce results consistent with the organization's needs.

USE OF INTERMEDIARIES

In an effort to pursue an active management program without committing the required time, energy, and resources, many institutions take the shortcut of using a fund of funds or a consultant. Unfortunately, the use of external agents (instead of an internal investment team) leads down a path to suboptimal results, as the interests of the fund of funds manager or investment consultant inevitably diverge from the interests of the institutional investor.

Deep understanding of markets based on meaningful interaction between fiduciaries and external managers provides the strongest foundation for investment success. Employing a fund of funds manager or engaging a consultant places a filter between those entrusted with responsibility for the assets and those making investment decisions. Without the confidence engendered by thorough, direct understanding of manager actions and market opportunities, investors judge competence of external agents primarily by the performance numbers, which constitute an insufficient, unreliable, and sometimes perverse measure. Risks associated with distancing fiduciaries from investment managers dictate that fund of funds and consultancy arrangements receive skeptical scrutiny.

Fund of Funds

Fund of funds managers provide the service of making investment decisions for fiduciaries. By pooling assets, usually from less sophisticated investors, fund of funds managers argue that economies of scale allow professional staff to manage monies in institutional fashion. Fund of funds firms range from multiproduct concerns that provide one-stop shopping to entities focused on specific niches, including nearly every asset class imaginable.

By providing manager selection and monitoring services, broad-based funds of funds suggest that they enable smaller organizations to tap into otherwise unavailable sophisticated investment strategies. Larger organizations sometimes hope to benefit by employing funds of funds to gain exposure to unfamiliar market niches.

In spite of the purported benefits from employing fund of funds managers, substantial risks stem from imposing a filter between the investment manager and the ultimate client. Regardless of the level of disclosure provided by the fund of funds manager, transparency in the investment management relationship declines dramatically. Clients unable or unwilling to understand the underlying manager characteristics rely solely on performance to evaluate investment strategies. When results disappoint, clients wonder not only about the investment managers, but also about the competence of the fund of funds advisor.

Faced with poor performance, the client loses the benefits associated with delegating responsibility to the fund of funds manager. Understanding the source of poor results requires investigation of the underlying investment management organizations, a task that the fiduciary hoped to avoid. Short of a thorough underwriting of the constituent managers, clients have no alternative other than simply reacting to the numbers, exposing the portfolio to the damaging prospect of selling low after having bought high.

When employing fund of funds managers, investors must search for firms with compatible professional and ethical standards. Delegating authority to engage investment managers carries enormous import. Even large, reputable fund of funds managers occasionally make staggeringly inappropriate judgments. Several years ago, a private equity vehicle launched by a multibillion-dollar fund of funds considered engaging an individual to manage an oil and gas program. Aside from the fact that the individual's resume showed little direct relevant experience, a criminal history clouded his past. Convicted of drug dealing, the purported energy manager had also been arrested and convicted for spousal abuse.

Most investors, when confronted with this set of facts, move on to the next opportunity. Under the best of circumstances, investing poses significant challenges. Hiring an inexperienced partner with a criminal past increases the difficulties immeasurably.

What motivated the staff to propose backing a poorly qualified manager of dubious character? While the full story likely contains a complex set of reasons, one obvious answer stands out. Fund of funds managers justify their existence in part by making nonstandard choices. Investing in the usual suspects provides less value added than does identifying emerging managers unavailable to most market participants.

Ultimately, the fund of funds decided to put the former drug dealer in the energy investment business. Not content simply to back this individual in the firm's standard format as one of a number of managers in a pool, the organization decided to devote the entire energy fund to this single manager. Life is too short to waste time making a concentrated bet on an individual with a checkered past, when the world provides countless superior alternatives.

In another extraordinary incident, Paloma Partners, a multibillion-dollar fund of funds, engaged John Mulheren's Buffalo Partners to manage a risk arbitrage portfolio. Mulheren gained notoriety in February 1988, when he packed his trunk with a .233 caliber Israeli Galil assault rifle, 9-millimeter semiautomatic pistol, .357 Magnum pistol, 12-gauge pistol-grip shotgun, and three hundred rounds of ammunition, intending to shoot Ivan Boesky. Alerted by Mulheren's wife, State of New Jersey troopers arrested Mulheren, preventing a possible tragedy.[2]

Since Paloma Partners refuses to disclose names of underlying investment managers, even to clients, most of the firm's investors were unaware of the relationship. Upon learning of the involvement with Mulheren, a potential client challenged the fund manager, arguing the investment did not meet institutional standards. "Mulheren's a great investor when he's taking his lithium," replied the manager.

Adding a layer to the investment management process decreases transparency, posing serious problems for fiduciaries. Instead of relying on someone's judgment in making investment decisions, the fiduciary relies on someone's judgment about someone's judgment in making the ultimate decisions. While commitments to convicted drug dealers and would-be assassins represent extreme examples of poor judgment, the incidents highlight the risk of using intermediaries to make decisions. The greater the number of layers, the greater the likelihood that outcomes deviate from the fiduciary's preferences.

Aside from the issues of transparency and delegation of authority, fund of funds suffer from burdensome fee structures. In the world of active management, the majority of assets fail to produce risk-adjusted excess returns as the certainty of manager fees and transaction costs overwhelm the false promise of investment success. Stated simply, the fund of funds manager adds another layer of fees to already debilitating charges, further diminishing the chances of realizing market-beating returns.

On top of the additional fee burden, the fund of funds faces the challenge of adverse selection, which limits the available opportunity set. Investment managers vastly prefer direct relationships with providers of capital. Funds of funds represent an inflexible and unreliable source of funding, because they do not control directly the monies they employ to make commitments. Since the highest quality investment managers enjoy the greatest ability to pick and choose their investor base, the fund of funds fights an uphill battle in accessing top notch investment firms.

Discrimination against funds of funds usually proceeds quietly, since prudent managers guard against the day when they might need to tap fund of funds' money, however unreliable it might be. Taking a rare public stand, in 2006, world class venture capital firm Sequoia Capital eliminated all funds of funds from its investor ranks.[3] By stating publicly what many managers practice privately, Sequoia Capital highlighted the problem of adverse selection.

Some evidence for the underperformance of funds of funds comes from the 2006 NACUBO Endowment Study.[4] Large endowments (with assets greater than $1 billion) reported hedge fund returns of 11.0 percent for the year ending June 30, 2006. Small endowments (with assets between $25 million and $50 million) posted hedge fund returns of 8.2 percent. What accounts for the difference? Funds of funds likely contributed to the relatively poor performance of smaller endowments. According to the study, only 2.7 percent of large endowments used funds of funds, while 47 percent of small endowments employed funds of funds. Apparently, a relationship exists between the use of funds of funds and substandard returns.

Further evidence on the poor returns generated by funds of funds comes from a study by Josh Lerner of Harvard, Antoinette Schoar of MIT, and Wan Wong of Harvard. In *Smart Institutions, Foolish Choices?: The Limited Partner Performance Puzzle*, the authors examine investment returns for private equity funds selected by various categories of investors. Returns on funds chosen by endowments produced "by far the best overall performance" with an average internal rate of return (IRR) of 20 percent. Funds of funds failed miserably, selecting partnerships with an average IRR of negative two percent.[5] The academic research backs up the *a priori* intuition. Investors sensibly avoid funds of funds based on issues of transparency, judgment, fees, and adverse selection.

Consulting Firms

Seeking to supplement internal resources, many institutions engage consulting firms to contribute to the investment process. The notion of employing qualified external resources strikes many fiduciaries as a sensible means to deal with the complexities of portfolio management. Unfortunately, the dynamics of the consulting business frequently drive clients to suboptimal outcomes.

Consulting firms maximize profits by providing identical advice to as many clients as possible. In the investment world, which demands portfolios custom tailored to institution-specific risk and return preferences, a cookie cutter approach fails. Clients must either identify a consulting firm that cares about goals other than profit maximization or manage the consulting relationship to achieve appropriately tailored advice.

Consultants express conventional views and make safe recommendations. Because consultants rarely espouse unconventional points of view, they provide more than adequate cover when dealing with investment committees. Decision makers rest comfortably, knowing that a recognized consulting firm blessed the chosen investment strategy.

Selecting managers from the consultant's internally approved recommended list serves as a poor starting point for identifying managers likely to provide strong future results. No consultant who wishes to stay employed recommends a start-up manager with all of the attendant organizational and investment risks. Because consultants seek to spread the costs of identifying and monitoring managers, consultants recommend established managers that have the capacity (if not the ability) to manage large pools of assets. Clients end up with bloated, fee-driven investment management businesses instead of nimble return-oriented entrepreneurial firms.

Unfortunately, the economics of consulting drive an unusual wedge between the interests of the consultant and the interests of the client. Ongoing demand for consulting services requires that clients remain dependent on the consultant, reducing incentives for consultants to move clients toward self-sufficiency. In extreme cases consultants recommend programs that, while ostensibly in the client's interests, simply serve to assure a continued stream of income for the consultant. For example, private equity consultants, also known as "gatekeepers," sometimes recommend direct co-investment programs to clients, which are obviously ill-equipped to handle the program.

(The client cannot even make a partnership decision without assistance; how could the client make an even more difficult direct investment decision?) Along with the co-investment recommendation, gatekeepers offer selection and monitoring services. If successful, the gatekeeper locks in a combination of partnership selection, co-investment advice, and monitoring services, creating an annuity stream lasting the life of the investment program.

In an even more troubling development, many consulting firms now offer fund of funds investment management services. The entire concept rests on an irreconcilable conflict of interest in which the purportedly objective consultant recommends that the client hire the consultant to manage assets. The combination of a self-interested consulting firm and the structurally flawed fund of funds business leads to an ugly proposition for the investment management client.

A former consultant summarizes the problems of the consulting industry in the following polemic:

> Ninety-five percent of institutions rely on a consultant to come in once a year, do a manager search that costs $18,000 conducted by someone with four years of industry experience, select a manager who is gathering assets, has good three-year performance numbers (how many times have you seen a consultant or committee pick a manager with poor three-year performance?) and has standard management fees. This scenario is repeated daily in the endowment and foundation world. The same institutions will fire the manager, who they barely know through their once a year client service presentation, when they underperform for two years.
>
> Consultants, for business reasons, cannot spend a lot of time on managers who will keep their asset base small. The economies of scale are not there. If there is a great manager who may have $50 million or $100 million of capacity per year, a consultant cannot cover them in detail. It just does not scale. Therefore, consultants are geared toward large managers with standard management fees that have lots of capacity going forward.

Interposing consultants between fund fiduciaries and external managers creates a range of problems that stem from a disconnect between the consulting firm's profit motive and the client's investment objectives. While consulting firms offer a shortcut that avoids the hard work of creating a dedicated investment operation, as is the case with many shortcuts, the end results disappoint.

DECISION-MAKING PROCESS

Reasonable decision-making processes give appropriate emphasis to the range of issues facing committee and staff. Charley Ellis describes a useful framework for categorizing various portfolio management decisions. Policy decisions concern long-term issues that inform the basic structural framework of the investment process. Strategic decisions represent intermediate-term moves designed to adapt longer term policies to immediate market opportunities and institutional realities. Trading and tactical decisions involve short-term implementation of strategies and policies.

In his wonderful book, *Winning the Loser's Game*, Ellis bemoans the fact that decision makers spend too much time on relatively exciting trading and tactical decisions at the expense of the more powerful, yet more mundane, policy decisions.[6] A decision-making process centered on making high quality policy decisions increases an investor's chances of winning.

Policy Target Focus

Policy asset allocation targets represent the heart of the investment process. No other aspect of portfolio management plays as great a role in determining a fund's ultimate performance. No other statement says as much about the character of a fund. Establishing a governance framework focused on policy decisions constitutes the most fundamental obligation of investment fiduciaries. Without a disciplined, rigorous process for setting asset allocation targets, effective portfolio management becomes impossible.

A robust discussion of asset allocation targets requires careful preparation. At the meeting prior to the annual review, staff members present to the committee a brief description of the issues they intend to analyze. The chair of the committee should encourage members to offer suggestions for issues that the investment staff could then consider along with the internally generated topics. A well-structured process underpins careful decision making.

Asset allocation targets ought to be reviewed once (and only once) per year. By concentrating the discussion of investment policy in one meeting, the most important investment decisions receive concentrated attention from both staff and committee. Perhaps equally important, limiting policy discussions to the assigned meeting diminishes the possibility of damage from ill-considered moves made in emotional response to the waves of gloom or euphoria that sweep over markets from time to time.

Yale and the 1987 Market Crash

The October 1987 crash in stock prices placed stresses and strains on decision-making processes. Yale felt the pressure. In spite of the fact that the university had followed a quarterly meeting schedule since the investment committee was established in 1975, two extraordinary meetings were held in late 1987 and early 1988 in response to the crash. Even though at the time of the meetings stock prices were substantially lower and bond prices measurably higher than at the time of the June 1987 policy review, the committee discussed whether to increase the policy allocation to bonds at the expense of stocks.

Yale made a disciplined late October, post-crash rebalancing purchase of tens of millions of dollars of equities funded by a corresponding sale of tens of millions of dollars of bonds. In the context of the gloom of late 1987, Yale's action appeared rash. Other institutions not only allowed equity positions to drift downward by the amount of the relative stock market decline, they further reduced equity exposure through net sales in November and December. Such sales seemed prudent in an environment where the *New York Times* published a weekly chart that superimposed 1987 stock prices on a chart of prices for 1929 through 1932.

Yale's internal committee dynamics proved difficult. In a written memorandum, one member characterized Yale's asset allocation as "super aggressive" and on the "far edge of aggressiveness." Citing bleak short-term prospects for equities, he commented that if Yale were right to have an aggressive equity posture, the university will get "little credit," but if Yale were wrong there would be "all hell to pay." Believing that "events of the past six months have diminished long-term prospects for equity markets," the committee member concluded that the university's assumptions regarding expected returns were overly optimistic. Hence, he suggested that both short-term and long-term considerations required downward adjustment of Yale's equity target. Another, more analytically inclined member, wondered if increases in historical volatility made stocks less attractive on a relative basis.[7] By questioning assumptions that had been examined as part of the annual policy review only four months earlier, committee members exposed Yale to the risk of an untimely reversal of strategy.

After much *Sturm und Drang*, Yale maintained policy targets, reaping attractive returns on its post-crash rebalancing trade. In spite of the university's success, behind-the-scenes discussions illustrate the potential danger of revisiting policy target levels too frequently, particularly in the midst of a market crisis. While trauma surrounding the 1987 stock market crash caused the university to violate past practice of limiting policy allocation discussions to one meeting per year, disciplined implementation of a sensible policy ultimately contributed to the pursuit of effective strategies in a difficult environment.

Although in retrospect the committee's actions appear innocuous, in other states of the world the positions taken by the investment committee members could have had severe repercussions for Yale's investment staff. In particular, the extraordinary memo containing a committee member's *ex post facto* criticism of the policy allocation targets had dangerous overtones. Had the market not recovered within a relatively short time frame, those staff members closely identified with the rebalancing trade might have suffered serious damage to their careers.

Strategic and Tactical Issues

While the committee meeting on policy asset allocation represents the focal point of the investment process, other meetings deal with important strategic issues. Following the close of the fiscal year, a meeting devoted to portfolio evaluation discusses the character and performance of the overall endowment and individual asset classes. Portfolio review memoranda describe individual asset classes in depth, placing results in the context of market conditions and identifying factors that influence significant investment opportunities. The positioning of an asset class relative to its benchmark with respect to fundamental characteristics—such as size, sector, and style—highlights significant portfolio bets that are evaluated retrospectively and prospectively. Active management efforts receive grades in the form of detailed report cards for each manager. The individual manager assessments include not only performance data, but information on reporting, transparency, fee structures, and co-investment. Analysis of strengths and weaknesses of portfolio strategies leads to an outline for future projects to improve portfolio management. In essence, the portfolio evaluation meeting provides a backward-looking assessment and a forward-looking strategic plan.

The remaining two quarterly meetings generally have a topical focus, frequently involving in-depth analysis of a specific asset class. Meetings centered on individual asset classes drill deep to provide a granular view, allowing committee and staff to evaluate thoroughly every aspect of asset class management. Decision-making assessments consider the impact of bets regarding size, sector, and style. One particularly effective exercise goes well beyond traditional performance evaluation by examining returns of terminated managers. In assessing performance of fired managers relative to benchmarks and actual portfolio results, investigators gain insight into the effectiveness of termination moves, a topic often comfortably ignored after completing the difficult task of severing ties.

Asset class reviews provide a chance for external investment managers to engage investment committee and staff in discussion of significant market issues. While sensible investors avoid the all-too-prevalent "beauty contest" (in which a series of managers make difficult-to-distinguish-between oral presentations in a hiring pageant), investment committee members do benefit from face-to-face interaction with managers. Creating a forum for lively interaction between managers and committee members adds value to the investment process. But, rather than allowing managers to present "canned" portfolio appraisals, investment staff should structure panel discussion to stimulate candid discussion of manager-specific approaches to asset class pitfalls and opportunities.

Occasionally, committee meetings deal with market issues that cut across individual asset classes. For example, the savings and loan debacle of the late 1980s informally influenced the private equity, real estate, and absolute return asset classes. In the late 1990s the Internet mania affected investments in the marketable equity, private equity, and absolute return asset classes. Focusing attention on the broad implications of a particular market phenomenon enhances the ability of an investment organization to pursue attractive strategies and to identify hidden risks.

Effective investors maintain focus on long-term policy targets, making the annual asset allocation review the centerpiece of an investment fund's agenda. Devoting the meeting after the close of the fiscal year to a thorough review of portfolio characteristics and performance provides a report card for the past and a road map for the future. The two interim meetings allow in-depth examination of a particular asset class or an interesting investment opportunity. Hewing to a well-defined schedule of meetings provides a structure for effective decision making and reduces the opportunity for committee and staff to make undisciplined moves.

DECISION-MAKING CHALLENGES

Effective endowment management processes encourage long-term investing. The universality with which investors proclaim themselves long-term in orientation matches only the startling degree to which short-term thinking drives investor decisions. Perhaps human nature dictates that short-term issues overwhelm long-term considerations. Time horizons shrink with the trauma of unexpected loss, the desire for immediate gratification, and the competitive need to win.

The human desire to make a visible contribution shortens time horizons. Because investment staff and trustees wish to leave their marks on the portfolio, potential problems exist if the investment fund's horizon exceeds a staff member's expected tenure or trustee's term. When managing perpetual life assets, explicit recognition of the discontinuity between personal and institutional time frames facilitates effective decision making. Continuity in management and governance provide another practical response.

Investors seeking short-term success will likely be frustrated by markets too efficient to offer much in terms of easy gains. Even if managers find short-term opportunities to exploit, they put themselves on a treadmill. As investors successfully exploit one short-term inefficiency, it must be replaced by another position followed by another and yet another *ad infinitum*. Creating wealth through a series of short-term investments is difficult, risky work. Moreover, managers hoping to beat the market every quarter dramatically limit their investment universe, pursuing only those mispricings likely to resolve themselves in the near term. Short-term players create opportunities for those few who attempt to invest based on considered long-term estimates.

True long-term investing dramatically broadens the investment opportunity set, allowing investors to profit from the irrationality of short-term players. Yet, because long-term investing involves an intrinsically higher risk profile, successful organizations must develop mechanisms to cope with the associated risks.

Short-Term Thinking

Too many market players operate with short time horizons. Anecdotal evidence abounds that many investment managers favor investment ideas that promise to pay off in three or six months. At the same time, fear of failure causes portfolio managers to hug the benchmark to *don't think short term*

avoid potentially disastrous falls to the bottom of the rankings. Mediocre performance inevitably results, as managers incur high transactions costs pursuing second-rate ideas within the context of an index-like portfolio.

Similar problems exist in the world of endowment management. Annual investment performance comparisons create (or reflect?) a horse race mentality. An audience of trustees, alumni, and faculty wait with great anticipation for the year-end results, comparing performance numbers to those from the peer group with which the institution competes. Short of beating an archrival at football, posting the highest one-year investment result ranks near the top of the list of institutional aspirations. As if the one-year numbers were not sufficiently short term, the consulting firm Cambridge Associates now publishes quarterly results for endowment portfolios. Obviously, judging long-term pools of assets by trailing three-month performance numbers induces the wrong kind of thinking, emphasizing short-term considerations over all else.

Performance competition causes some institutions to engage in bizarre behavior, including inflating published endowment values and reporting returns gross of fees. While secrecy surrounding overreporting of endowment levels prevents accurate measurement, a distressingly large number of institutions follow the practice of reporting gross returns. In the most recent endowment return survey conducted by Cambridge Associates 8 percent of those participating reported results before fees.[8] Of what possible use are such numbers? From a budgetary perspective, net returns provide useful data since institutions consume investment income after fees. From an investment perspective, net returns allow measurement of true value added relative to benchmarks. Barring a reasonable explanation, it appears that institutions report gross returns simply to gain a dubious advantage in the annual investment derby.

Consensus-Driven Behavior

Endowment managers engage in behavior similar to mutual fund benchmark hugging with peer group investment policies providing the stake to which an institution's asset allocation is tethered. Varying too far from the group consensus exposes the manager to the risk of being labeled unconventional. If the institution fails in its unusual approach, the policy will likely be abandoned and the investment staff will likely be unemployed. In contrast, had the institution failed with a standard institutional portfolio, policies may still be abandoned, but investment professionals would likely remain gainfully, if not happily, employed.

Concern regarding peer behavior rests, in part, on a rational basis. Educational institutions operate in a competitive environment, vying with one another for faculty, students, administrators, and financial support. Endowment size helps define an institution's competitive position, directly through provision of financial support and indirectly through creation of reputational capital. If dramatically different investment policies cause one university's endowment to decline precipitously, that institution may join a new, less prestigious peer group, losing not only financial assets, but also the confidence of important institutional constituencies. Conversely, unusual investment success enhances an institution's financial and reputational position. Trustees, generally a risk averse lot, may prefer prospective failure with a conventional portfolio to uncertain success with an unconventional approach.

However rational concern regarding peer behavior might be, if market participants weight heavily the consensus portfolio in asset allocation deliberations, change becomes quite difficult. In the extreme, fear of being different has everyone looking over their shoulder at everyone else's portfolio and no one looking at fundamental portfolio structure. Sensible portfolio management processes encourage the use of first principles to create portfolios appropriate for the institution, not mindless replication of other institutional asset mixes.

Contrarian Opportunity and Risk

The attitude of portfolio managers contributes to the success or failure of an investment program. Significant differences between successful investment operations and other well-run business activities cause standard corporate management techniques to fail in the investment world. Most businesses grow by feeding winners. Putting resources behind successful products generally leads to larger, increasingly impressive gains. Ruthless cuts of failed initiatives preserve corporate resources for more attractive strategies.

In contrast, investment success generally stems from contrarian impulses. View winners suspiciously; consider reducing or even eliminating previously successful strategies. Eye losers hopefully; consider adding to the out-of-favor approach.

Contrarian investing represents more than a reflex action causing investors to mindlessly "buy the dips." Out-of-favor positions must be supported by careful analysis of the fundamental drivers of value. Investigation of the contrarian alternative both provides a rationale for establishing the position and creates the conviction necessary to maintain the position in the face of market skepticism. Do not expect immediate gratification. In fact, going against the grain will likely appear foolish in the short run as already cheap assets become cheaper, leaving the true contrarian fundamentally out of sync with investors more in tune with the market.

Establishing and maintaining positions out of the mainstream requires decision making by relatively small groups. As groups increase in size, consensus thinking increasingly dominates the process. Behavioral studies identify a tendency for "group think." Most people so desire conformity that they embrace obviously wrong positions to avoid being at odds with the crowd.

Contrarian, long-term investing poses extraordinary challenges under the best of circumstances. In an institutional environment with staff and committees and boards, nearly insurmountable obstacles exist. Creating a decision-making framework that encourages unconventional thinking constitutes a critical goal for fund fiduciaries.

Unfortunately, overcoming the tendency to follow the crowd, while necessary, proves insufficient to guarantee investment success. By pursuing ill-considered, idiosyncratic policies, market players expose portfolios to unnecessary, often unrewarded risks. While courage to take a different path enhances chances for success, investors face likely failure unless a thoughtful set of investment principles undergirds the courage.

New York University and Bonds

Even the most well-meaning fiduciaries, motivated by altruistic intentions, sometimes pursue out of the mainstream policies which cause substantial economic and reputational damage. The story of NYU's endowment management over the past two decades vividly illustrates the dangers of implementing poorly founded investment strategies.

In the late 1970s and early 1980s, motivated by concerns regarding the fragility of the university's finances and the riskiness of the stock market, NYU allocated an average of 66 percent to bonds, 30 percent to stocks, and 4 percent to other assets.[9] NYU differed materially from her sister institutions by holding roughly double the average proportion of bonds and roughly half the average proportion of stocks.

Between 1981 and 1982, at the bottom of the equity market, NYU dropped its already low equity allocation from 33 percent to 7 percent of the portfolio, increasing the already high bond commitment from 62 percent to 90 percent of assets. Bonds continued to maintain a share in excess of 90 percent of assets through 1985, according to public reports on asset allocation, while stocks languished at single-digit levels, falling as low as 3 percent of the endowment. Even though after 1985 annual reports ceased to provide information on portfolio allocations, it appears that NYU persisted with its unusual portfolio structure throughout the late 1980s and early 1990s. After a nine-year disclosure hiatus, in 1995 the university reported holding 86 percent of assets in bonds and 9 percent of assets in stocks, indicating a continuing commitment to bonds. Only in 1997 did NYU begin to make a modest move away from fixed income to higher expected return assets.

Unfortunately, the bond-dominated portfolio left NYU on the sidelines during one of the greatest bull markets in history. From 1978 to 1998, stock returns exceeded bond returns in sixteen of twenty years, with stocks enjoying a 6 percent per annum advantage over bonds. Only in the aftermath of the 1987 crash did the fixed income strategy appear sensible, causing NYU board chairman Larry Tisch to receive a standing ovation at a NYU investment committee meeting. Market activity supported only a brief huzzah as the S&P 500 ended the 1987 calendar year 5.2 percent above the level recorded at the beginning of the year. Even when viewed from the perspective of a time frame as short as the twelve calendar months that included one of the all-time great stock market debacles, NYU's strategy failed to make sense.

As the bull market continued apace, Tisch turned away questions regarding the lack of equity exposure by responding that "the train has left the station."[10] Meanwhile, the opportunity costs for the NYU endowment mounted. From 1982 to 1998, an endowment wealth index for colleges and universities increased nearly eightfold, while NYU's endowment grew 4.6 times.[11] Had the institution's results simply mirrored college and university medians, in 1998 NYU's endowment would have been nearly a billion dollars larger than the actual level of $1.3 billion.

Beginning in the late 1990s, NYU began to reduce its overallocation to domestic fixed income, moving assets to domestic and foreign equities and absolute return strategies. Yet the legacy of the misguided bond bet endures, as NYU's 2005 portfolio shows scant exposure to the important asset classes of private equity and real assets. By failing to understand the relationship between the permanent nature of endowment funds and equity investments, NYU's endowment sustained long lasting, if not permanent damage.

Boston University and Seragen

Boston University's investment in Seragen, championed by the institution's former president, John Silber, posed a fundamentally different threat to the health of the university's finances. By funneling as much as $90 million of operating and endowment funds into a single biotechnology-based start-up company, Boston University made an unreasonably large bet on an extremely high risk investment.[12]

Silber first became interested in Seragen's "fusion toxins" at a 1986 lecture by Boston University scientist and Seragen founder Dr. John R. Murphy. In 1987, the university plowed $25 million of its $175 million endowment into the venture, buying a controlling interest from a Norwegian pharmaceutical company. Over the years, through further equity investments, operating support, and asset purchases, Boston University's exposure to Seragen went from excessive to irresponsible. In exchange for massive injections of funds, the university obtained control of the board, with Silber among the designated directors.

The institution's unusually concentrated, controlling position in Seragen attracted the attention of the Massachusetts attorney general who caused the university to dilute its ownership stake by pursuing public offerings. Even though share issuance raised more than $50 million in 1992 and 1993, Seragen's burn rate managed to outpace the cash inflows. By 1996, cumulative losses amounted to $200 million, causing Dr. Murphy to disassociate himself from Seragen, citing "business problems."

In spite of successes on the scientific front, Seragen's finances faltered, leading to delisting from the Nasdaq in September 1997. The stock, which went public in April 1992 at $12 a share and reached a high of $15 in January 1993, traded at ⅝ upon delisting. At the time, Boston University's stake amounted to little more than $5 million.

Desperate to salvage value, in December 1997, Boston University infused a further $5 million into Seragen by purchasing money-losing assets and providing ongoing support from the university's operating budget. By buying time, the institution managed to arrange an exit from the financially troubled company through a sale to Ligand Pharmaceuticals in August 1998. On September 20, 1998, the *New York Times* reported that the value of Boston University's position ultimately amounted to approximately $8.4 million, representing a loss of more than 90 percent on cost. Had the university's Seragen stake been invested in a diversified portfolio of stocks, the endowment would have benefited by avoiding the disastrous Seragen loss as well as by appreciation of tens of millions of dollars on the equity positions.

Ironically, Silber's positive assessment of Seragen's science appears well-founded. The firm's major drug, Interleukin-2, received FDA approval in February 1999. Yet the university stands to accrue little benefit from the drug's commercial success as Boston University's economic interest in the project diminished greatly with the Ligand takeover. Seragen's progress came too late and cost too much to reward the firm's shareholders.

By "rolling the dice" with endowment investments Boston University violated fundamental investment principles, providing a disservice to the institutions' constituents. Haunted by its failure to invest in Alexander Graham Bell's invention of the telephone, the university vowed not to repeat the mistake with Seragen. Unfortunately, spectacular investment success stories become clear only after the fact, forcing sensible investors to avoid outsized bets. A high risk, concentrated investment in Seragen, in the words of one faculty member, allowed Silber a shot at leaving "as a legacy a gigantic endowment." [13] Fiduciary requirements, no matter how liberally interpreted, fail to accommodate actions inconsistent with constructing a reasonably diversified portfolio.

In pursuing investment policies motivated by a desire to create an impact, NYU and Boston University inflicted serious damage on their portfolios of permanent assets. By playing a futile market valuation game, NYU missed the benefits of one of the greatest bull markets ever. In an ill-considered attempt to swing for the fences, Boston University suffered a dramatic direct loss and incurred even greater opportunity costs. Responsible fiduciaries best serve institutions by following basic investment principles, avoiding the temptation to pursue policies designed to satisfy specific individual agendas.

PERFORMANCE ASSESSMENT

Effective management of relationships between fiduciaries and investment advisors adds substantial incremental value to the portfolio. Strong relationships based on mutual trust and understanding allow money managers and clients to behave in an informed contrarian manner. In the absence of well-grounded relationships, money managers place their business at risk and clients run the risk of making ill-timed cash flow decisions, damaging the portfolio by buying high and selling low.

Successful portfolio management depends on client comprehension of the investment advisor's decision-making process. Without intimate knowledge of a firm's investment principles, clients simply react to performance, a no win proposition. If fiduciaries chase performance, funding a manager on a hot streak, disappointment results when the wind at the manager's back inevitably dissipates. When contrarian instincts cause fiduciaries to back a poorly performing manager, mediocre returns follow if poor performance persists because the manager lacks skill. Distinguishing between good fortune and good judgment demands thorough understanding of the manager's approach to investing.

Informed relationship management requires ongoing performance evaluation, incorporating both qualitative and quantitative factors. Monitoring the quality and commitment of a firm's principals plays a central role in assessing the ability of an organization to achieve excellence. Other significant issues include fidelity to investment principles and maintenance of an appropriate organizational structure. Regular face-to-face meetings between fund managers and external advisors constitute the most important tool for performance evaluation.

Portfolio return data provide essential hard input into the performance assessment process. By comparing manager returns to passive market benchmarks and active manager benchmarks, investors measure the successes and failures of an investment program. Sensible investors look beyond the basic return data to understand the risks associated with the portfolios that generated the returns.

Quantitative measures dominate performance evaluation exercises, reducing the complex web of portfolio construction decisions to a precise presentation of return data. The stark clarity of a set of historical performance numbers causes many investors to emphasize hard quantitative tools at the expense of fundamentally important soft factors. Striking an appropriate balance between quantitative and qualitative factors poses a challenge for fund fiduciaries.

Sensible investors impose thoughtful limitations on a portfolio. By limiting commitments to transparent, well-understood strategies, the universe of appropriate managers for a fund coincides with the scope of that institution's expertise. While investors need not acquire the depth of knowledge necessary to replicate an external advisor's investment management process, careful clients obtain a complete understanding of portfolio strategies. Without a firm grasp of the process, the client's role degrades to passive monitoring of performance, with the dangers inherent in placing investment results foremost in manager evaluation.

Assessing the viability of manager relationships requires continuous monitoring of a combination of qualitative and quantitative factors. Strong investment performance alone fails to justify maintaining a manager relationship. If the sense of partnership diminishes because of changes in people, philosophy, or structure, then tough-minded fiduciaries move on. Similarly, weak performance fails to justify terminating an investment management contract. If strong people in an appropriately structured firm pursue an intelligent approach to markets, elements critical to investment success remain in place. While understanding the causes of poor performance provides important insights for investment oversight, bad results in and of themselves present no fundamental threat to an otherwise sound investment relationship.

Qualitative Factors

Just as qualitative considerations dominate hiring decisions, those same qualitative factors dominate performance evaluations. If investment success simply required retaining managers with strong performance and firing managers with weak performance, life would be simple. Because the numbers provide only part of the story, difficult-to-evaluate qualitative factors play a central role.

Just as the quality of people drives manager hiring decisions, monitoring the people involved in the investment process drives relationship management. Short-run issues concern the enthusiasm, motivation, and work ethic of investment advisors. Responsible fiduciaries monitor the degree of an advisor's engagement, looking for warning signs of diminished interest or commitment. In the long run, generational transition issues loom large.

Generational Transfer

While thoughtful planning by investment management organizations increases the likelihood of successful transfer of responsibility from one generation to another, the process poses significant challenges, particularly for smaller organizations. The idiosyncratic nature of small entrepreneurial firms causes people to be far less interchangeable than would be the case at larger bureaucratic money managers. People dominate process at smaller firms, producing significant uncertainty in the period surrounding the old guard's retirement. Transferring responsibility to younger colleagues inevitably alters the nature of the firm as the new decision makers express their individual approach to markets. In short, the more attractive the investment manager, the greater the challenge in passing the baton.

The venture capital community exhibits an unusual number of entrepreneurial firms that succeed in spanning generations. By transferring responsibility seamlessly, early market participants Sutter Hill (founded in 1962), Greylock (1965), Sequoia (1972), and Kleiner Perkins (1972) each created and maintained leading positions in the venture capital community. As a result of smooth general partner transitions and sustained investment success, a number of well-established venture firms created franchise value, favorably positioning the premier partnerships relative to the rest of the venture community. Outside of the private equity world, few examples exist of small entrepreneurial investment firms retaining their character through several generations of control. Some grow large, abandoning investment goals to focus on asset gathering. Others, dependent on one or two individuals, fade away with diminished participation from those who drove the investment process. Perhaps firms built on the idiosyncratic brilliance of a successful investor stand little chance of transmitting essential skills to younger associates. In any event, assessing the energy, commitment, and enthusiasm of the individuals responsible for managing assets takes priority in monitoring relationships.

Firm Independence

The sale of an investment management firm requires immediate action. In a small, independent partnership, economic fortunes of the principals correspond directly to the success of the firm. The rewards associated with strong performance, and the penalties related to poor results, accrue to the decision makers. Sales alter the equation dramatically.

After the sale, external owners prefer retaining assets by moderating investment bets, increasing net client cash flow by enhancing marketing activities, and diversifying revenues by expanding product offerings. On top of concerns regarding changes in corporate strategy, the degree of commitment of investment professionals frequently wanes. Selling shareholders retire to focus on other interests. The most talented young people leave to pursue opportunities to create wealth, following in the footsteps of their now retired mentors. Those who remain tend to be less adept with fewer alternatives. No advantage accrues to clients from a sale.

Senior partners of successful independent investment managers face a dilemma. On the positive side of the ledger, the sale of a firm produces a handsome payday for the equity owners who walk away from the transaction with a small fortune. On the negative side, the sale sows the seeds of the firm's denouement.

By not selling the firm, senior partners fail to maximize the value of their stake. In what amounts to an act of *noblesse oblige*, younger principals receive equity interests for less than true economic value, creating the potential for the firm to continue as an independent entity. No guarantee of longevity exists, however, as the new owners now face the same dilemma their erstwhile senior partners did.

Investment Approach

Changes in investment approach raise yellow flags for fiduciaries. Increases in assets under management commonly alter investment methods. As assets increase, small-capitalization stock managers purchase more and larger securities, increasing diversification and becoming less small-capitalization-stock oriented. Some hedge funds, beginning as focused stock pickers, evolve into shops making macro bets, as increases in size dictate playing in broad, deep, and liquid markets.

Managers of all stripes face the temptation to become closet indexers. Running a market-like portfolio guarantees market-like results, reducing the likelihood of being fired for poor performance. When deep value managers report positions in growth companies, alert fiduciaries pose skeptical questions.

Disappointing results sometimes lead managers to alter approaches to portfolio management. Investment advisors may take greater risk, hoping to hit the long ball to recoup earlier losses. At the extreme, pursuit of risk to remedy past losses exposes assets to significant future losses as managers speculate in a desperate attempt to recover assets.

Poor results occasionally cause investors to undergo radical change, leading to bizarre transformations. The Feshbach brothers, Matt, Joe, and Kurt, developed a high profile in the 1980s based on impressive investment returns and controversial short-selling techniques. Using L. Ron Hubbard's Theory of Dianetics as an integral part of their investment strategy, the Feshbach brothers focused on identifying overvalued companies headed for a tumble. Using traditional securities analysis and private detectives to uncover fraudulent business practices, the Feshbachs were widely rumored to "talk down" stocks in their portfolio. Accused of "naked shorting" to establish illegal short positions when unable to access securities through legitimate channels, the brothers surrounded themselves with warning signs. Surprisingly, many investors, including the Frank Russell Trust Company, ignored the controversy, chased the Feshbachs' strong performance numbers, and committed funds to the brothers' pool, which peaked at nearly $1 billion in 1990.

In the early 1990s the Feshbach wizardry disappeared, as the strategy of shorting securities in a bull market produced the nearly inevitable disastrous results. After a spell of horrendous performance, losing 55 percent of assets in 1991 alone, the Feshbach brothers reinvented themselves.

In 1993, according to short seller David Rocker, the Feshbachs "publicly disavowed their short selling activities . . . to focus on a strategy of small capitalization growth stocks."[14] The change in strategy, by the "world's most notorious short sellers," akin to switching sides in the middle of a battle, attracted more interest in the press than with investors. By 1998, the firm managed $50 million, primarily in traditional long strategies, representing less than 5 percent of peak assets under management. Apparently, the passage of time did little to improve the Feshbach fortunes. A search of investment manager databases turned up very little beyond an SEC Form 13-F for Matt Feshbach's MLF Investments. The December 31, 2007 filing reported less than $60 million of positions.

Not all changes in approach bode ill for portfolio managers. For instance, a manager with a narrowly focused opportunity set rides the investment roller coaster, rising when opportunity abounds and plunging when deals dry up. Sensible managers adapt, altering strategy to exploit the full range of opportunities within the advisor's area of competence. Many absolute return managers began their businesses by focusing exclusively on merger arbitrage transactions. Recognizing the complementary analytical and legal skills required to assess reorganizations and bankruptcies, some firms started pursuing investments in the realm of distressed securities. By adding a fundamentally related activity, managers created a powerful tool for portfolio improvement. When merger and acquisition activity proceeded apace, portfolios held significant positions in risk arbitrage. In less robust economic times, when workouts and defaults littered the investment landscape, firms increased exposure to distressed investments. In contrast to investors expert in only one discipline, managers with more than one arrow in the quiver enjoy the opportunity to mitigate the cyclicality inherent in market activity.

Gradual, incremental changes in investment approach sensibly expand the scope of activity without abandoning the base upon which the firm's success rests. Natural, evolutionary improvement creates potential for enhancing portfolio results, benefiting external advisor and client alike. Fundamental change poses danger to client assets, demanding a dramatic response by fiduciaries.

Client Meetings

Regular face-to-face meetings between investment advisors and clients constitute the most important tool for relationship management. Meetings allow challenges to existing processes and exploration of new ideas. Frank discussion of advisor and client concerns contributes to early resolution of problems. While letters and phone conversations provide important input, nothing matches the benefits of sitting down with an investment manager for an in-depth review of portfolio activities.

Client responsibilities include being inquisitive without being intrusive. Respecting the boundary between advisor and client requires avoiding behavior that makes investment decisions difficult. Pushing advisors to take positions or discouraging specific investments crosses the line. Challenging a manager's thought process or encouraging a contrarian play contributes to successful relationships.

Investment advisor responsibilities include openness and honesty regarding portfolio activity. Complete transparency in portfolio matters provides an essential foundation for client understanding of the investment process. Occasionally, investment managers refuse to identify positions, expressing concerns regarding public disclosure on ability to manage a position. If a manager refuses to trust a client (or potential client) with portfolio information, the client should not entrust the manager with a portfolio. Advisors benefit from better-informed clients who tend to remain faithful during stretches of poor performance and facilitate sometimes difficult contrarian strategies.

Openness regarding business issues allows advisor and client to understand the present and to anticipate the future. Many business issues shape the character of a money management firm. Compensation practices influence motivation and retention of investment professionals. Succession planning tells as much about the character of the current generation as it does about the next. Firms that engage clients in discussion regarding sensitive business issues face stronger prospects of overcoming the difficulties inherent in running an investment management operation.

Continuing due diligence checks on investment advisors contributes to effective relationship management. Alert fiduciaries take advantage of opportunities to discuss with third parties the business approach and ethical standards of existing managers, always attempting to gain insight into external advisor characteristics. While less formal than the round of reference checks undertaken before hiring a manager, ongoing due diligence provides important insight into external advisor activities.

Regular interaction between client and advisor constitutes the most important tool for relationship management, providing ongoing input for qualitative assessment of manager activity. Constant reevaluation of the investment rationale contributes to effective oversight of external money managers, causing fiduciaries to maintain an attitude of healthy skepticism regarding active management activities.

Qualitative assessments of people, strategy, and structure lie at the core of relationship management. Sensible fiduciaries regularly revisit the premises upon which original hiring decisions rest, reviewing initial assumptions and subsequent behavior. Changes in an investment advisory firm's circumstances require particularly careful evaluation, causing prudent clients to underwrite once again the advisor's suitability.

Quantitative Factors

Beating the market, as described by a fair benchmark, constitutes the foremost objective of an investment manager. Mature, liquid marketplaces offer a host of well-structured benchmarks from which to choose. For example, U.S. equity markets boast a variety of broad-based indices, including the S&P 500, the Russell 3000, and the Wilshire 5000. The benchmark represents the passive alternative, a portfolio that faithfully replicates asset class performance. Active managers attempt to beat the benchmark, net of fees, in an effort to add value to the portfolio management process.

In contrast to marketable securities, illiquid assets have less-well-defined, market-related, performance measurement benchmarks. Private investments come from a wide variety of sources, ranging from divisions of publicly traded companies to family-owned businesses to entities in bankruptcy. Almost by definition, illiquid assets reside in markets without benchmarks since an investable benchmark requires well-established, liquid markets.

Investors pursuing private opportunities employ jerry-rigged benchmarks, generally using a derivative of a marketable securities metric, either explicitly as in the S&P 500 plus 500 basis points, or implicitly as in a real return of 12 percent (based, perhaps, on an expectation of 7 percent real returns for equities plus a 500 basis point premium).

Fiduciaries articulate a clear benchmark for each manager. In the liquid markets, a fair benchmark encompasses all investment opportunities from which an active manager chooses. The more liquid markets provide the best defined benchmarks, leading to the irony of precise measurement in the markets least likely to produce something worth measuring. Managers focusing on specific niches and investors pursuing activities in less efficient markets present benchmarking challenges. Ultimately, the index against which fiduciaries assess performance constitutes the manager's most important quantitative measure.

Benchmark Specialization

Investment consultants create and monitor an impressive number of specialized benchmarks, providing apparently precise tools to measure performance of a broad range of strategies and substrategies. Ranging from a reasonably standard matrix of style and capitalization indices to a somewhat motley collection of esoteric measures, consultant benchmarks assess even the most unusual approach to portfolio management.*

Specialized benchmarks occasionally provide valuable insight unavailable from broader measures of market activity. Consider the 2003 results for managers focusing on small-capitalization stocks. Median returns of 45.7 percent bested the S&P 500 return by more than 17 percent, on the surface an excellent result. When compared to a small-capitalization benchmark, however, the median results fall short of the passive alternative by 1.5 percent, a far less impressive performance. The use of a specialized small-capitalization benchmark provides a truer picture of active small-capitalization manager returns.[15] In the world of benchmark comparisons, apples-to-apples provides more insight than apples-to-pears.

Specialized benchmarks sometimes require careful evaluation. Consider the results of value investment strategies in the 1990s, a period when value managers generally failed to exceed returns of a value benchmark. For the five years ending December 31, 1997, the

---

*For example, consider the Bloomberg Football Index, an index of companies that own or operate English and Scottish football clubs.

value benchmark placed in the second decile of value manager results, an extraordinary showing for a passive portfolio.[16]

Why did the value index crush the results of value managers? The value index, created by a mechanistic screen that selected low price-to-book and low price-to-earnings ratio stocks, included a number of unattractive, washed-out companies. Because active managers often avoid obviously risky, distressed companies, typical active portfolios contain dampened value characteristics. When value stocks perform well, active managers frequently fail to match passive results, as markets reward the riskier profile of the mechanistically chosen portfolio. Only in times of severe market stress do outcomes favor the higher quality actively managed value portfolios.

Reasonable fiduciaries compare manager results to appropriate benchmarks. Examining small-capitalization manager returns relative to the S&P 500 distorts the story. Comparing value manager results to a broad-based index obscures the truth. Employing specialized passive benchmarks provides a richer comparison, allowing more direct evaluation of style-specific portfolios. When using specialized benchmarks, fair comparisons require an understanding of the differences in risk profile between the active portfolio and the benchmark.

Peer Comparisons

Peer comparisons provide another quantitative metric for performance assessment. While certain asset classes present less than satisfactory passive benchmarks, nearly every investment category contains a group of managers among which results can be compared.

Survivorship bias and backfill bias play an important role in peer comparisons, particularly in less efficient asset classes. Because market-related benchmarks provide so little short-term guidance for private assets and absolute return strategies, peer comparisons take on more significance. Unfortunately, in the absolute return arena, survivorship bias and backfill bias dramatically influence the composition and character of the peer group. Private asset peer groups suffer less extreme survivorship and backfill bias.

Risk Adjustment

Adjusting portfolio returns for risk plays at best a supporting role in performance evaluation. Managers tend to avoid discussing risk, unless explaining poor relative performance, as in "we did worse than the market, but we did it with less risk." Perhaps, the poor picture of risk provided by quantitative tools justifies the low level of discussion.

Standard deviation of returns, the measure of dispersion most commonly used to assess risk, fails to capture much of what concerns fiduciaries. Simply understanding the historical volatility of returns provides little useful information regarding the efficacy of a particular investment strategy. The fundamental risk of the underlying investment matters, not the security price fluctuation. In a world characterized by excessive price volatility, security prices mask true investment risk. In spite of its limitations, historical volatility is the most widely employed quantitative measure of risk.

Nobel laureate William Sharpe developed an analytical tool to assess the relationship between risk and return. By evaluating returns above (or below) the risk-free rate, the Sharpe ratio focuses on the generation of excess returns. Dividing the excess return by the standard deviation of returns produces a ratio describing the productivity of risk, quantifying the excess return generated per unit of risk incurred. However, Sharpe's ratio suffers from the same obvious shortcomings as do other measures of historical volatility.

The American Government Securities Fund

Consider the results of the Piper Jaffrey American Government Securities Fund (AGF), a mortgage bond investment vehicle, for the five years ending December 31, 1993. As shown in Table 10.1, AGF returned 19.3 percent per annum, representing a 13.7 percent annual premium over Treasury bills. Since volatility of 8.8 percent accompanied the excess return, AGF delivered a Sharpe ratio of 1.6 units of return for each unit of risk assumed.

From an investment perspective, AGF's 19.3 percent return appears at first glance to overshadow the 11.2 percent return of the Salomon Brothers Mortgage Index. However, because the mortgage index produced excess returns of 5.5 percent with substantially lower volatility than AGF, the bond fund and the index sport nearly identical Sharpe ratios for the period. In other words, AGF's higher returns appear to stem from accepting higher risk, not from generating superior risk-adjusted returns. Sharpe's ratio levels the playing field.

Even though the Sharpe ratio illuminates historical relationships between risk and return, backward-looking quantitative measures fail to capture fundamental risk factors other than those in the numbers.

Table 10.1 Alternative Bond Fund Characteristics
Mortgage-Backed Security Returns, 1989–1995

		Return	Excess Return	Risk	Sharpe Ratio
Five years ending	AGF	19.3%	13.7%	8.8%	1.6
December 31, 1993	Salomon Mortgage Index	11.2	5.5	3.5	1.6
One year ending	AGF	-28.8	-32.7	14.9	-2.2
December 31, 1994	Salomon Mortgage Index	-1.4	-5.3	4.0	-1.4
Five years ending	AGF	8.5	3.7	12.3	0.3
December 31, 1994	Salomon Mortgage Index	7.8	3.0	3.5	0.9
One year ending	AGF	25.9	20.3	5.8	3.5
December 31, 1995	Salomon Mortgage Index	16.8	11.1	3.2	3.5
Five years ending	AGF	11.3	7.0	12.2	0.6
December 31, 1995	Salomon Mortgage Index	8.9	4.6	3.3	1.4

Sources: Bloomberg and Yale Investments Office.

When the future differs in material ways from the past, investment choices based on quantitative analysis frequently disappoint investors.

The 1994 bond market debacle crushed the Piper Jaffrey AGF mortgage fund, causing losses of nearly 29 percent with a risk level of nearly 15 percent. The Salomon Brothers Mortgage Index fared somewhat better, as returns of -1.4 percent came with a risk level of 4.0 percent. AGF's Sharpe ratio of -2.2 for 1994 indicates risk-adjusted performance dramatically inferior to the index with its ratio of -1.4.

Quantitative characteristics of AGF's mortgage strategy change dramatically as the trailing five-year assessment period moves forward to include 1994. By including 1994's poor performance and volatility, returns drop from 19.3 percent for the five years ending December 31, 1993 to 8.5 percent for the five years ending December 31, 1994, even as volatility increases from 8.8 percent to 12.3 percent. Suddenly the double-digit return with single-digit risk becomes a single-digit return with double-digit risk.

The Sharpe ratio story reads even worse. Annualized returns for

AGF of 8.5 percent over the five-year period ending December 31, 1994 generate excess returns of 3.7 percent at a risk level of 12.3 percent. The resulting Sharpe ratio of 0.3 compares unfavorably to the ratio of 1.6 for the five years ending December 31, 1993. Even though the investment strategy remained firmly in place, market conditions caused what appeared to be a reasonably efficient, high-risk strategy into a low-return, high-risk technique.

In contrast, the five-year mortgage index return of 7.8 percent for the period ending December 31, 1994, along with excess returns of 3.0 percent and risk of 3.5 percent provides a superior set of characteristics. Although the risk-adjusted attributes of the mortgage index deteriorate with the addition of 1994's data, the index's Sharpe ratio of 0.9 indicates a material advantage over AGF's 0.3 level.

While quantitative risk assessment helps investors take a disciplined, analytical approach to assessing investment opportunities, the limitations of backward-looking number crunching become apparent when markets produce surprises. Based on data for the five years ending December 31, 1993, Piper Jaffrey's AGF and the Salomon Mortgage Index garnered identical Sharpe ratios, indicating roughly equivalent efficacy in translating risk into excess return. Moving forward one year makes the turtle-like index appear much more attractive than the hare-like mortgage fund.

In the case of the Piper Jaffrey mortgage fund, historical return and risk characteristics point investors toward poor timing decisions. In late 1993, attracted by high returns and index-like efficiency, investors saw ample reason to purchase shares of the fund. In late 1994, disappointed by terrible returns and poor relative efficiency, investors found clear justification to sell shares. Of course, in 1995, in spite of poor trailing five-year quantitative characteristics, the fund returned 25.9 percent, vastly exceeding the index returns and matching the index delivery of excess return per unit of risk.

The only defense against chasing the excellent 1993 numbers and avoiding the dismal 1994 returns lies in fundamental understanding of the nature of the investment activity producing the results. Investors making decisions based only on historical numbers focus exclusively on what has been, ignoring what will be. While looking into the future poses challenges fraught with peril, investors armed with a thorough grasp of the forces driving valuations face a higher probability of success. At the very least, investors cognizant of the nature of AGF's mortgage portfolio recognized the contribution of leverage to 1993's strong performance and considered the danger of an extreme reversal in a 1994 type of environment.

Risk adjustment matters. Unfortunately, reducing risk assessment to a single statistical measure fails to capture the essence of the concept. Prudent investors employ risk measure with care, supplementing the science with careful interpretation.

Rates of Return

The most basic financial tools measure returns either weighted by dollars or linked across time. Dollar-weighted returns, or internal rates of return (IRR), assess results considering the magnitude and timing of dollars invested. IRR calculations best measure returns for investment managers that control cash flow decisions, such as private equity investors who determine when and how much to invest in particular opportunities.

Time-linked returns derive from a series of periodic returns, without considering portfolio size at any point in time. Time-linked returns best measure results for managers that do not control cash flow decisions, such as marketable securities managers that accept contributions and withdrawals based on client decisions.

Barr Rosenberg's Value Added

Rosenberg Institutional Equity Management's (RIEM's) core equity product provides an interesting example of differences in dollar-weighted and time-weighted returns. As illustrated in Table 10.2 RIEM began corporate life with extremely strong returns on relatively small amounts of money. Following a pattern typical in the investment management industry, impressive results attracted large new accounts, with assets peaking at more than $8,100 million in 1990. As asset size created a headwind or as good fortune dissipated, poor investment performance followed, exposing large amounts of money to substandard management.

Over the firm's roller-coaster history, time-linked investment performance remained consistently positive. For the twelve years ending December 31, 1997, RIEM's core equity portfolio returned 17.3 percent per year, eking out a 30 basis point advantage relative to the S&P 500.

Dollar-weighted returns tell a less inspiring story. IRR calculations show a return of 11.8 percent per annum. Had RIEM's cash flows been invested in the S&P 500, the resulting IRR would have been 13.1

Table 10.2 Rosenberg Fails to Deliver Value to Clients

Portfolio Returns and Value Added, 1985–1997

Date (Year End)	Core Equity Assets (millions)	Excess Return (RIEM Return— S&P 500 Return)	Value Added (millions)
1985	$188	6.2%	$12
1986	1,037	-0.4	-4
1987	2,037	6.6	134
1988	4,222	-0.6	-23
1989	8,020	-4.8	-386
1990	8,157	-3.7	-304
1991	6,608	-0.8	-52
1992	3,692	3.9	143
1993	3,692	1.1	42
1994	1,838	-1.0	-19
1995	2,225	0.8	17
1996	2,023	-2.9	-58
1997	1,644	1.2	20

Source: *Nelson's Directory of Investment Managers, 1985–1997.*

percent per annum. Over the life of the core portfolio, REIM's clients lost 1.3 percent annually relative to the market, translating into approximately $500 million of opportunity costs.

In evaluating marketable security performance, both time-linked and dollar-weighted returns prove helpful. Time-linked returns provide evidence regarding a manager's investment acumen. Dollar-weighted returns shed light on cash flow timing decisions made by investors. When evaluating private investment performance, dollar-weighted returns provide the most appropriate measurement tool, as private investors control cash flow decisions.

Successful portfolio management combines art and science, requiring qualitative and quantitative assessment of investment strategies. While quantitative measures provide essential data for decision makers, reasonable fiduciaries guard against placing too much emphasis on easily quantified factors at the expense of less easily measured qualitative factors. Successful relationship management demands placing soft factors in a place of primary importance. The numbers, while important, play a supporting role.

Use of Performance Assessment

Investors employ performance assessment to hire managers, size accounts, and fire managers, with the choice of time frame providing a critical variable in the evaluation process. Thoughtful use of performance data creates opportunities to add substantial incremental returns, while misdirected actions readily destroy value.

The appropriate time frame for performance assessment depends on the asset class involved and management style employed. Feedback mechanisms operate over different cycles. Money market investments provide nearly immediate feedback, as assets mature within a matter of months, either successfully or not. The short cycle provides fiduciaries with substantial amounts of round-trip data. Unfortunately, in the highly efficient money markets, the information generates little opportunity to add value.

Private investing stands at the opposite end of the spectrum. Holding periods for assets span as much as a decade, forcing fiduciaries to make manager retention decisions well before meaningful feedback comes from recent investment activity. The long private investing cycle causes investors to make decisions based on factors other than near term investment performance.

Other asset classes fall between the money market and private equity extremes. The time necessary for feedback mechanisms to operate corresponds roughly to the manager's investment horizon. The shorter the horizon, the shorter the time needed to assess manager skill. In the marketable securities realm, high turnover indicates a relatively short-term horizon, suggesting short-term evaluation of the manager's trades. Consider the fact that 200 percent turnover corresponds to a six-month average holding period. In contrast, 20 percent turnover corresponds to a five-year average holding period. Low turnover strategies deserve longer-term evaluation, allowing time for the investment manager's strategy to play out. In the realm of private investing, time horizons appropriate for manager evaluation extend much longer.

While portfolio turnover identifies the average holding period for positions and suggests an appropriate minimum time frame for evaluating money manager trades, market forces often befog the view of manager performance. Multiyear moves in the relative attractiveness of small versus large and value versus growth highlight the importance of employing appropriate benchmarks and lengthen the time required to assess manager skill. Serious investors avoid hair trigger decisions, opting instead for careful, deliberate assessments that span the market cycle appropriate to a specific manager.

Performance evaluation ultimately determines the fiduciary's degree of confidence in an external money manager. Reassessing manager relationships places investors in an uncomfortable position, as reasonable investors engage investment advisors with a view toward establishing long-term relationships. Questioning the validity of the original hiring decision and examining the continued viability of the investment relationship causes some measure of cognitive dissonance. Careful fiduciaries seek stable, long-term arrangements, even while evaluating their dissolution.

The degree of confidence in particular managers influences portfolio allocations, with high confidence managers receiving greater funding levels. Periodic reviews of manager account sizes allow portfolios to reflect opinions regarding relative manager skill levels. Well-considered manager allocations incorporate factors other than confidence levels, including the appeal of the manager's particular strategy as well as the number of managers available to exploit a specific type of opportunity. That said, performance evaluation plays a dominant role in determining allocations.

With a clear grasp of a manager's approach to markets, clients obtain opportunities to add value through the portfolio rebalancing process. If manager account sizes generally reflect fiduciary preferences, recent performance might be used as a secondary indicator for targeting contributions and withdrawals. Even the most skilled managers experience periods of underperformance, attributable to positions that, once established, perform contrary to expectations. If, in the face of poor results, the original investment case remains intact, adding funds to an out-of-favor strategy increases exposure to a now even more attractively priced opportunity. Managers tend to react positively to the vote of confidence implicit in client cash flows arriving after a period of poor results.

In contrast, following periods of better than expected performance, thoughtful clients consider reducing account size. Extraordinary performance likely stems from a combination of manager skill and fortuitous market conditions. Reducing the account of an outperforming manager and reallocating funds to weaker performers generally enhances performance. While managers enjoy receiving cash flow, particularly when their investment style lacks favor in the marketplace, managers dislike disgorging funds. Managers frequently blame the market for poor results; skill completely explains their strong performance.

In any event, reasonable clients avoid costly disruptive cash flow requests. Withdrawals require particular care, since incurring unnecessary transactions costs dampens portfolio returns. Contributions to poor performers and withdrawals from strong performers might be made as part of a fund's rebalancing activity, generating only transactions already required for risk control purposes and facilitating low-cost repositioning of the portfolio.

Manager Termination

The impetus for manager termination generally falls into one of two broad categories. First, the initial hiring decision may have been a mistake. Regardless of the thoroughness of due diligence efforts, the true nature of an investment relationship emerges only after advisor and client work together for a period of time. Reexamination of initial assumptions causes fiduciaries to continue to learn about the manager's process, either reinforcing the work that supported the hiring decision or exposing shortcomings in the original analysis. Second, changes in people, philosophy, and structure require reassessment of manager relationships. Significant changes prompt sensible fiduciaries to take a fresh look at the manager, subjecting the relationship to a thorough reevaluation.

The most difficult part of managing a portfolio of external advisors involves termination of unsatisfactory relationships. The unpleasant nature of firing a manager causes many investors to stay with dysfunctional manager-client relationships far longer than prudent. Rationalizations for maintaining the status quo abound, providing superficial justification for avoiding the unpleasant task at hand.

Top-notch fiduciaries approach the manager evaluation task with a cool analytical mindset that borders on heartlessness. Once investors determine that mistakes led to the hiring of a manager or changes in circumstance cause the manager to be unfit, the termination notice must follow. In the final analysis, careful fiduciaries ask if the manager would be hired today. A negative answer points to termination.

CONTROL ENVIRONMENT

Back office operations represent a significant, yet often overlooked, source of risk. Operational controls do not appear on the radar screens of most institutional fund managers, as investors prefer to deal with the engaging issues surrounding portfolio management strategies. Fund managers ignore control environment issues at their peril; a major operational failure moves internal control issues from an obscure place in the background to an embarrassing role on center stage.

Endowment fund investors face control risks internally and externally. Internal control risks consist of exposures created at fund headquarters in the course of day-to-day portfolio management activities. If all assets were managed in-house, investors would face only internal control issues. Conventional audit procedures focus on internal practices, examining the efficacy and integrity of systems designed to support investment operations. External control risks consist of exposures created at outside managers. Traditional audit activities rarely assess directly the control systems of external investment managers, relying instead on work conducted by other professional service firms. Since a chain is only as strong as the weakest link, both internal fund operations and external manager back office operations require careful examination and oversight.

Inadequate control environments provide fertile breeding grounds for problems ranging in severity from continual imposition of small costs to sudden headline-grabbing disasters. Poorly conceived controls expose investors to the possibility of fraud and malfeasance. Pain avoidance requires careful planning. Unfortunately, institutions tend to focus on mundane back office operations only after incurring significant losses.

Investment organizations benefit from regular, independent, intensive external review of operational practices. For simple portfolio structures, internal and external auditors provide a comprehensive look at investment activity, examining relatively basic issues related to safekeeping portfolios of standard marketable securities. As increasingly sophisticated portfolio management activities add layers of complexity, generalist auditors face a dramatically more difficult task. To deal effectively with more complex investment programs, sensible fiduciaries engage high quality specialists to assess internal and external practices, providing an important tool for evaluating an often-ignored aspect of investment management.

A strong audit team from a first-class firm constitutes the first line of defense against internal control problems. While a thorough audit represents an important starting point, in today's investment management world, routine annual reviews no longer adequately assess portfolio practices. Occasional, "no holds barred" special audits by a team of experts provide important strategic insights into risks confronting fund fiduciaries, allowing remediation of existing issues and mitigation of potential problems.

Special Audits

Effective special audits engage high quality experts in an unrestricted, independent review of control practices. By bringing a fresh perspective to the oversight process, the investigative team causes staff members to revisit comfortable assumptions regarding internal operations, challenging individuals to improve existing procedures. Best practices provide a standard against which to measure current activities and future efforts.

Since 1990, Yale twice employed PricewaterhouseCoopers and once employed Deloitte & Touche to undertake top-to-bottom examinations of the university's investment operations. The first review provided a substantial amount of useful feedback, highlighting the risks in security lending activities. Prompted by the PricewaterhouseCoopers report, the university took a fresh look at the internally managed security loan program, concluding that structural changes in the market had transformed a once attractive opportunity into an unattractive risk-reward activity. As a result, the university discontinued its security lending operations, a move that appeared prescient when the Common Fund's security lending debacle became public sometime later.*

A second special audit of Yale's investment operations by PricewaterhouseCoopers concluded that, while industry "best practices" characterized the university's monitoring of external manager back offices, room for improvement existed. Standard industry practice involves relatively superficial investigation of internal controls at external man-

---

*Yale's security lending operation, managed much more conservatively than The Common Fund's, pursued a matched book strategy. That is, maturities of security loans matched maturities of investments, with the university generating returns by accepting credit risk in the reinvestment vehicle. Prompted to examine the issue by the PricewaterhouseCoopers study, Yale concluded that spreads were too thin to justify continuing the security lending operation. The Common Fund, motivated by the thin spreads in a matched book operation, took significantly greater risk in an effort to generate a meaningful return. See Chapter 6.

agers, if such controls receive any attention at all. Since external manager control processes contribute to the integrity of the overall control framework within which the endowment operates, the university's risk exposure depends on the quality of these sometimes superficially evaluated manager operations.

PricewaterhouseCoopers concluded that Yale had an opportunity to redefine industry standards by understanding and improving the financial control environment, internally and externally. The basic job description involves evaluating regulatory compliance, internal operations, accounting and trading systems, legal and auditing professional support, as well as policies for asset valuation, risk assessment, derivatives, and soft dollars. Yale's compliance efforts create opportunities to reduce risk by introducing superior practices identified at one manager to other managers, thereby improving control processes across the entire portfolio. Not only does the university benefit from evidence gathered when examining the control environment at outside managers, the evaluation process communicates the importance Yale attaches to strong internal operations. Such attention prompts managers to focus appropriate levels of time and energy on back office activities.

CONCLUSION

One of the most important distinctions in the investment management arena separates those investors with the ability to make high quality active management decisions from those investors without the resources to make such decisions. Active management opens up the possibility of employing asset classes that require superior investment skill—absolute return, private equity, and real assets. As an added attraction, active management provides the possibility of producing market-beating results in domestic and foreign marketable equities. In contrast, without active management skill, prudent investors limit choices to passively managed marketable security asset classes. Only foolish investors pursue casual attempts to beat the market, as such casual attempts provide the fodder for the skilled investors' market-beating results.

A disciplined framework for decision making underpins successful investment operations. Clear definition of the respective roles of staff and committee ensures that staff members drive the process, while committee members provide effective oversight. Without a rigorous process, informed by thorough analysis and implemented with discipline, investment portfolios tend to follow the whims of fashion.

Casually researched, consensus-oriented investment positions provide little prospect for producing superior results in the intensely
competitive investment management world.

An effective investment process reduces the inevitable gap
between the goals of the institution and the actions of the portfolio's
stewards. Trustees strive to make a difference during their tenure,
while staff members seek job security, with both aspirations potentially at odds with long-term institutional goals. By establishing and
maintaining investment operations as part of the fabric of the institution, fiduciaries increase the likelihood of placing institutional needs
ahead of personal interests.

Intermediaries, such as consultants and funds of funds, add
another layer to the investment process, introducing a dysfunctional
filter that serves to impair returns. Institutions that avoid employing
intermediaries and engage dedicated staff resources stand a far better
chance of success.

A sound decision-making process contributes significantly to
investment success, allowing investors to pursue potentially interesting, long-term contrarian investment positions. By reducing pressures
to perform quarter-to-quarter, liberated managers gain the freedom to
create portfolios positioned to take advantage of opportunities created by short-term players. An environment that encourages managers
to make potentially embarrassing out-of-favor investments and toler-
ates the inevitable missteps increases the likelihood of investment
success.

Long-term success requires individualistic contrarian behavior
based on a foundation of sound investment principles. An effective
framework overcomes the handicap of group decision making and
promotes well-considered risk taking. A thoughtful, high quality governance process serves as an essential underpinning of a successful
investment program.

Sensible investors assess investment advisory relationships with a
balance of soft qualitative attributes and hard quantitative characteristics. Qualitative factors play a central role in manager evaluations,
placing people at the core of portfolio structuring decisions. Critical
variables include the quality of investment professionals, the strength
of the investment philosophy, and the character of the organizational
structure. Regular face-to-face meetings constitute the most important
manager monitoring tool.

Quantitative management tools include return data on individual
portfolios, market benchmarks, and active manager universes. Overreliance on the neat precision of numerical results frequently leads to

poor decisions. Investors looking only at the numbers face the prospect of buying high and selling low, making commitments prompted by strong results and withdrawing funds based on poor performance.

Successful investment programs require open, honest relationships between institutional clients and external money managers. Direct, frequent communication allows investors to take advantage of market opportunities. When declining prices allow purchase of assets on attractive terms, high quality clients provide incremental funds to exploit the opportunity. Conversely, thoughtful money managers with relatively few attractive opportunities return funds to clients. Such activity takes place only when a high degree of confidence and trust exists between money managers and clients.

Performance evaluation drives portfolio allocation decisions, as conclusions regarding manager ability influence the confidence of fiduciaries. In many respects, the investor faces a binary decision. If confidence exists, fiduciaries muster the courage necessary to behave in a contrarian manner, supporting managers experiencing a spell of poor results. If a fiduciary lacks the confidence to increase exposure to an underperforming manager, either the manager or the fiduciary should go.

APPENDIX:
Impure Fixed Income

Fixed income alternatives dominate the population of well-defined markets that serve no valuable portfolio role. While default-free, non-callable, full-faith-and-credit obligations of the U.S. government play a basic, valuable, differentiable role in investor portfolios, investment grade corporate bonds, high yield bonds, foreign bonds, and asset-backed securities contain unattractive characteristics that argue against inclusion in well-constructed portfolios. Noncore fixed income asset classes command a sizable portion of the pool of investment alternatives. Many players allocate assets to corporate bonds and mortgage-backed securities, hoping to generate incremental returns without additional risk. Understanding the shortcomings of particular fixed income investment alternatives, particularly in regard to how those alternatives relate to the objectives of the fixed income asset class, helps investors to make well-informed portfolio decisions.

DOMESTIC CORPORATE BONDS

Owners of corporate bonds hold a piece of a loan to the corporation that issued the bonds to borrow the money. In a company's capital structure, debt obligations rank higher than equity interests, causing a company's bonds to exhibit less fundamental risk than a company's equity. Because bonds carry less risk than equities, fixed income investors expect lower returns than do equity investors. Unfortunately for investors, corporate bonds contain a variety of unattractive charac-

teristics, including credit risk, illiquidity, and callability. Even if corporate bond investors receive fair compensation for these unattractive
characteristics, astute investors recognize that the credit risk and callability of corporate obligations undermine the fundamental diversifying
power expected from fixed income holdings.

Credit Risk

Credit risk stems from the possibility that a corporation will not meet
the obligation to make full and timely payments on its debt. Rating
agencies, such as Standard & Poor's and Moody's Investor Service,
publish ratings for bond issues, purporting to grade the likelihood
that an issue will produce as promised. The most important factors in
assessing a bond issuer's ability to pay lie in the size of the equity
cushion supporting the debt and the amount of cash flow servicing the
debt. Investment grade ratings, assigned to the most creditworthy borrowers, range from triple A (the highest) to triple B. High yield or
"junk" bonds carry ratings of double B and below. Lower-rated bonds
embody greater credit risk and exhibit more equity-like characteristics.

Moody's describes triple-A rated bonds as being "of the best quality" and carrying "the smallest degree of investment risk," with interest payments "protected" and principal "secure." Double-A bonds
exhibit "high quality by all standards," while single-A bonds "possess
many favorable investment attributes." The bottom investment grade
category (triple-B) manifests adequate security "for the present," but
"lacks outstanding investment characteristics."[1] Despite the shades of
gray introduced by the description of the triple-B rating category,
Moody's paints a bright picture for investment grade debt obligations.

Unfortunately, from a corporate debt investor's perspective, triple-
A rated bonds can only decline in credit quality. Sometimes bondholders experience a downward drift in quality to less exalted, albeit
still investment grade ratings. Other times bondholders face a lengthy,
Chinese-water-torture deterioration in credit that results in exile to the
"fallen angel" realm of the junk bond world. On occasion, triple-A
rated obligations maintain their standing. In no case, however, do
triple-A bonds receive upgrades.

IBM illustrates the problem confronting purchasers of corporate
debt. The company issued no long-term debt until the late 1970s, as
prior to that time IBM consistently generated excess cash. Anticipating
a need for external finance, the company came to market in the fall of

1979 with a $1 billion issue, representing the then-largest-ever corporate borrowing. IBM obtained a triple-A rating and extremely aggressive pricing on the issue, which resulted in an inconsequential yield spread over U.S. Treasuries and (from an investor's perspective) underpriced call and sinking fund options. Bond investors spoke of the "scarcity value" of IBM paper, allowing the company to borrow below U.S. Treasury rates on an option-adjusted basis. From a credit perspective, IBM debt had nowhere to go but down. Twenty-eight years later, IBM's senior paper carried a rating of single A, failing to justify both the ratings agencies' initial assessment of IBM's credit and the investors' early enthusiasm for IBM's bonds.

Bond investors did not face an opportunity to lend to the fast-growing, cash-generative IBM of the 1960s and 1970s. Instead, bond investors considered the option of providing funds to the IBM of the 1980s and 1990s, when the company needed enormous sums of cash. As IBM's business matured and external financing requirements increased, the quality of the company's credit standing slowly eroded.

Contrast the slow erosion of IBM's credit to instances in which corporate credit quality declines dramatically. In early April 2002, WorldCom's senior debt boasted a single-A rating from Moody's, placing the fixed income obligations of the telecommunications company firmly in the investment grade camp. On April 23rd, Moody's downgraded WorldCom to triple B, one notch above junk status, as the company struggled with lower demand from business customers and concerns regarding accounting issues. A little more than two weeks later, following Chief Executive Bernard Ebbers's resignation, on May 9th Moody's chopped WorldCom's rating to double-B, junk-level status. According to Bloomberg, the firm thereby achieved the dubious distinction of becoming the "biggest debtor to ever be cut to junk."[2]

To the dismay of WorldCom's creditors, the rapid fire descent continued. On June 20th, Moody's assigned a rating of single B to WorldCom's senior debt, citing deferral of interest payments on certain of the company's obligations. One week later, Moody's dropped WorldCom's rating to single C, characterized by the rating agency as "speculative in a high degree." In the middle of the following month, on July 15th, the company defaulted on $23 billion worth of bonds. Finally, on July 21st, WorldCom filed for the largest bankruptcy in history, listing in its court filing assets in excess of $100 billion.

WorldCom's transformation from a single-A credit, possessing "adequate factors giving security to interest and principal," to a company in bankruptcy spanned less than three months. Most holders of bonds watched helplessly as the train wreck of WorldCom's bank-ruptcy demolished billions of dollars of value in what Moody's described as a "record-breaking default."[3]

During the final stage of the firm's death spiral, the WorldCom Senior 6.75 Percent Notes of May 2008 fell from a price of 82.34 in the week before the Moody's downgrade to a price of 12.50 after the firm's bankruptcy. Owners of equity fared worse. From the week before the downgrade to the date of the bankruptcy, the stock price collapsed from $5.98 per share to 14 cents per share. Measured from the respective peaks, equity investors took by far the rougher ride. The WorldCom sen-ior notes traded as high as 104.07 on January 8, 2002, resulting in an 88.0 percent loss to the bankruptcy declaration. Stockholders saw a price of $61.99 on June 21, 1999, creating a high-water mark that allowed investors to lose 99.8 percent to the date of the corporate demise.

Clearly, on a security-specific basis WorldCom's collapse hurt equity holders more than it hurt debt holders, consistent with the notion that equity carries more risk than bonds. Yet, ironically, equity owners likely found it easier to recover from the WorldCom debacle than bondholders. The key to this apparent contradiction lies in the superior ability of a portfolio of equities to absorb the impact of single-security-induced adversity. Because individual stocks contain the potential to double, triple, quadruple, or more, a portfolio of equities holds any number of positions that could more than offset one partic-ular loser. In contrast, high quality bonds provide little opportunity for substantial appreciation. The left tail of the negatively skewed distri-bution of outcomes hurts bond investors in dramatic fashion.

The deterioration in IBM's ability to pay over nearly three decades and the much more compressed collapse of WorldCom's credit stand-ing mirrored a broader trend in the corporate debt markets. In recent times, corporate debt downgrades far outnumbered upgrades, forcing bond investors to manage against substantial headwinds. For the two decades ending December 31, 2006, Moody's Investors Service down-graded 6,907 debt issues while the firm upgraded 4,087. In the last decade alone, $7,003 billion of debt deteriorated in quality relative to the $3,931 billion of debt that improved.[4]

The across-the-board decline in credit standards stems in part from the past two decade's relentless increase in leverage in corporate America. On June 30, 1987, the debt-equity ratio of S&P 500 compa-nies stood at 0.6, signaling that the constituent companies of the S&P 500 carried 60 cents of debt for every dollar of equity. As leverage increased in popularity, on June 30, 1997, the ratio reached 0.90. By June 30, 2007, the S&P 500 posted a debt-equity ratio of 1.03, indicating that debt levels exceeded the equity base by three percent. As the level of corporate borrowings increased, the security of corporate lenders decreased.

Not surprisingly, the increase in debt placed stress on the income statement. Consider the ratio between the cash flow available to service debt and a firm's interest expense. At June 30, 1987, the constituent companies of the S&P 500 boasted $4.70 of cash flow for every $1.00 of interest expense. By June 30, 2007, the ratio decreased to $3.80 of cash flow per $1.00 of interest expense, representing a dramatic impairment. Obviously, as cash flows decreased relative to fixed charges, the security of the bondholders decreased commensurately.

Balance sheets and income statements tell the same story. Debt-equity ratios increased markedly over the past two decades, signaling deterioration in corporate credit. Cash flow coverage ratios deteriorated significantly over the same twenty years, suggesting a decline in corporate financial health. Both factors contribute to rating agency downgrades far outnumbering upgrades.

In addition to fundamental factors, the particular nature of companies that issue corporate debt may contribute to the surplus of downgrades over upgrades. The universe of corporate debt issuers consists of generally mature companies. Relatively young, faster growing companies tend to be underrepresented in the ranks of corporate bond issuers, in many cases because they have no need for external financing. Bond investors cannot purchase debt of Microsoft, because the company sees no need to tap the debt markets for funds. Bond investors can purchase debt of Ford Motor Company, because the firm requires enormous amounts of external finance. If the group of corporate debt issuers excludes fast-growing, cash-generative companies and includes more-mature, cash-consuming companies, perhaps bond investors should expect to see more credit deterioration than credit improvement. Regardless of the cause, if history provides a guide to the future, bond investors can expect more bad news than good on credit conditions.

Liquidity

Liquidity of corporate bond issues pales in comparison to the liquidity of U.S. Treasuries which trade in the broadest, deepest, most liquid market in the world. Most corporate issues tend to trade infrequently, as many holders buy bonds at the initial offering and sock them away, pursuing buy-and-hold strategies.

Yet bond investors value liquidity highly. Compare U.S. Treasury issues and Private Export Funding Corporation (PEFCO) bonds. Even though both bonds enjoy full-faith-and-credit backing of the U.S. government, the less liquid PEFCO bonds trade at prices that produce yields of as much as 0.6 percent per annum higher than comparable-maturity Treasuries. The difference in yield stems entirely from the value that the market places on liquidity. Liquidity of most corporate bonds tends to stand closer to the PEFCOs than to the Treasuries, suggesting that lack of liquidity explains a significant portion of the corporate bond yield spread.

Callability

Callability poses a particularly vexing problem for corporate bond investors. Corporations frequently issue bonds with a call provision, allowing the issuer to redeem (or call) the bonds after a certain date at a fixed price. If interest rates decline, companies call existing bonds that bear higher-than-market rates, refunding the issue at lower rates and generating debt service savings.

The holder of corporate bonds faces a "heads you win, tails I lose" situation. If rates decline, the investor loses the now-high-coupon bond through a call at a fixed price. If rates rise, the investor holds a now-low-coupon bond that shows mark-to-market losses. The lack of parallelism in a callable bond's response to rising and falling rates favors the corporate issuer over the bond investor.

The asymmetry implicit in the corporate bond call provision prompts questions regarding relative market power and sophistication. Why do many bonds incorporate call provisions? Why do put provisions appear rarely?* Surely, if interest rate increases prompt bond price decreases, investors would like to put the now-underwater bonds to corporate issuers at a fixed price. The answer to the asymmetry no doubt lies in the superior sophistication of issuers of debt relative to the limited market savvy of purchasers of debt.

In point of fact, fixed income markets attract analysts several notches below the quality and sophistication of equity analysts, even though the complexity of the task facing the fixed income analyst arguably exceeds the difficulty of the equity analyst's job. Corporate

*A put option allows the put holder to sell a security at a fixed price during a specified period of time. If a bond issue contained a put option, the purchaser would enjoy the right to sell the bond (or put the bond) to the issuer at a fixed price during the period of time specified in the bond indenture.

bond investors need familiarity not only with the complexities of fixed income markets, but also with the full range of issues involved in equity valuation. Since understanding the cushion provided by a company's equity proves essential in evaluating a corporation's ability to service debt, bond analysts require a full assessment of a company's stock price. Ironically, because financial rewards for successful equity analysis far outstrip the rewards for successful fixed income analysis, the talent gravitates to the easier job of simply analyzing equity securities.

Negatively Skewed Distribution of Outcomes

Atop the perils facing investors in the corporate bond market stands a further handicap. The expected distribution of corporate bond returns exhibits a negative skew. The best outcome for holding bonds to maturity consists of receiving regular payments of interest and return of principal. The worst outcome represents default without recovery. The asymmetry of limited upside and substantial downside produces a distribution of outcomes that contains a disadvantageous bias for investors.

Shorter holding periods manifest the same distributional problem. Return of principal at maturity (or prematurely upon corporate exercise of a call provision) limits appreciation potential. The nearer the date of expected repayment, the greater the dampening effect. In the case of credit deterioration, bondholders experience an attenuated dampening effect. When corporate prospects deteriorate, bond prices decline as purchasers require greater returns for the now-riskier issue. In a worst-case default scenario, bond investors may face a total wipeout. Both when holding bonds to maturity and for shorter terms, bond investors deal with a decidedly unattractive, limited-upside, substantial downside, negatively skewed distribution of returns.

Investors prefer positively skewed distributions by a wide margin. Active equity investors prize positions with limited downside, perhaps supported by readily ascertained asset values, and substantial potential upside, perhaps driven by anticipated operational improvements. Under such circumstances, investors see a high likelihood of preserving capital with a considerable possibility of significant gains. Positively skewed distributions of expected investment results definitively trump negatively skewed distributions, creating yet another hurdle for fixed income investors.

Alignment of Interests

Interests of stockholders and bondholders diverge dramatically. Equity owners benefit by reducing the value of debt obligations. Equity owners suffer as the cost of debt finance increases. To the extent that corporate management serves shareholder interests, bondholders beware.

Consider the enterprise value of a corporate entity. Analysts assess company values by evaluating either the left side or the right side of the balance sheet. The left side of the balance sheet contains difficult-to-value physical assets. What price reflects the fair market value of the various and sundry facilities owned by Ford Motor Company? What value accrues to Ford from its world famous trademark? Even the most diligent analysts recoil at the thought of conducting the asset-by-asset inventory required to value the left side of a company's balance sheet.

The right side of the balance sheet contains easier-to-value liabilities. Summing the market value of a company's debt and the market value of a company's equity provides the enterprise value of a corporation. The enterprise value reflects the price an investor would pay to buy the entire company. If all equity were purchased at the market price and all debt and other liabilities were purchased at market prices, the purchaser would own the entire corporation (debt free!).

From this description of a firm's debt and equity positions follows the fundamental corporate finance principle that a firm's value stands independent of a firm's capital structure. Because an investor holds the power to undo what a firm has done with its capital structure or to do what a firm has not done with its capital structure, the enterprise value of a company must be independent of its financing. For example, an investor might undo a firm's leverage by purchasing that firm's bonds, thereby negating the effect of corporate leverage. Conversely, an investor might create a leveraged position in a firm by borrowing to buy the firm's stock, thereby creating leverage where none existed. Since investors can destroy or create leverage independent of a company's actions, the enterprise value must be independent of the company's capital structure.*

The description of enterprise value highlights the clear, direct trade-off between the interests of stockholders and bondholders. The

---

*If corporations enjoy superior access to debt financing, either because of creditworthiness or tax advantages, then the value of the corporation may be enhanced by increasing balance sheet leverage.

value of the enterprise lies in the sum of the value of the debt and the value of the equity. To the extent that owners of a company reduce the value of the bondholders' position, the equity owners benefit. Stockholders gain by imposing losses on bondholders.

Because interests of corporate management align with equity investors, bondholders find themselves sitting across the table from corporate management. Recognizing the vulnerability created by relying on corporate management to protect lender interests, bond investors employ complicated contracts, called indentures, that seek to cause corporate issuers of debt to serve bondholder needs. Unfortunately for bondholders, even contracts drafted by the most able lawyers prove insufficient to influence corporate behavior in the desired manner, particularly when the hoped-for actions run against the economic interests of management.

At times, the transfer of wealth from bondholders to stockholders occurs in dramatic fashion. When companies engage in leveraged buyout or leveraged recapitalization transactions, the debt levels of the corporations increase substantially. The increase in debt heightens the risk for existing lenders, leading directly to a decrease in the value of existing debt positions. KKR's 1989 RJR Nabisco buyout exemplifies the pain suffered by bondholders when debt levels balloon. During the bidding war for RJR, as the price offered for the company increased to ever-more-absurd levels, so did the prospective debt burden. Before the buyout, RJR Nabisco's liabilities amounted to something less than $12 billion. Post-buyout fixed obligations exceeded a staggering $35 billion. As a direct result of the dramatic change in capital structure, pre-buyout bondholders lost an estimated $1 billion of value while equity owners enjoyed a $10 billion windfall. The bondholder losses went directly to the equity owners' pockets.

In other situations, management employs more subtle methods to disadvantage bondholders. Simply by seeking to borrow at the lowest possible costs and on the most flexible terms, management acts to lessen the position of bondholders. Aside from working to achieve low borrowing rates, bond issuers might include favorably priced call options or attractively structured sinking fund provisions. Upon exercise of a call option, bondholders suffer and equity owners gain. Companies may negotiate indenture terms that grant wide operating latitude for management, including the flexibility to take actions that impair bondholders' interests.

The ultimate check on management's actions to disadvantage bondholders comes from a desire to retain access to the debt financing markets. Repeated, egregious actions that hurt bondholders may lead to a temporary hiatus in a company's ability to borrow on favorable terms. Yet the transactions most likely to raise bondholders' ire, buyouts and leveraged recapitalizations, occur infrequently, allowing the market's memory to fade before a company needs to borrow again. More subtle actions taken by management to pick bondholders' pockets seldom receive much notice. By taking a seat across the table from corporate management, bondholders expose their position to potential impairment.

Market Characteristics

At December 31, 2006, the market value of investment-grade corporate bonds totaled $1.7 trillion. Yield to maturity stood at 5.7 percent, with the proviso that future changes in credit quality contain the possibility of decreasing the forecasted yield. Average maturity and duration stood at 10.1 years and 6.1 years, respectively.[5]

Summary

Many investors purchase corporate bonds, hoping to get something for nothing by earning an incremental yield over that available from U.S. Treasury bonds. If investors received a sufficient premium above the default-free U.S. Treasury rate to compensate for credit risk, illiquidity, and callability, then corporate bonds might earn a place in investor portfolios. Unfortunately, under normal circumstances investors receive scant compensation for the disadvantageous traits of corporate debt. At the end of the day, excess returns prove illusory as credit risk, illiquidity, and optionality work against the holder of corporate obligations, providing less than nothing to the corporate bond investor.

Corporate bond investors find the deck stacked against them as corporate management's interests align much more closely with equity investors' aspirations than with bond investors' goals. A further handicap to bond investors lies in the negative skew of the potential distribution of outcomes, limiting the upside potential without dampening the downside possibility.

Safe-haven attributes justify inclusion of fixed income in well-diversified portfolios. Unfortunately, in times of duress, credit risk and optionality serve to undermine the ability of corporate bonds to protect portfolios from the influences of financial crisis or deflation. In troubled economic times, a corporation's ability to meet contractual obligations diminishes, causing bond prices to decline. In declining rate environments, caused by flight to quality or by deflation, bond call provisions increase in value, heightening the probability that companies call high-coupon debt securities away from bondholders. Sensible investors avoid corporate debt, because credit risk and callability undermine the ability of fixed income holdings to provide portfolio protection in times of financial or economic disruption.

Historical returns confirm that investors received insufficient compensation for the array of risks inherent in corporate debt. For the ten years ending December 31, 2006, Lehman Brothers reports annualized returns of 6.0 percent for U.S. Treasury bonds and 6.5 percent for investment-grade corporate bonds. While index-specific differences in market characteristics and period-specific influences on market returns cause the comparison to fall short of a perfect apples-to-apples standard, the 0.5 percent per annum difference between Treasury and corporate returns fails to compensate corporate bond investors for default risk, illiquidity, and optionality. U.S. government bonds provide a superior alternative.

HIGH YIELD BONDS

High yield bonds consist of corporate debt obligations that fail to meet blue chip standards, falling in rating categories below investment grade. The highest category of junk bonds carries a double-B rating, described by Moody's as having "speculative elements," leading to a future that "cannot be considered as well assured." Moving down the ratings rungs, single-B bonds "lack characteristics of the desirable investment," triple-C bonds "are of poor standing," double-C bonds "are speculative in high degree," and the lowest class of bonds (single-C) has "extremely poor prospects of ever attaining any real investment standing." [6]

High yield bonds suffer from a concentrated version of the unattractive traits of high-grade corporate debt. Credit risk in the junk-bond market far exceeds risk levels in the investment-grade market. Illiquidity abounds, with the lowest-rated credits trading by appointment only. Callability poses the familiar "heads you win, tails I lose" proposition for owners of junk bonds with an added twist.

Holders of both investment-grade and junk bonds face callability concerns in declining rate environments. Lower rates prompt refunding calls in which the issuer pays a fixed price to the bondholders and reissues debt at lower cost. Holders of high quality paper and junk bonds face interest-rate-induced refunding risks of similar nature.

Above and beyond the possibility that junk bondholders lose bonds in a declining rate environment, callability potentially thwarts the junk bondholder's ability to benefit from an improving credit. One of the goals of junk-bond purchasers involves identifying companies that face a brighter future, leading to greater ability to service debt, improved marks from the rating agencies, and higher prices in the market. Fixed-price call options serve to limit the ability of junk-bond investors to benefit from improving credit fundamentals, marking yet another means by which equity holders benefit at the expense of bond-holders.

Packaging Corporation of America

Consider the fate of investors in Packaging Corporation of America (PCA) 9.625 percent Series B Senior Subordinated Notes of April 1, 2009. Issued by a highly leveraged manufacturer of containerboard and corrugated cartons, at the initial offering in April 1999, the bonds carried a coupon rate approximately 500 basis points above compara-ble maturity Treasury notes and boasted a rating at the bottom of the single-B category. According to Moody's Investors Service, the single-B rating indicated that "[a]ssurance of interest and principal payments or of maintenance of other terms in the contract over any long period of time may be small."[7] Purchasers of the bonds no doubt hoped for a better future, one in which the likelihood of maintenance of contract terms might be larger rather than smaller. Perhaps investors foresaw a future characterized by an improvement in corporate fundamentals, a bull market in bonds, or both.

The PCA 9.625s of April 2009 provided more than $530 million of proceeds to help finance private-equity-firm Madison Dearborn's leveraged buyout of Tenneco's packaging business. The single-B rating flowed naturally from the highly leveraged nature of the buyout trans-action. At the time of the bond issuance in the second quarter of 1999, PCA carried net debt of $1,639 million, representing a borrowing level equal to 4.9 times the company's equity base.

In January 2000, PCA floated equity shares in an initial public offering conducted near the peak of a two-decade-long bull market. Underwritten by Goldman Sachs, the 46.25 million shares offered at $12 each raised a total of $555 million in proceeds for the company. As for the bondholders, the 9.625s of April 2009 retained a single-B rating and a price near par.

Shortly after the company's IPO, the hoped-for improvement in

PCA's credit picture began. Second quarter 2000 net debt declined to $1,271 million, improving the debt-equity ratio to 2.2. In April 2000, Moody's increased the company's senior subordinated note rating from single B3, the lowest rung of the single-B category, to single B2, the middle-rung rating. More good news followed in September 2000, when Moody's boosted the rating of the PCA 9.625s of April 2009 to B1, the top of the single-B category. In a mere eighteen months, the quality of the senior subordinated securities showed significant improvement.

Positive momentum in PCA's financial situation continued. By the third quarter of 2001, the company paid down enough debt to bring outstanding borrowings to $751 million, resulting in a debt-equity ratio of 1.1. Moody's Investors Service recognized the improvement by assigning a mid-range double-B rating to PCA's senior subordinated debt, moving investors from the "small assurance" of single-B paper to the far-more-exalted "uncertainty of position" of double-B obligations.

By the second quarter of 2003, bondholders faced far better circumstances than they confronted in January 2000. Over that period, net debt declined from $1,292 million to $607 million. The debt-equity ratio decreased from 2.4 to 0.9. Credit fundamentals moved dramatically in favor of PCA's junk-bond investors.

Not only did the PCA 9.625s of 2009 benefit from the company's ability to pay down debt, thereby improving the credit standing of the remaining obligations, but the bonds also profited from a dramatic decline in interest rates. In January 2000, ten-year U.S. Treasury rates stood at 6.7 percent. By June 2003, ten-year Treasury yields halved, promising investors only 3.3 percent. The powerful bond market rally and the dramatic credit improvement combined to move the price of the PCA 9.625s of 2009 from approximately par in early 2000 to around 108 in June 2003.

Unfortunately for bondholders, call provisions of the PCA 9.625s of April 2009 dampened the security's appreciation potential. On April 1, 2004, the company enjoyed the right to purchase the outstanding bonds at a fixed price of 104.81. Because of improved credit standing and lower interest rates, PCA would almost certainly exercise its right to call the bonds and refinance at lower rates. Investors evaluating the bonds in mid 2003 knew they would almost certainly lose the bonds at a price of 104.81 on April Fool's Day in 2004, placing a limit on the amount they would reasonably pay for the securities.

In fact, holders of the PCA 9.625s of April 2009 did not need to wait until April 2004 to relinquish their bonds. On June 23, 2003, the company announced a tender offer for the securities at a price of

110.24, representing somewhat more than a two-point premium to the pre-tender market price. The company opted to pay 110.24 for the bonds on July 21, 2003 instead of waiting to pay 104.81 on April 1, 2004, because the combination of the firm's improved credit condition and the market's decreased interest rates made it too expensive for PCA to leave the bonds outstanding. The tender proved successful, as holders of 99.3 percent of the notes surrendered their bonds to the company.

PCA issued new bonds to refund the PCA 9.625s of April 2009, paying much lower rates of 4.5 percent on the five-year tranche and 5.9 percent on the ten-year tranche. The dramatically reduced coupons saved PCA tens of millions of dollars of interest expense over the remaining term of the original financing. Both refinancing bond issues eschewed fixed-price call provisions, as the junk-bond investors firmly demanded that the company close the barn door after the stalls had emptied.

From an investor's perspective, accepting the company's tender maximized returns. Based on the bond's coupon, the tender price, and the call price, if investors held the securities until the call date, they faced an expected return of only 60 to 65 basis points over comparable-maturity Treasuries. Rational holders of the PCA 9.625s of 2009 had no choice but to tender their holdings.

The call provision proved costly to PCA's senior subordinated bondholders. In June 2003, the bonds traded in a close range, from a low of 108.2 to a high of 108.6 averaging approximately 108.4. Based on lower interest rates and PCA's improved credit standing, had the PCA 9.625s of 2009 not had a call provision, the price would have been in excess of 125. The company's fixed-price call option dramatically reduced the potential for junk bondholder gains.

In spite of the dampening effect of the PCA 9.625s call provision, bondholders received handsome holding-period returns. Buoyed by improving credit fundamentals and declining interest rates, the junk-bond investors garnered a return of 49.2 percent from January 28, 2000, the date of the company's IPO, to July 21, 2003, the date of the completion of the tender offer. Junk-bond investors could not hope for better circumstances or better results.

How did the PCA junk bond returns compare to results from closely related alternative investments? Strikingly, a comparable-maturity U.S. Treasury note produced a holding period return of 45.8 percent, as the noncallable nature of the government issue allowed investors to benefit fully from the bond market rally. The 3.4 percent holding period increment, realized by PCA bondholders over the three-and-one-half years, represents scant compensation for accepting a high degree of credit risk. U.S. Treasuries produced risk-adjusted returns significantly higher than those realized by holders of the PCA 9.625s.

Holders of PCA stock faced a tough set of circumstances. In contrast to the strong market enjoyed by bondholders, equity owners faced a dismal market environment. From the date of PCA's IPO, which took place near the peak of one of the greatest stock market bubbles ever, to the bond tender-offer date, the S&P 500 declined a cumulative 24.3 percent. Bucking a decidedly adverse market trend, PCA's equity rose from the initial offering price of $12.00 in January 2000 to $18.05 on July 21, 2003, representing a holding period gain of 50.4 percent. Even in the worst of worlds for equity holders and the best of worlds for bondholders, the equity owners of PCA eked out a victory.

Upon reflection, the superior returns garnered by PCA's equity holders might be expected. Improving credit fundamentals for junk bond positions necessarily correspond to an increase in the equity cushion supporting the company's fixed liabilities. An increase in the stock price provides one means of enhancing the underlying support for the firm's debt burden. Since improving credit fundamentals frequently go hand in hand with rallying stock prices, investors face better odds by owning unlimited-upside stocks as opposed to constrained-potential bonds.

In the case of deteriorating credit fundamentals, junk bond investors attain little or no edge relative to equity investors. Recall that the PCA 9.625s of April 2009 entered the markets in 1999 at the bottom of the single-B rating category, precariously positioned with a "small assurance of maintenance of contract terms." Credit deterioration would likely damage the investments of bondholders and stockholders alike.

Junk bond investors cannot win. When fundamentals improve, stock returns dominate bond returns. When rates decline, noncallable bonds provide superior risk-adjusted returns. When fundamentals deteriorate, junk bond investors fall along with equity investors. Well-informed investors avoid the no-win consequences of high yield fixed income investing.

Alignment of Interests

Junk bond owners face misalignment of interest problems even more severe than those faced by investment-grade bondholders. In the case of fallen-angel junk issues that began life as high quaility bonds and suffered a fall from grace, declines in credit quality correspond to reductions in equity values. In distressed situations, corporate managements usually work hard to prevent further erosion in the company's equity base. Tools available to management include revenue enhancement and cost reduction. Obviously, reducing interest expense and otherwise decreasing the value of debt obligations represents one important means by which management can improve the equity position. Holders of fallen angels find their interests at odds with the interests of corporate management.

In the case of new-issue junk bonds, particularly those employed to finance leveraged buyout deals or leveraged recapitalization transactions, bondholders confront even more highly motivated, adversarial management groups. Sophisticated, equity-oriented financial engineers bring numerous tools to bear on the problem of increasing equity values substantially and rapidly. As the financial operators work to limit the cost of debt, the bondholders realize the mirror image of cost reduction in the form of return diminution.

Market Characteristics

At December 31, 2006, the market value of high yield corporate bonds totaled $657 billion. Yield to maturity amounted to 7.9 percent, with the market showing an average maturity of 7.9 years and an average duration of 4.4 years.

Summary

Junk bond investors face a concentrated combination of the factors that make high-grade corporate bonds a poor choice for investors. Magnified credit risk, greater illiquidity, and more valuable call options pose a triple threat to bondholders seeking high risk-adjusted returns. The relatively high cost of junk bond financing provides incentives to stock-price-driven corporate managements to diminish the value of the bond positions in order to enhance the standing of share owners.

As protection against financial accidents or deflationary periods, junk bonds prove even less useful than investment-grade bonds. The factors that promise incremental yield—credit risk, illiquidity, and callability—work against junk bond owners in times of crisis, undermining the ability of junk bonds to provide portfolio protection.

The recent historical experience of junk investors confirms the inadvisability of owning debt positions in highly leveraged corporations. For the ten years ending December 31, 2006, Lehman Brothers High-Yield Index produced annualized returns of 6.6 percent relative to 6.0 percent for U.S. Treasuries and 6.5 percent for investment-grade corporates. While structural differences in the indices (most notably differences in duration) make the comparison less than perfect, the fact that junk bond investors took far greater risk for insignificant incremental return comes through loud and clear.

ASSET-BACKED SECURITIES

Asset-backed securities consist of fixed income instruments that rely on a broad range of underlying assets (the backing in asset-backed) to provide cash flows and security for payments to bondholders. While the most commonly used asset in asset-backed securities consists of home mortgages, bankers employ assets ranging from credit card receivables to commercial lease payments to automobile finance obligations as collateral for asset-backed deals.

Asset-backed transactions exhibit a high degree of sophisticated financial structuring. Driven by a security issuer's desire to remove assets from the balance sheet and obtain low costs for the financing, the asset-backed security purchaser sits across the table from a formidable adversary.

In the case of mortgage-backed securities—financial instruments that pass through mortgage payments from homeowners to security holders—investors face an unappealing set of responses to changes in interest rates. If interest rates decline, homeowners enjoy the opportunity to prepay and refinance the mortgage. Just as discharging a high-rate mortgage favors the borrower, it hurts the holder of a mortgage-backed security by extinguishing an attractive stream of high interest payments. Similarly, if rates rise, homeowners tend to pay only the minimum required principal and interest payment. Holders of mortgage-backed paper lose high-return assets in a low-rate environment and retain low-return assets in a high-rate environment.

In exchange for accepting a security that shortens when investors prefer lengthening and lengthens when investors prefer shortening, holders of mortgage-backed securities receive a premium rate of return. Whether the premium constitutes fair compensation for the complex options embedded in mortgage securities poses an extremely difficult question. Wall Street's version of rocket scientists employ complicated computer models in a quest to determine the fair value of mortgage-backed securities. Sometimes the models work, sometimes not. If financial engineers face challenges in getting the option pricing right, what chance do individual investors have?

Optionality proves even more difficult to assess than credit risk. In the case of fixed income instruments with credit risk, sensible investors look at bond yields with skepticism, knowing that part of the return may be lost to corporate downgrades or defaults. In the case of fixed income instruments with high degrees of optionality, everyday investors hold no clue as to the appropriate amount by which to discount stated yields to adjust for the possible costs of the options. In fact, many professionals fail to understand the difficult dynamics of fixed income options.

Piper Capital's Worth Bruntjen

In a celebrated case of the early 1990s, Worth Bruntjen, a fixed income specialist at Piper Capital in Minneapolis, built an enormous reputation as a manager of mortgage-backed securities. Based on stellar results in the early years of the decade, Bruntjen attracted significant amounts of capital from retail and institutional investors alike.

Bruntjen managed the Piper Jaffray American Government Securities Fund (AGF), one of a group of mortgage-bond investment vehicles for retail investors. Driven by a powerful bull market in bonds and a portfolio highly sensitive to interest rates, for the five years ending December 31, 1993, the fund returned 19.3 percent per annum, representing a substantial increment over the 11.2 percent annual return of the Salomon Brothers Mortgage Index. Bruntjen's top-of-the-charts returns prompted Morningstar to name this "visionary and guiding force" runner-up in its portfolio-manager-of-the-year competition.[8]

Public records indicate that Bruntjen counted the State of Florida among his institutional separate account clients. In fact, Florida pursued a perverse investment strategy with its conservative operating funds, taking assets from poorly performing managers and adding assets to market-beating accounts. As a result of Bruntjen's stellar results, by January 1994, the State of Florida's account with Bruntjen totaled in excess of $430 million, more than double that of the nearest competitor.[9]

Bruntjen explained his strategy: "We buy government-agency paper that has a higher interest rate than the 30-year bond, but has an average life of only three to five years."[10] The fund manager's "paper" included mortgages and mortgage derivatives with a bull market bias. Nonetheless, Bruntjen's something-for-nothing explanation of his investment approach found a receptive audience. Funds under Bruntjen's management rose rapidly until early 1994.

Unfortunately for fixed income investors, the fall of 1993 marked a high point of the bond market rally, with ten-year U.S. Treasury yields reaching a twenty-six-year low of 5.3 percent. Within a few short months, by May 1994, a wrenching decline in bond prices drove yields to 7.4 percent. The *Wall Street Journal* described the spring meltdown in the mortgage market: "The bloodbath in mortgage derivatives is claiming new casualties as investors and dealers continue to rush for the exits, feeding a vicious cycle of falling prices and evaporating demand." [11] The bear market that rocked bond portfolios laid waste to Bruntjen's approach.

During calendar year 1994, Bruntjen's individual investors in AGF experienced losses of nearly 29 percent. In contrast, the Salomon Brothers Mortgage Index posted a modest 1.4 percent loss. Between January and September, the Bruntjen's State of Florida account incurred losses of $90 million, an entirely unacceptable result for supposedly conservatively invested operating funds. Frustrated by the dismal returns, Florida announced that it would pull nearly $120 million from Bruntjen's account. Retail and institutional investors suffered side by side.

The bond market carnage turned Bruntjen's strategy on its head. When rates rose, the mortgage specialist's use of "significant investments in volatile derivatives like inverse floating-rate bonds and principal-only strips" caused his funds to behave like long-term, thirty-year bonds, not like the shorter-term bonds he cited in his strategy description. [12] Heightened sensitivity to interest rates in a rising rate environment doomed Bruntjen's investors.

Worth Bruntjen, Morningstar's "visionary," failed to understand the risks of his strategy as did his superiors at Piper Capital. Supposedly sophisticated institutional investors at the State of Florida failed to understand the risks of his strategy. Mutual-fund consulting firm Morningstar failed to understand the risk of his strategy. The complexity inherent in understanding and evaluating mortgage-related securities argues for avoiding exposure to the potentially harmful options imbedded in mortgage instruments.

Florida's Sub-Prime Folly

In 2007, after clearly failing to learn from the Piper Capital debacle, the State of Florida once again embarrassed itself in mishandling a short-term investment portfolio. This time, Florida's Local Government Investment Pool (LGIP) produced the dismal results by exposing the fund to highly structured investment in low quality, sub-prime investments.

Prior to the mishap, at the end of 2007's third quarter, the fund contained $27.3 billion[13] in 2,168 individual accounts maintained by 995 local government participants.[14] In the words of the Florida State Board of Administration (SBA), the pool sought "to provide stable returns for participants with an emphasis on safety and liquidity of principal."[15]

Belying its conservative mandate, the LGIP pursued a yield chasing strategy, characterized by *Bloomberg Markets* as "more aggressive than most states." In October 2007, Florida's 5.63 percent yield represented the "highest return of any public fund in the U.S."[16] The next month, in November, Florida's high posted yield appeared less promising. Dogged by rumors of impaired holdings, Florida responded with a November 9th "Update on Sub-Prime Mortgage Meltdown and State Board of Administration Investments." The report begins to address the acute problems with the LGIP on page 11 with the Pollyannaish observation that "[w]e are pleased to report that none of the SBA's short-term portfolios have any direct exposure to sub-prime residential mortgages." Talk about a distinction without a difference. As LGIP participants were about to find out, indirect exposure holds the potential to harm as much as direct exposure.

Prompted by concerns over holdings of downgraded and defaulted debt, in November participants began leaving the fund, ultimately withdrawing $12 billion, or 46 percent of the fund's assets. Closing the chicken coop door after losing a substantial portion of the flock, on November 29 the state froze withdrawals. The once-largest and once-highest-yielding fund stood in disarray.[17]

Florida hired BlackRock to deal with the mess. BlackRock separated the pool into a prime pool, Fund A, with approximately $12 billion, and a less-than-prime pool, Fund B, with approximately $2 billion. Fund B contained a variety of toxic waste, including structured finance company paper issued by KKR Atlantic Fund Trust and KKR Pacific Fund Trust (sponsored by buyout firm KKR), Axon Financial Fund (sponsored by buyout firm TPG), and Ottimo Fund (registered in the Cayman Islands). On top of the asset-backed commercial paper, Fund B included substantial holdings in CDs issued by Countrywide Bank, the troubled (and downgraded) mortgage lender, due to the CDs' "significant" credit risk.

Fund A, with its high quality asset pool, allowed limited withdrawals a week after the freeze, beginning on December 6th. Participants promptly withdrew nearly $2 billion. The State of Florida made a mess of its short-term fund pool. Florida erred first, just as in the Piper Capital case, by aggressively chasing yield without regard to risk. Florida erred second by allowing a run on the bank, paying out $12 billion to early movers at par and leaving all of the impaired assets with the laggards. Florida needs to rethink its approach to investment management.

Clearly, many investors lack the capacity to understand the options in mortgage-backed securities. From a broader portfolio perspective, option-related and credit-related issues in mortgage-backed securities work against investors who wish to use the bonds to hedge against deflation or financial distress. The prepayment option held by the homeowner works like a call option on a corporate bond. If rates fall, prompted by deflationary forces or financial distress, the holder of mortgage-backed securities may lose the investment, along with protection against unfavorable circumstances. Similarly, defaults on mortgages, most likely in times of distress, undermine the value of fixed income's crisis hedging attributes.

Alignment of Interests

Holders of asset-backed securities stand opposite some of the marketable securities world's most sophisticated financial engineers. At best, asset-backed security investors buying newly minted securities should anticipate low returns from the issuer's use of a complex structure to further the corporate objective of generating low-cost debt. At worst, the complexity of asset-backed securities leads to an opacity that prevents investors from understanding the intrinsic character of investment positions. In extreme situations, the Rube Goldberg nature of asset-backed security arrangements causes serious damage to investor portfolios.

Market Characteristics

At December 31, 2006, the market value of asset-backed securities totaled $105 billion. Yield to maturity amounted to 5.3 percent, with the market exhibiting an average maturity of 3.2 years and an average duration of 2.8 years.[18]

Summary

Asset-backed securities involve a high degree of financial engineering. As a general rule of thumb, the more complexity that exists in a Wall Street creation, the faster and farther investors should run. At times, the creators and issuers of complex securities fail to understand how the securities might behave under various circumstances. What chance does the nonprofessional investor have?

Many mortgage-backed securities enjoy the support of government-sponsored enterprises, causing investors to assume that the securities carry low levels of risk. Investor assumptions may prove false on two counts. First, the credit risk may ultimately prove greater than market participants assume. Second, the GSE-induced investor complacency may mask significant risk of exposure to hard-to-understand options. Investors beware.

Just as with other forms of fixed income, the issuer of asset-backed securities seeks cheap financing. Cheap financing for issuers translates into low returns for investors. Combine low expected returns with high complexity and investor interests suffer.

As with many other segments of the fixed income markets, investors in asset-backed securities appear not to have reaped rewards for accepting credit and call risk. For the ten years ending December 31, 2006, the Lehman Brothers Asset-Backed Security Index returned 6.0 percent per annum, essentially matching the Lehman Brothers U.S. Treasury Index return of 6.0 percent per annum. Like other comparisons of bond index returns, the numbers do not account for differences in index composition. Nonetheless, over the past decade asset-backed bond investors appear to have fallen short in the quest to generate risk-adjusted excess returns.

FOREIGN BONDS

By asset size, foreign-currency-denominated bonds represent a formidable market, falling just short of the aggregate market value of U.S.-dollar-denominated debt. Yet, in spite of the market's size, foreign bonds offer little of value to U.S. investors.

Consider bonds of similar maturity and similar credit quality, with one denominated in U.S. dollars and the other denominated in foreign currency. Because monetary conditions differ from country to country, the two bonds would likely promise different interest rates. An investor might expect that different interest rates and different economic conditions in different countries would lead to different investment results. If, however, the investor hedges each of the foreign bond's cash flows by selling sufficient foreign currency in the forward markets to match the anticipated receipt of interest and principal payments, then the U.S. dollar cash flows of the dollar-denominated bond match exactly the U.S. dollar cash flows of the foreign-currency-denominated bond hedged into U.S. dollars. In other words, an unhedged foreign currency bond consists of a U.S. dollar bond plus some foreign exchange exposure.

Foreign currencies, in and of themselves, provide no expected return. Some market players, as part of so-called macro strategies, speculate on the direction of foreign exchange rates. Foreign bond mutual funds provide a vehicle through which investment managers sometimes take speculative positions. Top-down bets on currencies fail to generate a reliable source of excess returns, because the factors influencing economic conditions, in general, and interest rates, in particular, prove far too complex to predict with consistency. Sensible investors avoid currency speculation.

In a portfolio context, foreign exchange exposure may produce the benefit of additional diversification. Even with no expected return, the lack of full correlation between currency movements and other asset class fluctuations reduces portfolio risk. However, investors should obtain foreign exchange exposure not through foreign bond positions, but in connection with an asset class expected to produce superior returns, namely foreign equities.

Since foreign currency positions, *per se*, promise a zero expected return, investors in foreign bonds expect returns similar to returns from U.S. dollar bonds. Yet, unhedged foreign bonds fail to provide the same protection against financial crisis or deflation enjoyed by holders of U.S. Treasury securities. In the event of a market trauma,

U.S. investors have no idea what impact foreign exchange rates will have on the value of foreign bond positions. The unknown influence of foreign currency translation forces investors hoping to benefit from fixed income's special diversifying characteristics to avoid unhedged foreign bond exposure.

Alignment of Interests

Holders of domestic Treasury bonds expect fair treatment from their government. Unlike the inherently adversarial relationship between corporate issuers and corporate creditors, governments find no reason to disadvantage their citizens. If investors purchase foreign-currency-denominated bond issues held largely by citizens of the country of issue, those investors may well benefit from a reasonable alignment of interests.

However, if a foreign government debt issue resides primarily in the hands of external owners, the alignment of interests breaks down. In fact, if political considerations trump contractual obligations, external holders of foreign government paper may suffer worse consequences than owners of troubled corporate debt. When international politics enter the picture, foreign bondholders may suffer.

Market Characteristics

At December 31, 2006, foreign-currency-denominated bonds totaled a substantial $14.5 trillion, of which $9.2 trillion represented issuance by foreign governments and $1.9 trillion represented investment grade issues of corporations. Foreign-currency-denominated, high yield corporate issues totaled a paltry $114 billion, reflecting the market's relative immaturity.

Yield to maturity for foreign-currency-denominated government paper amounted to 3.2 percent, with an average maturity of 8.2 years and duration of 6.2 years. Foreign-currency-denominated investment-grade corporate bonds promised yields of 4.3 percent with average maturity of 7.0 years and duration of 5.3 years.

Summary

Foreign-currency-denominated bonds share domestic bonds' burden of low expected returns without the benefit of domestic fixed income's special diversifying power. Fully hedged foreign bonds mimic U.S. bonds (with the disadvantage of added complexity and costs stemming from the hedging process). Unhedged foreign bonds supply investors with U.S. dollar bond exposure plus (perhaps unwanted) foreign exchange exposure. Foreign-currency-denominated bonds play no role in well-constructed investment portfolios.

2007 PERFORMANCE UPDATE

Based on data presented in the summary section for each of the fixed income alternatives, Treasury bonds appear to provide superior risk-adjusted returns. The return comparisons fail to provide a completely fair test, however, because differences in duration throughout the ten-year measurement period cause the comparisons to fall short of the apples-to-apples standard.

Domestic corporate and high yield returns for the ten years ending December 31, 2006 produced inadequate margins over Treasuries to compensate for illiquidity, credit risk, and call risk. Asset-backed securities actually show a small deficit relative to Treasuries. Although the shorter duration of asset-backed instruments explains part of the return deficit, even after adjusting for the shorter duration,

Table A.1 Treasury Bonds Trump Riskier Alternatives

Ten-Year Returns of Fixed Income Indices

	Period Ending December 31,		Index Duration (Years)
	2006 (%)	2007 (%)	December 31, 2007
U.S. treasuries	5.97	5.91	5.2
Domestic corporate	6.52	5.96	6.3
High yield	6.59	5.51	4.6
Asset-backed securities	5.95	5.43	3.4

Source: Lehman Brothers

investors received insufficient compensation for straying from the full faith and credit of the U.S. government.

The credit crisis during the second half of 2007 emphatically reinforced the superiority of Treasury bonds. Trailing Treasury returns scarcely moved as the ten-year measurement period advanced from the end of 2006 to the end of 2007. In contrast, corporate bond returns declined by 56 basis points to a level of only five basis points above Treasuries. High yield bond returns dropped by 108 basis points per annum for the ten-year period, falling a full 40 basis points below the Treasury return. Similarly, asset-backed securities lost 52 basis points per annum, increasing the deficit relative to Treasuries to 48 basis points.

One lesson of the 2007 credit crisis concerns the fact that investors in bonds with the unattractive characteristics of illiquidity, credit risk, and call risk underperformed Treasuries for the year ending December 31, 2007. The other lesson concerns the timing of the dramatic short-term underperformance of corporate, high yield, and asset-backed securities during the second half of 2007. Just when investors most needed protection provided by bond positions, non-Treasury holdings disappointed.

CONCLUSION

A host of fixed income markets fall short of the diversifying power inherent in default-free, full-faith-and-credit obligations of the U.S. government. Factors including credit risk, call options, illiquidity, and foreign exchange limit the attractiveness of investment-grade corporate bonds, high yield bonds, asset-backed securities, and foreign bonds. Sensible investors avoid the sirens' song that promises something (in the form of hoped-for incremental return) for nothing (in the form of ignored incremental risk).

Notes

CHAPTER 2: ENDOWMENT PURPOSES

1. Brooks Mather Kelley, *Yale: A History.* (New Haven: Yale University Press, 1974.)
2. The Governor and lieutenant governor continued to serve ex officio as Fellows of the Corporation, although in the modern era they have not participated actively in Yale's governance.
3. Merle Curti and Roderick Nash, *Philanthropy in the Shaping of American Higher Education* (New Brunswick, NJ: Rutgers University Press, 1965); Frederick Rudolph, *The American College and University: A History* (Athens: University of Georgia Press, 1962).
4. Hugh Davis Graham and Nancy Diamond, *The Rise of American Research Universities* (Baltimore: Johns Hopkins University Press, 1997).
5. Ibid.
6. Howard R. Bowen, *The Costs of Higher Education: How Much Do Colleges and Universities Spend per Student and How Much Should They Spend?* (New York: McGraw Hill, 1980). See also Graham and Diamond, *Universities*, p. 97.
7. Denise LaVoie, "School Year Begins with New Unification Church Affiliation," *Associated Press*, 28 August 1992.
8. *New York Times*
9. Joseph Berger, "University of Bridgeport Honors Reverend Moon, Fiscal Savior," *New York Times*, 8 September 1995.
10. Lynde Phelps Wheeler, *Josiah Willard Gibbs* (New Haven: Yale University Press, 1951), 91–92.
11. Leonard Curry, "Congressional Hearing Puts Stanford Officials on Hot Seat," *The Orange County Register*, 14 March 1991.
12. The 0.5 percent increment was designated "to support renewal of campus

buildings and infrastructure." See *Stanford University Annual Financial Report, 1995.*

13. The unpublished survey of endowment size and institutional quality relies on research conducted by the Yale Investment Office.
14. "The Fortune 1,000 Ranked Within Industries" *Fortune,* 28 April 1997.
15. "Best Colleges 1998," *U.S. News & World Report,* 1 September 1997. USNWR ranks 28 of the 29 Carnegie Universities. Rockefeller University, because it does not grant degrees, is excluded from the study.
16. The National Center for Education and Statistics, *Directory of Post Secondary Institutions, 1987–1997,* vol. 1.

CHAPTER 3: INVESTMENT AND SPENDING GOALS

1. James Tobin, "What Is Permanent Endowment Income?" *American Economic Review 64,* no. 2 (1974): 427–432.
2. Harvard University, *Managing Harvard's Endowment.* (Harvard University, 1990).
3. Even though Harvard's 1974 spending policy rationale contains flaws, in practice the university spends at prudent levels, producing payouts similar to those of comparable institutions.
4. Yale University, *Report of the Treasurer, 1965–66,* ser. 62, no. 19 (New Haven: 1966), 6–7.
5. National Association of College and University Business Officers (NACUBO). Data are from various *Endowment Studies.* Prepared by Cambridge Associates, Inc.
6. In the 2006 NACUBO survey, 335 institutions reported using target spending rates.
7. See Table 2.2 for additional information.
8. Karen W. Arenson, "Q&A. Modest Proposal. An Economist Asks, Does Harvard Really Need $15 Billion?" *New York Times,* 2 August 1998.
9. Henry Hansmann. "Why Do Universities Have Endowments?" *PONPO Working Paper* No. 109, Program on Non-Profit Organizations, Institution for Social and Policy Studies, Yale University. January 1986, 21.
10. Ibid., 23.
11. Tobin, "Endowment Income," 427.

CHAPTER 4: INVESTMENT PHILOSOPHY

1. Roger G. Ibbotson and Paul D. Kaplan, "Does Asset Allocation Policy Explain 40, 90, or 100 Percent of Performance?" *Financial Analysts Journal* 56, no. 1 (2000): 32.
2. Ibid., 29.
3. Charles D. Ellis, *"Winning the Loser's Game" Timeless Strategies for Successful Investing,* 3d ed. (New York: McGraw Hill, 1998), 11.
4. William N. Goetzmann and Philippe Jorion, "A Century of Global Stock Markets," *Journal of Finance* (forthcoming).
5. Stephen J. Brown, William N. Goetzmann, and Stephen A. Ross, "Survival," *Journal of Finance* 50, no. 3. (1995): 855.
6. Robert Lovett, "Gilt-Edged Insecurity," *Saturday Evening Post,* 1937.

7. Cambridge Associates, Inc. *1997 NACUBO Endowment Study.* Washington, D.C.: National Association of College and University Business Officers, 1998).

8. John Maynard Keynes, "Memorandum for the Estates Committee, King's College, Cambridge, May 8, 1938." in Charles D. Ellis, ed., *Classics. An Investor's Anthology* (Homewood, Ill.: Business One Irwin in association with the Institutie of Chartered Financial Analysts, 1989), 79–82.

9. Gilbert Burck, "A New Kind of Stock Market," *Bank Credit Analyst*, April 1998, 22. First published in *Fortune*, March 1959.

10. Ibid.

11. Endowment asset allocation figures come from Cambridge Associates, a consulting firm specializing in advising not-for-profit clients.

12. See Robert J. Shiller, *Market Volatility* (Cambridge: MIT Press, 1989).

13. Ibid., 2–3.

14. Burton Malkiel and Paul Firstenberg, *Managing Risk in an Uncertain Era: An Analysis for Endowed Institutions* (Princeton, NJ: Princeton University, 1976).

15. Brady Commission, *Report of the Presidential Task Force on Market Mechanisms, January 1988.* (Washington, D.C.: GPO, 1988), 53.

16. Keynes, *The General Theory of Employment, Interest and Money.* (New York: Harcourt and Brace, 1964), 155.

17. Ibid., 160.

18. Ibid., 151.

19. Benjamin Graham, *The Intelligent Investor* (New York: Harper Business, 1973), 279.

20. See Eugene Fama and Kenneth French, "Size and Book-to-Market Factors in Earnings and Returns," *Journal of Finance*, 50, no. 1. (1995): 131–155, and Eugene Fama and Kenneth French. "The Cross-Section of Expected Stock Returns," *Journal of Finance* 47, no. 2 (1992): 427–465.

21. Graham, *Intelligent Investor.*

22. Keynes, *General Theory*, 157.

23. Douglas Appell, "GMO's Grantham not worried about the bulls," *Pensions & Investments*, 5 March 2007.

CHAPTER 5: ASSET ALLOCATION

1. Moody's Investor Service, *Moody's Transportation Manual* (New York: Moody's Investor Service, Inc., 1973), 358–370.

2. Richard Michaud, "The Markowitz Optimization Enigma: Is 'Optimized' Optimal?" *Financial Analysts Journal* 45, no. 1 (1989): 31–42.

3. Richard Bookstaber, "Global Risk Management: Are We Missing the Point?" (paper based on presentations given at the Institute for Quantitative Research in Finance, October 1996 and at the Internal Models for Market Risk Evaluation: Experiences, Problems and Perspectives Conference, Rome, Italy, June 1996.)

4. Keynes, *General Theory*, 1964, 155. The full quote from Keynes is: "The social object of skilled investment should be to defeat the dark forces of time and ignorance which envelop our future."

5. Jeremy Grantham. "Everything I Know about the Stock Market in 15 Minutes," Internal Memo.

6. Vijay Kumar Chopra and William T. Ziemba, "The Effect of Errors in Means, Variances, and Covariances on Optimal Portfolio Choice," *Journal of Portfolio Management* 19, no. 2 (1993): 6–11.

7. Roger G. Ibbotson and Rex A. Sinquefield, "Stocks, Bonds, Bills, and Inflation: Year-by-Year Historical Returns (1926–1974)," *Journal of Business* 49, no. 1, (1976): 11–47.

8. Paul M. Firstenberg, Stephen A. Ross, and Randall C. Zisler. "Real Estate: The Whole Story," *Journal of Portfolio Management* 24, no. 3 (1988): 31. Apparently, the article continues to be highly regarded as it appears in the 1997 publication, *Streetwise. The Best of the Journal of Portfolio Management*, Peter L. Bernstein & Frank J. Fabozzi, editors, Princeton University Press.

CHAPTER 6: ASSET ALLOCATION MANAGEMENT

1. Linda Sandler, "Endowments at Top Schools Bruised in Market," *Wall Street Journal.* 13 October 1998.

2. Sowood Capital Management: Sowood Alpha Fund (pitch book), 2004.

3. Gregory Zuckerman and Craig Karmin, "Sowood's Short, Hot Summer," *Wall Street Journal*, 27 October 2007.

4. Ibid.

5. Sowood letter to investors: 30 July 2007.

6. Roger Lowenstein, *When Genius Failed. The Rise and Fall of Long-Term Capital Management* (New York: Random House, 2001): 224–25.

7. John R. Dorfman, "Report on Common Fund Cites Warning Signs," *Wall Street Journal*, 17 January 1996, C1.

8. Keynes, *General Theory*, 157.

CHAPTER 7: TRADITIONAL ASSET CLASSES

1. Ibbotson Associates, *Stocks, Bonds, Bills, and Inflation 2006 Yearbook* (Chicago: Ibbotson Associates, 2003): 27–28.

2. Jeremy Siegel, *Stocks for the Long Run* (New York: McGraw Hill, 2002): 6.

3. William N. Goetzmann and Philippe Jorion, "A Century of Global Stock Markets," NBER Working Paper Series, Working Paper 5901 (National Bureau of Economic Research, 1997), 16.

4. Robert Arnott, "Dividends and the Three Dwarfs," *Financial Analysts Journal 59*, no. 2, (2003): 4.

5. James K. Glassman and Kevin A. Hassett, *Dow 36,000: The New Strategy for Profiting from the Coming Rise in the Stock Market* (New York: Random House, 1999).

6. Siegel, *Stocks for the Long Run*, 210.

7. Geraldine Fabrikant and David Cay Johnston, "G.E. Perks Raise Issues About Taxes, " *New York Times*, 9 September 2002.

8. "Jack's Booty," editorial, *Wall Street Journal*, 10 September 2002.

9. David Leonhardt, "Reining In the Imperial C.E.O.," *New York Times*, 15 September 2002.

10. Steve Lohr and Joel Brinkley, "Microsoft Management Tells Workers There Will Be No Breakup," *New York Times*, 26 April 2000.

11. Jathon Sapsford and Ken Brown, "J.P. Morgan Rolls Dice on Microsoft Options," *Wall Street Journal*, 9 July 2003.
12. Data from Wilshire Associates.
13. Ibbotson Associates, *2004 Yearbook*, 224, 234.
14. Carole Gould, "Better Understanding of Bonds," *New York Times*, 27 August 1995.
15. Publicdebt.treas.gov, "Treasury Calls 8-¼ Percent Bonds of 2000–05," http://www.publicdebt.treas.gov/com/com114cl.htm.
16. Bureau of the Public Debt, Press Release of January 15, 2004: "Treasury Calls 9-⅛ Percent Bonds of 2004–09."
17. Stephen J. Brown, William N. Goetzmann and Stephen A. Ross, "Survival," *Journal of Finance* 50, no. 3 (1995).
18. Antoine van Agtmael, *The Emerging Markets Century* (New York: Free Press, 2007): 307–8.

CHAPTER 8: ALTERNATIVE ASSET CLASSES

1. The amount of the capital required to execute the Newell Rubbermaid trade ranges from an aggressive value of the Rubbermaid price less the net proceeds from the short sale of Newell (31¹³⁄₁₆ - 2.28 = 29.5325), to a conservative value of the Newell short position (.7883 x 43.26 = 34.10). Choosing the value of the Rubbermaid share (31¹³⁄₁₆) represents a middle-of-the-road position.
2. Roger G. Ibbotson and Peng Chen, "The A, B, Cs of Hedge Funds: Alphas, Betas, and Costs," Yale ICF Working Paper No. 06-10 (Yale International Center for Finance, September 2006), 2.
3. Burton G. Malkiel and Atanu Saha, "Hedge Funds: Risk and Return," *Financial Analysts Journal* 61, no. 6 (2005): 82.
4. "Merrill Lynch Factor Index. An Alternative to Investable Hedge Fund Indices," Merrill Lynch, Global Markets and Investment Banking Group, September 2006.
5. Kevin Mirabile and Rosemarie Lakeman, *Observations on the Rapid Growth of the Hedge Fund Industry*. (Barclays Capital, 2004): 2.
6. Treas.gov, "Key Initiatives," http://www.treas.gov/offices/domestic-finance/key-initiatives/tips.html.
7. Data from Bloomberg; LehmanLive; National Association of Real Estate Investment Trusts.
8. National Association of Real Estate Investment Trusts, "Forming and Operating a Real Estate Investment Trust," http://www.nareit.com/aboutreits/formingaREIT.cfm.
9. Marc Cardillo, Robert Lang, Maggie Patton, and Andrew Heath, "U.S. Real Estate and REIT Investing. Executive Summary," *Cambridge Associates*, 2007.
10. Green Street Advisors, "REIT Share Price Premiums to Green Street NAV Estimates," http://www.greenstreetadvisors.com/premnav.html.
11. Matt Terrien, "Investing in Direct Energy: A Diversification Tool for Portfolios," (Prepared for Merit Energy Company) Ibbotson Associates. 11 October 1999.
12. "Warburg Pincus Completes Acquisition of Bausch & Lomb," Bausch & Lomb newsroom. www.bausch.com, 26 October 2007.

13. *2006 Investment Benchmarks Report: Buyouts and Other Private Equity* (New York: Thomson Financial, 2006).

14. Steven N. Kaplan and Antoinette Schoar, "Private Equity Performance: Returns, Persistence, and Capital Flows," *Journal of Finance*, no. 4 (August 2005): 1791.

15. *2006 Investment Benchmarks Report: Buyouts.*

16. Josh Lerner and Antoinette Schoar, 17 January 2008.

17. Keynes, *General Theory*, 160.

18. Andrew Metrick and Ayako Yasuda, "The Economics of Private Equity Funds," (September 9, 2007). Swedish Institute for Financial Research. Conference on The Economics of the Private Equity Market.

19. Estimated numbers, based on data collected by Cambridge Associates. Controlled capital is defined as current net asset value of the aggregate partnerships plus aggregate undrawn capital. All data refers to the U.S. market only.

20. Randall E. Stross, *eBoys: The First Inside Account of Venture Capitalists at Work* (New York: Ballantine Publishing Group, 2000): 182.

21. Ibid. xv.

22. *2006 Investment Benchmarks Report: Venture Capital* (New York: Thomson Financial, 2006).

23. Kaplan and Schoar, *Journal of Finance* 40: 1792.

24. Kaplan and Schoar, *Journal of Finance* 40: 1809.

25. Estimated numbers, based on data collected by Cambridge Associates. Controlled capital is defined as current net asset value of the aggregate partnerships plus aggregate undrawn capital. All data refers to the U.S. market only.

CHAPTER 9: ASSET CLASS MANAGEMENT

1. Keynes, General Theory, 155–56.

2. The information on Granville is drawn from Rhonda Brammer, "10 Years After He Peaked, Will Joe Granville Rise Again?" *Barron's*, 24 August 1992.

3. James J. Cramer, "The Bull Case of the Individual Investor," *TheStreet.com*, 28 January 2000.

4. Ibid.

5. James J. Cramer, "Cramer the Contrarian Remains Unconvinced, Part 1," *TheStreet.com*. 14 February 2000.

6. James J. Cramer, "Cramer the Contrarian Remains Unconvinced, Part 2," *TheStreet.com*. 14 February 2000.

7. James J. Cramer, "Scrutinizing the Value Managers," *TheStreet.com*. 11 February 2000.

8. James J. Cramer, "Cramer the Contrarian Remains Unconvinced, Part 4," *TheStreet.com*. 14 February 2000.

9. Bill Alpert, "Shorting Cramer," *Barron's*, 20 August 2007: 23–25.

10. Thyra Mangan, "Comments of T. Mangan on S7-12-06," 28 March 2007: Sec.gov.

11. Bill Alpert, "Shorting Cramer," *Barron's*, 20 August 2007: 25.

12. Irving Fisher, *The Rate of Interest. Its Nature, Determination and Relation to Economic Phenomena* (Macmillan Company, 1907): 217.

13. "Buffett's Job Description: 'They May Be Hard to Identify,' " *Wall Street Journal*. 28 April, 2007.
14. The discussion of entrepreneurial capitalism draws heavily on a 1997 essay by G. Leonard Baker, General Partner of Sutter Hill Ventures, "How Silicon Valley Works: Reflections on 25 years in the Venture Capital Business," 1997.
15. Joseph A. Schumpeter, *The Theory of Economic Development*, trans. Redvers Opie (Cambridge: Harvard University Press, 1934), 66.
16. Joseph A. Schumpeter. *Capitalism, Socialism, and Democracy*, (New York: Harper & Brothers, 1950), 83.
17. Ibid.
18. Fortress Investment Group LLC, *Form S-1*, 8 November 2006: 4.
19. Fortress Investment Group LLC, *Form S-1/A*, 2 February 2007: 2.
20. Fortress Investment Group LLC, *Form 10-K*, 31 December 2006: 82–3.
21. Fortress, *Form S-1/A*, 62.
22. Ibid., 106.
23. Ibid., 15.
24. United Asset Management, *United Asset Management Annual Report, 1997*, 2.
25. Sara Calian and Laura Saunders Egodigwe, "Old Mutual Agrees to Acquire Asset-Management Firm UAM," *Wall Street Journal*, 20 June 2000.
26. Ibid.
27. Douglas Appell, "Old Mutual Affiliates to Gain More Equity," *Pensions & Investments*, 16 October 2007.
28. Andrew Ross Sorkin and Michael J. de la Merced, "Home Depot Said to Cut Price of Supply Unit by $2 Billion," *International Herald Tribune*, 27 August 2007.
29. George Anders, "Captive Client: Morgan Stanley Found a Gold Mine of Fees," *Wall Street Journal*, 14 December 1990, sec. A.
30. Ibid.
31. *Wall Street Journal*, 4 June 1991, 6.
32. Ibid.
33. Ibid.
34. Ibid.
35. Jenny Strasburg and Katherine Burton, "Goldman Global Equity Fund Gets $3 Billion in Capital," Bloomberg.com, 13 August 2007.
36. Henny Sender, Kate Kelly and Gregory Zuckerman, "Goldman Wagers on Cash Infusion to Show Resolve," *Wall Street Journal*, 14 August 2007.
37. "GS—Goldman Sachs Conference Call," Thomson StreetEvents, Final Transcript; 13 August 2007: 4–5.
38. *Wall Street Journal*, 14 August 2007.
39. Jeffrey Taylor, "SEC Wants Investment Managers to Tell Clients More About 'Soft Dollar' Services," *Wall Street Journal*, 15 February 1997, 5, 21.
40. Ibid., 40.
41. Barry B. Burr, "Soft Dollar Managers Pay." *(Chicago) Pensions and Investments*, 10 August 1998, Editorial section, 10.
42. SEC, *Inspection Report*, 3.
43. Advisory Council on Employee Welfare and Benefit Plans, *Report of the Working Groups on Soft Dollars/Commission Recapture*. (Washington D.C., 13 November 1997), 5, 21.

44. Sec.gov, Christopher Cox, "Speech by SEC Chairman: Address to the National Italian-American Foundation" (Washington, D.C., 31 May 2007).
45. Sec.gov, Christopher Cox, "Speech by SEC Chairman: Address to the Mutual Fund Directors Forum Seventh Annual Policy Conference" (New York City, 13 April 2007).
46. Roger Lowenstein, *Buffett: The Making of an American Capitalist* (New York: Random House, 1995), 62.
47. Josh Lerner, "Discussion of 'The Economics of Private Equity Funds' by Metrick and Yasuda," Harvard University and NBER.
48. Andrew Metrick and Ayako Yasuda, "The Economics of Private Equity Funds" (9 September 2007). University of Pennsylvania, The Wharton School, Department of Finance.
49. Gretchen Morgenson, "It's Just a Matter of Equity," *New York Times*, 16 September 2007.
50. *Wall Street Journal*, 15 July 1992.
51. Ibid.
52. "The 400 Richest Americans: #215 Neil Gary Bluhm," Forbes.com: 21 September 2006.

CHAPTER 10: INVESTMENT PROCESS

1. Keynes, *General Theory*, 157–158.
2. James B. Stewart, *Den of Thieves*. (New York: Touchstone, 1992): 421.
3. *Private Equity Analyst*, August 2006: 32.
4. TIAA-CREF, *2006 NACUBO Endowment Study*, www.nacubo.org.
5. Josh Lerner, Antoinette Schoar, and Wan Wong, "Smart Institutions, Foolish Choices? The Limited Partner Performance Puzzle," Harvard University, National Bureau of Economic Research, and MIT (2005): 15–16.
6. Ellis, *Successful Investing*.
7. The 1987 stock market crash was a 20 standard deviation event. Backward looking estimates of volatility would naturally increase for periods in which the extraordinary data from October 1987 were included.
8. Information comes from the 2005 survey of investment returns sponsored by Cambridge Associates.
9. New York University, *New York University Financial Report, 1977–1997*, 20 vols. (New York: New York University, 1977–1997); New York University, *New York University Annual Report, 1977–1985*, 9 vols. (New York: New York University, 1977–1985).
10. Roger Lowenstein, "How Larry Tisch and NYU Missed the Bull Market's Run," *Wall Street Journal*. 16 October 1997.
11. The NACUBO (National Association of College and University Business Officers) Endowment Wealth Index reflects median annual changes in the aggregate endowment market value of institutions participating in the group's annual survey. Year-to-year change in wealth includes the impact of investment returns, gifts, and spending.
12. David Barboza, "Loving a Stock, Not Wisely But Too Well." *New York Times*, 20 September 1998, sec. 3.
13. *New York Times*, 20 September 1998.

14. David A. Rocker, "Refresher Course. Short Interest: No More Bullish Bellow," *Barron's*, 1 May 1995, 43.
15. Data from Russell Mellon and Bloomberg.
16. PIPER: Pensions & Investments' Performance Evaluation Report (PIPER), *Managed Accounts Report, December 31, 2007: Quarter End* (New York: Pensions & Investments, 1997).

APPENDIX: IMPURE FIXED INCOME

1. Marie Nelson, "Debt Ratings," *Moody's Investors Service*, 23 July 2003.
2. "WorldCom's Credit Rating Sliced to Junk by Moody's," *Bloomberg*, 9 May 2002.
3. Sharon Ou and David T. Hamilton, "Moody's Dollar Volume-Weighted Default Rates," *Moody's Investors Service*, March 2003.
4. Data from Moody's Investors Service.
5. Data from Lehman Brothers.
6. Nelson, "Debt Ratings," *Moody's Investors Service*.
7. Ibid.
8. Andrew Bary, "Paying the Piper," *Barron's Chicopee* 74, no. 15 (1994); Morningstar, *Morningstar Closed-End Funds* 10, no. 7 (March 1994).
9. Bary, "Paying the Piper," *Barron's Chicopee*.
10. Jeffrey M. Laderman and Gary Weiss, "The Yield Game," *Business Week*, 6 December 1993.
11. Laura Jereski, "Mortgage Derivatives Claim Victims Big and Small," *Wall Street Journal*, 20 April 1994.
12. Bary, "Paying the Piper," *Barron's Chicopee*.
13. "Update on Sub-Prime Mortgage Meltdown and State Board of Administration Investments," SBA Florida, 9 November 2007: 5.
14. "Local Government Investment Pool Newsletter," SBA Florida, Q3 2007: 4.
15. Ibid., 1.
16. David Evans, "Peddling Tainted Debt to Florida," *Bloomberg Markets*, February 2008.
17. Ibid.
18. Data from Lehman Brothers.

Acknowledgments

Carrie Abildgaard, my writing aide-de-camp, cheerfully and competently converted my ideas and scribbles into this book, good naturedly transforming a sometimes harrowing process into a joyful exercise.

Len Baker, my role model, forces me to bring my best to Yale's investment process (and entertains me) by constantly questioning, analyzing, and debating every aspect of endowment policy.

Bill Brainard, my teacher, constantly reminds me of what it means to be a good university citizen, setting an incomparable example day in and day out.

Charley Ellis, my chairman, graces Yale's investment process with his presence and ideas, consistently informing our decisions with intelligence and wit.

Rick Levin, my leader, contributes to Yale (and Yale's investment activities) in so many ways, particularly in fostering an environment that promotes (and demands) excellence.

Meghan McMahon, my companion and soul mate, steadfastly supports me managing the improbable feat of both keeping me grounded and inspiring me.

Dean Takahashi, my co-conspirator and friend, challenges me and the entire Yale Investments team to put forth the best possible effort, most importantly by adhering to personal and professional standards of the highest order.

Index

absolute return, 182–99; and active management, 112, 180, 182, 190, 191, 192, 193, 198, 199; and alignment of interests, 197, 198; and alternative asset characteristics, 112–14; and asset allocation, 100, 101, 112–14, 135; and asset class management, 284, 285–86; and backfill bias, 192–95, 198; benefits of, 181, 198; bottom-up, 113; characteristics of, 242; and compensation arrangements, 284, 285–86; definition of, 198; and diversification, 181, 182, 186, 187, 189, 192, 198, 242; and domestic equities, 114, 191, 192; and event-driven strategies, 112, 182, 183–87, 197, 198, 242; and expected return, 114, 188–96; and hedge funds, 112–13, 190, 191, 192–96, 198, 199; and historical data, 113, 192–95; and inflation, 197; and investment process, 299, 330, 334; and leveraged buyouts, 193, 227, 228; and market characteristics, 197; and merger arbitrage, 112, 182*n*, 183–87, 188, 197; overview about, 182–83, 198–99, 242; and performance assessment, 334; quantitative attributes of, 192–95; and rebalancing, 135; and risk, 112–13, 114, 182, 186, 187, 192, 195–96, 198, 199, 242; and short sales/positions, 112, 113, 182, 182*n*, 188–91, 192, 198; and survivorship bias, 192–95, 198; and value approach, 112, 113, 182, 183, 188–90, 191, 196, 197, 198, 242

Acadian Asset Management, 263

active management: and asset class, 136, 137, 138, 245–96; and chasing performance, 93–97; and client base, 254–55; and compensation arrangements, 272–94, 295–96; costs of, 245; fully loaded hurdles for, 80–82; game of, 246–51, 294–95; and independent organizations, 260–70; and investment process, 297, 298–99, 309, 317, 345; and normal portfolios, 138; performance assessment of, 193, 246–51, 273, 317, 332, 333, 334, 346; personal characteristics of, 246, 251–54; and return, 75–77, 137, 245, 247, 274, 297, 298; and risk, 137, 247, 273;selection of, 243–44, 246, 251–54, 259, 295, 296; and size, 254–55. *See also specific topic*

adaptation, and asset class management, 255, 257–58

administrators, academic, 10, 22, 43

adverse selection problem, 312

About the Author

David Swensen, Yale's Chief Investment Officer, manages the university's $23 billion in endowment assets. Under his stewardship the Yale endowment generated returns of nearly 17 percent per annum, a record unequalled among institutional investors. Mr. Swensen, who earned a Ph.D in economics from Yale, leads a staff of 20 located near the Yale campus in downtown New Haven.

Prior to joining Yale in 1985, Mr. Swensen spent six years on Wall Street—three years at Lehman Brothers and three years at Salomon Brothers—where his work focused on developing new financial technologies. At Salomon Brothers, he structured the first swap, a currency transaction involving IBM and the World Bank. Mr. Swensen authored *Pioneering Portfolio Management: An Unconventional Approach to Institutional Investment* and *Unconventional Success: A Fundamental Approach to Personal Investment*, both published by The Free Press.

Well regarded by peers and competitors alike, high praise comes from Vanguard founder Jack Bogle ("Swensen is one of only a handful of investment geniuses on the planet"), former Harvard Management Company chief executive Jack Meyer ("David is the best in the business"), former Morgan Stanley investment strategist Barton Biggs ("Swensen has become big money's Warren Buffett"), and Princeton professor Burton Malkiel ("Swensen is a true investment leader").

In 2007, Mr. Swensen received the Mory's Cup for conspicuous service to Yale and the Hopkins Medal for unparalleled loyalty to Hopkins School. His alma mater, the University of Wisconsin—River

Falls, awarded him an honorary doctorate in 2008. In that same year, he became a Fellow of the American Academy of Arts & Sciences.

Mr. Swensen is a Trustee of TIAA, a Trustee of The Brookings Institution and a member of the Investment Board of the University of Cambridge. He has advised the Carnegie Institution of Washington, the Carnegie Corporation, the Hopkins School, the New York Stock Exchange, the Howard Hughes Medical Institute, the Courtauld Institute of Art, the Yale New Haven Hospital, The Investment Fund for Foundations, the Edna McConnell Clark Foundation and the States of Connecticut and Massachusetts. At Yale, where he teaches students in Yale College and at the School of Management, he is a Fellow of Berkeley College, an Incorporator of the Elizabethan Club, and a Fellow of the International Center for Finance.